WORLD POSTMODERN FICTION

To S

Light, love, life

WORLD POSTMODERN FICTION

A GUIDE

Cristopher Nash

LONGMAN
London and New York

Longman Group UK Limited
Longman House, Burnt Mill,
Harlow, Essex CM20 2JE, England
and Associated Companies throughout the world.

Published in the United States of America
by Longman Publishing, New York

First published in hardback as
World Games: The Tradition of anti-realist revolt
in 1987 by Methuen & Co. Ltd
Paperback edition first published in 1993
by Longman Group UK Ltd
Second impression 1994

ISBN 0 582 20910 2

British Library Cataloguing-in-Publication Data
A catalogue record for this book is
available from the British Library

Library of Congress Cataloging-in-Publication Data
Nash, Cristopher.
World postmodern fiction : a guide / Cristopher Nash.
p. cm.
Originally published as: World games, 1987.
Includes bibliographical references and index.
ISBN 0-582-20910-2 (pbk.)
1. Fiction – 20th century – History and criticism. 2. Realism in literature. I. Nash, Cristopher. World games. II. Title.
PN3503.N38 1993
809′.912 – dc20 92–39356
CIP

Printed in Malaysia by PA

CONTENTS

FOREWORD

So we are to live in each other's language for a space of time. As is often said of situations like this – my having written, your having read – we have already entered into a kind of 'agreement'. Let me say a few things then, for my part, about some of the hazards that might otherwise lie hidden in the obscurity of this 'contract's' fine print or of its 'co-signers'' expectations. About what this volume tries and does not try to do, and something of what it must fail to do in spite of all its efforts.

Historical crises don't guarantee their solutions, and even an openly acknowledged crisis doesn't promise a simple single response. What follows is not the chronicle of a movement toward one kind of fiction, but the display of the products of a movement *away from* (what its proponents have tended to regard as) one sort of fiction, namely Realism, and *toward* several *different alternative sorts*. Here is not an analysis of authors' whole works, nor a 'coverage' of all the apparently relevant texts; it's an exploration into a vast-ranging modality of thinking and writing, touching on what strike me as the most efficient illustrations of that modality.

If I didn't think that the writing I have in mind was palpably different from literature that had previously held sway I shouldn't have bothered to begin this book. But I must be frank in owning that I'm not particularly attracted to the notion that anti-Realist writing is 'new' writing. It would be quite wrong to say that all 'experimental' projects are anti-Realist, and right to point out from the start that a number of reputedly 'unconventional' earmarks of anti-Realist activity have in fact played a long-standing role in conventional fiction, designed to preserve the intentions of Realism itself. Vital features of an anti-Realist impulse and its strategies have existed side-by-side with the impulses and strategies of Realism since the dawn of literature in the West. (This would be what one recent 'innovative' writer means when he says that "the new tradition coexisted with the old tradition from the beginning, not as the exception that proves the rule but as an alternative rule".[1])

Thus while this work gives its closest attention to fiction emerging in the second half of the twentieth century, its deeper concern is with a species of writing and thinking-about-writing and not narrowly about a neat historical moment, even while one of its principal hopes is ultimately to incite contemporaries to consider why anti-Realism should have caught fire in our time, and what that betokens.

This text takes the descriptive form as its model, even mimicking in its early chapters the format of the conscientious cumulative inductive style of enquiry. Every description involves an interpretation, but textual interpretation is not my leading purpose. I talk not so much about 'what' texts try to say, but more about 'how' they try to say anything, and the implications of that. The book offers itself less as an explication and more, literally, as a guide – a 'topology', with whose heuristic companionship (citing conceivable routes, landmarks, asking questions as it goes) the reader might find his or her *own* way through the literature's terrain. Nevertheless, one of its liabilities is that it does work toward what the physicist of optics would call 'high resolution', the sorting out of perceptions (and conceptions) we tend to confound. Any argument seeking resolving power is bound to suffer the ill of all powerful expository systems: the appearance of categorical orderliness at the expense of a nuanced expression of overall, ever-altering continuity, of how one thing merges into another and of the provocative and lively instability of the relations between texts that so stimulates critics to write about writing. My defence must rest in the fact that a governing concern here is the sense of difference and the sense of the difference it makes when we fail to see differences.

It's not easy to start an exposé essentially from scratch and build to a reasonable level of sophistication on a broad front, as I feel logically compelled – by the nature of the material – to do, without chronically understating some cases and overstating others. The reader will be advised to take all possible corrective action. To the anxious I can only offer the mixed sweetener that this book was written between the summers of 1982 and 1984 and reflects my thinking at that time, and that in a subsequent book on 'the limits of anti-Realist revolt', developed as a conclusion to the same project, my argument becomes yet less quietistically pluralist than I have tried – in the apt immediate spirit of the 'play of signification' and in spite of my own social instinct – to keep this one.

I talk a great deal about 'theory' and 'theories'. This seems literally impossible to avoid – if only on historical grounds, if we are to register adequately anti-Realist fictionalists' own frequent insistence that distinctions between theoretical ('non-fictional') and fictional utterances are illusory – and I cannot bring myself in honesty to apologize for it.[2] Alongside anti-Realist fiction another, kindred wave of 'non-fictional' writing (notably of course in poststructuralist criticism) is still in full spate and must be met. But an essential struggle here is to keep to the fiction itself and to writing directly devoted to it. One good reason for this, quite apart from the obvious aesthetic attraction and intellectual challenge for me of the appearance of unity and integrity in a book about writings often avowedly against the aesthetics of unity and integrity, the reader will immediately acknowledge who physically hefts this already sizeable tome. Another has to do with a historical twin detail: that writing of that 'other, non-fictional' sort (with a few exemplary exceptions of which I take up cases) seldom gives its attention at length to its sibling contemporary fiction, for good though 'paradoxical' reasons we'll eventually broach; and that it rarely produces qualitatively radical discourse itself, for causes that are pragmatically substantial, however hard to find self-consistent. This is not, then, to provide a compendium or even a fair bibliography of, say, poststructuralist critical texts – of which splendid instances in any case exist in abundance and to which I warmly recommend the reader to turn for comparison. My hope is that in the end readers may instead have felt called upon to think about those forms of writing that make up the keen, dark and flashing narrational cutting edge, and not just the seated expository haft, of the instrument that current culture has been engaged in shaping in its effort to hammer out and whet a discourse suited to its mind.

In these pages, devoted to what is doubtless the most deliberately complex fabric of ideas and writing processes in the history of narrative, much is simplified or outrightly omitted in the interests of that two-headed, treacherous thing, clarity. One among many infelicitous acts committed here in clarity's name is surely to be lamented by readers believing that all *lettres* should be *belles* – in the area of diction. The fiction at hand has endured the hectic proliferation of appellations usual in the seed-time of each new critical enthusiasm – 'anti-Realism', 'post-Modernism', 'Metafiction', 'Surfiction', 'Superfiction', 'Transfiction', 'Fabulation', 'Literature of Exhaustion', of 'Information', of 'Replenishment', of 'Silence' . . . . Few forms of literary busy-ness are less helpful than the disproportionate expense of energy on the gush of jargon. But in search of something approaching accuracy, I allow myself certain terms, including neologisms, of sometimes peculiar sorts. A shorthand, to forestall as far as possible the begging of questions, for the purposes of this particular discussion alone. (I make no excuse that in some quarters that is fashionable; often I use fashionable terms in unfashionable ways or set them aside altogether when perhaps least expected as unsuited to the context, and equally often go for the cliché, for its richness.) The word 'Postmodern', for instance, fails to communicate – as 'anti-Realist' ultimately can – the full force and array of ideas motivating works so vastly diverse as those popularly covered by the label 'Postmodernism', and I've chosen to address the phenomenon of the postmodern in fiction from now on as a manifestation of *anti-Realism*, in the hope that through this term we can share an understanding of the broader (and perhaps more penetrating) sort that so brazen a title as *'World Postmodern Fiction: A Guide'* might lead one to hope for. In this word-gaming, what might seem to solicit sterile if not indecent habits of public intercourse is meant only to brace useful habits of private thinking, for the most part my own. I have no interest whatsoever in adding my *ad hoc* coinage to the permanent treasury of literary prattle; I hope never to see it again.

To lend point to this last caveat, I'll mention one central example of the perils bound to come with any too solemn export of my nomenclature into the world of literary debate beyond the reaches of this book's own network. As its first-edition title reflected in its play on the 'word/world' nexus (*World-Games: The Tradition of Anti-Realist Revolt*), this new volume exhibits an old prejudice: that is, the inveterate sense that books seem simultaneously about, and are themselves, *things*; the prepossession with the substantive. In literature this is itself a relic of a Realist (*rēs*-ist) manner of regarding experience. I am actually more interested in writing not as object but as act. By nevertheless adopting that *chosiste* vocabulary I have merely allowed my language to reflect the (predictable) phenomenon: that the anti-Realist movement is itself ensnared in – is the shadow of – the habits of thinking of the literature, and indeed of the culture, that it seeks to subvert. So, for polemic and other reasons that will eventually become apparent, my own writing is on every page unblenchingly committed to playing out as legitimate – as well as to questioning – certain customs of expectation. (To wit: my candid use not merely of a host of worn discursive conventions, but also of certain lemmas – springing for example from what I believe to be the actualities of reading experience – that are left unargued here, as they are left unargued by most writers throughout their lives, and that are addressed in that subsequent volume to which this is in some respects a prolegomenon). The reader should note that that is so, and at every turn beware.

I hope that feminists (who have the best chance) will find better ways of communicating convincingly ideas that in this book are couched in 'patriarchally' rationalistic form. As to content, it would be a mistake to think I've not been continually mindful of the fact that – particularly under the heading of 'fantasy' as recuperated by recent critical theory –

a great deal of non-realistic fiction has been written with either tacit or explicit feminist intent, just as in the past much fiction bearing non-realist traits has sprung from, for example, political and/or sectarian religious impulses. While among the writers to whom I give important attention there are leading women fictionalists and critics, I've become convinced that issues raised by its theory and praxis (like say Marxist or indeed orthodox Christian writing pressing parallel claims for consideration in their endeavour to 'explode' modern readers' conventional expectations) make innovative specifically feminist fiction a matter so complex as to permit no full and fair treatment of it within the confines of this book. But the real point is that the present study's subject is the *general* practice of a literature whose aim is to overturn positivist Realist thinking, and not any of the many concerted political or metaphysical programmes whose interests anti-Realist strategies may have been – or might in the future be – made to serve. I wish, in other words, that what follows may help to reveal the broad conceptual and formal *foundations* on which radical fictional activity of many sorts may be based and with which, in actuality, it may inevitably if unwittingly be entangled.

In important ways what's here is dedicated to the many – students, teachers, friends – who worked with me in those obscure and heady years when we were the first group in a British university to tangle with this range of fiction in a course established for that purpose, in perhaps the first university in any country having so daringly (rashly?) trusted as to *require* literature students to undergo the experience; years when we had, to our ceaseless excitement, virtually nothing concerted to read in the field but the fiction itself. And to those of more recent times who've observed with me the flood of critical texts rise to engulf such fictions like stark scattered islands in a swelling sea of glittering speculation. I leave them – together with, most of all, the precious life-breathing spirit of those glowing days that made all meetings and questions sing and that stays ever in my mind – unmentioned or named only in the notes to save their being hauled down with me into the maw of Error's Comeuppance where I alone must be called to reckon; you know who you are. Of Malory, her toleration and belief in this writer as a human being (despite all indications to the contrary) were both the warmest support and strongest ultimate critique anyone writing could hope to know; for her love, honesty, wits-about-her, and courage all through it – I'm sure she doesn't need me to say more.

About sources

My main text is unequivocally populist in its handling of foreign-language materials; I present them universally in English translation.

Already enough obstacles stand in the way of contemporaries' awareness of how their word/world models are shared and/or answered by others whose cultures seem different. After long thought I see no excuse for preserving language barriers in the name of a fleeting (and anyway debatable) scholarly precisianism which I have myself in narrower contexts fought for. Every passage I cite can be consulted in the language of origin by specialists and I *beg* them to set their readings beside my own; but they aren't – or should not be – the people who might most profit by such evidence as this book offers, however roughly, of what is going on abroad. In the case of quotations, page references are to the editions (translations for example) from which the relevant passages have been finally reproduced. Details of publication affecting these as well as the original editions on which they were based are given in the Bibliography. Wherever not otherwise indicated in this way, translations from the French, Italian and (in fewer cases) Spanish are mine, with the original texts' phrasing in brackets (or given in full in the notes) in situations of doubt or possible misrepresentation.

Acknowledgements

We are grateful to the following for permission to reproduce copyright material:

Harcourt Brace Jovanovich, Inc. for an extract from *Of Other Worlds* by C. S. Lewis. Copyright © 1966 by The Executors of the Estate of C. S. Lewis; University of Illinois Press, the translator and Author for "Leafs" by Gerhard Rühm, translated by Rosmarie Waldrop in Charles Russell (ed.) *The Avant-Garde Today* (1981); The Ohio University Press/Swallow Press, Athens for a table paraphrased by Jean Ricardou (from Baudry's *Personnes*), translated by Erica Freiberg in *Surfiction*, edited by Raymond Federman (Swallow Press, 1981); the Author, Gerhard Rühm for his "The Lion" translated by Eugene Williams in *Breakthrough Fictioneers* by Richard Kostelanetz, published by Something Else Press; Southern Illinois University Press for "Taboo" from *The Other Side of the Mirror* (El Grimorio) by Enrique Anderson Imbert, p 69. Translated by Isabel Reade. Copyright © 1966 by Southern Illinois University Press.

INTRODUCTION
The Realist tradition

Are we real?

At the moment when you'd read only that question, you grasped a great deal less about me than you do now that your reading of this second sentence is finished.

What had appeared in those first three words to be scarcely more than a sign that we had a language in common, and that I might be vaguely musing – or crying aloud in my solitude – about the nature of existence, has now by the end of our second sentence been altered and amplified in many ways. That dim, seemingly metaphysically speculative 'we' – did it refer to 'mankind'? – has taken on the personalized clarity of a 'you' and a 'me'; and you know that I believe in 'us' and in some communication between us.

And you may see (for example, when you notice the contraction 'you'd') that I seek, moreover, a particularly informal, perhaps even intimate relationship with you. You can sense, too, something of the cultural background behind me, and the 'social' level of exchange between us that I'm aiming at – by, say, my use of the rather special word 'grasp' instead of simply 'know', and by the phrase 'a great deal' rather than, say, 'a lot' on the one hand or 'conspicuously' on the other.

In addition, you know things about where I stand philosophically – that I believe, for instance, in the positive effects of time ('when' and 'now'), and in the capacity of reading to increase our 'knowing'. And you're better placed to relate to me, to take a shrewdly if provisionally appropriate stance with regard to me as you no doubt instinctively hasten to do – consciously, unconsciously – with every person that you meet in life. Certain details about the way I've proceeded seem to pose a positive challenge: the contrivance of my second sentence (standing unfinished for you until you'd read the word 'finished'; seeming empty of information about me yet claiming to tell much; deferring any palpable relation to the question which the preceding sentence had emphatically posed) – was it only an eye-catcher? a ruse? Perhaps all kinds of rhetorical motives, venal ones too, underlie my approach to you. The very network of these words suggests that I may have been toying with words, or with you yourself. That I may be playful, capricious, 'deep', or downright dishonest.

By the standards of your 'normal' experience of the world, you would be right in thinking to yourself: 'I must watch my step with him.' I have become a person who poses a human situation of a rather precisely recognizable sort. In a couple of sentences (whose commentary could indeed have been longer and richer) I have, without seeming to do so, answered in my fashion the question you thought I was declining to answer. The reality of you as a thinking, sorting, enquiring being has been reasserted, and I myself have become 'real'.

But is any of this as true as it seems?

The 'personality' of the 'me' that the preceding words describe is 'real' – we may be sure of that. It's perfectly reasonable to string together all the odd bits of information that those words intimate into a shape which you may call – as a form of shorthand – a person. It is even reasonable to attach to the 'me' they indicate the personal name that you find on the title page of this book. So there you have me. One author, one voice, me. But are we sure? Are you positive that the person whose name appears there did not create a *character*, whose 'voice' you're now hearing? How do you know that even the name is not an invention of yet a third person – or persons – who believe(s) quite different things, whose 'reality' you may never encounter?

Now we are in deep trouble. Because, having planted this suspicion, this doubt in your mind, however passionately I may struggle to persuade you that 'I mean' what I say, I'll never be able to convince you wholly that I do, or – what is worse – that 'I' am here at all, behind these words, in the way that the words themselves suggest that I am. We are in different worlds. You; the you that I think I'm addressing; the you that you think you are; I: the I that you think I am; the me that I think I may have created in the words on this page.

What is 'real' about what happens in this book or any book is the shape that it may lend to the thoughts in the mind of whoever reads it, by virtue of *the assumptions that it stirs there*: that a certain kind of 'person' is speaking, and so forth. But this does not necessarily tell the person reading anything real about what is outside the book in the way that it may seem to at first glance – about the writer's life, for example, or about the reader's. Indeed, 'my' postulating the existence of a 'you' whose customs of thought 'I' have so confidently described raises problems about the relations between language and reality which 'we' may never resolve. In a situation like this, where both of 'us' are in some sense linguistic fictions, who are 'we' – to coin a phrase – to judge?

This, then, is a taste of what's to come, and a way of saying that here is not a book about reality, but a book about books and the assumptions about reality that they seek to stir and contest. When I speak of Realist and anti-Realist fiction, I do not have in mind books that are more like or less like real life, but *books* (and I use the capital R to signal this distinction) *of certain sorts* whose assumptions differ concerning *what things and how things ought to be said* about reality. Readers find themselves continually wanting to say, and writers astonishingly often do say, 'But this (however crazy) book is so *true to life* – it *is* realistic.' That must often – it may even in some sense always – be right. Yet how easy it is for other readers to say the opposite thing about the same book – and feel equally right. To one reader the *Divina Commedia* or *Gulliver's Travels* or *Der Prozess* or *Catch-22* is sheer fantasia, to another it is the spitting image of life. Insofar as it's a question of truth, that is a tough nut to crack. What we can hope to do here is hard enough: to come to grips with the ways in which a great and growing number of writers of books today lay a challenge to *that movement in literature that called itself or has come to be called* Realism and that sought to represent 'reality' in what they believe now to be a quite distinct and limited manner.[1]

Realism, we're often told, cannot properly be defined. There are many arguments for this, not a few of them offered in schools of literature with weighty authority. A favourite, coming in frequently sophisticated guises, is essentially that realism is about reality, and reality is nothing more definable than 'everything humans experience'. An important variant of this theme is that language is nothing but symbols signifying what's real, and that anything in language must be realistic or it's gibberish. Another argument points out that, throughout history, the most extravagantly diverse sorts of artists – including artists whom we may intuitively consider the most extravagantly 'unrealistic' – have claimed or had it claimed for them that they were the greatest realists. We remember le Douanier Rousseau's declaration, to the astonishment of his Realist critics – and perhaps to the public at large – that only he and Picasso were the true realists. "Homer thought he was being realistic. So did Virginia Woolf".[2] So Alain Robbe-Grillet, with a surprise for some of his critics not unlike that raised by Rousseau, calls his own apparently radical fiction "a return to the real". "Every writer", he says, "thinks he is a realist" (1962, 154, 153). There is truth to that, and complications burgeon forth from it.

Among those seeking a more refined combination of these propositions, it's asserted that if Realism *were* to be defined it would have to be called a mode that is not simply *about* reality but *mimics* it – but this 'mimesis' (as made famous in modern times by Erich Auerbach) is to be found virtually everywhere, from the Bible and Homer to early Latin and medieval texts and Shakespeare, and thus cannot be historically *located*. It's "a perennial mode", says J. P. Stern (1973), in his turn perhaps the most resolute apologist for realism in more recent decades. But there is another part to this historically-orientated proposal: literature is realistic insofar as it is 'true' to the age in which it's written. But each age has its own, different reality. Realism, then, changes; a work that is realistic for one culture eludes precise and accurate description as realistic for another.

Yet one more case is made, then, whose aim is to 'cover' realism – to shelter the term from the charge that it lacks definition – and whose effect is once again to obscure its description. It takes as its basis the idea that what is real is what is true, and that 'true reality' may be given to us even when it seems other than real. Along with other prominent critics at this end of the century, Stern – whose book *On Realism* was written partly in reaction to the onset of the anti-Realist movement – advances what to him is a crucial distinction: there is the "realism of description" which Auerbach puts forward and by which a work of art provides "the serious representation of everyday reality"; and there is something else, the "realism of assessment", in which departures from the 'externally real' are permitted, by reason of its compensatory insight: it affords us a 'reliable evaluation' of events in life, of how things (inwardly) are (130ff.). This unquestionably high-minded supposition reflects an earnest – and much needed – attempt to account for our sense that Henri Rousseau and Robbe-Grillet may be right: that if a work 'feels right', 'feels true', even when it is not realistic in the 'descriptive' sense, it is not to be dismissed as '(regrettably) unrealistic'. It would be patently absurd for us to cordon off from the ranks of finally worthwhile literature an *Odyssey* because it describes a goddess Circe, skilled in enchantments, or a *Paradise Lost* for depicting the fall of an angel from Heaven. The difficulty with the realism-of-assessment view is that it fails to tell us by what criteria we may ourselves assess a text's 'assessments' or 'insights' – how we might in practice exclude *any* work from the category of realism. Or indeed why, for reasons other than sentimental ones, we *need* – in order to 'save' them – to dub Homer or Milton realists. "To call a work 'realistic' is to commend it", Stern tells us; how can we be sure that he does not in fact mean that to commend a work is to call it realistic? We want this theory of realism to work, but the 'stronger' it seems as a comprehensive concept, the more ineffective it comes to be as a description. In practice, it constitutes another firm gesture in the direction of the indefinability of realism.

Throughout the run of objections to the effort to describe literary realism, the one recurrent theme is that to define the thing is to lump together works that are not the same. What is illuminating is that it is most typically the advocates of realism who adopt this energetically as an objection (even while they remain the most liberal practitioners of the 'lumping together' activity). It's the healthy impulse to say that each work of art that we like stands on its own special merits and not by reason of its association with a school or a programme, of which it could not and would not seek to be merely a neat exemplar. Great books are better than movements. The classification of a group of books as those-that-are-our-favourites, or as those-that-are-about-everything-we-can-experience, had its weak points as a definition, but a 'realistic' attitude might well be that the best you can do is to admit this and get on with it.

Yet here is where anti-Realists enter the scene.[3] They will vigorously declare that Realism is not always the best that is written and is not actually about everything – or even nearly everything – at all.

'Ah, but', their opponents quickly answer, 'they're thinking only about one kind of realism. That of the fiction of a particular movement in Europe and the Americas in the nineteenth and early twentieth centuries.' The fact is that no one denies this. (Realism with that capital R comes downstage centre, into the spotlight.) Anti-Realists of all sorts positively express in a variety of ways the opinion that the right target of *their* objections to what has happened in the history of imaginative writing is not 'realism' in any all-encompassing sense, but a delimitable literary *convention*, Realism, manifesting itself above all in 'the Novel' as it came to be known from the time of its avowed supremacy over other narrative forms in the nineteenth century.

It's in this sense that Stern, too, has felt free to say that "realism hasn't been the dominant mode of writing during most periods in the history of literature", that "there is no assurance that there will be a realism tomorrow' (157), and that "only among the realists of the nineteenth century and their heirs do we find a complete commitment to the mode" (122).

My aim is to set out a picture, a synthetic construct, whose function is *not* to provide a definitive historical representation of the exact nature of all Realist texts, but to offer a frame of reference, an over-all 'perspective' on Realism of the sort that I think an *anti-Realist* would largely recommend. In this 'description' of the Realist tradition, there's no pretence towards a final and absolute 'objectivity'. Much of what anti-Realists write is openly polemic – not to say propagandistic – in its intent, and I don't think it's a particular part of my duty to conceal assertions of theirs which may reveal that. My point is to record here a generalized view of the *range* of limitations to which anti-Realists may regard Realist writing as subject, not universally but in ultimate effect. No anti-Realist will find all of these limitations true of Realism, or – finding them to be traits of Realism – will consider them all to be limitations; some will welcome a number of them as indispensable to their own writing processes. An important aspect of our description of any particular fictionalist-in-revolt will, in other words, arise from our perception of the particular features of Realism with which he/she seems especially to take issue.

Special effects ensue from the fact that anti-Realists take a partisan stand. When writers from among the variety discussed in the next chapters speak of the Realist tradition, the authors to whom we'll find them commonly referring are those nineteenth-century masters they were 'taught' – and who, for that matter, are taught in schools and universities today – as representing the foundations of the modern fictional heritage. That is to say ones on some list that might be headed by Balzac, Stendhal, Flaubert, Dickens, George Eliot, Tolstoy, Dostoyevsky, Zola, together with those authors (perhaps sometimes psychologically more important) of "received" and popular formulaic fiction who are at present, as Stern says, "their heirs" and who frequently may appear to the new writer as the mainstays of an established machinery of taste in which he or she feels his/her creative activities to be involuntarily enmeshed.[4] But where anti-Realist writers themselves address Realism, either in theory or in their fiction, they are inclined to commit all the sins those uncomfortable with the term dread most. They fail to escape the charge of over-simplification, of 'lumping texts together'.[5] This is a pitfall I would surely do my utmost to avoid if my aim were to propound a definition of Realism that would stand against all tests as the historically 'proven' one.

But that wouldn't, once done, be of much use to us here. What's needed is something else. The suggestions to come are offered not as a *comprehensive* description of Realism but only as groundwork for the consideration of what *subsequent* fictionalists cite as differentiating their work from it. Any validity which the picture of Realism that follows may have on its own, independent of its utility as an articulation of its opponents' views, will be for others to test or leave in obscurity, according to taste, as time goes on.

The operation of this book thus has a certain circularity to it. For readers to whom this offers less delight than it might to anti-Realists themselves, some patience is needed. It's their own behaviour, their work seen up close (which is the meat of later chapters), that alone can give real substance – or give the lie – to anti-Realists' perception of Realism as I outline it in these introductory pages.

There is, on the other hand, an artificial polarity in the organization of the ideas that follow at which some might be appalled. I speak, as many have before me, of 'worlds' and of two kinds of worlds in particular. Of the 'world' presented – narrated – within a book: a world presented at some level as the pre-existing 'facts in the matter' (even though this may in the next moment be denied at some other level); a world that we might 'imagine ourselves into', 'live in', whether more or less comfortably. We can talk – always in an imagining way – of such a world's mountains, its people, its people's ideas. And I speak of the 'world' of the book itself; the narration, the writing by which, in its own unique form, we are presented with – among other things – that 'fact-world'; the world of the book that is actually a part of the world in which we live. We can talk of its words, the organization of these words, even of its printing and the way its pages are bound – or not bound – together.

This perennial distinction is in many ways the crux of the formal argument of a number of anti-Realists (whether a distinction can be drawn between the two worlds, what is to be learned from any distinction between them, and so forth). We can hold a book, love a book as a book; we can imagine ourselves to love the 'people and things that happen' within it; and we can do either one of these without the other. "This claybook, what curios of signs (please stoop), in this allaphbed! Can you rede (since We and Thou had it out already) its world?" We wouldn't have needed Joyce thus to remind us of the tension between 'words' and 'worlds', and it's only in one sense 'lightly' that I've expropriated as epigraph Nabokov's phrase "the game of worlds".[6] It may be as though – if it's the world at large that we care gravely about, desperately even – the book that we hold between us and that world is one of the archetypal 'games' through which we may play with or play out our relations with that world. On a certain plane, twentieth-century criticism has subscribed to this convention in the differences described by French structuralism between "*histoire*" and "*discours*", by Russian formalism between "*fabula*" and "*sjužet*", between "story" and "narration" as it's often been put in English.[7] An important part of the story of anti-Realist activity to be narrated in this book will be concerned with the ways in which the distinction comes to lose its seemingly universal and simple utility.

Realist ideas

In the view of the writers ahead of us, the premisses underlying Realism would in broad terms be expressed in this way.[8] First, that there is a positively determinable world – which we can call that of 'actuality' – external to the work of fiction, and which it's the fundamental responsibility of fiction to represent 'as it is' or 'has been'.[9] (We'll have reason to discuss this at considerable length later, as the '*referential*' motive: the book refers to the world outside it.) Second, that this world is a *cosmos* – that is, a complete, integrated system of phenomena governed by some coherent scheme of rules (such as those of natural law, the assembled forces of history), whose only obscurity derives from its vast diversity and complexity, and whose truthful delineation depends ultimately on the comprehensiveness and rationality of its description.[10] (Thinking of Realism in its modern forms, theorists find it convenient from time to time to speak of this notion as at least in spirit affined to that of nineteenth-century positivism.[11]) Third, that the essentially right procedures for referentially-motivated fiction are those of *mimesis*, by which in this book I mean the material transcription of the empirically verifiable data (the objects) of the physical senses.[12] Fourth (and fifth) that, just as in the 'actual' world at any one moment we may not have access to *all* the information we may seek on a given subject and consequently must strive to assess the probable truth based on the most exhaustive collection of information possible – fiction too should direct its attention towards an *exhaustive* disclosure of the 'facts' ('the whole truth') and the presentation, finally, of what is most *probable* according to our past experience of the actual world, particularly as exemplified by the procedures of history and science. And sixth that, since among the greatest obstacles to our perception of the truth is the complexity – and inclination toward *parti pris* – of each individual subjective consciousness and the diversity among the 'subjectivities' that compose human experience taken collectively, the greatest effort must be made towards the ostensibly most '*objective*' articulation of the data as possible ('nothing but the truth'), with the minimal visible intervention on the part of the 'teller'.[13]

While these postulates would appear to make Realism concerned solely with the novel's relationship to the world it reports and not with its relation to the reader (though this appearance turns out to be quite illusory), two further intentions essential to the Realist mode, in this view, bear specifically on the kind of process it seeks to set in motion in the reader's mind. A Realistic narrative is to be an *illusionistic* and *declarative* mode of telling. That is, it must operate in our reading with the full force of the illusion that we are 'within its world'; and it should be taken as one containing *truth that may be unambiguously paraphrased*. These features need some elaboration.

If the world within a novel is to have the semblance of a world 'always already there' ('*toujours déjà là*'), existing objectively – and if it's to be taken as essentially identical or 'assimilable' to the actuality outside it – then it must convince the reader (entertainment apart) that it's a world he might enter into, that he might 'live in'.[14] This sense of the necessity to make fiction 'livable' – which I'm calling the illusionist motive – is fundamental to Realism.

The process of establishing an illusion for the reader arises from – and contributes toward the satisfaction of – an intention on the part of the Realist text that's complementary to but not the same as the motives of entertaining and of imparting (didactic) information. Aristotle, for whom the illusion was central to the success of the drama and from whom, in essence, an Auerbach derives his conception of mimesis, argues that an orderly structure is indispensable to illusion itself. At bottom, the orderliness of an *unambiguous causal* conception of the universe is essential. The Realist hope pivots on the assumption that a similar order of relations – linear, temporal – operates between the book and the reader, that similar rules of cause and effect operate in both. That is, that they may *cause the reader, in time*, to respond as a mind within the book's world would respond. The preservation of the story's illusion throughout the duration of the reading – far from being merely a happy by-product of the novel's other processes – may indeed be the principal mechanism by which the causal continuity, the very logic of the Realistic narrative's system of 'forces', is confirmed for the reader.

To its opponents, a further fundamental intention of Realism is that it operates for us in what I've just now called a *declarative* mode. It purports to (be in a position to) *make clear*, without prejudice, what the reader will *recognize* (because it fits his/her established experience) but simply cannot have known or determined without the narrator's aid. It addresses us characteristically in the firm, clear, unperplexedly assertive narrative voice of someone who knows that as soon as we have heard what's to be told, we will perceive it to be demonstratively (apodictically) true. It proposes to be 'transparent'. And it achieves this effect in a manner which may strike us, looking back – depending on our viewpoint – as either paradoxical or as a manifestation of some double-dealing: however it claims to reveal to us something *new*, it persuades us of its reliability by speaking to us in language that is largely clear because it is of a familiar sort, in terms that vary little from the old ones in which we're accustomed to think. "Miss Brooke had that kind of beauty which seems to be thrown into relief by poor dress" says the first line of *Middlemarch*; "Happy families are all alike; every unhappy family is unhappy in its own way" is the famous opening of *Anna Karenina*. We are asked to look 'through' the language of the text at a predetermined 'real world'.

But we can't help but feel that this is achieved by the grace of a tonality that seems simple and self-effacing yet asserts a subtle kind of authority, seated in the certitude that we share the same world and already agree – or will soon agree – with the narrator as to its qualities. In a favoured distinction among some anti-Realists, this is the nature of a 'readerly' (*lisible*) text – as opposed to a 'writerly' (*scriptible*) one of sorts we'll find espoused later. Only the statements narratives make, and not the narrations themselves, are to be scrutinized for 'honesty' or 'fair play'. The relation between the words as signifiers and the 'things signified' is a track that is – as Terence Hawkes says – "well-worn, established and compulsory" (1977, 114). This is not to be taken as a contradiction to our common experience that Realist fiction is complex, that it is 'about characters who' are unstable and caught in a world of contrarieties. Anti-Realists speaking about this argue only that there is an overwhelming (indeed overweening) deception lodged in the gap between a *histoire* concerning such characters, for whom existence may be as problematic as you please, and a *discours* that is as clear cut and reassuring as you could imagine. (Some rule of 'homology' has been broken.) The narrative is, in a philosophically significant sense, 'positive'. The reader would have 'said' the same things had he/she been there, and he/she *would* have been there only the narrator makes it his business – and the reader counts on him – to get there first. It is a compact between reader and narrator to the effect that the latter will declare what is 'truly' happening and the former will go – will be carried – along.

One of the features most often ascribed to such fiction is that it's rigorously chronological at the story level. This is correct and must not be confused with the fact that it is *often* at least modestly achronological in the telling. The narrator's 'play' with time is itself habitually the product of the declarative (rather than some 'ambiguative' or 'problematicist') motive. It's done for our own good – our better ultimate understanding of a matter too tangled for direct presentation to the uninitiate. Zigzags in the telling make us 'see the (straightforward) truth unfold' in a way that is all the more emphatically convincing by virtue of the clarity and seeming 'dramatic inevitability' with which complicated relationships thus develop before our eyes, resisting all artifice, adamantine behind the teller's 'mere veil of words'.

In writing to someone of a fifty-page section of *Madame Bovary* he had just completed, Flaubert said: "It is an uninterrupted portrayal of a bourgeois existence and of a love that remains inactive – a love all the more difficult to depict because it is so timid and deep ..." (1953, 144). In these few words the fictionalist discloses a number of primary beliefs concerning the way in which his novel is to be taken, and among these is the final one I've mentioned and one that needs amplification. For Flaubert, *Madame Bovary* is not only referential (it 'depicts' an external 'bourgeois existence') and illusionistic (Emma is 'real' enough to 'love' and her love is concretely characterizable – is 'inactive', 'timid' and 'deep' – in precisely the way that the love of actual persons might be characterized); it is *rationally paraphraseable*. Those fifty pages are "an uninterrupted portrayal of ...". The implications of this, for example from an anti-Realist standpoint, are vast.

First of all, Flaubert is 'interpreting' his work. And what's more, he's implying that the substance and justice of this interpretation is based upon an interpretation which he has already placed upon life outside the work. (That there is a bourgeois existence, that people in it love, etc.; even if he were referring only to life as conventionally represented in other books – which we know by other means he is definitely not doing – this would still be an interpretative act of the same sort.) Now, we are thoroughly familiar with this way of talking and thinking about novels. People say, 'Such and such book is about ——', and in a few generalized, conceptually abstract words ('bourgeois', 'love') often quite different from those of which the book is typically composed, they state what is to them the book's import. In fact, where Realist fiction is concerned, what people most often seem to say in commending it is that it *has* import of this sort; they say it has 'depth' (e.g. 'psychological depth'); they say that 'it's a great work because it conveys universal human truths such as ——'.[15]

This embodies an intimation of a very special sort about books. It suggests that 'There is a truth contained herein, of so widespread a sort that it is – once perceived – in the final analysis "free" of what happens between these covers and may be restated in the form of a rational proposition and applied wherever one likes for the understanding of the world outside.' This idea about novels does not necessarily follow from the nature of narratives or of language, taken as a whole. We can imagine – and we'll certainly later hear – a novelist saying, for example: 'This story tells nothing but itself, this language means only what it says.' The Realist mode, it would seem, is concerned not merely with 'presenting facts' but also with the notion of truth in an additional sense. It invites us to believe that interpreting and conceptualizing – both about books and about life – are right things to do. That, indeed, generalization, paraphrase, is the necessary 'equals sign', the *trait d'union*, the pathway between the book and the reader's own life. I may say of Emma Bovary, 'There but for the grace of God, but for the slightest wrinkle in fate, goes sister Kate. Unlike Emma, Kate is not pretty, Kate does not wear spectacles, Kate does not read – but Kate is bourgeois and habitually loves in a way that is inactive, timid and deep. Nothing about their histories is the same and yet I know that in depth, in general, they are profoundly alike. Flaubert shows me the real truth about our Kate.' "The preponderance of message over code is one of the basic conditions of any realistic fiction", Stern tells us (161). And – as an anti-Realist may say – in such fiction there is always buried the proposition not simply that it contains general truths, but that it is worth reading (is right) because it represents what *is* in a way that shows that what is, at some level, *makes sense*. That the book bears concrete testimony to the 'fact' that the world is so constructed that it is possible to be right, to make sense of what is. The invitation to paraphrase, to interpret rationally, in other words, itself constitutes a philosophical statement about existence.

One further item that should be added to this list of premisses – one that is not always openly expressed but that appears to be intuitively inextricable in the nineteenth-century Realist mind from those that *have* been avowed – is that for a world (fictional or real) to make sense to humans, it must make sense *for* humans. That in a world in which God has fallen – or been pushed – into the background, *Homo sapiens* must come into the foreground. The apotheosis of science and of human history as 'the two muses of the age', and the putting forward of a conception of literature as a quasi-scientific 'anatomy' (as Flaubert would say) or as a historical 'chronicle' (as Stendhal, Balzac and so many others will do), are but manifestations that, whatever nature's will in the matter, humanity – and humanity's experience of reality – must now be the measure of things. Perhaps *because* it seems such a commonplace that we take it for granted, anti-Realists might have us bear in mind that, for the Realist, it's not the truth merely of nature, but of human nature, that fiction claims to show. Realism, they will like to say, is anthropocentric.

Realist worlds: their shape and substance

Realist theory and practice appear to support these observations. As to the *world* presented within a Realist novel, it will regularly be so designed, first of all – Realists themselves propose – as to have about it a certain *probability* with respect to our own (as Auerbach says) 'everyday reality'. Things are what they normally seem; this is part of what Stern refers to when he speaks of "that middle distance to which realism is committed" (161). What matters and what's true is to be found buried in the details of 'common', 'typical', 'average' people and events, set in the day-to-day middle range of quotidian experience.[16] "Common language, common knowledge, common experience", these are the qualities Stern puts forward as those of Realism (89). "I have purposely avoided the accidental and the dramatic", says Flaubert (1953, 247). There will be no 'ineffable', no supernatural, no dragons, no paradise, no hell – except those that may be accounted for by 'natural law', in other words those that are products of some character's mind. No kings and no queens – unless they're 'basically like everybody else'; no saints, as George Eliot would put it; "no monsters", as Flaubert says, "no heroes!" (1953, 247); and nothing that is finally 'naturally' inexplicable.[17] What's to be presented as true of men and women within such a novel must somehow fit with what we know – or think we know – to be true of 'mankind as a species'.

Realist narrative, then, centres above all on 'character'. (Readers feeling that this must perforce be the very foundation of all fiction, anti-Realists will say, have another think coming to them.) "It is with individuals that the social truth of realism is concerned" – says Stern – "not with trends or inchoate masses of humanity, and not with fragments of consciousness either" (121). And this raises the question of psychology. "The psychological development of my characters is giving me a lot of trouble", says Flaubert speaking of *Madame Bovary*, "and everything, in this novel, depends on it" (1953, 142). We hear – and perhaps think – endlessly of the 'psychological realism' of such novels as this. What is it that can so encompass treatments of 'mind' such as Dickens' 'caricatures', on one hand, and Flaubert's Emma, on the other, and yet that so sets them apart in our impressions – at least in our *first* impressions – from Nabokov's Shade, Beckett's Molloy, and Robbe-Grillet's Mathias?

What, if anything, 'characterizes' Realist characterization lies somewhere in this. At whatever level of 'internality' the Realist addresses his/her characters, what they seem to have in common is that these are never portrayals of 'pure, raw mentality', but are rather narratives of personality. That is, they all share, in a crucial sense, a conception of person which *contains*, which confers on the flow of represented 'thought' (however vacillating the array of its percepts and intentions), a persistent shapeliness, consistency, and even moderate predictability within the context of the world about it.[18] Personality in this respect, we might say, is an 'institutionalization' of the 'forces', the continuity, of private experience that is as characteristic of Realism as social institutions are (as we'll see) in containing and defining the forces of public moral, spiritual, political and sexual behaviour. This sense of character as person is another aspect of what Stern is talking about when he says that Realism is concerned with showing things in "the middle distance". "'The purpose of the whole' ... that determines the middle distance of realism ... is the fictional creation of *people*, of individual characters and lives informed by what in any one age is agreed to constitute a certain integrity and coherence. ... The realistic attitude ... only makes sense and works ... in a world in which there are *people*, individuals of some degree of integrity and coherence of character" (120–1).

Psychology of character, therefore, becomes a principal basis for the meaningful and orderly organization of experience within a Realistic world. As Flaubert implies in asserting that in *Madame Bovary* he has ruled out "the accidental" – in a world in which humankind is taken to be the measure of things, it is also made out (oddly in the name of verisimilitude) to be the agent behind things. We may take the case of the traditional critical objection to the apparently gratuitous coincidence of the flood at the end of *The Mill on the Floss*: that it was a flaw in Eliot's Realism. If instead of "the rains" some character – raging, say, against the world of St Ogg's – had destroyed the banks of the Floss, then the narrative would have been saved. The subtlety of the problem is often missed. 'The point', the Realist critic may insist, 'isn't that the flood shouldn't have happened except by human agency, but that by it Eliot avoids resolving the book in its own terms, which are human–ethical.' The net result, however, is identical. If, positing the flood, Eliot had been willing to draw around it a world large enough to embrace consistently forces beyond those of the human–ethical she'd have been true to Realism's (and the Realist critic's) cosmic attitude; but she'd have created a cosmos that was not realistic.[19] Better a flawed Realism, she decides, than a betrayed one. Narrative events are generated within the sphere of human intentions: external forces (of nature, of spirit) are largely evoked only insofar as they have concrete reference to human affairs. And nothing happens that is humanly inexplicable. "Realistic fictions", as Stern says, "are created on firm ground which reveals no epistemological cracks, and . . . when such cracks appear, they are not explored but transformed into the psychology of characters: realism doesn't ask whether the world is real, but it occasionally asks what happens to persons who think it is" (31).

Realism's narrative *situations*, then, revolve around character and the activities and perceptions of characters ostensibly seeking physical well-being and psychological self-fulfilment – this almost universally through sometimes ambiguously, sometimes sharply defined but shift-ing, notions of romantic or erotic love and/or material achievement. Here, individual human conceptions of value are both personally and publicly circumscribed by rather distinctive, restrictive notions of a social order and ethos, and by the complex mechanism of human interrelationships which they in turn generate. In particular this mechanism is based on the distribution and manipulation of social, political and – often above all – sexual influence, and of wealth, property, employment, and prestige of personal image. To anti-Realists it's a heavily structured, hierarchically regulated world in which the form and meaning of life are taken to be embodied in – and tested in terms of – a limited number of more-or-less fixed and readily defined institutions: marriage, family, law, church, government, and the educational, commercial, industrial, agricultural, military and medical establishments. Both the texture of this world and the character of those living in it are customarily treated as most fully 'revealed' when seen in the light of – or put to the proof in the arena formed by – such institutions.[20] Narrative turning points, crises, centre typically on their inadequacies, and on transgressions against the norms they represent.

In this view – as if 'human truth' must be incomplete until it accounts for the individual as a member of his/her 'species' – where physical settings are concerned in Realism there's an emphasis on locations in which the operation of the forces of the 'typical human collective' predominate. *Locales* (as contrasted with those of the most influential pre-Romantic and Romantic works, for example, such as *La Nouvelle Héloïse*, *Paul et Virginie*, *Werther*, *René*) are ones of dense and finely interdependent population, notably centres of metropolitan or provincial bourgeois – or closely nucleated agrarian – society.

Beyond this, to a remarkable degree, Realist novels seem to express a need to contextualize. Like the Realist's notion of nature, they abhor any intimation of a void. When Balzac introduced us in his first sentence to the universe of *Le Père Goriot* by saying "For the last forty years the elderly Madame Vauquer, *née* de Conflans, has kept a family boarding-house in the Rue Neuve-Sainte-Geneviève between the Latin Quarter and the Faubourg Saint-Marcel" (27) – or indeed from the moment that we've read the subtitle of *Scarlet and Black; A Chronicle of the Nineteenth Century* – we have entered into a story that has a '*megastory*'. Far from providing only a decorative colouration to the stories of Julien, Rastignac and Raskolnikov, all those references to the story of the deceased but 'true' *Napoleon* make sensible to us vital actions in their respective fictional narratives which might otherwise be quite incomprehensible. Always behind the immediate '*histoires*' of the novel's characters there is an '*extra histoire*' – an 'already written *histoire*', a system of 'givens' that is either 'common knowledge' or readily verifiable, which we 'know to be real'. The very substance – or substantiality – of this fiction is thus meant to be not only positively but continuously rooted for us in the larger world which is ours.

And between the megastory and the story there is something else, which we might at least informally call a *parastory*:[21] that is, a mass of narrative (not merely descriptive) matter that's offered in the same way as essential to our understanding of the primary story as it unfolds in the (punctual) present – essential to our acceptance of its causality, particularly of its psychological ground rules of cause and effect – but that's *not* externally 'verifiable'. It supplies not only the past biography of characters, but often such information as their genealogy, their family and personal traditions, their tics, their formative traumas, and the whole picture of the hereditary and environmental forces at work 'behind' them. It supplies a probable, plausible fictional background to fill up any residual void that might otherwise lie between what 'fictionally happens' and what we know to have happened, outside.

One of the salient features distinguishing a 'typical' Realist novel from other earlier forms of narrative in terms of its sheer *bulk* at the level of *histoire* would lie in the relative absence of megastory and parastory in the latter (think of *The Faerie Queene*, *The Pilgrim's Progress*, *Candide*). A reading of the worldly adventures first of Candide and then of Pierre in *War and Peace* – or simply a glance at the two volumes side-by-side on the shelf – tells the tale. A major cluster of anti-Realists in our own century will play upon this.

But as Realist criticism continually reminds us, it's what goes on within the characters that gives focus for us to all that world around them in a Realist novel. What is 'felt' by the characters is what matters, to the extent that it takes on a value of its own, a kind of numinous primacy, even while it comes under a narrator's sharply sceptical scrutiny. In even the outwardly most radical Realism, the narrative's dynamics pivot on a sometimes deeply conservative convention (in often the most positive sense) of the sanctity of the human sentiments. The story that emerges comes to be governed by a more or less routinely assumed code of *narrative decorum*, of *sentimental formulae* in the representation of certain central aspects associated with the common life, a code which anti-Realism will often make it part of its principal business to suspend, throw into question, or attack. What's 'told' about those whose feelings count most is conditioned and regulated by preceptive notions of the virtues of 'normal'/'natural' love and sexuality; maternity; parental and filial affection; fidelity to a person, a faith, a principle, a cause; personal magnanimity and social caritas; steadfast courage in adversity; notions of the inviolability of the body, of the innocent (children, the aged, the naive, the virginal) and of the right to life and freedom from suffering; notions of the dignity of the individual and specifically of the underdog, and the dignity of simple faith and hard labour; and of the urgency of conscious awareness and enlightenment. And in tandem with all this there's the sense of narrative ambivalence and/or frustration if not arid rage (and some of the greatest narrative tension) when these precepts threaten to prove aesthetically exclusive, repugnant, elusive or illusory.

Without seeking here anything like a thorough or methodical list, we can in the most informal way readily think of a wide but distinctive spectrum of *thematic topoi* that persistently recur in such fiction. Grounded on an assumption of the special efficacy of dialectical interaction, of the articulation of 'dramatic tension' or 'conflict' as an ideal mode for the declarative elucidation of thematic values and of that equilibrium and completeness that constitutes a cosmos, these are characteristically expressed in antithetical pairs, out of which it is the task of characters – and of the reader – to draw a meaningful synthesis or ultimate truth. The class system (or the mercantile system) is the basis of a stable social (or economic) order / is a web of intrigue, a machine of oppression. Marriage or the family (or the old regime) is the seat of love and eternal values / is a mesh of prescriptions and the snare of social and personal progress. Nature (or history, or the law, or the church, or technological progress) is the material expression or counterpart of human ideals / is the expression of irresistible universal material forces operating with remorseless indifference to private human ideals. The adoption of models of heroism (or saintliness) is the way to personal self-development / heroism (or saintliness) is impossible in modern times. Poverty is a trial conferred by fate upon man as a test of character / is a product of senseless socio-economic forces crushing character. The quest for power (or for the gratification of passion, or self-assertion through illicit action) is a means of establishing personal identity / sets the individual inexorably apart from human fellowship. Innocence is an intrinsic virtue / ignorance obstructs justice and self-actualization. The enactment of personal ideals is 'man's' ultimate salvation / solidarity with the community of humankind is the individual's ultimate salvation. The attainment of a creative synthesis of these and similar antitheses is the ultimate source of nobility / the failure of such a synthesis engenders mediocrity and banality of the most degrading forms. Realist narrative reifies these apprehensions of the way human experience is organized, treating them as universal and eternally abiding *natural objects* of psychological and moral perception, rather than as the historically contingent conventions of a particular cultural world-view.

We can recognize in addition certain types of *incidents* that reappear with rather striking frequency as the narrative correlatives of *topoi* such as these. Among them might be scenes depicting: an established domestic routine (e.g. the family at home); a character's sensation of restlessness/injustice; the marriage of convenience, of illusion; fantasy – the recourse to historical–imaginary models of being; the departure – for a better way of life; the unfamiliar world – the innocent blunder; the initiation, indoctrination; the shock of disenchantment; the declaration of war against the establishment; the adoption of rules; the temptation (of beauty, of power, of *luxe*); the seduction; the winning of a (social, political, sexual) foothold; the pursuits of labour; the fall into compromise (of native virtue, of ethical ideals); the celebratory summons to the simple life; the refusal – the disowning of old values; the betrayal; the realignment/reversal of alliances; the appearance of the rival, the new contender; the mutilation of the guiltless (the family, the innocent bystander); the unforeseen abandonment (the letter of rejection, the failed rendezvous); the submission to addiction (to luxury, to power, to alcohol or narcosis, to idyllic delusion, to sexuality); the collapse of old fortunes; the past announces itself (the detective, the avenger, the usurer, the blackmailer); ostracism; flight; the cul-de-sac; the past catches up; the happy prospects of the new alternative 'generation'; the confession, the surrender / the refusal to 'see'; the reformation of character / the retreat from the world / death in disillusionment; the working out of the terms of settlement or accord between those who remain; the earth-rooted endure; the wheels of 'progress' roll on.

If there has seemed to be any sort of order to the brief catalogue of incidents I've given, it was intended merely to simplify my own immediate aim of making clear – by a casual juxtaposition of examples – what I meant by each among a purposely free-ranging collection of examples. For instance, the two solitary words "ostracism" and "flight", in following the fairly menacing "the past announces itself . . .", needed no further explication, as they might have done had they followed, say, "the winning of a foothold" or "the departure – for a better way of life". An odd effect, however, has been that, in laying things out in such a way as economically to communicate with 'sense' otherwise undecipherably 'bare events', I've constructed a kind of story. A second effect has been that I've unmistakably told a story that carries with it a *particular*, *over-all* sense; that is, of a rather bleak view of existence. I have no doubt that together we might have cited other 'typical Realist' incidents contributing a more positive aura within such a context. Yet I am pretty confident not only that this is a fairly representative selection (if only because the Realist mode is inclined to be surreptitiously preceptive – along the lines I've indicated – in its setting forth of 'human truths' and hence to single out incidents that have a cautionary flavour), but – more importantly – that I could have arranged these same given events in a 'narrative order' that would have communicated a quite different vision of things. It's for that very reason that – having candidly adjusted our sights in this way – I'm prepared to let the paragraph stand. It serves an obvious point: the events in a story – the traits of a fiction's 'inner' world (the subject of the past half-dozen pages) – play a limited role in the impression we get of its over-all nature from our reading. It's the way that it's told that's finally 'telling'.

Realist words: their aims and strategies

Behind all that we can say about the *form* of Realistic fiction, anti-Realists will argue, there lies a constant feature. It positively invokes the conception that its 'telling' leaves what is told untouched. As a transparent medium (a window, a mirror) it has no qualities other than clarity. Since it claims to offer as its 'subject' a reality that is always already there, it *disavows the influence of 'form' (discours) upon 'content' (histoire)*. So we're in a variety of ways invited to feel that what's represented is a somehow random 'cross-section' (*tranche de vie*) taken straight out of life. Thus for example at the level of *histoire*, efforts are made to convey the impression that life is going on when we enter (*in medias res*) and life goes rolling on as we leave. In support of this renunciation of responsibility on the part of the novel's form (which itself obviously constitutes a formal rule of its own), Realist texts will call upon further specialized principles of narrative procedure. Central among these will be notions of the *objectivity*, the *comprehensiveness*, the *equity*, the *uniformity*, the *irony*, the ultimate *univocality*, the *figurality*, and the *effacement* or '*innocence*' of discourse. Until we've surveyed them with something like 'anti-Realist' disengagement we'll be unprepared to grasp much of what happens in anti-Realist fiction itself.

In contrast with an alternative major traditional conception of art (one fundamental to the attitude of Romanticism), that its function is 'expressionistic' – that is, that its purpose is to express the artist's own feelings and ideas – the Realist view is dualist in a very special sense. It asserts an inherent separation between the artist and the things he/she portrays. The artist and we stand 'here' together; reality stands 'over there'. The idea of detachment is essential. Reality is the *object* of our (subjective) attention. To the extent that subject and object get mixed up together, Realism fails in its duty. However much the illusionist intention invites us to enter the scene, we do so by the grace of the fact that the artist has stood firm and has endowed it with the qualities of a concrete, objective existence, distinct from his or her own. At least three different processes are involved. The convergence of attention or *concentration on objects*; the *objectification of the abstract*; and the *objectification of the subjective*.

It's been a favourite observation over the past few decades that the word 'real' stems etymologically from the Latin *rēs*, 'thing'. However we may squirm under this conflation of meanings, the notion that Realism is in some sense a kind of 'thingism' somehow clings.[22] Desnoyers, one of the heralds of the movement in art, defined Realism with what seemed utmost simplicity as "*la peinture vrai des objets*" (1885).[23] Consonant with this, a typical chapter of Realist narrative is surcharged with the minute and sedulously accumulated detailed description of characters' physiques, facial expressions, mannerisms, idiosyncracies of personal and regional speech, their dress, dwellings, possessions, diet, the flow of objects from person to person, and the tangible minutiae of social customs and manners. Objects and the 'detached observation' of them take on a virtue of their own.

But if – by reason of the declarative motive, say – the writer has some ('subjective') opinion to express? If we were to look at fictional narratives in the way that a teacher in the great tradition might wish – to see them as the embodiments of preconceived sets of abstract ideas, as a *Pilgrim's Progress* or a *Candide* undoubtedly in some important sense was – we'd be struck with the difference between the ways in which a Bunyan or a Voltaire and a Realist handled things. There is something cursory and schematic in their disposition of data, in comparison with the Realist's. 'Write a passage', says our imaginary teacher to, say, an apprentice Flaubert, 'showing how irresponsibly capricious and egoistically oblivious to the human realities a human can be.' Flaubert writes: 'Emma went to the house of the wet-nurse who was boarding her baby. Emma didn't care that the woman's way of living was a hazard to her own child's life.' 'Too abstract!' cries the teacher, '*be concrete*!' So Flaubert writes:

> One day Emma felt a sudden desire to see her baby. ... It was a little low house with a brown tiled roof; a string of onions was hanging down from the attic window. Some faggots propped against the thorn hedge surrounded a bed of lettuce, a few head of lavender and some sweet-peas trained on sticks. Little runnels of dirty water trickled over the grass, and all round were various nondescript rags, woollen stockings, a red calico night-dress, a large thick sheet spread out on top of the hedge. The squeak of the gate brought out the nurse, carrying in one arm a baby that she was suckling. With her other hand she dragged along a puny little boy with scabs all over his face, the son of a Rouen draper, left in the country by parents too engrossed in their business.

His narrative goes on for a page with no report of any speech from Emma until she leaves:

> 'Very well, very well!' said Emma. 'Good day, Madame Rollet.'
> And she wiped her feet at the door as she went out.
>
> (1857, 105–6)

To a Realist the passage would be an acutely effective one; by the standards of a Bunyan or a Voltaire it would be uneconomical. It illustrates the Realist's movement not only toward plenitude but toward the objectification of the abstract.

But the matter goes further still. In the Flaubert paragraph above – making my first point – no fewer than one in every six words is a noun designating some concrete object. In the Stendhal paragraph below, of an almost identical length, there is scarcely one.

> Obliged to spend a week in Strasbourg, Julien sought distraction in thoughts of military glory and devotion to his country. Was he in love, then? He had not the slightest idea, but in his tortured heart he found Mathilde the absolute mistress of his happiness as of his imagination. He had need of all his strength of mind to keep himself from sinking into despair. To think of any subject that had nothing to do with Mademoiselle de la Mole was beyond his power. Ambition, and the minor triumphs of vanity had in the past taken his mind off those feelings Madame de Rênal had inspired in him. Mathilde had absorbed all; he found her everywhere in his future.
>
> On every hand, in this future, Julien foresaw failure. This individual whom you have seen at Verrières so full of presumption, so full of pride, had fallen into an absurd extreme of self-depreciation.
>
> (1830, 398)

Realist fiction is often treated by contemporary critics as though 'description' were its solitary function. The segment above from *Le Rouge et le Noir* is clearly not descriptive in the sense that the *Madame Bovary* paragraph is. But it's not 'story-telling' either. Yet – however broken and erratic its 'flow' from sentence to sentence, however fitful and shifty its apparent 'subjects' from phrase to phrase, however uncertain (or undefined) its movement or status in terms of punctual time – we're deeply at home with the kind of passage it is. In fact, *because* of these modulations we're able to find a precise place for it among our expectations of traditional fiction: it *is* a description – of a fluid 'state of mind'. However 'subjective' this 'content' may have been made to seem, we have not been 'living' Julien's turmoil with him – we've been observing him, like one of those butterflies he's tacked "mercilessly" in a cardboard box he's made, a specimen writhing under the pin.[24] Nowhere have we 'seen him', materially, in this passage – but we've seen his subjective experience as an object, an insect in its 'paper showcase'.

We must make no mistake about this: the illusion holds throughout. It does not need to do so by keeping us within the mind of the character – Realism rarely in fact works this way. It does so by holding us within a perspective, a world of which the character's thinking is but one intelligibly related part.

As this third permutation of the objectivist inclination shows, one doesn't have to claim that to be a Realist is to assume that what's 'materially there' is both the source and the manifestation of everything that it's meaningful to tell (though we may at times feel that there's some justice to the claim if not to the assumption). What counts is that by an intriguing process of thought, certain speculative and pragmatic intuitions in a certain epoch appear to have fallen into a surprising syncretic blend: *to be objective* (it's believed) *is to look at objects; to see things as objects* (it's believed) *is to be objective*. The two views have little logical connection; their psychological attraction to one another is potent. In Realistic discourses, a materialist vision and a rationalist vision for a historical moment coalesce. In telling what is after all always unreal because it's fiction, the solution is to reify it.

Following from this, then, certain objects – in keeping with the conception of a world composed of things *containing declarable* meaning – take on privileged status in nineteenth- and twentieth-century Realist narrative. *Histoires*, in this perspective, revolve with striking frequency around 'things', often initially missing or enveloped with secrecy, which it is the dramatic task of characters to *discover*, to turn into *currency*, to *make clear*. The central furniture of the story is a repertoire of objects (a letter, a will, a diary ...[25]) whose leading feature is that they are in some crucial sense 'containers'. That they hold for those within the *histoire* – as the text would for its reader – contents substantiating a pre-existent reality, value, truth.

'Bulking large' on our shelves, Realist novels provide us with far more raw data than would ever be needed for the telling of the story. The narrative describes how and where, in what season and at what time of day, in what sorts of rooms, at what speed and with what kinds of utensils people do their work, eat, sleep, pace about, reason things out, cry and cough and adjust their spectacles and blow their noses. No other literary mode before the Renaissance began has ever claimed to do this – has ever wanted to claim to do this. Yet we customarily believe that the plethora of material somehow belongs there. A principle of *comprehensiveness* resides here, sustained by the text's intentions to seem objective, probable, exhaustive and cosmic.

The principle would seem to impel our reading experience in two opposite directions at once – toward a sense of chaos and toward an excessive sense of sameness. For, on the one hand, in its effort toward the appearance of non-selectivity, a novel may actually present us – we may come to wish it to present us – with details for which there seems to be absolutely no narrative or aesthetic significance. The very fact that they have none bears witness to the book's fidelity first-last-and-always to life itself.[26] The 'meaning' of the data it contains is part of the *world*'s meaning and belies any impression we might otherwise have had that any motives on the narrator's part determine what is told. But on the other side, having a 'totalistic', 'globalistic' intent, the text seeks not merely plenitude but positive *redundancy*.

> The realist's first pitfall is an overburdening of intimation [writes Stern].... Courting ephemerality, the realistic writer must hope that cultural gaps will be bridged by repeated intimations. Literature which does not enable us to bridge such gaps is not necessarily meaningless, but the meanings it yields don't have the continuity of realism. ... Banality ... is the realist's second pitfall.[27]

In other words, lest, by reason of some shift of culture between the writing and the reading, the reader is inclined to question the sense of an event as first described, the iteration of it in other forms with added details will eventually provide him/her with the experiential link that renders sense. 'He put on his castor——' What? we ask, he put on a small swivelling wheel? some perfume of musk? The narrator adds: '——a great hat from the fur of the beaver his father had killed one winter on the banks of the Volga.' Through the experience of that 'aha!', the 'euphoria of recognition' and the growing conviction of the internal causal coherence of the book as a whole, the sheer weight of data that the narrative drags along the track of its story consolidates, packs down, sets firm, the track itself. Thus a formal strategy of 'overprovision' re-enacts the vision of an integrated universe, in which everything fits – a universe whose creative and proliferative capacity is entirely matched by its orderliness and harmony.[28] The point is not merely that abundant details are given but that the feeling of abundance itself is reinforced; while clarity must be there, much effort is bestowed on conveying the impression that effort is needed to produce it. Justice is seen to be done.

We apprehend this in another way, in terms of Realistic discourse's *equity* or *levelness of regard.* Just as it may 'view things' from a middle distance, so it strives to seem to keep a kind of constant horizon of perception. While it often has large things to say, it works hard not to allow its 'angle of vision' to stray upward, for instance, into cloudy oversimple generalities.[29] When Flaubert gives all that attention to describing Charles Bovary's hat, we may like to say that it must have some metaphorical significance; but we're being very sophisticated when we explain it that way, and the fact is that an unsophisticated reader accustomed to Realism doesn't feel that that long passage is out of place without such an explanation. We've been induced to believe that this *is the way* to talk about 'reality'. 'Elevated concepts' are not merely disguised, they are dissolved in a continuous flow of detail by which the impression is given that a principle of parity operates throughout. No event or idea is privileged, nothing is omitted that 'has happened', or so it's implied. This is not a matter of Realistic discourse's 'consistency of tone', which is quite different, but of its assumption of an evenness of attention and evaluation (hence my adoption of the word 'regard' with its double-entendre), of 'equality of (material) representation'. This added feature of its 'telling' contributes toward the bulkiness we expect of such fiction. (The Realist short story, as to the proportion between story and telling, is no exception.) Where every party seeks or seems to be accorded 'equal time', little will seem to be told that's of much moment, or the broadcast may seem to go on forever.

Yet this semblance of liberality in the treatment of 'matter' conceals what is actually a powerful constraint. Realistic 'levelness' of discourse has another aspect, as we quickly see when we compare it with writing in other fields. We don't need (illusionistically) to 'get into' the life of a snail – or indeed of Napoleon – to credit a narrative about either of them by a biologist or a historian. A large part of our acceptance of non-fictional narratives (including a great number of normally highly 'improbable' events that science and history recount) derives from their expertise-based external authority, together with their allusion to certain axiomatic 'laws' (e.g. of nature) which we also believe in for similarly external reasons. In return for failing to create an uninterrupted illusion, 'non-fictional' narrative guarantees its external 'truthful' authority. And in return for being 'only fiction', fiction demands that the illusion of its internal coherence be uninterrupted. But – we say – surely both modes of telling allow for interruptions. Balzac's, Eliot's, Tolstoy's – and, yes, Flaubert's – narrators are always intruding and, usually, getting away with it, just as the scientist frequently interrupts to interpret his experimental observations. Here's the heart of the matter. In Realist fiction, we accept intrusions in the *narration* of the 'making forces' at work within the *histoire*; but these must not appear to interfere with those making forces themselves. This is one of the areas in which *discours* and *histoire* must collaborate with great delicacy and tact. Once again, telling must not seem to tamper with story. What Realism does not tolerate is a mixed discourse in which faithful narrative of *histoire* and any other kind of discourse operate according to mutually exclusive premisses. There must not be, for example, on one side: a premiss that the 'laws of making' are God's or nature's or human history's (the world of the *histoire* is always already there); and on another side: a premiss that the laws of 'making' are the narrator's (the world of the *histoire* is actually created by the narrator). A prime target for anti-Realist attack will be that Realist narration is characterized by a *uniform, unmixed discourse* whose purpose is the constant and punctilious preservation of a cognitive distance between *histoire* and itself.

But how can that stable impression – or indeed the impression of openness to the plenum of experience – be maintained within a text that's nevertheless cosmic and declarative, that aims to promote our perception of a 'correct' ('true') perspective from which the sum of its events may 'most intelligently' be observed?[30] Realism's 'tact' and subtlety unfold. In its outward assertions, it is univocal; in its composition it is ironic and often figural.

If the raw data of human experience tend to scatter and fly apart, literary convention has a compelling mechanism ready to hand in tropism – in, above all, metonymy and metaphor. The centre can be made to hold by the synthesis, the synthetic use of rhythmically recurrent imagistic motifs producing the effect of a global harmony, of a unified meaningfulness – without the aid of overt statement. The Naturalists' well-known theoretical qualms about the imposition of metaphor on 'real' events only remind us of the challenge it inherently poses to the mimetic impulse. As means of thematically organizing our perception of otherwise potentially amorphous experience on the part of their characters, Stendhal's use in *Le Rouge et le Noir* of such devices as the bird of prey and the *Mémorial de Sainte-Hélène*, and the function of Goriot's silver, are deeply familiar, as are Emma's blind man, Anna's old peasant with the iron, Eliot's images of the web and the pier-glass, Zola's le Voreux and the germination of the seed, Dickens' fogs and railways, Verga's railways and malaria and his *contadini*'s notion of *la provvidenza*. But Realism's *figuration of data* presents its own problems, as the last example I've mentioned foreshadows.

In pre-Realist narrative, notions of Fate and Fortune as transcendent influences are entirely consistent with each text's over-all propositions about the nature of existence. But in a fiction in which man is the measure and the force of a supernatural system is put aside, such references must be perilously out of place. Verga, like Zola in his treatment of the *topos* of germination, takes care to 'naturalize' his constant reference to providence; *la provvidenza* is always on the lips and in the minds of his *characters*; he's not responsible for it. Yet on another plane we know that he is. A cosmic view (the dynamic creative and destructive powers of determinism in human affairs) is in full-scale operation. But now, in the interests of 'objectivity', it must be concealed. As Stern says, Realism refuses "all invitations to journey into the ineffable"; there's to be no "dominance of intimatory meaning"; "symbolism" must be eschewed (184, 156–7, 84). Realism avows itself to be liberated from the life-falsifying rigidity which fixed allegorical systems may entail. As a window, a novel must appear unclouded by double meanings of its own. Things are (to the reader though rarely to the characters) what they seem. Words and the images they convey, however patterned they are, must be capable of passing as merely linguistic products of the effort to elucidate, to cast needed light on the empirical human foreground and not to intimate a transcendent background. Realist fiction therefore makes use of the strategy of *disambiguation* wherever it can. Not only are the supernatural and the naturally inexplicable erased, and natural forces made to provide the rationale for events, but events and characters appearing ambiguous are all eventually (quickly, some critics argue) 'accounted for'. If there's a mystery, it's there *in order* to be solved. A Realist novel, anti-Realists will say, is 'the text in a hurry' (*pressé*) – to explain. Coupled with this is the process of the *familiarization of the exotic* (Dorothea in Rome, Emma and Rodolphe at La Vaubyessard and in the forest). The potentially extra-ordinary (or 'Romantic') is made – with often obvious, often quite subtly linked thematic implications – to conform to or be dissolved in an overriding notion of what is ordinary.

A bizarre trait of Realism, then, from the standpoint of the anti-Realist is that where it appears superficially to be complex, it moves – beneath that surface and by *oblique* procedures – towards the simplicity of a unitary vision. In this view, an extraordinary feature is that it puts apparent equivocality to the service of an ultimate univocality. Above all, to this end, in a way that is not charmingly casual or incidental but constitutional and irreducible, Realistic fiction is an ironic mode.

> Realism [says Stern] is hostile towards ideology and conceptual language generally ... yet there appear to be no restrictions on the kind of vocabulary it may press into its service: aren't these two claims incompatible? The paradox is resolved as soon as we recall ... literature's freedom ... to treat [conceptual terms] ... as though they were 'objects' or data: as contents of a fictional consciousness, or as the play of authorial irony. (132)

Ostensibly, some special privilege obtains with irony in Realism. By tacit convention, where there is some *doubleness of voice* – where the narrator tells us in effect that in some sense he is *not* saying (only) what he appears to be 'telling' us – we absolve him of the onus of intrusion.[31] Where irony enters (when, for example, Stendhal's narrator lets us know that though we may on one level have sympathy for Julien, on another we must remember that he is proud, vain, and so forth – while all the time he *purports* to be telling us just one thing, namely what Julien thinks of and to himself), it is as though some kind of self-denying ordinance has taken effect.[32] It's by virtue of this waiver of final responsibility, the *systematic and sustained ironization of histoire at the level of discourse*, that we're able to 'live with' both the ostensible textural neutrality and the 'cosmic' propositionality of Realist texts in general. In each text, beyond *topoi* articulated at the level of *histoire*, there is some residual larger notion, on a higher organizational level, touching on such concepts as the positive meaningfulness of personality, social exchange, psychological awareness and/or moral seriousness, together with hints tendered in support of individual aspiration, energy, the advancement of society by an enlightened elect. ... Propositions are ventured at a 'cosmic level' which the narrator in each case does not *thematically announce* or may even appear to disown. Overarching attitudes are broached which only the ironic modality – by its seeming mutual annulment or neutralization of conflicting views at the local plane where *histoire* and *discours* meet – can release.[33]

Here is the realm in which fiction seeks to establish its 'innocence', to *efface* itself, to obliterate those signs by which it would seem to be governed by a unitary personal world-view.

Further textural strategies emerge. Throughout cosmically-motivated narratives from *Gilgamesh* onward, the protagonist 'grids' the horizon of our expectations. It's through the clarity of the protagonist's insight and/or the protagonist's values and desires that the potential for a plurality of meanings for the text as a whole is reduced. He or she may contribute more than any other single feature towards the disambiguation and the readerliness of the text. The protagonist can show us what to look for, what it all 'means'. But again the tension within Realism makes itself felt. The perspective, the focus the 'hero' or 'heroine' puts upon things must not be too narrow, too sharp – or too all-encompassing – or the idea will overrule the 'facts'.

So we encounter the *defocalization of the protagonist*. The 'true hero' disappears. We're given more than one protagonist (Anna – but also Levin). The protagonist's view is cross-filed with a view of events not 'focalized' by one protagonist (in *Bleak House*, Esther's narrative – but also the interwoven third-person omniscient narrative). The protagonist fails to put his/her whole vision (however wholesome) into effect. He/she is deflated, has defects of physique, of perception, of intellection, of feeling, of morality. The protagonist's aims themselves (even when told in the first person) are faulty when regarded from the distance at which we are subtly, ironically placed by the over-all concatenation of events and the nuanced selection and interplay of language by which his/her subjectivity and behaviour are displayed. The very protagonist is described as wavering, uncertain – his/her own values, view and very identity are momentarily but repeatedly, regularly obscured.

Yet so long as the 'world' to be described has the kind of breadth, diversity and intricacy that the Realist envisions it as his/her task to represent, Realism seems caught in a paradox. What 'person' could a Balzac or a Tolstoy set loose in the universe he retails, with the apparent span-of-knowing of a Balzac or a Tolstoy, without overwhelming its objective existence with the evident thunder of his wisdom? The Realist, then, moves steadily towards the 'depersonalization' – the *defocalization of the narrator*. As with its treatment of the protagonist, the text's information, its 'truths' as a whole, are now reapportioned and distributed. Other characters than the narrator are delegated as responsible for sharing and showing the 'knowing'. Information essential to the *histoire* is dispersed – by the device of the *narrative alibi* – among a vast range of readily familiar specialist characters, experts who form a now standard part of our experience of Realist reading: the old veteran or local sage, the doctor, lawyer, teacher, postman, midwife, shopkeeper or general gossip who knows everybody else's business. And with this come scenes of revelatory exchange between the knowers and the inquisitive uninitiate: the narratively indispensable questions are 'naturally' put by the curious or ignorant, the child, the newcomer, the voyeur, the raw recruit or apprentice, the disciple or hanger-on, the searcher or researcher, the spy, the suspicious – the rival, the aroused parent, lover, spouse or in-law. Other scenes appear in which the stress is not on the ignorance of the listener but on the assertiveness of the speaker: the curse, the complaint, the recrimination, the boast. And crises crop up in which the 'perplexed' is significantly all alone and must 'learn for himself': the uncovering of evidence, of a clue, of a sign, of a secret.[34] The passage of information from text to us is disguised as the outcome of the dramatized circulation of information within the story itself. The process makes for some of the most common sequences in Realist fiction – as well one of the foundational rules of the Realist-based manual of the 'craft' of writing: 'Don't tell it, dramatise it!'

But information about characters of a sort which can't 'in probability' be known by other characters must be relayed to us by some narrator 'himself'; there's no other way out. Yet, among other things, that vast reservoir of 'human truth' discovered by psychological insight, on which the Realist text trains its eye, lies of necessity in this realm. Once again, by one of the great sophisticated strategies in literary history, Realism masters that sleight of hand, of word, *free indirect discourse (style indirect libre)*. The narrator becomes so defocalized that we think there's no 'voice' but the character's; standing at the window peering in at the scene, we fail to see the source of the whisper at our ear.[35]

Still, there are things the narrator needs to say which 'he' or 'she' can blame on no one but 'himself' or 'herself'. Impossible as it may seem, the fiction's very language makes shift now to dissemble, to dissolve the 'himness/herness', the overbearing personal character of its speaker. Two classes of strategems in particular illustrate Realism's response to the dilemma. One of these gives shape to the relation intended between the telling and what's told. In the phrase 'impossible as it may seem' I've employed a gesture commonly used throughout literature to show that the speaker is on the side of the listener. The thing we look at is equally far from us both, and we stand together. But a feature of 'modalized' language such as this – affecting questions of belief, knowledge, certainty and ignorance, of obligation and permissibility, of truth, necessity, contingency and possibility – is that it distances the speaker not from *what* he or she tells – from the *histoire*, say – but from the sense of the rightness or truth of it. This is exactly what the Realist doesn't want to happen. Rightness and truth are what 'he's' there to give us, and, to the extent that 'he' puts this into question, he puts (the appearance of) personal self above what he tells. Realist narrative, then, seeks the *demodalization* of the text. It takes trouble to avoid language betraying its evaluative activity – phrases, for example, such as surely, probably, possibly, seems, perhaps, admittedly, so to speak – and all that standard apparatus (exclamation marks, quotation marks, italics and the like) by which with disdain or some other sign of personal opinion we imply that the given utterance is not ours.

The second – and oft-cited – strategem expresses the relation sought between teller and listener. When a narrator informs us that a character is a 'villain' or 'pitiful', that a room 'stinks' or is 'gorgeous', that an action is 'charming' or 'brave', the language threatens not the rightness or truth of what happens in the story but, rather, the status of the narrator as more directly regarded by us. Who is 'he', the Realist demands, to tell us what to think? The spectrum of discourse by which the narrator might be judged to be judging must, he says, be pared from the text.[36]

> Star of descending night! fair is thy light in the west! thou liftest thy unshorn head from thy cloud, thy steps are stately on thy hill. What dost thou behold in the plain? The stormy winds are laid. The murmur of the torrent comes from afar. Roaring waves climb the distant rock. The flies of evening are on their feeble wings; the hum of their course is on the field. What dost thou behold, fair light?

> It was raining. The rain dripped from the palm trees. Water stood in pools on the gravel paths. The sea broke in a long line in the rain and slipped back down the beach to come up and break again in a long line in the rain. The motor cars were gone from the square by the war monument. Across the square in the doorway of the café a waiter stood looking out at the empty square.

As the contrast between these two passages may suggest – each equally elegaic in its mood, each with its evocation of the silent regard following the upheaval of war now past, each equally 'poetical' in its own way, the first (so stirring to Werther and Lotte) the opening section of the last segment of "*The Poems of Ossian*", the second from the opening paragraph of Hemingway's "Cat in the Rain" (Macpherson, 1926, 409; Hemingway, 1944, 136) – once the Realist had set our horizon of expectations at the level of 'ordinary everyday life', any exotic departure risks appearing an encumbrance imposed on it by the narrator as person. The proposed solution is the *detonalization* of the text. Not only in its sometimes notorious twentieth-century purist permutations (in Hemingway, for example) but in Stendhal and Balzac,

Dostoyevsky and Tolstoy, there is a gesture soliciting us to take the narrator's 'report' as reportorial. To render diction and syntax 'flat', mono-tonous even, to strip it of the unrestrained colouration of the subjective imagination associated with Romanticism except insofar as these may be naturalized as the products of character psychology. The Realist has in mind the model of the objective scribe, setting down simply what's 'present'.

Ultimately, here as before, to speak of a work of fiction as being 'objective' – about fictional, by-definition non-existent 'objects' – is of course just plain silly. To an unexpected extent the posture of objectivity is an artificial means to another end. No one is being particularly 'objective' about anything. The narrative voice isn't a mirror or a window – it's another character. A voice that's characterized (by such rhetorical conventions) as that of a 'neutral personality type', that 'type you can really trust'. The 'objective precision' of the text is a strategy by which it dramatizes the belief that reality is solid and *can* be meaningfully mimicked. The way Realist narrative performs resembles the way a mime on the bare stage works when he or she makes us 'believe' by the precision of his/her gestures that a door is there, a balloon is there, a policeman is there, a fire is there and has its own objective being. The gesture toward objectivity, in other words, far from having so much to do with scientific truth or moral impartiality, is often largely called up to satisfy a very different motive – as another contribution towards illusionism and the cosmic attitude that illusionism underwrites. As soon as we've 'bought' some book's 'objectivity' and thus its illusionism, an anti-Realist may insist, we've purchased – at some price – a view that holds our own actual universe to be one that is finite, orderly, sensible and complete.

The case against Realism

Historical distinctions in the theoretical illumination of literature can obscure what is otherwise fundamentally straightforward. For example: that in any era the Realist impulse in its *broad outlines* exists side by side with its alternatives. Barthes sees it in Madame de La Fayette, Auerbach sees it in Boccaccio and Homer. What makes it and narrative in the novel form *come together* in the nineteenth century has to do with historical forces that support their fusion and cultural prepotence in that time, supportive forces that no longer cohere for late-twentieth-century writers. 'The nineteenth century', then, *means* something in an emblematic way to some of 'our' writers which they and we may or may not, almost according to taste, attribute to La Fayette, to Homer. Yet by what oversight can anti-Realists have let slip by the whole Modernist movement? Or, to be more accurate, why should one large group of them these days in fact be frequently called not 'post-Realists' but 'post-Modernists'? (It's actually because they do represent only one sort of reaction to Realism that I've declined to appropriate that term.)

Broadly speaking, the truth is that 'post-Modernists' acclaim Modernists among their favourite influences, and we can find them objecting to Modernism only in terms of those characteristics which it shares with Realism as I've described it. In all major respects except a very few that should become apparent, the leading figures of Modernist fiction and its immediate forerunners – James, Joyce, Proust, Mann, Faulkner, Woolf (and we may add, as many do, Lawrence, Hesse, Svevo, Céline, Malraux, Sartre, Camus and Kafka) – intelligibly fall well within the ambit of the principles of Realism set out in these pages. And Modernists have not, as Modernists, ever participated, at the level of fundamental issues, in the 'struggle against' Realism as we'll find anti-Realists determined in a variety of ways to do.[37]

My reasons for saying these things may be briefly put in this way. First, where the matter of Realistic referentiality is concerned, we don't need to make appeal merely to the very broad assertions of the apologists of Modernism to recognize that it is the "shock of recognition" that such fiction seeks to afford us.[38] It is difficult to imagine any literature that's more mimetically referential – however stylized their presentation may be – than the descriptions of the 'worlds' of Joyce's Dublin, Proust's Paris or Mann's Hamburg. Or that does so in a more massively comprehensivistic fashion ('informational' and 'probabilistic'). We recall Proust's prodigious embrace of 'a whole section of society' in one historical moment, of the Joycean novel as a self-proclaimed "farraginous allincluding chronicle", of Mann's introducing his massive *Der Zauberberg* with the announcement that "only the exhaustive can be truly interesting"; no matter how mannered and deeply ultimately symbolic his vision of it, Faulkner's multi-volume portrayal of Yoknapatawpha in structure and detail is patterned after the great tradition of the Realistic *roman-fleuve*, and however fictitious his 'parastory', it's anchored in a 'megastory' which he persistently invites us to verify. Even when Ike Snopes courts a cow, the text is insistently burdened, for all its 'mythicism', with the linguistic impedimenta of an appeal to the sentiment of material probability. Mann's sustained insistence on, above all things, the "mediocrity" of his protagonist has not simply thematic but explicit mimetically probabilistic intentions, and the same can be demonstrated to be true of Joyce's voluminous treatment of the minutiae of Bloom's, Molly's and Stephen's quotidian experience. The Odysseus myth has its explicit ironic function only to the degree that it resonates behind this foreground.[39]

At the level of *histoire*, then, what in Modernism may seem *invraisemblable* is naturalized by means of thoroughly conventional Realist notions of character and of character's centrality to experience. Illusionism dominates as before. While the 'I' of *A la recherche du temps perdu* (or indeed even of *Der Steppenwolf* or *The Waves* or *The Sound and the Fury*) is unstable or uncertain, the intuition of a 'self' is a constant on which the narrative's operation relies; it's offered without question as an entity to be 'identified' according to thoroughly consistent 'laws of causality and probability'. While there's every likelihood in Modernist fiction that the sense of an oncoming Deluge of external phenomena on one hand, and of the contingency and frailty of consciousness and artistic action on the other, threaten the meaningfulness of form, there is no final abrogation of either the illusion or of the Realist's renunciation of formal influence. The 'reality' is still 'always already there'. 'Anthropocentric' psychology comes more rather than less to the fore, and while there's progressive slippage and dislocation of the conception of personality at a superficial level, little is more typical of Modernist fiction than its unremitting insistence that we organize and recuperate the text's data by means of the differentiation it calls for between, for example, Leopold/Molly/Stephen or Hans/Joachim/Settembrini/Naphta as personalized notations, as personae in a drama, as *characters*. Narrator and narrator's protagonist now may even routinely come into the foreground and fuse to such an extent that the *histoire* – such as it is – seems to be subsumed under one subjective experience. But this is only part of a larger illusion. The *histoire becomes* the story of that narration as James would have had it – yet the same 'laws' (natural laws in every significant Realistic sense) govern all levels of *histoire* and (by identity) *discours*. We see a struggle over – and increased plurality of – form, but these are wholly circumscribed within the rules of a 'natural' megastory and parastory. There's an elaborate matrix of data – everything from the full spectrum of Realist human institutions to geography, biology, meteorology – that completely and definitively explicates the dynamics of that subjectivity in terms of rational materialism; there's a *race, milieu and moment* that would entirely satisfy a Balzac, a Taine, a Zola. To lose sight of this in a rush to say that fiction is now '*about*' time, memory, consciousness, myth, risks missing what such novels are made of and what makes them work as narratives.

On the same grounds that we consider Realism 'declarative' it would be fruitless to argue that the extremes (perhaps unequalled in narrative history) to which Modernists carry the discursive, expository and explicitly propositional features of their prose are not indicators of its immanent intention to be taken as profoundly declarative and paraphrasable. That its discourse, perhaps more than any in previous history, is extensively occupied with the precisianist qualification, modification and modulation of its 'statements' only reinforces our sense that it's so intended, in the terms I've mentioned earlier. Its accent on the fluctuations of personality serves well the conventional Realist aim at the defocalization of the protagonist as well as of the narrator. Beyond this – the distinction between 'who focalizes what's told' and 'who actually, behind it all, tells' is crucial – its ultimate 'voice' strives firmly to teach us to bring with Tolstoyan clarity what we think we know and say into register with what we ought to know and say.

Apart from its emphasis on the processes of consciousness and its obvious corresponding experiments in fluidity of discourse, and, naturally, its new stress on certain perennial thematic *topoi* (time, memory, the cult of place, the place of art), the most marked development in Modernism lies, we must say, in its approach to the old tension between the objective and the totalistic motives, the urge to submit to data and the urge to organize them. We've no problem in discerning the gargantuan yearning here to 'capture objects', the autonomously 'pre-existing' causally coherent material substance of the fictional world. We easily spot the traditional Realistic prepossession with the figurative operation of objects: Bloom's kidney and bar of soap, 'Marcel's' *madeleine*, Hans' Hippe-pencil and Clavdia-X-ray. Nor could any Realist resist applauding the determination with which the Modernist unfolds and explores subjectivity 'as an object'; or the manner in which he or she seems capable at will of finding a way of 'objectivizing' the abstract. It's Modernism that gives us the words for these Realistic processes – the 'objective correlative', the 'epiphany', the 'archetypal symbol'. Further, the conception of the objective correlative stems from and intimately implies its association with a vision of the connectedness of things (in the symbolist theory of *correspondances*) which, while it's anti-Naturalistically transcendentalist, invokes that very cosmic faith which Realism aims to promote.

The notion of the epiphany Joyce draws from a deeply structured and organized, totalistic vision of existence (as the reader of its originator, Aquinas, will know) to which a Balzac – an avowed Swedenborgian, after all – would have gladly pledged himself. If Modernism ever reflects any revolt against the Realist spirit, it is to affirm not a more radical but a more metaphysically orthodox credo toward which Realism yearns.

There's no doubt that, as I've suggested, this way of seeing things can in a Joyce or a Mann serve an ironic motive (a further and profound link with Realism) that differs from that of a Stendhal or a Flaubert or a George Eliot in the degree of its elaboration: in Joyce's whole conception of Bloom's and Stephen's story against the background of the *Odyssey*, for example, or in Mann's idea of Hans' story as a variation on the myth of the Quest. We might argue then that we've found one capital respect in which Modernism parts with Realism. But Modernists, theoretically anchored as they are in the tradition of Vico, Goethe, the Schlegels, Coleridge, Baudelaire and Mallarmé, would insist that nothing is further from the duality implied by metaphor and allegory than their idea of symbol and myth; that, to the contrary, the latter literally objectify the transcendent, that truth resides *in the object*; that in a profound sense Realism and Modernism are devoted to the same end – the retrieval, the recovery of that ultimate reality lying imminent in objects that (they might claim) has been obscured and falsified by man's rigid classical, classificationally dissective conceptualization of experience.

One may accept this, or judge it wrong or inadequate. We *may* discover that one whole 'wave' of anti-Realism adopts something resembling this notion of symbol as a basis for its own movement. The fact remains that we don't find Modernists seeking to demolish, overturn or upset the course of Realism. Rather, it seems more economically in keeping with the evidence to say that Modernism is in some compelling or compulsive way a last-ditch effort to trace the figure in the carpet, to 'make do' with, to salvage some sense of order from the rubble and debris of Realism's own surviving materials.

There will be more to say about Modernism as we go along.

The ground rules for the success of a new movement are straightforward and, like any good dance or game, involve three or four basic steps. Anti-Realism (however broadly we come to define it) has isolated the literary opposition, and it has identified it with what it considers a discrete system of values. The third step would be to show from as many angles as possible that this system of values is unsuited to the views and needs of the culture in which it now hopes to move. Anti-Realism takes that step too. Its argument is that from the standpoints of the philosophy of science, mathematics and language, of art, of history, and of literature itself, Realism can no longer work as it was once believed to do.

Philosophically, we don't think about things, we're told, in the way that writers did in the nineteenth century. First of all, we now live with 'relativity'. In fact, temptingly simple though it might be to believe otherwise (it would be a quixotically heroicist and unhistorical belief), the surge of relativistic feeling in the twentieth century was never a product or a reflection or even a misrepresentation of Einstein's General Theory of Relativity (1916); it was an expression of the already widespread attitude that had made that theory possible. Decades before the emergence of the movement we're to consider, radical postulates had been advanced concerning perception and cognition whose implications for the human sciences may have been even more far-reaching. One set of these has received vociferous if belated attention among recent literary critics. In 1927 the physicist Werner Heisenberg's paper on the uncertainty principle appeared. It was "necessary for the first time to recognize", he was to say, "that the physical world differed from the ideal world conceived in terms of everyday experience." The vision of reality from 'the middle distance' was finally in question.

> The resolution of the paradox of atomic physics can be accomplished only by further renunciation of old and cherished ideas. Most important of these is the idea that natural phenomena obey exact laws – the principle of causality. In fact, our ordinary description of nature, and the idea of exact laws, rests on the assumption that it is possible to observe the phenomena without appreciably influencing them.

Such traditional ideas of both causality and of objective observation were defective.

> The law of causality, because of its very nature, can only be defined for isolated systems, and in atomic physics even approximately isolated systems cannot be observed.

Totalistic perspectives could not hold.

> There exists a body of exact mathematical laws, but these cannot be interpreted as expressing simple relationships between objects exist-

> ing in space and time. . . . It is not possible to decide, other than arbitrarily, what objects are to be considered as part of the observed system and what as part of the observer's apparatus.
>
> (Heisenberg, 1930, 1053–4)

To put it in comparable literary terms at the risk of trivializing it, by reason of this principle of uncertainty or indeterminacy no *discours* (observer's apparatus) can relate any *histoire* (observed system) without the likelihood of so interfering with it that the *histoire's* 'inherent truth' must be obscured. And in fact, while there are natural forces at work in the universe, these are ones, as Heisenberg had put it, "to which every approach from the world of natural experience" (such as that of Realistic discourse) "is lacking" (1958, 101).

In 1931 the mathematician Kurt Gödel published a paper on 'formally undecidable propositions' – now popularly known as the 'incompleteness theorem' or simply 'Gödel's proof' – that had as vital an impact on the world of pure mathematics as Heisenberg's has had in the realm of physics. In essence it argues – and has not since been shown not to prove in substance – "that it is impossible within the framework of an even relatively simple mathematical system – to demonstrate the internal consistency (non-contradictoriness) of the system without using principles of inference whose own consistency is as much open to question as that of the principles of the system being tested" (Newman, 1956, 1616). There are formally undemonstrable arithmetical or logical truths; the consistency of arithmetic or of logic cannot be established by any meta-mathematical or logical reasoning which can be represented within arithmetic's or logic's system. "The resources of the human intellect have not been, and cannot be, fully formalized", as Newman and Nagel say (Nagel, 1956, 1695); "formal deduction has as its crowning achievement proved its own incapacity to make certain formal deductions" (Newman, 1956, 1616).

Put crudely, as Heisenberg's and Gödel's evidence (and that of the many in both fields who've worked in their wake) would have it, it looks as though both our powers of empirical *per*ception and our powers of pure logical *con*ception are logically incapable by any rational means at any one time of ever making 'total' sense of – or even of observing – all the facts that make up 'the truth'.

In the philosophy of language, dominant twentieth-century trends are so intimately analogous to those I've described in physics and mathematics that it would be abortive merely to outline them here; as an inextricable part of current literary theory itself, their movement will be a central subject throughout the remainder of this book.

Whether or not we're inclined to speak of this sceptical turn as a reflection of 'absolute decay' in the status of science – or of rational materialist thought – science's and philosophy's own revision of their limits was made possible by an even larger shift in Western culture's perspective as a whole.

> After having proclaimed the omnipotence of scientific observation and deduction ... and after asserting that for its lenses and scalpels there did not exist a single mystery ... [m]an is still walking about in the midst of the same enigmas, in the same formidable unknown. ... A great many scientists and scholars today have come to a halt discouraged. They realize that this experimental science, of which they were so proud, is a thousand times less certain than the most bizarre theogony, the maddest metaphysical reverie, the least acceptable poet's dream, and they have a presentiment that this haughty science which they proudly call 'positive' may perhaps be only a science of what is relative, of appearances, of 'shadows'....

This passage – in spite of its apparently explicit references to 'uncertainty' and 'relativity' – was published in April 1892; and it was written in support not of a philosophical or a literary position, but of the Symboliste movement in painting.[40] As with literature, there has always in the wider sphere of art as a whole, including music, been a powerful impulse that has proclaimed that mimesis was never art's greatest or proper province. That, to the contrary, art's true interest was not in mimicking external, material reality but in either the 'trans-real' or in what it, art itself, can and does do with its own inherent materials. That it is there to express what is within the artist or what is in nature but behind nature's outward contingent appearances, or to compose what is beautiful and/or evocative, whether by reason of the qualities of the art's own materials or by virtue of relationships (harmonies, for example) on one of these other planes.

Already, from the end of the nineteenth century onwards, this perspective had come into the theoretical foreground in every aesthetic or quasi-aesthetic medium except literature itself. "An objective representation, having objectivity as its aim", said Kasimir Malevich in 1927, the year of Heisenberg's indeterminacy paper, "has nothing to do with art. ... The Suprematist ... ignores the familiar appearance of objects."

> Objectivity, in itself, is meaningless to him. ... The visual phenomena of the objective world are, in themselves, meaningless; the

> significant thing is feeling, as such, quite apart from the environment in which it is called forth. ... If one insists on judging an art work on the basis of the virtuosity of the objective representation – the verisimilitude of the illusion ... he will never partake of the gladdening content of a work of art. ... Art ... no longer wishes to illustrate the history of manners, it wants to have nothing further to do with the object, as such, and believes that it can exist, in and for itself, without "things".[41]

Realistic mimesis is not merely illusionist; it's illusory. "Nature and art", Picasso had already said, "being two different things, cannot be the same thing. Through art we express our conception of what nature is not".[42] "It is time", added Naum Gabo, "for the advocates of naturalistic art to realize that any work of art, even those representing natural forms, is, in itself, an act of abstraction, as no material form and no natural event can be re-realized."[43] "*The great hidden laws of nature*", Piet Mondrian declared, "are more or less hidden behind the superficial aspect of nature. Abstract art is therefore opposed to a natural representation of things. ... In art one cannot hope to represent in the image things as they are."[44]

Art therefore turns away from the strategies of probabilistic illusion by which Realism had 'naturalized' its data for us. "In order that art ... should not represent relations with the natural aspect of things, the law of the *denaturalization of matter* is of fundamental importance. ... 'Art' is not the expression of reality such as we see it, nor of the life which we live, but ... is the expression of true life ... indefinable but realizable in plastics."[45] And art refuses declarative transparency ('readerliness'). Artists now "know that humanity is not served by making art comprehensible to everybody; to try this is to attempt the impossible. One serves mankind by enlightening it. Those who do not see will rebel, they will try to understand and will end up by 'seeing'. In art the search for a content which is collectively understandable is false."[46]

Art, in this view, finds that rational efforts to distinguish – to 'anatomize', as Flaubert would have said – objective facts or to establish moral principles are bound to deceive. "Life knows neither good nor bad nor justice as a measure of morals," said Gabo. "Life does not know rationally abstracted truths as a measure of cognizance."[47] "Today [1930] one is tired of the dogmas of the past," Mondrian argued, "and of truths once accepted but successively jettisoned. One realizes more and more the relativity of everything, and therefore one tends to reject the idea of fixed laws, of a single truth." Yet here then lies art's answer: "This is very understandable, but does not lead to profound vision. For there are 'made' laws, 'discovered' laws, but also laws – a truth for all time."[48]

So art elects a leap, a Pascalian *pari*. Which direction it chooses will determine two leading strains in non-realistic art and, incidentally, the two central modes of anti-Realist literature. It may hope to explore the qualities of *form* itself: "Pure painting", as Delauney called it; "plastic purity". "Having always been more profoundly moved", as Stanton MacDonald Wright put it in 1916, "by pure rhythmic form (as in music) ... I cast aside as nugatory all natural representation in my art. ... My inspiration to create came from a visualization of abstract forces interpreted, through color juxtapositions, into terms of the visual. In them was always a goal of finality."[49] Or – as had been foreshadowed by Gauguin as early as the 1880s and passionately developed by Kandinsky by 1912 – it may set out freely on the course of a private, non-consensual (for example non-probabilistic) vision in the name of that *transcendent truth* with which it may be in harmony: "The breaking up of the soulless-material life of the nineteenth century. ... The building up of the psychic-spiritual life of the twentieth century", these are art's "procedures" as Kandinsky saw it.[50] In Mondrian's view "As a pure representation of the human mind, art will express itself in an aesthetically purified, that is to say, abstract form. ... We shall see a reconciliation of the matter-mind dualism."[51] Through "subjectivity", art can make 'the absolute appear in the relativity of time and space'.[52]

As we'll see, insofar as it was a subjectivist and symbolist objective, in search of the absolute, one branch of anti-Realist fiction was to take the second of these 'directions', which after all has much in common with Romantic theory and has indeed, as an idealistic mode of thought, persisted throughout literature since Plato. In pre-war fiction the Surrealist movement was a major manifestation of it. As to the first, formalist orientation – and as to the second insofar as it was 'abstract' in its intention – though there were earlier moves in that direction fiction has largely had to wait until our own 'historical moment'. But the foundations were laid for a concerted literary attack upon Realism based on a conception of a fundamentally non-mimetic *raison d'être* in art as a whole.

In the meantime another argument has arisen to the effect that – as matters are described by current writers in the social sciences – present-day conditions outside of literature itself disqualify the Realistic mode. It has two parts to it: first, that Realism is inadequate to the expression of contemporary realities; and, second, that Realism is superadequate.

As it's described by one proponent of revolution in the narrative, "the conventional totalizing novel" of societies in the process of industrialization sought to present "secular substitutes for religious absolutes" (Zavarzadeh, 1976, 5). But, Mas'ud Zavarzadeh goes on,

> the new communicating technologies make the formulation of any encompassing authoritative visions increasingly more difficult, since they produce an information overload which gives such diverse and disparate views of reality that no single interpretive frame can contain them all and still present a coherent vision of experience. The information revolution also expands the range of the probable to the extent that it blurs the boundaries of fact and fiction. . . . The present seems to be more a mutation than a continuation of the past.

The contemporary period in fact "lacks an all-encompassing view of itself. . . . Cultural actualities cause the very notion of order to be regarded as a superstition" (7, 9–11). What's more, contemporary man "faces a redefinition of his own basic psychic conditions". The "humanistic concept of the self, its distinction between normal and abnormal, and its prescription for regaining a temporarily obscured selfhood" (as exemplified by the Freudian outlook) has now been eclipsed by theories that shatter "many of the protective distinctions, such as rational/irrational; appearance/reality; interior/exterior; fact/fiction" (17). The function of characterization as a device, for example,

> has become obsolete today, when a less anthropomorphic [sic] view of the world dominates our imagination. The individual has lost his centrality in a world where the very survival of the human race is at stake. . . . Character . . . today cannot fulfill its traditional narrative functions, which were to portray a fully individuated person so rooted in a 'community of thought and feeling' shared by his fellow human beings that he could also typify a particular group of people. (30–1)

Moreover, the very conception of "contradiction-free Aristotelian causal logic has been replaced by multivalued logics" (16).

> "Valued ends" . . . are set not according to pre-established human goals but by the self-augmenting, self-perpetuating needs of the new technology itself. . . . The old organic world of man and the new world of technology . . . "obey different imperatives, different

> directives and different laws which have nothing in common". ... Such developments create an open-ended and indeterminable system which defies all historical and totalizing frames of reference.[53]

> An air of irrelevance and immateriality has surrounded the contemporary interpretive novel.
>
> (26)

> The scientific discoveries of the recent past have overthrown the traditional views of facts as the understandable, tame, verifiable, and familiar sunny core of reality ... and instead have revealed them to be as wild, indeterminate, arbitrary, dark, and elusive as the most outrageous fantasies of speculative fiction.
>
> (21)

Seen against such a background, the continued reassertion of the 'old probabilities' would seem to be not merely foolish but treacherous. Realism becomes superadequate (my graceless term, not Zavarzadeh's) – it may accomplish more than is sanely wanted of it. We're thoroughly familiar, or should be, with the way in which (in the tradition of Lukács' energetic conception of it, for example) Realism is advocated as a medium for the promulgation of attitudes under the rubric of objective mimesis. (Socialist Realism, for one, wouldn't care to pretend to be instructing the converted.) The effect that socio-politically motivated endorsements of Realism have had in stirring some of today's strenuous reactions against it has not yet been explored and is likely to be vast. But what's important is that, to be false, Realism doesn't, in the perspective before us, need to be 'seeking to sell' anything more partisan than 'natural commonsense truth'. By the very force of its creditable illusionistic processes, it may impose on the reader's consciousness otiose and indurate ways not only of seeing but of *looking* at things and of interpreting and acting upon things.

The essential arguments against Realism on 'purely literary' grounds are quite simple. The first is that Realism isn't all that good at mimesis anyway. The second is that Realism is, on the empirical evidence of the past, far from all that literature has usually 'done' and can be hoped to 'do'. And the third is that Realism isn't on logical analysis all that literature should be expected to do.

The first idea begins by asserting that there is fictional literature and there is non-fictional literature. If there had never been any doubt (as it's now suggested there is) that literature performed its best service as a mimetic medium, there seems to be some innate difficulty in the notion that Realistic narrative could be the acme of fiction precisely to the extent that it is least fictional. Where what one wants is 'the facts', especially in an 'information rich' culture that's thought to be egalitarian in the dissemination of its information, certainly one has only to turn to the up-to-date, comprehensive, accurate and objective (as can be) and limitlessly detailed volumes published in biology, geography, geology, oceanography, astronomy, physics, chemistry, engineering. . . . Who is the fictionalist, to presume to proclaim his/her guesses at the truth in a few frail novels when the whole universe of material facts lies broadcast about the reader for the price of a – more than likely free – library card? Even in the area of the social sciences, a Balzac's picture of the mechanisms of society must have its limits beside the assembled work of trained historians, biographers, psychologists, economists, sociologists, anthropologists, the infinite journals of government, business, religion, philosophy and the superabundant general press. Surely there must be some reason beside its author's observational and expository expertise that makes one seek out a novel. Why doesn't fiction face up to doing what it – inherently – does best? Not reporting facts, but making fictions.

The second charge, that Realism isn't all there is to literature, draws the response: 'But what else is there?' Invited to consider the traits we've ascribed to Realistic fiction, its preoccupation with social institutions, for example – marriage, law, education, commerce – and with "common language, common knowledge, common experience", one can say 'But such is life! surely this is all that stories of human beings can be about'.

One answer would be: are these what *Gilgamesh* is about? or the Book of Job, or the *Odyssey*, or *Daphnis and Chloë*, *Metamorphoses*, *Beowulf*, *Tristan et Iseult*, *La Chanson de Roland*, *Le Roman de la Rose*, *Troilus and Criseyde*, *Gawain and the Green Knight*, *Morte d'Arthur* – you'll admit they 'feel' different – *The Faerie Queene*, *Hero and Leander*, *Orlando Furioso*, *Gerusalemme Liberata*, *Paradise Lost* – or *Gargantua et Pantagruel*, *Don Quixote*, *Pilgrim's Progress*, *Candide*, *Gulliver's Travels*——?

Something has happened. The anti-Realist would recall as witness J. P. Stern, the committed pro-Realist, who candidly finds unconvincing, as he says, "the view that realism is the sole carrier of truth in literature"; "there is no assurance that there will be a realism tomorrow. . . . Realism hasn't been the dominant mode of writing during most periods in the history of literature" (156, 157). However basic and all pervasive its stuff may appear to be in 'the ordinary life of man', says the anti-Realist, scarcely a semblance of the Realist world seems to occupy any significant space in a large part of the world's past narratives. Except as 'background' or as casualties of irony, such institutions, themes and strategies as we've mentioned seem displaced or dispelled there by other concerns. Viewed in the context of what might well be called the great fictional 'mainstream', the Realist mode was a cul-de-sac, an anomalous momentary 'hiccup' in the history of literature. A thing, as John Barth put it, "that has just about shot its bolt" (1967, 32).

But – as the third line of reasoning would have it – even if fictional literature in the past had always in practice given us nothing but Realism, is that categorically all there is for fictional literature to give? "The works of realism", says Stern, "bear witness more directly to life in the world than any others we know" (179). But is life in the world – as a 'subject' or as an idea – fiction's sole option? Stern contrasts the Realist mode with what he calls an 'idealist' one. "In realism the relation that obtains between a work of literature and the world outside is positive, expressive of a fundamental assent, whereas in idealism it is negative, expressive of a problematic attitude towards the world. . . . What such [an idealist] system requires for its elaboration is a radical alienation and distancing from those realities of life: a distancing which . . . runs counter to and challenges the practice of realism"(54). As we'll know from the evidence of modern theories of art, it is exactly this "fundamental assent" to "life in the world" that will prove a sticking point for at least half of those who feel that literature should be more wholly open to the expression of human experience.

And the question of 'idealism' apart, literature might conceivably be included among those arts whose subject may be nothing more or less than itself. In one unusual paragraph Stern gives a summary of the history of dramatic and narrative literature in nine movements (with Realism near the mid-point). This he portrays, as many conventionally do, in terms of fluctuations down through history in the way of internal 'themes' and dramatis personae's attitudes, seen from within the illusion-worlds of the plays and novels themselves. It's an evolving story of literature eventually "dissolving all persons other than the individual self, ending up in our own time with the fragmentation of that self, too, into a series of drives, 'tropisms', microscopic episodes, and linguistic ploys" (175–6). Imperceptibly – as if compelled for reasons he can't explain – Stern has moved from speaking of what characters (in their worlds) undergo to speaking of what novels (in our world) undergo. What he's not foreseen, yet that his diction uncovers in these last five words, is that a *radical* turning in fiction is in view, in which the internal-illusionist perspective itself is – or seeks to be – set aside. As the tangle of levels of his sentence shows, here's a shift that his Realist vocabulary (taking characters' experiences as its foundation) can't articulate or accommodate coherently.[54] It's a shift in which finally it is not theme or the illusion of self or of mind but *language* – the language of the text as a composition – that has become the organizing principle.

We have before us, then, two related kinds of crisis within literature's view of itself. "Realism ... is philosophically incurious and epistemologically naive", says Stern. "The realistic writer has no contribution to make to any discussion about 'models of reality', for he has no doubt about the singularity of the world in which realism lives, in which we all live"(54). But – we can hear his opponents saying – it's not good enough. On aprioristic grounds, there's logically more that literature can address itself to than this 'single world'. Dr Johnson foreshadowed half of it: "If the world be promiscuously described, I cannot see of what use it can be to read the account; or why it may not be as safe to turn the eye immediately upon mankind as upon a mirror which shews all that presents itself without discrimination" (Johnson, 1750, 20). If illusion's aim is merely to produce an undistinguishable duplicate of the world we already know, Realism risks proliferating monotony, unaccountability, banality and experiential and conceptual triviality. The other half, the other side of the coin, is that if the illusion is to be the end in itself, Realism risks betraying the causes of both life-in-the-world and art.

So now, this last argument goes, we've every reason to expect – to ask, even – that fiction be willing and ready to break with probablistically mimetic illusion, in at least one of two ways. As a still illusionistic mode it may feel free to pretend, or even think right to set out to demonstrate, that there's more than everyday life-in-the-world to feel and think about. Or, as an anti-illusionist mode, it may unfold and explore – whether for the sake of beauty or some further kind of truth or pleasure – the one thing fictional illusions can't cope with: the fictionality of the fiction itself, and all that it's 'composed of'.

I've mentioned that the success of a movement rests in part in its attesting in some three stages that the one it would displace is unsatisfactory. There's yet another step wanted. It must try to prove that it has the answers to fill the void it's thus created.

Anti-Realists would, I think, for their various reasons, speak in a fairly unified voice – some stressing one thing, some another – in support of the objections to traditional fiction I've described. From this point on they'll diverge widely. Yet they do now seem to coalesce, in vital respects, into two essential groups. They'll try to show us 'what else there is' by breaking our conventional relations with 'this world', or by moving us to other hypothetical worlds altogether.

1

SHAPES

Fiction-games people play

This is a superficial chapter; an oblique first glance across the surface of books.

It's plain enough that the variety of contemporary texts working in some fashion to unseat Realistic expectations in reading is vast and growing. Here are several sample cases – models for future reference.

One kind of narrative would place us in a quasi-historic, prehistoric or legendary time in which human behaviour is different from that which we'd readily understand in the context of the Realist tradition. (A Carolingian knight circulating in the world of common men – in Calvino's *Il cavaliere inesistente* [*The Nonexistent Knight*, 1960] – is little more than a suit of armour; the armour dismantled, the knight ceases to exist.) Another story takes us to a setting proposed to exist side by side, temporally, with our own actuality yet in which events occur that fail to coincide with the natural and social 'laws' essential to the workings of Realist narrative. (A civilization is described – in Borges' "Tlön, Uqbar, Orbius Tertius" (1964) – for whose citizens objects have no continuous reality and whose conception of existence constitutes "a new world that finally replaces our present world".[1]) A third story posits events that – though they're offered as occurring in a time and a setting encompassed by the world as it might be described in a Realist novel – depart from the conditions on which Realist narrative rests. (In Barth's "Night-Sea Journey" (1968), at the start of

Lost in the Funhouse, a "voice" portrays itself as swimming in an endless sea towards a nameless shore, in language intimating that it may 'speak for' a spermatozoon – or for an idea, an *élan*, such as the writer's creative impulse – seeking, and simultaneously abhorring the impulse to seek, a realization of itself which it may or may never achieve.)

We may be "removed", in other words, to a "space" in which normal Realistic understandings with regard to time, place and – or – action are "replaced" by quite different ones. In Nabokov's *Pale Fire* – a book composed of a poem of 999 lines and of a 190-page indexed 'commentary' on that poem – we're invited to entertain the perhaps mutually exclusive possibilities that the place, "Zembla", from which its commentator says he has come, exists only in his imagination; and/or exists on the same level of reality as the place, "Appalachia, U.S.A." where he says he's more recently lived, which may, in some third alternative, also be a product of his imagination; and/or exists as a product of the imagination of the writer about whose poem 'he' writes, who lives in Appalachia or some other unnamed place; and so forth. In another novel the relatively stable, Realist, conventional notions of space, time and action may themselves be put into question, as if this were the very 'subject' of the narrative. It is often impossible – in Robbe-Grillet's *La Jalousie* [*Jealousy*] or Sollers' *Le Parc* [*The Park*] – to ascertain whether, in relation to each other, events described are occurring in the present, the remembered past, or an anticipated future; in 'real life', in a 'still life', a photograph, or in the mere unfolding of language having no 'serious' relation to 'reality'. One half of the account of which Beckett's *Molloy* is composed begins with the statement "It is midnight. The rain is beating on the windows" and ends – closing the book – with the statement that this did not happen: "It was not midnight. It was not raining." In Calvino's *Se una notte d'inverno un viaggatore* [*If on a Winter's Night a Traveler*] the reader is asked on ten different occasions to believe he/she has begun a novel of a certain sort, only to discover that one is each time reading only the first chapter of a different novel about different characters, different times, different places, by a different 'author'.

Each of literally thousands of narratives written since the end of the Second World War, then, turns irrevocably on some written 'event' – at the level of *histoire* or of *discours* – that would be grossly incompatible with the writing premisses of a *Madame Bovary*, a *Père Goriot*, a *Middlemarch*, an *Anna Karenina*.[2] But our perception of this 'gaming' is so generalized and vague – and covers so many possibilities, so many kinds of possible meanings – as to leave us with no immediately 'natural' way of rationally describing in a concerted manner what it is that we may intuitively feel underlies and unites so diverse an array of texts. The problem is rendered acute by the fact that – while analyses of individual authors or nationally grouped authors or clusters of texts of one or another of these sorts abound – no research has been produced attempting the kind of 'synthetic overview' we need, a topology of this varied landscape, so to speak, of 'alternative fiction'.

We might try to redress matters by looking to the writers' – and their advocates' – emphatic public statements on the subject of Realism and its modern heritage. "The true shock", a recent critic has written in speaking of new fictionalists, "is not how far their novels have gone, but rather how far we let the old novel desert the true ideals of artistic representation in favour of a wholly unreal documentation, which was satisfactory to neither reader nor writer and potentially destructive of the genre itself" (Klinkowitz, 1981, 179). In fact, for us a second but equivalent shock must lie in how many astonishingly diverse minds, among novelists themselves, we find speaking so dogmatically and sweepingly in unison in this way on this matter. "Of all the interesting subjects for meditation offered us by the attitude of the public towards literary works", wrote Nathalie Sarraute in 1956, "is the admiration ... for acknowledged masterpieces" (121). In the realm of the novel, if we had to designate all of the writers of such sworn masterpieces "by one name, it would have to be that of 'realists'" (128). Yet, she went on, there was one very disquieting point:

> what they described was not reality. ... It was only a surface reality, nothing but the flattest, most commonplace sort of semblance ... [126]. Nothing but habit of long standing, that has become second nature, in addition to our submission to all generally accepted conventions, our continual absent-mindedness and haste, and, above all, the avidity that impels us to devour the appetising foods these novels offer, make us agree to let ourselves be taken in by the deceptive surfaces that this form sets shimmering before our eyes ... [131]. We end up accepting the immorality that, in literature, results from a negligent, conformist, hardly sincere, hardly honest attitude towards reality. ... By presenting readers with a reality that is mutilated and a snare, an indigent, flat appearance in which ... they find nothing that really constitutes their lives – neither the real difficulties with which they must cope nor the real conflicts they have to face – we alienate them and arouse their distrust, we discourage them in their efforts to find in literature the essential satisfaction that it alone can give them [134–5].

Already, by 1947, another novelist who would scarcely be considered in any other context as likely to fit comfortably in the world of Sarraute had with equal passion published lines about what his countrymen regarded as "serious" literature – and there's no question but that he has the same fictional tradition in mind:

> the expression of 'real life' ... seems to fall short of academic standards. The notion that motor-cars are more 'alive' than, say, centaurs or dragons is curious; that they are more 'real' than, say, horses is pathetically absurd. ... For my part, [J. R. R. Tolkien wrote] I cannot convince myself that the roof of Bletchley station is more 'real' than the clouds. ... Much that [the academic] would call 'serious' literature is no more than play under a glass roof by the side of a municipal swimming bath. ... We are acutely conscious both of the ugliness of our works, and of their evil.
>
> (Tolkien, 1964, 55–6)

Two decades later, one of the most radical fictionalists of our own time, and one whose work is among the most explicitly devoted to the exclusion of conventional ethical concerns from his novel, is as ardent as these others in his implicit association of Realism with an insidious immorality. "From now on", Philippe Sollers wrote "the novel repudiates its false gods (Balzac and Tolstoy)" (1968b, 59). The anger – the sense of cultural delusion and betrayal perpetuated in traditional fiction – is clear: we are surrounded by, entrenched in, the effects of "the bourgeois novel", as Alain Robbe-Grillet, among many, has put it. "The only conception of the novel that is current today is, in fact, that of Balzac", Robbe-Grillet wrote in 1956.

> Most of our contemporary traditional novelists ... could copy long passages from *The Princess of Cleves* or from *Old Goriot* without arousing the suspicions of the vast public that devours their products. ... One can hardly believe that this art can survive much longer without some radical change ... [1962, 50–1]. The nineteenth-century way of composing a novel, which corresponded to life a hundred years ago, is now no more than an empty formula ... [136]. The word thus functioned as an ambush into which the writer lured the universe and then delivered it into the hands of society ... [57]. We thought we had come to terms with [the world around us] by giving it a meaning, and the whole art of the novel, in particular, seemed dedicated to this task. But that was only an

illusory simplification. ... What we have to do now, then, is to build a literature which takes this into account [56].

This attitude crosses all national cultural bounds in the West. "People have lost faith in the novel", said the American Ronald Sukenick in 1970, "they don't believe it tells the truth anymore, which is another way of saying that they don't believe in the convention of the novel."[3] "It's hard to believe the novel has a future", he added in 1975. "What we think of as the novel has lost its credibility – it no longer tells what we feel to be the truth as we try to keep track of ourselves. ... I would like to propose the invention of a new tradition of fiction" (Sukenick, 1981, 36).

> The novel [wrote Susan Sontag] is (along with opera) the archetypal art form of the 19th century, perfectly expressing that period's wholly mundane conception of reality, its lack of really ambitious spirituality, its discovery of the 'interesting' (that is, of the commonplace, the inessential, the accidental, the minute, the transient). ... While music and the plastic arts and poetry painfully dug themselves out of the inadequate dogmas of 19th century 'realism' ... the novel has proved unable to assimilate whatever of genuine quality and spiritual ambition has been performed in its name in the 20th century. It has sunk to the level of an art form deeply, if not irrevocably, compromised by philistinism.
>
> (1969, 108–9)

"The world of serious fiction is very narrow," said C. S. Lewis in Britain. "Too narrow if you want to deal with a broad theme'", added Kingsley Amis in this conversation between them (Lewis, 1966, 91). The brand of narrative for which Lewis argued as an alternative, a kind he considered to be liberated from the strictures of Realism, "really does deal with issues far more serious than those realistic fiction deals with; real problems about human destiny. ... What is a footling story about some pair of human lovers compared with that?" (89). "We must not allow the novel of manners", he had already declared in 1955, "to give laws to all literature: let it rule its own domain. We must not listen to Pope's maxim about the proper study of mankind. The proper study of man is everything. The proper study of man as artist is everything which gives a foothold to the imagination and the passions"(65). As if to echo this, the Argentinian Jorge Luis Borges describes a writer–character in one of his stories as feeling that "irreality" is "one of art's requisites" ("*la irrealidad, que es condición del arte*").[4] "As Borges would say ... this irrealism", John Barth adds, "is all that I would confidently predict is likely to characterize the prose fiction of the 1970s. I welcome this ... because unlike those critics who regard realism as what literature has been aiming at all along, I tend to regard it as a kind of aberration in the history of literature" (Bellamy, 1974, 4).

In these passages, while there are nascent signs of divergence of views as to where a non-Realistic fiction ought to go, we've reached one of those moments in history where a common cause makes strange bedfellows. In fact a blurring of boundaries characterizes the moment in important ways, and this seems to present very real problems for us.

One of these appears at first to involve chronological anomalies. Among the generalized expressions of disillusionment with Realism quoted, a number were first uttered – in conversation, in lectures, in articles, in fiction itself (the Tolkien, Sarraute, Lewis, Robbe–Grillet, Borges) – on occasions considerably, even decades, before their ultimate publication in book form some time in the mid-1950s or after. Certain further texts central to arguments to come were written as far back as the last quarter of the nineteenth century yet found their 'public voice', their first general circulation and both their popular and their 'serious critical' reception in exactly the period from the mid-fifties of our century onward. It's in the late twentieth century that there exists a concerted cultural context and a conscious intellectual framework capable of supporting them and that 'appropriates' and presumes to validate them.

The other and more immediately crucial 'blur-effect' affecting those statements is one I've referred to as the 'lumping-together' phenomenon: "the old novel", "acknowledged masterpieces", "serious fiction", "Balzac and Tolstoy", "the bourgeois novel", "*The Princess of Cleves* and *Old Goriot*", "contemporary traditional novelists", "the convention of the novel", "the novel of manners" ... Everything we know of their contexts and of their authors' views as expressed elsewhere makes it plain that what's intended by this array of epithets is fictional Realism. But when it comes to our trying to grasp what it is that actually produces the outcome I mentioned a few pages ago, that 'unseating of our customary (Realistic) expectations', as points of reference such sweeping negative generalities leave us mouth-agape. Our best hope in the first instance, then, to gain a footing, is to identify in a bare, uncomplicated way the fiction before us – the *narrative* qualities *taken globally* – together with the sorts of *overt premisses* on which such texts basically depend *as narratives*.

Of the works we're to consider, a small but particularly well-publicized number are openly inclined, on some plane, toward the naive and/or the kitsch. We'll need eventually to consider the question of the status of narratives about which 'serious critics' throughout the culture increasingly pour forth volumes of treatises each year yet whose appeal – in fact whose concerted pitch in some cases – seems often to be to the young, to the literarily irrecondite, and to the sentimental and sensation-seeking in readers at large. Inasmuch as this trait can truly be laid at the door of much in Tolkien, Lewis, White, Buzzati, Beagle, Le Guin, Heller, it can as readily be said, applying the same intuitive criteria, of much of Borges, Golding, Vonnegut, Lem, Barthelme, Pynchon and Calvino. Indeed, as the difficulty I have in drawing up two separate lists of writers here shows, it's hard to know by what rational principle we might unmistakingly distinguish the kitsch and naive from the 'genuinely sophisticated' in them, even while we feel unquestionably that both kinds of properties are there in plenty. For the moment it suffices to say that some unexpectedly fluid commixture of the 'high' and the 'low' (as Frye might have put it), of the esoteric and the popular formulaic, now runs in the literary vein, for perhaps profound and complex reasons. And to keep alert to the fact that sophistication is not merely one of the qualities a work can *have*, but is also fundamentally one of the things a work of art may *do*. That sophistication itself is a rhetorical modality; that both the recondite *and* the vulgate formulae may be functional strategems, like any others, by which the work may choose to work upon us.

What seems uncustomary seems in some respect 'unnatural'. Realists' prepossession with the 'natural' world, and with the effort to give a 'natural' description of it, is a turning point around which perhaps all anti-Realistic activity might be imagined to revolve. Anti-Realism seeks to confront and displace what Husserl called 'the natural attitude'. Put in the most primitive terms: what we think we see 'in nature' – what we take to be 'natural' – is largely a product of our projections. We assume to be 'out there' certain pre-existing and continuous (always already there) phenomena which are in fact contributed by our consciousness; our consciousness is in turn determined by, among other things, cultural forces; and among these is the force that language itself has in structuring our thinking. When we speak, therefore, of 'things' in language we believe to be the most 'natural' – that is, innocently self-effacing and 'transparent', mere media for the reproduction of 'real', im-mediate and absolute events outside it – we are already engaged in the act of *producing*, shaping, attributing predetermined systems of meaning to, the universe. In this view, when we speak – or write – 'naturally' of what appears to be 'most natural', we are, in fact, most likely to be merely re-enacting the thought-habits of our culture. Realist fiction, therefore, as a medium pretending to mimetic transparency and to objectivity – and committed as it is to the continuity of illusion, to the most 'probable', to the most familiar and the most 'readerly' – would be the most likely to perpetuate what may be only, in the final analysis, conventional delusions. To write Realistically would be to 'naturalize', to bring under our control, to domesticate, and to cease thereby to see or question events as they are. What is to distinguish anti-Realist modes from one another may well come to hinge on the divergence of their responses to this problem and the variety of the ways in which they may seek to set before us events (in the wide sense of the word I've indicated[5]) that are 'unnatural' and consequently more genuinely 'real'.

"What language would escape this insidious, incessant language", says one writer, "which always seems to be there before we think of it?" "We need", says another, "to clean our windows; so that the things seen clearly may be freed from the drab blur of triteness or familiarity – from possessiveness. ... this triteness is really the penalty of 'appropriation': the things that are ... familiar, are the things we have appropriated. ... We say we know them. ... We laid hands on them, and then locked them in our hoard, acquired them, and acquiring ceased to look at them."

The first of these quotations is by Philippe Sollers (1968b, 61); the second by J. R. R. Tolkien (1964, 52). That they speak as though with one voice on the issue I've just described should be instantly apparent; that they also stand, in their fiction, at opposite ends of the spectrum of the literature we're to discuss will become increasingly plain. That they happen to be 'extremists' strikes me as unimportant; nor do the two seem to me (though others will variously disagree) supereminent as artists among those around them. What matters, I think, is rather that they are simply exemplars of two elementarily different courses that, as I've already implied, anti-Realism is to take.

New-world games: gaming with worlds

If we'd had no other intimation of it, we could have readily made out from the first three examples referred to (pp. 48–9) that, to open things bluntly, certain books appear to seek to build before us 'other worlds' as alternatives to the sort portrayed in Realistic narrative. A fiction of alternative worlds is not a new idea.[6] And if one wished in a work of fiction to supersede the 'natural-world' of Realism, one could hardly conceive of a more obvious and direct way than this.

But I think it's essential that we see from the start that both species of fiction ahead of us are in a vital sense deeply conservative – each in its own fashion.

With the outstanding exception of the apparent question of *probability*, what we can temporarily call the alternative-world model in contemporary fiction is, put simply, typically compounded of virtually all the standard narrative features that are well within the tolerances of the Realistic mode.[7] It will turn out to be comprehensively illusionistic, declarative, exhaustive in its movement toward informational amplitude, and it renounces the influence of form upon content. It conserves the principles of the objectivist stance; of uniform, unmixed discourse; of the familiarization of the exotic; of the defocalization of the narrator. It avails itself commonly of the tactics of the narrative alibi, free indirect discourse, and the demodalization of the text. It is, above all – as we'll have cause to search into at length – cosmically totalistic in configuration, and mimetic in its strategy.

I've omitted the issue of external *referentiality*, and for a substantial reason. As we must come to observe at close hand, when a work of fiction proposes any detachment from or incompatibility with whatever is commonly assumed in the world (of fiction or of actuality) external to it – whether by virtue of its story's improbability or of any other exception it may bring to the rule – as anti-Realistic narrative is about to do, it's inclined to make the question of its referentiality (in what way is it referential? is it referential at all?) its unique and central problem. Chapter 2 broaches that cask. But one point related to the matter needs clarification right away.

What I've said about alternative-world fiction's being "mimetic" must raise a quizzical eyebrow or two. It's necessary now to consolidate an idea implicit in what I said in the last chapter yet that was purposely left ambiguous. I proposed there that Realist fiction expressed both a referential and a mimetic motive. This seems redundant – and in most common usage it would be. (A book speaks of the world outside it; a book imitates the world outside it.) But – in the way that I'd like to treat these terms – that is not necessarily so at all. A novel is referential when it claims to tell us something about the world outside it. A novel is mimetic when it *makes appeal to the verbal conventions* by which we 'imitate' the world outside. In a subtle but absolutely crucial way these are not the same. We know from experience – and speak quite ordinarily in a way that shows we know it – that narrative literature frequently claims to be referential yet is scarcely mimetic. *Paradise Lost* claims to intend to justify the ways of God to man, yet it often offers us what we would by no stretch of the imagination call a 'material transcription of the empirically verifiable data of the physical senses'. To discover whether it is meant to be taken referentially we need to supplement our reading of its descriptions with other evidence, of which the purely expository abstract phrase "to justify the ways of God to man" is one. On the other hand, the following passage clearly uses the language by which a Realistic novel habitually 'imitates' the world outside it: "In a leather arm-chair, to the right of the fireplace and the standard lamp, a man is sitting in profile, glass in hand. In front of him is a woman". Yet other evidence within the text from which I've taken it – Sollers' *Le Parc* (7) – positively protesses that it is *not* meant to be taken referentially.

The implication is that writing may be imitative in its strategy – borrowing, for example, the formulae of a literature that is referential – without in fact seeking to report to us anything other than itself. Let's think, for instance, of the word 'scribe'. A scribe is one who writes down something – who 'scratches marks'. We have come to *use* the word, *in addition*, for one who *tran*scribes with these marks, who *copies* something that exists before those marks are made. The anti-Realist may suggest that we have added to the meaning of the word 'writer' a similar *supplementary* presumption – that the writer 'copies the world' – when this is excessive and not necessarily true. We need other information before we can be sure of the 'motivation' underlying the words of a text – the *status* of the thing to which the words 'refer'. Whether it's to be taken, for example, as something 'real', something 'purely fictional', or some linguistic play within the text.

In life, when I say something aloud that seems self-pitying to the man next to me, he may respond by *putting on* a face of self-pity. He frowns, he pouts his lips, he clasps his hands – he represents by detailed concrete gestures what he feels I myself am doing. He makes a comment on my self-pity by frankly stating – by the peculiar quality of his gestures – that he is *imitating* me. The whole effect of his otherwise bizarre activity is lost if he does not include these *extra cues*, making it plain that he's not simply writhing about for his own comfort but has moved into a *mode of imitation*. By, for example (and perhaps above all), a specialized intensification – amplitude, repetition, diversification, exaggeration, recapitulation by the redundant addition of different but analogous words, gestures – of detail. We have a full vocabulary of indicators in life by which, quite obviously, quite subtly sometimes, *we declare that we are imitating*.[8]

Literature has such a conventional vocabulary at hand. Its appearance manifests a *choice* on the part of the narrator. (My friend could as easily have left out that special exaggeration of detail – and I would not have known he was imitating me but would have thought he was merely, in and for himself, writhing.) In life, a lady of a given background may say to me "I've just tried on the most beautiful dress!" and when I ask her to describe it she may say "It was simple and yet elegant, like a Cinderella gown – it reminded me of the picture of my grandmother at her first ball. I felt like I was floating, in a dream." This 'description' may give me a rich sense of what the dress was like, but it is not a mimetic description. The 'strategies' the teller uses are ones based on personal (both 'real-life' and, you notice, 'literary') *associations*; the 'object in view' is not the dress but the teller's private and subjective impressions. A mimetic description might begin "It was an ankle-length Empire-style sapphire blue silk gown" or "a close-bodiced crinoline with sweeping skirt of embroidered white Swiss lawn, over-embroidered with seed-pearls". The basis of these reports – from recent women's-wear journals – is a register of discourse (here that of couture) conventionally deemed specifically appropriate to the object at hand and indeed to the whole class of objects to which it belongs, and not (so much) to the unique experiences of the particular teller; a language adapted to, referring to the properties by which the thing itself is imagined to '*express itself*'.

There is a host of textual strategies by which a book, now, can refer us to the conventional language of reporting (detailed inventories of material data, the adoption of a rhetoric of objectivity, of technical jargon associated with the topic, and so forth) and it *may* be imitating the world outside it. But it may simply be imitating imitative language. As we do in life, it borrows the rhetoric of imitation not always to convey – imitate – a *truth* but to convey the impression *about ourselves* that whatever we say, it can be trusted because we seem to be in possession of the language used by those expert in the relevant area of 'truth'. Whatever the text's reasons for doing so – and there may be many – all that we know without further evidence is that it has moved into an imitative mode.

This is what Flaubert has done in the passage I've pointed out in the preceding chapter, where Emma visits the nurse. He's shifted gears, he has moved into the mimetic mode.[9] 'But', one may say, 'Flaubert's is serious business; the example you give of your friend's "putting on a face" is merely a case of mockery. Flaubert was not shifting gears as your friend does, he wrote that way because that is the way that any serious narrative must be written. Mimesis is not an "imitation mode" – it's simply *the* mode of the language of "telling" anything, which is *always* representing something other than itself!' Yet this we know is not the case. Language and imitation are not so inextricably linked as that. In the nineteenth century it was taken to be more so than in other centuries. As I've indicated speculatively in the last chapter, Voltaire (as an arbitrary example) did not view uninterrupted mimesis as the universal mode of fiction. The choice not to be mimetic has always been with us. This is one point that Sterne was making in his famous parodies of gestural mimesis in *Tristram Shandy*. To write mimetically is to write according to a special convention; one may accept it – or not.

It's essential that we see that a decision is involved. The implications are sizeable. When, for example, a mimetic modality is elected, its appearance on the scene constitutes not merely a 'representation' of the things it signifies but – as a *conventional signal*, a promissory note ('this text promises to imitate') – one of the text's very credentials. That is, it's one of the articles on which our credence is (hoped) to be founded. When, by contrast, a narrator of Voltaire's kind says merely 'Being an eccentric, X did Y', he submits a different kind of credential: the inner logic of the text – and also, surreptitiously, the *logical* reasonableness of his tonality. (He *is* of course in this way mimicking a 'reasonable person', and here some of our troubles will arise. . . .) In each case – in a 'Voltairean mode', in a 'Flaubertian mode' – the choice discloses much concerning the particular bases, the premisses on which our reading of the text is intended to be founded.

It's easy for us to forget that in the history of imaginative narration taken as a whole, 'Once upon a time' has been the norm, the normal initiating 'cue'. Realism's 'on the thirteenth of January 1848, at nine o'clock in the morning' is, all-in-all, the exception. It represents a departure from a longer tradition, a departure whose aim is to serve as a signal that we have now moved from the 'old story-telling mode' to the imitative mode. But once we have discerned the choice and its many implications, we are not yet assured of knowing whether the text's intentions are referential or not. Mimesis and referentiality *in this sense* do not *logically* entail each other. Mimetic prose can be recognized instantly on the page, by its texture. Its referentiality remains to be seen. A mimetic text is one that borrows the strategies of imitation and may intend to be referential or it may not. A referential text is a text that may be replete with such strategies but it need not be so and – in the history of narrative – often is not.

We may in fact end up with authentic doubts as to whether in practice this distinction holds. What's important for us now is to be prepared, for the moment, hypothetically to entertain the possibility of the logic of it, or we'll be unable to cope with much that's to be claimed by any anti-Realist narrative.

In 'alternative-worlds' fiction we can straight away see the effect of this, the limited aspect of mimesis – which criticism has failed fully to recognize. Here is a fiction that 'depicts unnatural worlds naturally'. At the opening of the first example I mentioned on p. 48, Calvino's *Il cavaliere inesistente*, the narrator introduces the title-character as "a knight entirely in white armour; only a thin black line ran around the seams, the rest was light and gleaming, without a scratch, well finished at every joint, with a helmet surrounded by a plume of some oriental cock" (1962, 288). The description is unmistakably mimetic. But probability – the satisfaction of Realist prinicples of natural causality – and mimesis are no more the same thing than mimesis and referentiality are. In the course of the same passage we are told, too, that the knight doesn't exist. Here 'his probability' halts, and his story – told mimetically – goes on. ("Well", says Charlemagne as they meet, "for one who doesn't exist you're in great shape."[10]) Alternative-worlds fiction operates congenitally in this fashion. Mimesis is no guarantee of probability any more than it guarantees referentiality; it may induce credence, but it guarantees not the what-and-how of a story but the manner of its treatment. Probability, to put it very crudely, is about rules of being and happening; mimesis is about rules of telling. However things are and happen, these can be reported mimetically, whether Realistically probable or not.[11] Further, they can be referential, whether mimetically reported or not, whether probable or not (the 'improbable' knight can, for instance, be offered as a metaphor for something 'real'). This is why conventional criticism fails to make the needed distinctions. A novel may be 'an accurate description of life as we know it', as Realism claims. But there are actually *three* claims here – that the novel is mimetic ('accurate description'), that it is referential ('of life'), that it is probable ('as we know it') – and a novel need not be any more than two or one or it may even seek to be none of these things. Positive materialist Realism, with its supporting criticism, alone maintains them to be inextricable: the mimetic track – and it solely – will lead to external truth of a probabilistic sort. Alternative-worlds fiction here takes its leave of Realism.

Lest we feel uneasy about this – since in actuality, 'in real life these days', almost anything sometimes seems possible and since in narratives things have often been described that seem 'improbable' yet somehow 'true to actual life' – let's be clear: (1) probability is concerned – as it is in the physical sciences – with nothing more or less than the question of the degree to which a relationship between events is 'true to a customarily agreed or expected type' (given conditions of X sort, Y is more likely to occur than Z); and (2) the customarily agreed or expected type of relationship to which we refer in this book is not that of actuality but that characterized in certain – namely Realist – fiction. (We'll have more to say about this notion of 'custom' later.) Thus for *our* purposes 'probability' is concerned with the notion that, for example, a human being may become a husband, a doctor an adulterer, but not a horse – not because this may not happen in actuality but because it does not happen in Realistic novels.

Superficially, then – so long as we set the problem of referentiality aside – alternative-world narrative appears to leave all Realism's premisses except probability unquestioned. It's this that puts it into trouble, into perturbation, that makes it what it is, against the background of Realistic expectations. We sense that it's to stand or fall by its handling of that mad, often astonishing transgression.

How can such fiction work?

In some sense, every story of this sort is in part an 'etiological theory' – a theory of how things within it come to be. Its universe is what it is by virtue of the special system of causality at work within it. It 'works' with us by persuading us that this system is workable, that for the duration of our reading it makes its own sense. Our understanding of alternative-world fiction (to hold to this awkward term for just a bit longer) as a whole depends on our insight into the hypothetical causal system supporting its various narratives. And these are many.

It's commonplace to speak of narratives governed by the naturalistically improbable as 'fantasy' literature, and to describe this as hingeing on 'the supernatural'. There's some etymological logic in saying so (what is not 'natural' may be 'the supernatural'), though I think it will turn out not to fit our experience of the kind of contemporary narrative we're to talk about generally. (Recent theories of '*fantasy*' raise other qustions we must discuss.) But certainly something that characterizes one group of such texts is that they partake of an unbroken literary tradition running throughout history in which some metaphysical order implicitly holds sway. Because this particular group does represent so readily recognizable – and currently popular – a mode, it gives us a useful point of departure.

'Metaphysical' systems

Here – in a fiction working consciously in the classic Christian allegorical tradition, flourishing as such in the period following the First World War and becoming progressively more secularized as the Second World War comes and goes – forces outside the natural universe are portrayed as irresistibly giving shape to events in the natural world itself.

(1) In a chain of novels by Charles Williams (e.g. *War in Heaven*, *Many Dimensions*, *The Place of the Lion*) life in essentially middle-class society is transformed by the emergence of powers that, for example, momentarily transmute men and women into beasts – a lion, a serpent, an eagle, a unicorn, a phoenix, a lamb. In C. S. Lewis's "cosmic trilogy" (*Out of the Silent Plant*, *Perelandra*, *That Hideous Strength*) a Cambridge philologist is kidnapped and taken to Mars and to Venus; in a new phase in the history of the universe, assisted by the organized puissances of Deep Heaven, he plays a major role in the obviation of a second Fall. In works such as these, the Ideal in the form of an invisible divinity comes for a limited time to reshape the parameters of the material world, to assert its own immanent positive presence.

(2) In David Lindsay's *A Voyage to Arcturus* (without a recognizable parallel at the time of its publication in 1920, exerting enormous influence on writers of the preceding and subsequent major groups – such as Williams, Lewis, Tolkien – and now popularly reissued and the subject of increasing critical discussion: see, for example, Pick, 1970, and Sellin, 1981) a man is taken from England to a place in another solar system where he has new physical shapes and psychological traits thrust upon him, and journeys relentlessly in quest of someone or something he cannot define. He struggles to survive - and make sense of – encounters with creatures of extravagant monstrosity, beauty and cruelty and, in his death, invokes the perception (though the enigmatic quality of the book persists to the end) that a perfect, sublime but materially unknowable system exists and renders both natural forms and the very values normatively associated with them (goodness, reason, beauty, the value of life itself) meaningless.

(3) Dignified in critical circles by classic Modernism's continued use of its narrative themes and devices, another class of fiction persistent throughout the twentieth century (of which Henri Bosco's 'Hyacinthe' series, Dino Buzzati's *Il segreto del Bosco Vecchio* and Peter S. Beagle's *The Last Unicorn* may be taken as diverse examples) attaches itself to the tradition not of allegory but of the literature of "faëry".

Here the natural universe is depicted as having 'behind' it a transmundane world, intrinsically benign, amoral, spontaneously orderly and self-contained, but whose figures may be drawn or provoked into action with swift and often irrationally preternatural force in the environment of men. Initially summoned to gratify human egoistic drives, through the very strategies of metamorphosis, enchantment and the like by which it has satisfied these, the stability of Creation is ruptured. The forces thus unleashed, through the progressive and often phantasmagorically violent destruction of the overreachers who have called them forth, characteristically proceed toward the restoration of a new provisional equilibrium and the semblance of a return to the natural order – to a 'normal' reality (as though nothing had happened), but one tentatively cleansed of its disruptive influences.

(4) In a further body of fiction, this time freely derived from the tradition of 'Gothic' or Romantic horror literature (and of which the dozen or so of H. P. Lovecraft's stories centring on "the Cthulhu Mythos" may serve as a representative example), the world of humankind becomes subject to the will – and/or ritual worship – of a universal hierarchy of autochthonous or extraterrestrial super-beings. At the 'interface' between the natural and this negative ("unmoral", as Lovecraft puts it) supernatural system, anomaly and monstrosity are produced – ghouls and changelings, exchanges of bodies, invasions by the living dead. By its contact with humanity this otherworldly system – coherent in itself – throws into jeopardy the standard vision of cultural order, with which it's inherently incompatible. A process is engendered that threatens to bring about human civilization's disintegration into chaos. An apocalypse is for the duration of the story held in abeyance by the restitution (on the plane of 'Creation' as a whole) of a kind of perilous and intricately composed deadlock between 'forces' and (at the level of the narrative crises in which the immediate protagonists are entangled) the provision of an apparently 'natural' resolution of the story's initial mysteries.

'Historical' systems

(1) A substantial body of modern fiction makes appeal to the literary tradition of the epic as the history of a 'folk' (borrowing from the conventions of the saga, the *chanson de geste*, and from the heroic stock of late medieval romance) – fiction of which T. H. White's five-volume Arthurian cycle, E. R. R. Eddison's *The Worm Ouroborus* and Tolkien's *The Lord of the Rings* can be seen as popular examples. Here superhuman acts and supramundane events take place by virtue

of the *donnée* of a Golden or Antediluvian Age in which nature was richer and/or more plastic and elemental in its forms. A protohistorical condition obtains, where culture is imagined to stand still at the brink of annihilation by nature's primeval forces – the forces of the wilderness and of the primitive mentality of 'proto-humanity' itself. Resolution, or the possibility of it, is subject to humankind's ability to generate a civilization for iself: to win rational dominion over nature within a more limited sphere, to establish boundaries of influence, to relinquish its claim to supernatural powers, and to secure a tacit if uncertain pact of accommodation with the forces of nature (both those of the external environment and those inherent in humanity's own nature) which had heretofore been primordially fluid and uncontained. The narrative in a sense dramatizes, *inter alia*, the evolution of the realistic outlook.

(2) In the tradition of the Renaissance mock- or pseudo-epic descending from Ariosto and Tasso and of the utopian/dystopian *conte philosophique* typified in the work of Swift and Voltaire, fiction as divergent as James Branch Cabell's eighteen-volume *Biography of Manuel*, Joseph Heller's *Catch-22*, John Barth's *Giles Goat-Boy* and Italo Calvino's *Il barone rampante* [*The Baron in the Trees*] break formally with the probabilistic formulae of Realism. Gods and heraldic beasts come alive in profusion among human beings; an airman beset by the madness of war and the machinery of human institutions that have induced it sets out in a boat to row from Italy toward the salvation of his soul which he calls "Sweden"; a campus revolution is set in train by a boy reared as a goat; an eighteenth-century aristocrat lives his whole life in the trees and disappears at last into the heavens suspended from a balloon. Born at a historical moment of cultural stress into a highly perceptive and ceremonialized civilization-in-transition, each text's protagonist begins essentially as a *tabula rasa* – an individual in whom no value is 'prescribed'. The quasi-historical model instigated by the text sets the scene in which he or she, as 'hero' or 'heroine', may find and commend to us a form of withdrawal, a minimally moral private system of elementary standards in response to the exotic intricacy and artificiality of the civilization in which he/she finds him- or herself caught. In the same way, the text's own over-all violation – largely by exaggeration – of the norms of the Realistic *histoire* directs the reader's attention to the excesses of the socio-political codes prevailing in the actual, external 'contemporary history' which Realism may have seemed designed to consolidate and confirm.

'Anthropological' systems

But the fabrication of worlds whose events spurn the quotidian probabilities of Realistic narrative does not always rest strictly upon the displacement of Realist notions of natural physical law. Quite standard conceptions of evolution may in fact provide the rationale for the invention of a *histoire* whose givens are nevertheless radically different from those of the "everyday life" of a Realist text. In Giorgio Saviane's *Il mare verticale*, prehistoric figures emerge out of bestial forms and obsessively perceive fire as the virtue of certain stones and the sea as a vertical wall. In William Golding's *The Inheritors* a species of *participation mystique* governing the mental processes of its Neanderthoid characters pre-empts Realistic rules of differentiation and contradiction; it impels them not to think but to "picture", to partake of the images in one another's minds, and to apprehend objects as phenomena quite different from those of which the Realistic world would be constituted. In John Gardner's *Grendel* the world is conceived as seen by a narrator – Grendel – who is himself a product of the projections of the minds of the denizens of a Dark Age existence. Here it's not the material events themselves that would be imcompatible with the standards of probability controlling a *Madame Bovary* or an *Anna Karenina* but rather it's the narrative construction placed upon them by the characters focalizing our attention. The strategy is one based on principles made current in twentieth-century literature by the quasi-anthropological theories of thinkers such as Tylor, Frazer, Lévy-Bruhl, Van Gennep, the Cambridge School of Anthropology and of Freud and Jung. 'Reality' is offered operationally as a construct of the mind that observes it, and to all intents and purposes the model of narrative reality selected is in turn in these cases the product of a vision in which the quality of mind itself is a function of a temporal (evolutionary) paradigm. 'Primitive mentality' engenders an 'alternative reality'.

'Natural-history' systems

Taking its lead from a set of narrative conventions typically associated with what is now called 'science fiction' but that has persisted as a formal tradition in literature at least since the time of Lucian, another branch of 'alternative-world' fiction represents new, heterodox settings and life-forms as the logical outcome of imaginary 'natural conditions' different from those native to the universe as it's formulated by Realism. In Ursula Le Guin's *The Left Hand of Darkness*, the prevailing features of the planet Gethen – its eternal winter climate, the functional effects of light and darkness on its inhabitants' behaviour, and the inhabitants' constitutional androgyny – govern both the narrative's plot-development and its thematic organization. Typically the polarization of societal values only latent in Realistic fiction is thus so intensified as to accentuate a conception of the urgency of a transcendent holistic outlook for the physical and spiritual survival of living beings. In the most clearcut illustration of this kind of text's working procedure, Calvino's *Cosmicomiche* [*Cosmicomics*], each story of which it's composed commences with a brief passage, typographically set off (in italics) from the main text, setting forth a general statement of physical conditions or laws currently held to be true by experts in some pertinent field of scientific knowledge.[12] In this way, in each of the book's stories we are prepared to read of a universe that stands at the brink of 'naturalistic' coming-into-being, where 'characters' that are little more than raw mental states make signs in the void, chase one another through space, stumble into emergent clumps of matter, and observe themselves taking on material form.

The debate as to what if anything distinguishes science fiction from other modes flourishes and raises important questions.[13] For our purposes, some notion of the operation of a scientistic point of view is crucial here. The naturalization of events by means of a consistent theory of material rules of causality (e.g. biological, astrophysical) is what makes narratives of this sort tick.

Our habits of thinking about science fiction, though, may mislead us where 'alternative-world' literature is concerned. For one thing, at a superficial level, our association of 'the marvellous' in 'sci-fi' with a futuristic vision may in this area deceive us. What is Realistically improbable now has in fact only the most tangential basis in expectations, technological or otherwise, concerning 'the world of the future'. That science may some day put us in a position to *witness* worlds such as these is at this level virtually irrelevant: what provides the rationale for the narrative is that a (different) world, such as that in Calvino's or in Le Guin's text with its extra-ordinary dynamics, is *given* as 'always already there', whether anyone will 'get to see it or not'. At a deeper level, the terms of science indeed provide the model from which this imagined alien existence springs; here is a fiction arising from a systematic vision of a world with a different natural history. Significantly, in alternative-world fiction (in *The Left Hand of Darkness* as in *The Inheritors*, where in the end the 'new people', *Homo sapiens*, characterized by their rational–material mentality, very certainly 'win') the construction placed upon things by the nature of the alternative world is often in some serious respect treated as one that the living can not only ill afford to lose but cannot intelligently replace with a purely positivistic, 'scientific' world-view.

'Epistemological' systems

Fictional worlds have been invented whose characteristics are envisioned as being determined by the horizons of perception of their inhabitants – by the specific qualities of their capacity for knowing. Here the effect of time's operation may be offered as an interesting detail, yet it promises nothing in the way of a resolution of the narrative's fundamental problems. To imagine or even to be 'given' how time might have brought about the conditions that now appear to obtain seems irrelevant to the story's dynamics and its final implications.

In Edwin A. Abbott's *Flatland: A Romance of Many Dimensions*, first published in its fullest form in 1884 (no doubt under the influence of the writings in mathematics and physics of William Kingdon Clifford and Clerk Maxwell), re-released in at least twenty-six English, German, French, and Italian editions since, and having had powerful impact on more recent fictionalists,[14] a world of intelligent beings is described whose total experience is confined to a single plane, a two-dimensional space, in much the way that we are described by modern physicists as inhabiting a four-dimensional space of which we can directly perceive only three. Wholly lacking faculties by which they might become aware of anything outside that plane (and incapable of moving off the flat surface they inhabit), they have no conception, for example, of the solidity of objects. Should a sphere approach, they can be conscious only of the circle in which it cuts the plane of their perceptions. By extending the conception of this initial flatland Abbot constructs a universe in which the dramatis personae are geometrical figures, working and conducting war according to powerful laws of angular relations. In a subsequent section called "Other Worlds", sex and revolution and oppression are carried out in terms of lines and lustrous points, the narrator – indefinitely imprisoned for his radical intuitions – ends by conceiving of even the realities of a flatland as "no better than the offspring of a diseased imagination, or the baseless fabric of a dream" (Abbott, 1884, 102).

In Borges' "Tlön, Uqbar, Orbis Tertius", Tlön is a "cosmos" whose people subscribe to a "complete idealism" that "invalidates all science". "The world for them is not a concourse of objects in space; it is a heterogeneous series of independent acts. ... Objects are convoked and dissolved in a moment, according to poetic needs." No one believes in the reality of nouns; some think that "only what happens every three hundred nights is true" and others that "while we sleep here, we are awake elsewhere and that in this way every man is two men" (Borges, 1964, 8–10). In contrast to this, in "Funes el memorioso" ["Funes the Memorious", 1964], the boy Funes is "almost incapable of ideas of a general, Platonic sort". His perception and memory of discrete events appear to be total. He is unable to "think ... to forget differences, generalize, make abstractions". He is the "lucid spectator of a multiform, instantaneous and almost intolerably precise world". He hopes in vain to reduce each day to some seventy thousand memories. He dies "of congestion of the lungs" – or of "the heat and pressure" of reality. As in the case of Tlön, the narrator describes Funes's inner world as one that threatens "sooner or later" to take over our own (64–6).

Beyond the ultimate possibilities of extreme idealism and extreme realism, there lies the possibility of a world in which relativity – the uncertainty of the point at which, of the relationship by which, the two might be imagined to meet – is equally beautiful and ominous. In Calvino's story "Ti con zero" ["ti zero", 1967] the narrator has launched an arrow at a lion: "the arrow A suspended in midair at about a third of its trajectory, and, a bit farther on, also suspended in midair, and also at about a third of its trajectory, the lion L in the act of leaping upon me, jaws agape and claws extended". The narrator would "inhabit forever this second" of time, aware of everything around him – the "endless deserts with the position of each grain of sand". But to establish for himself the "configuration" of this time-zero, he perceives that he must move to time one, t_1. "To stay still in time I must move with time, to become objective I must remain subjective" (117–18). Certainty and uncertainty are inextricable. In the story "L'inseguimento" ["The Chase", 1967], in a car speeding along a highway, the narrator is "prisoner of the general system of moving cars, where neither pursuers nor pursued can be distinguished", with the possibility that "all of a sudden the center of the city will be transformed into a battlefield or the scene of a massacre" (135, 131–2). In a series of tales clearly built upon relativistic conceptions of perception from Xeno's paradox to Einstein's General Theory Calvino's figures pursue one another through universes whose space is shaped and reshaped by their own presence, glimpsing one another at once behind themselves and – looking ahead – simultaneously racing off with their backs turned.

In such narratives, relativity and paradox seem at first to extinguish the possibility of a whole – cosmic – overview. Yet what distinguishes them is that what they make out to be indeterminate is only indeterminable within the frame of reference of perception's limitations. Science does not actually behave as though the apparent mutual exclusivity of wave and particle observations entails any actual mutual exclusions of one (natural) truth by another, any more than the logician behaves in desperation as though he has to conceive of things solely in the way that Xeno's paradox proposes. As the texts' constant concentration on thematic *topoi* associated with signs, manifestations, sensations and memory shows, the problem lies not in nature as a whole, in this view, but in the nature of observation and 'registration'. Defects in our ways of apprehending things, then, are seen as *part* of the nature of nature as a whole – an epistemological dilemma and not a metaphysical one – and are comprehended within a potentially (even when not fully demonstratedly) unified nature.

'Ontological' systems

Modern fiction – the offspring of a relativistically orientated culture – might stop here. "Creation" is what the mind chooses to see. But – perhaps, again, unprecedented in literature – a fiction devoted to the creation of alternative Creations may now take this as only a starting point, a jumping-off place. Narratives begin to appear that are concerned with worlds containing heterodox forms engendered not by standard physical laws newly applied but rather by the immanent character of their very being. Kinds of being, that is, may produce corresponding physical forms. Historically, narrative has always made room for this possibility, in the allegorical tradition; the way a thing (a character, for example) *is* determines the shape of its material form and its behaviour (the evil a character represents is manifested in his ugliness). But whereas in allegory the abstract, ideational 'meaning' of a character typically brings about his physical form, in the fiction before us now, any ideational 'content' associated with a form is at most only an incidental aspect – one of the casual traits – of the form itself which its inward being has produced.

We are confronted with a rich permutation of a theme that has deeply preoccupied twentieth-century thought and narrative since at least the emergence of Existentialism: the question as to whether independent being can obtain, prior to the 'act' of existing. Not surprisingly this fiction – like that of Existentialism – often shows an intimate concern with the idea of the force of volition in the shaping of reality.

In Joseph McElroy's *Plus* (1977), a man's brain, the object of a technological experiment, is suspended in a container and sent in a satellite into space. Stage by stage, in a manner outside the intentions of the experimenters and by dint of its spontaneous life-will, the brain generates physical organs of a kind hitherto unknown, and with them the ability to perceive and manipulate its immediate environment in previously unforetold ways. In Calvino's "La spirale" ["The Spiral", 1965] a blind creature in the primordial sea yearns to be desired by another, an equally sightless one. It proceeds to evolve about itself an exquisite spiral shell whose beauty generates in others the necessity and ultimately the capacity to behold it.[15] The creature's overwhelming will – a function of its subjective being – creates in the objective universe the faculty of sight. In Stanislaw Lem's story "Les Robinsonades", the Robinson Crusoe hero has for a lover on his island a woman part of whose very nature is the "law" that she is untouchable; this law, in turn, like the woman herself, is an artefact of his imagination, where the admissibility of touching her physically would entail the inevitable and intolerable acknowledgement of her material unreality. The story, we're told, is "an ontological tale of the necessity of permanent separation" (1971, 371).

We may be tempted to take fictions of this sort as dramatizations in rather peculiar forms of the standard Realist theme of the interaction between the personal will and a hostile environment. But it's indeed apparent from the texts themselves that what is at issue is nothing less than the positive force of ontological being itself. Speaking of the creation of his shell, Calvino's narrator says "I had no idea of making it because I needed it; on the contrary, it was like when somebody lets out an exclamation," it was a kind of "self-expression". "So", he says, "I can say that my shell made itself, without my taking any special pains to have it come out one way rather than another" (1965, 176–7). For the protagonist of *Plus* a fundamental discovery is that "the more that was all around came from him"; the new "parts of his sight ... had come of themselves, yet they were always himself"; his sight comes "at will, if not his"; with a jolt he perceives "that not only could he think his own growth, he must" (McElroy, 1977, 58, 115, 124, 138). As Lem's Robinson "prepares to create himself a world from zero", we learn that "if he is a prisoner, it is only of his own creation", "each being, as it were, a captive of his own myth"; "these persons are fragments untying themselves", Robinson realizes, "from my being" (Lem, 1971, 359, 363, 364, 358).

Essential to the formation of Realistically improbable events in such fiction, the action of the will-to-be thus takes precedence over any particular form which it may actually produce. In Calvino's *Il cavaliere inesistente* the peasant Gurdulù flings himself into a pond, mistaking himself for one of the ducks paddling there; subsequently he confuses himself with leaves, with the earth itself. "All is soup!" he later cries, clambering into a cook's cauldron, and an onlooker is unsettled by the possibility of "the world being nothing but a vast shapeless mass of soup in which all things dissolved and tinged all else with itself". The system upon which these alternative probabilities rest is spelt out for us: "World conditions were still confused in the era when this took place", the narrator tells us: "the world was pullulating with objects and capacities and persons who lacked any name or distinguishing mark. It was a period when the will and determination to exist, to leave a trace ... was not wholly used up" (Calvino, 1960, 322, 307).

'Alternative-world' texts may all have something to do with the very question of creation; those mentioned here inescapably do. But the activity of creating need not play an obvious role in the narrative itself – as it does in the preceding examples – for the text to pivot on an 'ontological' premiss. In Carlos Feuntes' massive novel *Terra nostra*, the same character (with equal freedom from the norms of Realistic probability) may appear during the course of the narrative in many different epochs and locales – sixteenth-century Mexico, twentieth-century Paris – and in any one narrative era may even materialize in two or more incarnations. Once again, standard logical canons of identity, differentiation and non-contradiction are held in abeyance. With its own inherent and minutely detailed features (including those we'd conventionally ascribe to the influence of history – people's dress, habits, attitudes and the like), each setting is given in some sense as exclusively occupying all time. Realist notions of how the place 'came to be what it is' in historical terms are set aside. The dynamics of time, and with them the ordinary principles of chronological evolution that characterize Realistic narrative itself, are dis-placed in favour of a cult of place itself: the world of the book is constituted of a congeries of worlds each of which is represented essentially as eternal and eternally discrete. The destructive force with which history in Fuentes' view annihilates living patterns of being is disallowed. The immediate 'ontological' value system of each place governs with an a-historical autonomy, with literally extraordinary narrative results.

'Linguistic' systems

In a sense, so far as the narration of the 'improbable' is concerned, where there is language anything is possible. There is an increasing body of literature rooted in the premiss that heterodox worlds may be produced in fiction by the generative function of language itself.

The narrator of Borges's "La biblioteca de Babel" ["The Library of Babel", 1964] posits the existence of a Library that contains "all verbal structures", including a book "which is the formula and perfect compendium *of all the rest*". "I cannot combine some characters", he says (and cites the example *dhcmrlchtdj*) "which the divine Library has not foreseen and which in one of its secret tongues do not contain some terrible meaning" (56–7). This certitude that everything is already written, the writer declares, makes phantoms of us all. What distinguishes Borges's piece is that it is itself a play upon the words "already written": what is uttered equals what is predetermined. The 'narrative twist' is a *product* of a verbal twist. The narrator is making deliberate appeal to the tenacious association in human cultures – of which mythological narratives give widespread evidence – of the act of naming, uttering, with the act of creating. In the beginning was the Word.

Fiction built upon the conception of the power of the Logos – sometimes and not surprisingly in the spirit of *Alice in Wonderland*, often in the tradition of Joyce, Queneau and Gadda – becomes itself neologistic. Language, it tends to intimate, is characterized by a potential for the infinite expansion of relations between it and its referents – or for the outrunning of its referents and the ultimate evolution of its own autonomous worlds. Sense is now forever on the brink of breaking down – or out – into nonsense, only to be drawn back into the recuperative vortex of language's own ever-expanding internal sense. In Robert Pinget's *Graal Flibuste*, superficially a simple picaresque tale of the travels of its unnamed narrator and his coachman, a world unfolds filled with flowers that tremble with desire, plants that attack men, beasts of monstrous shape and behaviour (turkey-seals, sobbing lyre-birds, a herring with the head of an olive tree, and a cow's tail that lifts up the sea and floods five continents). It's a world that evolves out of its own language.

> Loristyche gave birth to the palm-tree Sbur, who has the trunk of a man and the sex of a dog. He engendered the three Asters, goddesses of the dance and of moonless nights. Aga is a blond, Ada brunette and Ara a redhead.
>
> (Pinget, 1956, 58)

In this scant passage, translated here as literally as possible and quite randomly selected but perfectly representative of many in a book whimsically full of genealogies and lyric inventories, we can see the process at work as well as anywhere. The goddess-children of a fabled tree are flowers; fair enough: that's a 'natural' outcome. But goddesses then of moonless nights – and of the dance? why? If we insist on a natural explanation, we're not only free simply to accept this as arbitrary, we're obliged to. It's by the obviousness – the terribleness – of the punning intended that the text collars us: *Asters* are not only flowers, they are stars. Word-play has begun to institute new narrative data: these asteroid goddesses – of course – reign brightest when the moon is down. A natural (historical) resemblance has created a linguistic 'efflorescence' of which Pinget is quick to make capital. It becomes laughably clear now. Deities of the dance? The Asters are 'stars', too, in the way that Fred and Adele (read: Ada?) were, particularly as pronounced in (Pinget's) French:[16]

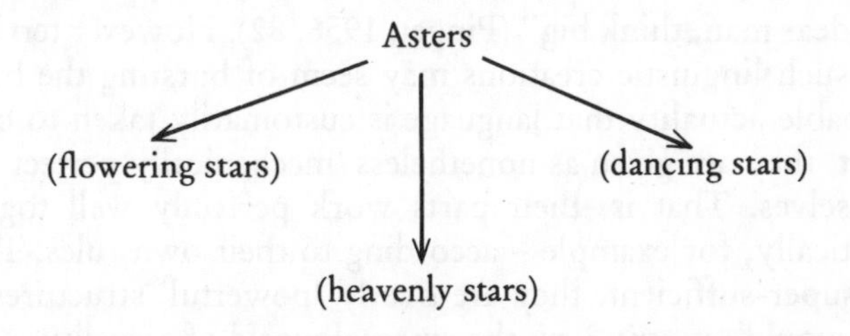

It's not a wholly natural but a verbal medium we've moved into now; we're in the realm of Max Müller and the theory of narrative – specifically mythological narrative – as a product of an infectious, a metastatic 'disease of language'. Limits exist for us – but they are those inhering in linguistic systems.[17]

As we already have glimpsed, to think of narratives as controlled by the nature of language is to begin to think of them at least partially as the offspring of literature itself. In Calvino's "Il conte di Montecristo" ["The Count of Monte Cristo", 1967] Edmond Dantès lies prisoner in the Chateau d'If, dreaming of escape. Among the many ways he tries in his imagination, the closing one entails his hope of (re)constructing the process by which Dumas has created the novel of which he is a part. "The concentric fortress, If-Monte-Cristo-Dumas' desk, contains us prisoners, the treasure, and the hypernovel *Monte Cristo* with its variants and combinations of variants in the nature of billions of billions but still in a finite number. . . . To plan a book – or an escape – the first thing to know is what to exclude."[18] *Two* world-systems, two verbal systems here intermesh, and Dantès' problem is precisely to determine their exact points of intersection – to find his way out of his immediate world into the world of Dumas' novel, in which he 'has already' – as a character – escaped.

For the moment, each 'world' we've looked at so far seems meant to be taken as having some kind of rational completeness, or potential for completeness, about it. The number of choices for Edmond Dantès is "finite", and either the prison-world he's in is perfect (will contain him forever) or he will escape by virtue of its failure to coincide with the perfect plan of a prison he will design. The 'universe' of the Library of Babel is defined by its 'bookishness', the hierarcho-maniacal orderliness with which its 'world's' data are ranged by tacit fiat – letters within words on pages in books upon shelves along corridors up the tiers of the universal edifice. If one character in *Graal Flibuste* says that he fails to comprehend its genealogy, he is told by another to look at "the great beauty of the world" which contains it, to observe "the total effect, the mechanism of the total effect. Think big, my dear man, think big" (Pinget, 1956, 82). However terrifyingly capable such linguistic creations may seem of bursting the bonds of the probable actuality that language is customarily taken to be made to report, they are given as nonetheless 'mechanically perfect' worlds in themselves. That is, their parts work perfectly well together – grammatically, for example – according to their own rules. They are merely super-sufficient, they are overly 'powerful' structures as the logician would say, *vis-à-vis* the external world of actuality.

While the last three clusters of 'alternative-worlds' (epistemological, ontological, linguistic) appear to raise questions concerning what modes of perception are the right ones, or appear to set aside in large part our standard notions of the referential responsibilities of language, they each still 'plump for' the virtual primacy of one kind of vision. Each declares that a delimitable system operates which accounts for *everything, including* the inadequacy of our contingent perceptions.

What I've said about 'alternative-world' fiction is not in any way put forward as a sophisticated inventory, with regard to either precision or exhaustiveness. Nor is it offered as an interpretation of texts. In spite of his obvious interest in historical processes (as evidenced in *The Sot-Weed Factor*), both John Barth and his readers would be as astonished to hear anyone say that *Giles Goat-Boy* was 'about' history, as Golding and his readers would be to hear that *The Inheritors* was 'about' anthropology. However intimately they're linked, we can't afford to confuse narrative with thematic premisses. A story's narrative argument is not the same as its thematic argument.

Just as is the case with Realist fiction, a work of the sort I've been talking about may assert at the narrative level that, for example, certain physical laws make the chain of events possible, yet that quite different ethical, psychological, political, or metaphysical principles are what make it meaningful. And in point of fact, Realists/Naturalists

(Balzac, Eliot, Zola, Verga, Tolstoy) are far more likely actually to be authentically interested in historical, anthropological or natural-historical processes than any of the writers touched on in the preceding pages. By the same token, writers we look at in the next section are more likely than some of these latter to be genuinely concerned with epistemological or linguistic issues *as thematic issues*. Our subject, for the moment, has been the functional, fictional-world-building use made of conventionally agreed systems of human conceptions. In writing a new preface to a novel he had first published nine years before, *Il visconte dimezzato* [*The Cloven Viscount*, 1960], a story of an aristocrat who has been blown in half in combat and returns to his domain as two men, one 'good', one 'evil', Calvino announced to those among his critics who had seen in this an ethical allegory that he "had never thought even for a moment of good and evil. . . . I had used a well-known narrative contrast to give substance to what interested me, namely dimidiation. Contemporary man is divided, mutilated, incomplete, an enemy to himself".[19] The writer seizes on a received moral–allegorical formula in much the robust and casual way that, earlier, allegory had traditionally taken up whatever popular narrative formula lay at hand at the time – for example the protocol of the literary land of faëry as it was when Spenser found and appropriated it – and puts it to the service of his own different thematic intentions.

So, not only does there exist a wide spectrum of fiction that responds to Realism by trangressing particularly against Realism's canons of probability, but each work of its sort does so according to some premiss that can be readily expressed in abstract declarative terms. This premiss, this rationale, is fully contained within the text's *histoire*, and this *histoire* pre-scribes a 'world' whose internal coherence remains unquestioned.

We can now replace that ungainly term 'alternative-world fiction' with another that, for all its own awkwardness, has as one advantage that it tells more, without belying the nature of the fiction it refers to. Both Realistic and alternative-world texts hold with the model of the perfect (complete and integrated) machine – the mechanical paradigm, in which no event is produced by any 'cause' outside the given world's own unified system. The difference between them is that the fiction now before us posits a 'new' world system; it is "neocosmic" in its impulse. I mean this in a triple sense. First, a narrative putting forward a neocosmic view behaves in every respect as though *a world is there*, prior to the text's articulation of it (and in spite of our practical, material, commonsense hesitation as to its probability), and remains simply to be 'discovered' by us in much the way that Columbus and

Magellan found their improbable 'New Worlds'. Second, this kind of text asserts that, as a world, this one (in keeping with the larger philosophical conception of the '*cosmos*') is an ordered, integrally meaningful whole in the way that Realist worlds are meant to be. And third, the text (like narratives produced by other schools of literary thought but *not* by Realism) implies that works of its sort – putting the new representation of an imaginary world above the dictates of quotidian probabilism – in some manner make way for a 'new world' for the reader or humankind at large. The pretentiousness of the term "neocosmic" (as against the 'soft' popular connotations of words such as 'fantasy') is there to reflect a seriousness ascribed by such texts to their own status among narratives.

I stress that the notion of a neocosmic fiction – like the notion attaching to the fiction I'll be talking about in the next section – bears not in the first instance on a theory of the nature of actuality but on a theory of the configurations of books. The word 'cosmic' here refers to a variety of narrative in which the universe described is implied to have a complete, integrated and autonomous order at the level of story. And a 'neocosmic' narrative sets its particular cosmos over against not 'the real world' but against the kind of universe customarily proposed in Realist fiction.

Any idea of a 'world', of course, nevertheless raises the question of a 'world-view'. Because the qualities of different anti-Realist narratives will turn out to be so deeply determined by their different relations to the conception of cosmos, we're immediately entangled in at least one philosophical issue that must be considered front-on. "The fact is", Susan Sontag has said, that

> all Western consciousness of and reflection upon art have remained within the confines staked out by the Greek theory of art as mimesis or representation. ... None of us can ever retrieve that innocence before all theory when art knew no need to justify itself, when one did not ask of a work of art what it *said* because one knew (or thought one knew) what it *did*. From now on to the end of consciousness, we are struck with the task of defending art.[20]

Much as we must feel in sympathy with the *largeur* of this perspective and much as it seems to fit with the anti-mimetic cry in our own times (of which heavy evidence lies ahead for us), I think we must recognize that this *historicist* model (the terms of her argument make it clear that it's based on that) falls short of the truth. There's as little justification for the idea that art's ability to make copies of natural things was its first or only excuse for being as there is for the idea that the Greeks invented such an excuse. Sontag's notion of some past time of irretrievable innocence in this respect is a theory of a Golden Age for which we have no evidence. To the contrary, it's hard to think of the 'non-representational' art – whether 'fabulous' or geometric – of Mesopotamia, or indeed of any *pre*historic culture we can name, as not having been generated and authorized by some cultus allowing the maker to believe 'we make this object because it has a place in the world of experience outside it'. We are actually compelled to 'defend' art or any of its modes from the moment we feel impelled to *find a place for anything*. A place for everything, and everything in its place. It's *this* – the much larger and more profound 'cosmic' motive – and not the historical rise-to-hegemony of some specific theory about art that leads to such 'defensiveness' as Sontag speaks of. The representationalist philosophy of art has never been more than one among the many brought to bear by a species in search of order; and the idea of mimesis, to 'do' mimesis or not – the notion that art needs a rationale, whether this or some other – becomes truly problematical the instant we decline to say that our sense of experience needs to be coherent.

It's precisely at this point, at this brink, that literature stands or claims to stand today. Realism has congenitally said 'Yes' to the possibility and desirability of total coherence. Neocosmic fiction says 'Yes but not in Realism's terms.' And fiction we've now to consider says simply 'No'.

Anti-world games: gaming with words

To fulfil its special intentions, neocosmic fiction is readable, even readerly. Of the fiction we're now to consider, many texts will have it acclaimed as one of their distinctions that they are among the most radically unreaderly in the history of literature. Rather than constructing worlds alternative to Realism's, couched in Realism's language, its writing can in a sense be generically described as 'dis-integrative' in its operation. In whichever of the many courses it may take, it *seeks to dismantle* – and lead us to observe at some distance – our customary expectations of narratives. As will be apparent from the four last cited examples at the start of this chapter (p. 49) by Nabokov, Beckett, Robbe-Grillet, Sollers, it *wants* in some way to disrupt our 'normal' ways of reading.

Some may be keenly surprised then to find that as a class it is typically extremely conservative when it comes to the question of verisimilitude, of probability – that is, in just that respect in which neocosmic fiction is 'radical'. Nothing seems less to the 'dismantler's' taste than a prolonged or consistent, univocal recourse to 'the fantastic' or 'the marvelous'. In fact there seems in this case to be a persistent preoccupation (at the level of *histoire*) with the standard, 'natural', even banal quotidian conception of existence that we conventionally expect of Realism. We'd be hard put to find a text where, to start with, 'setting' and 'situation' depart in essential character from ones to be found in Realist fiction. Not simply to make this point plain but *because* their local effects render their global outlines increasingly difficult to recall the more we explore them, I set down here the bare narrative shapes or 'pre-texts' of principal texts now to be considered as samples.

On a modern African plantation a husband jealously watches the movements of his wife and the man who may be her lover; straying about a northern European city a second-rate detective seeks a lead by which to investigate a supposed – but in fact as yet unmaterialized – murder; a travelling salesman rides a bicycle around a dreary island trying to sell watches and contemplating a murder that may or may not have happened by the time he sails away again on the mainland steamer (Robbe-Grillet's *La Jalousie* [*Jealousy*], *Les Gommes* [*The Erasers*], *Le Voyeur* [*The Voyeur*]). Two middle-aged men sit in different rooms, one writing of his journey to see his mother, the second writing of his search for the first, each telling of the encounters and the physical and mental impairments that have occurred along his way across country; a man lies in bed in "a plain private room" in "a plain ordinary house", gazing out his window onto an ordinary street and sky beyond – and another reposes at the side of a similar "quiet street near the shambles" – each contemplating his condition as he stares around him (Beckett's *Molloy*, *Malone Dies*, *The Unnamable*). A young Argentinian passes time among acquaintances in the flats and streets of Paris, has a love affair, and returns to Argentina where he takes a job and has another affair (Cortázar's *Rayuela* [*Hopscotch*]). A boy travels with his middle-class family to a coastal resort and finds himself getting lost in the boardwalk funhouse (Barth's *Lost in the Funhouse*). A writer stands at his window communicating wordlessly with a working-man in the city street below (Mauriac's *L'Agrandissement*). A man of arcane reading interests, living a materially straitened life in a rural backwater, in the hope of money kills an old man and finds the country through which he moves increasingly emptied of its intelligibility, to the point where his own 'death' only signals his having to circle continually through the ever hopeful, ever senseless round of life (O'Brien's *The Third Policeman*). On a summer's evening in a town a man writes and relives now lost relationships while the traffic goes by beneath his balcony and figures move past windows across from his own (Sollers' *Le Parc*). A university lecturer and her students discuss their approaches to literature and consider their relationships in the light of more-and-less possible ways of re(de)constructing them in words (Brooke-Rose's *Thru*). A group of Parisians' lives are portrayed in terms of their distribution in the building which they tenant; a man examines his relationships in terms of the organization of the *lycée* class of which he's the instructor (Butor's *Passage de Milan* and *Degrés*). A man settles down of an evening to read a book, finds that the volume he has is imperfect, in subsequent days goes in search of a correct copy, encounters a woman with similar interests, marries her, and in bed with her finishes reading his book (Calvino's *Se una notte d'inverno un viaggatore*). A middle-aged man in a provincial town hunts for some pretext to have the malicious schoolmistress put away in an asylum; a hearing preliminary to a criminal investigation is conducted, and the verbal transcription of it sets forth the common and quirky behaviour of the province's local inhabitants (Pinget's *Le Libera* [*The Libera Me Domine*] and *L'Inquisitoire* [*The Inquisitory*]). On a September day a man in New York shuts himself in a six-dollar-a-week room to write about an immigrant who's come to take up 'the American way of life', while another sets out to record the writer's diurnal story (Federman's *Double or Nothing*).

We can and no doubt should dispute these brutal one-sentence accounts (I can personally accept them only with varyingly restive shades of dismay); but no number of alternative constructions we put on the actual texts could ever bring their postulated 'worlds' into line with those neocosmic ones I've cited. As the epigraph to Sollers' *Le Parc* declares (of 'the park' which the book takes as its presiding motif), "It's a composite of places (*lieux*) ... in which everything appears natural except the com-position (*assemblage*)". And it's true: in this at first deeply perplexing novel (which street is this, the one in place X or the one in place Y? who is this woman in line 20? is she the same as the woman in line 19?) nothing could appear more 'natural' than the parts of which it's composed (the evening breeze, the sounds in the street, the woman in the window, the woman in the room). As the quasi-situational scaffoldings of what will turn out to be quintessentially anti-Realist works of narration of a second sort, these and comparable *histoires* or pre-texts for *histoires* are unequivocally Realistic.

This Realistic 'shadow' behind the 'dismantler's' text is not merely casual but in fact essential to its enterprise. It begins to look as though contemporary fiction, in the array of its reactions to Realism, may be inclined to polarize, to display some kind of powerful, two-directional symmetry. If it's in some sense true of neocosmic narrative that in it there may be "fantasy, but the freedom granted to [its] matter is counterbalanced by the strict classicism of [its] manner", as Vivian Mercier says, we may now be bound on another course altogether (1971, 383). Expressed technically, it may be "obviously true", as Brooke-Rose puts it, that in literature "the freer the paradigmatic axis, the more rigid the syntagmatic, and vice versa".[21] Now there is no effort to offer alternative worlds, but rather a move towards alternative presentations of 'the received standard world'.[22]

The narrative mode before us, characteristically setting aside conventional articles of faith in coherent systems of causality in the relation between events, may seek above all to separate itself from any abiding interest, except negatively, in story causality. It is not – it says – in the choice we've made (under Realism) among the possible coherent causes behind existence that we've been mistaken, as neocosmic narrative may be proposing. It is rather in the choice we've made in speaking and writing about existence as though it had such coherent causes. The correct way of writing about series of events must therefore be some way that puts that *kind of speaking and of writing* into question. This fiction, then, tends to take as the basis of its departure from Realist narrative the radical perturbation of narration itself – of the ways in which the story is transmitted ('spoken') to us.[23]

This different orientation is not incidental but fundamental. The text will deliberately seek to divert us, in two senses of the word: to redirect our attention away from the story's matter – its illusion – and towards the 'means of production' of it; and to 'occupy' us with the 'intrigue' of the latter, with the 'story of the story'. The criteria here, in abandoning the outlines of Realist texts, generate a repertory not of kinds of worlds (with the *histoire*-level rationales that support them) but of narrative perspectives (with the *discours*-level norms that sustain them).

We need to be careful about this. It's not to say that such fiction is ultimately to be described as not having story elements (and thematic *topoi*) at the level of *histoire* that are very much its own. We'll come to that in later chapters. Nor is it a matter of the radicalization of discourse only; *stories* here *are* often to be 'deformed' at every turn. Rather, what may finally set this mode apart from those of Realistic and neocosmic fiction is that the questions it raises are simply, crucially, not all answered on the plane of the *histoire*. What, then, does the narration on the page *do* with the narrative *histoire*, the 'natural world', to which it claims to refer?

Narrative range

It's a critical commonplace that for the Realist the movement of narration has its analogy, *par excellence*, in the movement of the perceiving eye. That vision is taken to be *the* 'realistic sense'; and that the Realistic novel takes as its overriding metaphors the window, the mirror, the lens (of a telescope, a microscope, a pair of spectacles). If the Realist's 'regard' typically places the objects of its attention into a 'middle distance', much anti-Realist narrative is inclined to explore and exploit this expectation. It will seek to replace the novel's conventional 'field of view' with one of a different kind. Recalling the lines by which Stern (via Lichtenberg) illustrates what he means by Realism's 'middle distance' the possibilites become instantly clear: "'I see in the distance a strange mass . . . I come closer and find that it is a castle. . . . If, unfamiliar with the purpose of the whole, I were to continue investigating, I would soon find myself analysing the stones, which would only lead me further away'" (120–1).

(1) The 'dismantler' may move toward a *contraction of the standard perspective*. In a now famously typical passage at the beginning of *Le Voyeur*, directing our attention towards a section of the steamer's landing slip, Robbe-Grillet writes:

> The stone rim – an oblique, sharp edge formed by two intersecting perpendicular planes: the vertical embankment perpendicular to the quay and the ramp leading to the top of the pier – was continued along its upper side at the top of the pier by a horizontal line extending straight toward the quay. . . .
>
> (1955, 6)

For some four hundred words the text focuses in this way on the spatial arrangement of the stonework of this pier. Mauriac's *La Marquise sortit à cinq heures* [*The Marquise Went Out at Five*] sets its whole action at the junction of five streets, in the space of one summer evening hour; Butor's *Degrés* turns on one hour in a classroom; Mauriac's entire novel *L'Agrandissement* takes place in a character's mind in the space of two minutes, making up one single paragraph. The conception of the narrative as an "agrandissement", a photographic "blow-up" of a minute event, was already by the 1950s a fully developed theme within fiction itself – as Cortázar's short story by that title shows – and haunts anti-Realist narratives of this second broad kind. As we can already recognize, in texture it seems significantly (against the background of Realism) hyper-informational, and anti-schematic. Which leads us by contrast to the second predictable variation in the matter of 'field of view'.

(2) The 'dismantler' may seek a *dilation of the standard perspective*. Instead of a narrower ('microscopic' or 'telescopic') view of things, the telescope may be inverted (as Pirandello's narrator in "La tragedia d'un personaggio" commends to the character that appears before him in his study); we look at things 'through the wrong end'; we get a wide-angle perspective.

This needs watching. The 'middle distance effect' may momentarily be thought of as a function of the ratio between the extent of the object described and the amount of detailed information given about it. But as the Stern quotation means explicitly to show, up close we are "further away" from a sense of "the purpose of the whole" of the thing; and this is precisely the effect sought, for example, by Robbe-Grillet. 'Middle distance' is actually a function of the ratio between the extent of the object described and the amount of detailed information provided *plus* the instructions we're given as to its over-all, diagrammatic nature, "purpose", its meaning in its setting. It's this 'plus' that the 'dismantler' may aim to withhold.

We might expect what we nowadays call *minimal* fiction to be a sort that is especially suited to the aims of the writer seeking to 'dilate' our view. Complete yet brief, the minimal narrative – we may think – encourages us to get a lot out of a little. This is sometimes its intention; and it's true that minimal fiction represents an effort to subvert the wide perspective, the broad informational scale of Realist fiction – the *War and Peace*, the *Comédie humaine*. But in truth – as our experience of *haiku* had long ago shown us – minimal writing is nearly always of a sort (for example epiphanic in intent) that is indeed merely middle-distance fiction in miniature.[24]

In anti-Realist fiction of the kind before us, however, another cluster of texts searches to provide us with diagrammatic, abstract instructions concerning the event's whole to such a degree as radically to reduce the 'standard proportion' of detailed concrete information about its particular qualities. A narrative by Giles Gordon entitled "Genealogy" (1973) begins:

> a man a woman a man and a woman lovers a couple a son
> a family a man a woman a man and a woman lovers a couple

> a son a family a man a woman a man and a woman lovers a couple a son a family a man a woman a man and a woman lovers a couple a daughter a family a

and for twenty-six lines continues with similar permutations of the same words, to end with the following:

> man a man and a woman lovers a couple a mongol

A narrative, "Post-Scriptum", by Jean-François Bory, begins

> And after the subject, the verb, followed by an adjective agreeing in gender and number with the subject. The same subject, an adverbial pronoun, an auxiliary verb, an article, a noun, an object of the predicate, an indefinite pronoun and an infinitive verb. An adverbial clause, a prefix, a verb in the third person singular of the indicative; a comparative adjective, a subordinate proposition agreeing with the adjective of place

The text continues thus for nearly four hundred words, concluding:

> The same subject, an adverbial pronoun, an auxiliary verb, an article, a noun, an object of the predicate, an indefinite pronoun and an infinitive verb.[25]

Pierre Guyotat's *Éden, Éden, Éden*, an effort in the same general direction as these – and dignified by prefaces by Barthes, Leiris and Sollers – is a book composed of one sentence.

What is the reader to *do* with fictions of these kinds? *Modernists* have frequently called upon the tendency in the reader to 'deduce' further unuttered 'information' from otherwise highly diagrammatic texts; this was an intention behind Gertrude Stein's "Rose is a rose is a rose ... " as much as it lay behind the elliptical narrative tactics that such as Hemingway may have learned from her. But the Modernist text ultimately produces its 'objective correlatives' – those particularized data that confer on narrative events their potential for naturalization, their Realistic (thing-ish) substantiality. The diagrammatic usage of the 'dismantler' has clearly other ends in view.

In one of these two contrasting but complementary anti-Realist procedures, we may have the *thing* but no sense of its status in the totality of things. In the other we may have a sense of that totality but it seems momentarily empty, a void. As the anti-Realist often likes to say of the quantum physicist's hesitation, of the perpetual vacillation between the perception of the particle and the perception of the wave, in the broader view – or the stricter view – the solid cosmos has somehow lost its integrity, its conviction.

Narrative specification

Much of what we say about the text's range is in fact deeply linked to its specification – to what it actually, substantively, tells or does not tell us about the events within its purview. In a typical statement, Mercier says of Beckett's *The Unnamable* – a *locus classicus* in this respect – that it "reveals once and for all the minima of the novel: no plot, an almost nonexistent protagonist, no setting" (1971, 20). Carrying forward the strategies of Modernism, where – in its omission of data (personal names, place-names, dates and so forth) normally associated with the massive megastory and parastory of Realist fiction – the aim was conventionally to suggest that here was an 'everyman' in a 'universal situation', the anti-Realist now seems almost to intimate that we are face-to-face, rather, with a 'no-man' in a no-man's land. In his Mortin cycle of novels, Pinget makes little effort toward consistency of characterization or of the presentation of events in a specifiable place or time; people's and places' names change almost *ad libitum*, and as often as not anything reported to have occurred in the past is described as having 'happened ten years ago', no matter how this may put our normal understanding of chronology and causality into disarray. Laying Realism's free indirect discourse aside, the novel experiments more and more frequntly with free *direct* discourse; the very speaker becomes fluid: is it a man? a woman? a dog? does it live or is it dead, does it speak of what it is or in fact of what it is not? As Robbe-Grillet says of his characters in his preface to the English edition of the film script of *L'Année dernière à Marienbad* [*Last Year at Marienbad*],

> we know absolutely nothing about them, nothing about their lives. They are nothing but what we see them as. . . . Elsewhere they don't exist. As for the past . . . we sense [that the hero] is making it up as he goes along. There is no last year, and Marienbad is no longer to be found on any map. This past, too, has no reality beyond the moment it is evoked with sufficient force; and when it finally triumphs, it has merely become the present, as if it had never ceased to be so. . . . What we see on the screen *is in the act of happening*, we are given the gesture itself, not an account of it.
>
> (1961, 12)

The intentions behind such statements are rich and complex. For the present it's enough to observe once again that the writer seeks to undermine the process by which we assume that the events within the fiction have some integral and verifiable relation to a stable, totalizable world outside it.

It is possible to make more ado over the axis of specification than it justifies, as early enthusiastic commentaries on anti-Realism (obviously still under the influence of Realist expectations) tended to do. In some regard, once the omission of physical incident has been observed one feels one may have said most of what there is to say about experiments in *non*-specification. What may actually turn out to be most vital to the writer is not what is positively 'missing' but what is present by implication but relationally uncertain. This is essentially, as we see next, what the ordeal (through which the 'dismantler' puts the reader's standard narrative expectations) is about.

Narrative 'units'

(1) A 'dismantler's' text may be a kind of palimpsest, on which events, treated *positively*, seem somehow to be inscribed on top of one another. In Sarraute's *Martereau*, as in Moravia's *L'attenzione* [*The Lie*], the objective story the narrator seeks to relate comes to lose its grip as we become aware of the likelihood that the occurrences he solidly describes (concerning the relations between himself, for example, and the members of his family) are in fact inventions which he has superimposed on 'more real' events outside his mind. *Martereau* at vital moments sets before us disparate versions of the same scene. In Robbe-Grillet's *La Maison de Rendez-vous* [*The House of Assignation*] – as this typical passage shows:

> The door of the apartment is ajar, the apartment door is wide open, despite the late hour, the apartment door is closed
>
> (1965, 151)

– the narrator unremittingly sets before us chains of mutually exclusive data, episodes, whole 'plots' even, which we struggle largely in vain to bring into standard accord. In Barth's *Lost in the Funhouse* (1968) the 'adventure' of the boy is told in continual counterpoint against the background of the narrator's effort to tell it and the growing sense that the more readily we accept the latter's terms of reference the less likely it is that the former and his adventure can be taken to have 'happened'. In his "Menelaiad" (1968) Barth constructs a series of narratives within narratives in each of which certain events tend to displace their counterpart events in the narrative before it. In all of these, for the duration of our reading, it's the multiplication of positive statements that inclines to dissolve our assurance as to the meaningfulness of positive assertion.

(2) By contrast, a text may successively negate its previous assertions:

> And once again I am I will not say alone, no, that's not like me, but, how shall I say, I don't know, restored to myself, no I never left myself, free, yes, I don't know what that means...
>
> A and C I never saw again. But perhaps I shall see them again. But shall I be able to recognize them? And am I sure I never saw them again?
>
> ... There is no need to despair, you may scrabble on the right door, in the right way, in the end. It's for the whole there seems to be no spell. Perhaps there is no whole. ...
>
> ... The pale gloom of rainy days was better fitted to my taste, no, that's not it, to my humour, no, that's not it either. ...
>
> Yes, even then, when already all was fading, waves and particles, there could be no things but nameless things, no names but thingless names. ... Saying is inventing. Wrong, very rightly wrong. You invent nothing. ...
>
> Then I went back into the house and wrote, It is midnight. The rain is beating on the windows. It was not midnight. It was not raining.

Here, in passages taken as typical samples from the initial pages and the last page of *Molloy* (Beckett, 1951, 12, 15, 31, 35, 37, 240) – and clearly echoed over a dozen years later in the first paragraph of Robbe-Grillet's *Dans le labyrinthe* [*In the Labyrinth*] "I am alone here now, safe and sheltered. Outside it is raining ... outside it is cold, the winds blows between the bare branches. ... Outside the sun is shining, there is not a tree" (1959, 7) – we recognize the pattern of the side-by-side *assertion-and-negation* of events that's become one of the mainstays of 'dismantler' discourse. The foundation of Realist narrative in the declarative mode is – by a concerted process of statement and revocation of statement – rendered (hopefully) 'null and void'. Robbe-Grillet's *Les Gommes* [*The Erasers*] comes to pivot thematically on a fantasy about a kind of 'eraser' by which one might expunge errors that have occurred 'in life', to be replaced by more 'correct' acts or interpretations of acts. We are left to ask, Can such corrections ever be definitive?

(3) But the ultimate way to test the search for the definitive event may in fact not lie in the multiplication or the negation of possibilities.

In Christine Brooke-Rose's novel *Thru* (a title that plays not only on the idea of the creation and dissolution of a character, Ruth, through the mutation of the letters of her name, but also on the mutation of the word 'truth' itself), the question is recurrently posed: Is the narrator the creator or the creation of her characters? In *Le Parc* – and more forcibly in later fiction of Sollers' – the very antecedents of the narrative's pronouns shift so that we are repeatedly placed in a state of uncertainty as to whether, for example, "I" stands for a character, for the narrator, or for the text itself which the narrator writes. The exploitation of *ambiguity* causes our standard narrative certainties to recede. The reader must constantly ask, 'What is "actually happening"?' 'What event is this?'

Narrative 'lines'

In a medium – literature, language itself – that ineluctably discloses itself to the spectator in a linear, chronological fashion,[26] yet where its practitioner looks to throw time and causality into question, there is bound to be trouble. The anti-Realist may be expected to 'trouble' the waters – the directional, progressive current, the narrative line or lines of which his work as a whole is composed. Where the over-all *sequence* of his text's events is concerned, he may be thus inclined to seek some combination of similar strategies (positive, negative, ambiguous) to arrest or occlude the process of naturalization.

(1) *'Positive' strategies* (a) A novel may contain one narrative line (or more than one) whose continuity seems unexceptionable and straightforward, yet in which, finally, some normally crucial (in Realist theatre jargon, 'obligatory') event is missing. If the tale could be told in a sentence, some 'copula' some 'conjunction' would be missing: it has what we might call *paratactic* linearity. In Realist and Modernist fiction ellipsis seems to occur often enough. In *Bleak House* (and in detective fiction generally) the central murder doesn't happen where it 'should'; but this is only a momentary gap; eventually the whole account is supplied. In *Der Zauberberg* [*The Magic Mountain*] we're led to ask, What happened between Hans and Clavdia that magical or

awful night? But the dramatic and thematic fabric of the narrative as a whole is so constructed that we cannot conceive of an answer that would substantively alter our reading of it; the story stands intact and complete. In 'disintegrative' fiction, lacunae are at some level not merely apparent but authentic.

In *Se una notte d'inverno un viaggiatore* none of the ten 'novels' the reader–character picks up ever end. In *Rayuela*, while we're told *where* physically in the first half of the book to place the diverse chapters ('nodules') printed in the second half, we're rarely given a hint as to *how*, narratively, to integrate them into 'the story'. If in reading *Molloy* we take Molloy's and Moran's separate stories as thematically one (a not uneconomical way of making sense of their conjunction in one novel) with their positions reversed, Moran's being the story of the making of a Molloy, then there is a narrative ellipsis between parts I and II. In *Le Voyeur*, at the point (between parts I and II) where the purported murder would have been committed, there is (in the original) a blank page, and a corresponding "hole" in the protagonist's memory. In *Le Parc*, as Sollers' colleague Ricardou has nicely observed, there is "at the end of the first period of the book ... a large blank", the "ideal center of the book", "the ideal place where the transmutation occurs that transcends, at their point of junction, both Night and Day" (Ricardou, 1967, 276). In *The Third Policeman* what begins as an omission of a central 'fact' (the narrator's death) ends – with the provision of the fact – as an admission of its vacuity (death is narratively meaningless).[27]

(b) 'Stories' within texts may, in oscillating, parallel series, present us with a kind of *multi-linearity* of apperception.

In Borges's "El acercamiento a Almotásim" ["The approach to al-Mu'tasim", 1970a] a book by that title is described and interpreted by the present speakers only to be replaced by another narrative from a subsequent edition, with an alternative interpretation. In "La otra muerte" ["The other death", 1970a] we're told the story of a 'cowardly' young man, which – it becomes apparent – may be confused by its tellers with the story of another, who was a 'hero'. In "Abenjacán el Bojari, muerto en su Laberinto" ["Ibn Hakkan al-Bokhari, dead in his labyrinth", 1970a], we encounter the tale of the death of a man as it occurs in some five different versions, entailing as many motives and as many interpretive themes. The same process (wrought in other ways) lies at the centre of Pinget's *L'Inquisitoire* (where literally hundreds of character-linked narratives are imbedded in the matrix of the interrogated man's reminiscences), in Robbe-Grillet's *La Maison de Rendez-vous*, and in Calvino's *Se una notte d'inverno un viaggatore* and *Il castello dei destini incrociati* [*The Castle of Crossed Destinies*] (where the tarot cards with their fixed personae yield different stories to their different card-tellers). A number of short stories (or rather, invented 'critical essays' in which the novels they discuss are 'summarized' in story-form) revolve around this tactic in Lem's *A Perfect Vacuum*, 1971, a volume that is – the reputed 'editor' tells us – "the model of the Universe as a game. . . . that is to say, a book 'about nothing'" (353–4).

The multiplistic mode of narration, too, has a long tradition. Browning's *The Ring and the Book* is of course a classic example of a pattern whereby plot A and plot B (and in this case eight further plots) are put forward successively as alternative paraphrases representing a single *histoire*. But Browning's is specifically intended as a collection of 'either/ors' within a generic, collective Romantic–Realistic scheme evoking the variety of possible psychological (cosmically integrable) understandings of a given situation. In the fiction we're now discussing there is a positive inclination to commend to our attention – instead of the 'story A *or* story B' view – a 'story A *and* story B' conception of how we should read the text. We are made aware of the '*or*ness' (the contradictoriness) of each successive alternative; but that's not all. As in the case of Nabokov's *Pale Fire*, for example, we *think* the plot as a whole can make sense – if we'll concede that one of these versions and not another takes precedence, 'is the real one'. But the predominant feeling is not so much one of our having a choice, but of the over-providing (indeed, overly provisional), supersaturated, 'hypersemic' quality of the text as a whole. And, above all, here is not the merely pleonastic quality of the Realist novel, where redundancy makes for clarity. Rather, the work generates a particular kind of superfluity in which the progressive surcharge of signs eventually leads literally to an overload, an 'inordinate' diffusion of overlapping possibilities that merge into one another, so that definition and the chance for choice are somehow, somewhere along the line, lost.

(c) But in a narrative, by means of some form of self-referentiality, much may be asserted of a positive, lucid and apparently consistent and even complete sort, yet that leaves us unsatisfied as to its meaningfulness.

Thus on the plane of the *histoire*, a linear text may be *regressive*. In Butor's *L'Emploi du Temps* [*Passing Time*, 1960], the protagonist–writer compulsively returns again and again to the time in which he'd written earlier parts of his narrative, and in so doing goes back into the time of which he had (at that time) written; events from these three 'levels' of time become intermingled. Mauriac's *L'Agrandissment* is in large part ostensibly 'about' the writing of – and is a reconstruction and reassessment of – Mauriac's three previous novels, as seen by the writer who is a protagonist in each of those novels. In Pinget's *Quelqu'un* [*Someone*] the linear time-scheme is marked by repeated false starts, in which the narrator – forgetful, obsessive, confused – goes back over the same events 'time and again'.

And on the plane of the *discours*, a linear text may be *recursive*. The conception of infinite regress is one that haunts disintegrative fiction. Yet, in spite of an almost universal critical habit of assuming otherwise, far from all regressive texts are recursive ones. It's one thing for the narrative to refer to events from which the currently described event has sprung; it's another for a narrative to refer to other passages of narration from which the current passage springs. These may blur into each other – and it's a penchant among anti-Realists philosophically most committed to the *regressus ad infinitum* to make this happen – but the former is clearly concerned with the relations between story events (with physical causality, for example), and the latter with the relations between narrative utterances (with the ways, for example, that words may by their own nature generate narration). We must return to this issue later but, for the moment, 'I am my father's son' is a regressive statement; it declares that I am defined by the nature of my relationship to someone else, who in turn is defined (in the phrase 'my father') by his relationship to me. The following, on the other hand, are recursive; the utterance refers not to matters of relationship outside it, but rather to relationships within it and to the way it works in the reader's mind; it is not a question of me being created by my father and my father being in a sense created (made a father) by me, with the sentence merely stating this 'pre-existing fact' external to it, but rather a question of the sentence's creating the 'facts' that it states:

> "Do you think anybody has ever had precisely this thought before?"
> "'yields falsehood when appended to its quotation' yields falsehood when appended to its quotation".
> "The reader of this exists only while reading it."
> "Does this remind you of Napoleon?"
> "This prophecy will come true."
> "I am not the man I pretend to be."[28]

Mid-century anti-Realist fiction is replete with gestures of this sort. Borges' "Magias parciales del *Quijote*" ["Partial magic in the *Quixote*", 1964] speaks of the king of *A Thousand and One Nights* as one who "hears from the queen his own story. He hears the beginning of the story, which comprises all the others and also – monstrously – itself", so that "if the characters of a fictional work can be readers or spectators, we, its readers or spectators, can be fictitious" (1964, 195, 196). Barth's *Lost in the Funhouse* and *Chimera* advance stories in which this motif is elaborately amplified, the quotes-within-quotes-within-quotes pattern of "Menelaiad" being but one permutation. *L'Agrandissement* is described by its narrator as "the story of a gentleman who is asking himself how he's going to write a novel that I have already written".[29] There lurks here more than a hint that the struggle to capture a definitive truth contains its failure; within or beyond each story there must remain a story yet to be told.

(d) Still, a 'positive' narrative may not be self-referential and may yet put its assertions into question. It may, in its totality, seek to be *circular*. I say 'seek to' because, seen against the background of the extreme difficulty in composing a narrative that is actually both intelligible and circular, the energy expended in anti-Realist fiction in generating the impression of circularity is remarkable. Every linguistic utterance in fact has a beginning, a middle and an end, and insofar as the middle is different from the beginning, the end that any reader reaches by way of this middle must be different from the start. This reality – so essential to the enterprise by which the Realist represents the human condition as the product of a dynamic process of evolution, of change – is a challenge to anti-Realists.

The interrogation forming *L'Inquisitoire* starts and ends with the same question. The nightmare experience comprising *The Third Policeman* ends with the realization that the same nightmare is beginning again. Molloy's story is the narrative of how he's journeyed to his rudimental, nonage state, in his 'mother's room'. *Les Gommes* begins with the firing of a shot and the stopping of a watch at 7.30 and ends twenty-four hours later upon the restarting of the watch at 7.30, with the firing of a second shot. *Le Voyeur* is the narrative of the circular (or figure 8) journey of the protagonist away from and back to the steamer on which he had come. Borges's "Las ruinas circulares" ["The circular ruins", 1964] tells of a man in a circular temple who sets out "to dream a man ... and insert him into reality" and who comes to perceive "that he too was a mere appearance, dreamt by another" (1964, 46, 50). Furthermore, where circularity of *histoire* is abandoned there will be alternative efforts in 'disintegrative' fiction towards circularity of *discours*. The palindrome (by which, for example, the Napoleonic mythos that so haunts nineteenth-century Realist fiction might be reduced to the inanity 'Able was I ere I saw Elba') becomes – as it was for Saussure – an ideal model, and mechanical aids will be brought to bear. Reminiscent of *Finnegans Wake* (where the last sentence breaks off midway to be completed by the end-of-sentence phrase with which the book begins), the *first* narrative of *Lost in the Funhouse* appears on the two sides of a page in the form of a printed phrase which we are to cut out and paste in the shape of a Möbius strip that will read (endlessly) "once upon a time there was a story that began once upon a time there was a story that began ..." (Barth, 1965, 1–2).

Here are 'positive' narratives, then, with a difference. By obliging us to work over and over the same *assertions* or by appearing to bring us ever to the same point – and doing either or both of these with literally *a-prioristic* analytical rigour – texts may begin to divest clarity, shapeliness and order of that intelligence, even that intelligibility, normally associated with them. The integrated, systematic relations between past, present and future, between here and there, between this and that, appear hollow; completeness seems (once more) empty.

(2) *'Negative' strategies* If a novel can throw into doubt the occurrence of a given event by 'contradicting itself', it may deny any sequence of events in the same way. This is of course the final effect not only of examples I've already mentioned but, on a larger scale, of total works like Pinget's *Le Fiston [Monsieur Levert/No Answer*, 1959] and *Mahu ou le Matériau* [*Mahu or The Material*, 1952], where an alternative story comes along in the second half to replace the first. "I'm starting over", says a new first-person narrator in *Le Fiston*; "I must have made a mistake at the beginning" (69). "I lied a great deal at the beginning of this book to get to this point", says the 'writer' of *Mahu*. "Between you and me, the first part was a novel that didn't work out" (144). "The story", Robbe-Grillet wrote later of *La Jalousie*, "was ... constructed in such a way that any attempt to reconstitute an external chronology was bound to end, sooner or later, in a series of contradictions, and hence in a dead-end" (1962, 150).

But the attack on the coherence of narrative 'lines' may embody a conception quite distinct from that entailed by the mere revocation of events, a conception of an altogether different cast. The question is no longer simply one of the actuality of occurrences. Because words must occur on a page not all together but one at a time, must the writer be taken to mean that many things may never happen at once? At least since the onset of the *symboliste* movement writers have repeatedly been dogged by the intransigence with which linear modes of articulation are contaminated with intimations of time, of a temporality which they have not 'intended'. It's not how things come about in life but the very nature of literature that's at issue. Must writing, compelled by its linearity to imply things which it may not wish to say, inevitably express causality, for example, or temporality, however much its very words semantically disown these things?

Writers now will struggle in ever-increasing ways to break out of this prison. One may invent – and imitate the ways of – a world in which novels of a different sort operate. "On Tralfamadore", says a character in Kurt Vonnegut's *Slaughterhouse*-5, "when a person dies he only *appears* to die. He is still very much alive in the past. . . . All moments, past, present and future, always have existed, always will exist." In Tralfamadorian novels "each clump of symbols is a brief, urgent message – describing a situation, scene. We Tralfamadorians read them all at once, not one after the other. There isn't any particular relationship between all the messages. . . . There is no beginning, no middle, no end, no suspense, no moral, no causes, no effects. What we love in our books are the depths of many marvelous moments seen all at one time" (1969, 25, 62). Calvino's narrator in "Ti con zero" fights to "live forever" in one "interminable second" (1967, 118–19). The symbolist impulse toward instantaneity, simultaneity, perpetuated in Surrealism, becomes a vital urge in 'disintegrative' fiction. "All duration cancelled", as a Mauriac character says, "time no longer passing, no longer existing, only this prodigious simultaneity" (1961, 71). In writers as diverse as these and Sanguineti, Cage, Claude Simon, Nabokov, Robbe-Grillet, Sukenick, Sollers, there'll be a movement toward the selection of narrative situations in which time would on psychological grounds appear to stand still. Not only are the durations of *histoires* reduced (from the conventionally attractive 24-hour span of *Ulysses* to one of 1 hour, to 2 minutes, to a second). The narrative is contextualized in terms of some object borrowed from another, visual medium (a photograph, a painting), together with the notional preoccupation with the time-freezing aspects of the visual media. Discourse will adopt grammatical and syntactic strategies by which to crush out, to expel the linear implications of linear construction – by the cobbling together of clauses without conjunctions, the replacement of indicative predicates with their participial and infinitive counterparts, the reduction of punctuation, the conflation of data within seemingly 'endless' paragraphs.

In its reach for the at-once static and global effect, fiction – sometimes with fear and trembling, sometimes with a kind of ecstatic abandon – tentatively approaches the extinction of the apprehension of causality on which the Realist text depends for its coherence. Once again (wave versus particle) the indicated signs are that you can't have both the event and a rational, organized savvy of its relationship to other events.

(3) *'Ambiguative' strategies* The ambiguation of events will readily produce ambiguity in the sequential train of a novel as a whole. Our conventional inclination to distinguish one narrative line from another in terms of persons – who is active in this line, who in that – may now lie at the heart of the matter. In Sarraute, Mauriac, Federman, Sukenick, Sollers, Brooke-Rose, events may at first be associated with particular times or places or 'people', yet may cease to be consistently co-related and coextensive in the ways that we've been led to expect. An occurrence, in other words, may happen to one person in different times or places; at one time to different people or in different places; in one place but to different people or at different times; a single occurrence may seem variably to form part of two or three or more different sequences of events.

A new issue arises. Theoretically, an *event* taken by itself may happen or not happen, or may be of one kind or another; but an event seen as part of a larger narrative has another aspect – it may be (in fact conventionally always is) assessed as to 'where it belongs'. The matter of narrative 'belonging' thus now too becomes subject to 'radicalization'. The classically cited case of *metalepsis* occurs in Cortázar's "Continuidad de los Parques", where the reader of a novel is killed by one of his characters.[30] By a literal 'leap' between *histoire* and *discours*, events unexpectedly arise that are not confined within the story's causality but (breaking the Realist canon of 'uniform discourse') erupt rather into the imagined realm of causality of the hypothetical writer and reader themselves. Narrative linearity is made ambiguous – and more. For 'writer' and 'reader', in such stories, *are* of course only hypothetical – they too are only part of the fiction. Just what, if anything, does 'belonging' mean where fiction is concerned? Who is to deny a Sollers the right to such striking fluidity of narrative as his texts' instability of pronominal antecedents engenders, where "*elle*" may equally allude to a woman or a page (*la page*) in the book 'about her'? Who says we were right, the 'dismantler' may say, to have devoted ourselves so diligently to this person-orientated way of sorting things out? It's plain that there is a rule – a Realist rule – to this effect: the one that declares perhaps instinctively within us that it is impossible to conceive of an action (the basis of *histoires)* without a clear agent to define it by. But is this instinct appropriate to the experience of reading? Are narratives necessarily 'descriptions of actions' after all? Surely they're merely words, and the sole agent behind them is their writer . . . ?

Narrative arrangement

Things move swiftly now. The shifting of the centre of creative emphasis from story to discourse opens the way for experiments controlling the disposition of the language in which fiction is couched, the very array of the words on the page.

(1) *Locutionary programmes* A novel may challenge us to recognize an open and frank disparity between its *histoire's* apparent principles of organization and the principles by which its data have actually been produced by the narrator. A 'story', in other words, is told that seems to spring from 'natural' internal relations between events, yet we're made aware that in fact these have been generated by the narrator according to some other principle altogether.

(a) A narrative may thus still be more-or-less clearly a product of language (which makes sense), but now the *linguistic event* comes first, and not 'the thing that it represents'; the initiating activity takes place not in 'the world' but in the words.

The 'story' may thus arise out of occurrences at the level of the most basic units of language; that is, out of (1) *orthographic or phonetic* operations: puns, anagrams and the like may 'create' it. A prototype often cited is Raymond Roussel's gaming with the phrase "*Napoléon premier*", which leads him to write "*nappe ollé ombre miettes*"; a miniature narrative transformation of this sort in English, offered by Culler, is this one: "The sons raise meat"→"The sun's rays meet".[31] We've seen 'Mülleresque' signs of this process emerging in Pinget. Or the narrative may be generated by (2) *grammatical and syntactic* transformations, such as those pronominal ones I've mentioned in Sollers. Or it may unfold out of (3) *lexical* permutations; a pre-ordained word-list may elicit a tale. Cortázar, for example, turns a standard surrealist dictionary exercise into a narrative within his protagonist's mind. "the shipworm", he thinks, "shirked among the shirts and shivered deep within the shittim wood; the worst of it was that the shifty shingle was shimmying up and down his shin, in some Shinto shire that could be shirred for a shilling".[32]

(b) In a different way, narratives may be regulated by what we might call *transcriptional* events. They may claim to be composed partially of occurrences constituting the process of narrating, itself. The narrator's act of writing or otherwise 'recording' his/her words becomes part of the *histoire*. Echoing *Tristram Shandy*, in *Molloy*, *Lost in the Funhouse*, *Pale Fire*, *Le Parc*, the narrator tells us of the paper he writes on, his movements, the circumstances and conditions of his writing. In Cage's "Where Are We going? What Are We Doing?" (1961) and Cortázar's *Rayuela* the activity of registering the narrative on a recording tape (the operation of the machine, the stopping, the rewinding) becomes an intercut part of the narration.

(2) *Non-locutionary programmes* Programmes of yet another sort involve disparities between the apparent rules of organization of *both* the story *and* the discourse contained within a text, on one hand, and the rules behind the *physical arrangement* of the text's matter as a whole, on the other. Rules of the latter sort may in truth be of a formal, extra-literary, and quite non-discursive kind.

a) A novel can be ordered according to an arithmetical strategem. As Mercier long ago pointed out, French writers in particular may be especially indebeted to Queneau for the example he set in *Le Chiendent* [*The Bark-Tree*]. Here is a novel that – as he himself publicly stressed – "contains seven chapters, each divided into thirteen sections; the last section in each of the first six chapters stand apart, being non-narrative, whereas the last section of the seventh becomes narrative to round out the book" (Mercier, 1971, 28–9). Butor's novel *Degrés*, then – as he himself diagrams it – is "divided into three parts, each containing seven divisions. Characters are introduced by three in each section of the first part. ... Fourteen more students are introduced two by two in the seven sections of the second part, and seven more one by one in the third part. ... "[33] Jean-Louis Baudry's *Personnes* ends with a full-page tabular representation of its structure according to the dominance of sections by pronominal combinations.[34] And Sollers's novel *Drame* is composed of sixty-four sections on the model of the chessboard, while his *Nombres* is made up of one hundred passages, each after the first four (since the book is governed by a cyclic order with a period of four) opening with a numbered notation – for example, "4.36" – corresponding to a "predetermined, arbitrary, numerical space".[35]

b) Whether because the 'dismantler', unlike Mann, Joyce and other Modernists, may be inclined to turn for his/her formational premisses not to the linear models of music (the ballad, the symphony) but to the visual modes (the so-called static, flat-surfaced, simultaneistic experience of photography, painting) – or because above all he or she may be concerned to remind us that the book is itself not a transparent, illusionistic medium but rather one of those *objects* of which actuality is made – 'disintegrative' texts are often ones in which the narrative is subject not only to verbal but to graphic patterning, physically, on the page. *Typo*graphic strategems may take over. Like

Queneau, Cortázar introduces passages in which orthodox spellings are replaced with phonetic ones, and passages in which the printed lines of two narratives alternate on the page:

> IN September of 1880, a few months after the demise of my
> AND the things she reads, a clumsy novel, in a cheap edition
> father, I decided to give up my business activities, transferring
> besides, but you wonder how she can get interested in things[36]

In Federman and others letters, words, paragraphs may be set upside down or in varying typefaces; words may (reminiscent of Apollinaire and Marinetti) be arranged to form objects – a tree, a snake – or geometrical shapes, sometimes 'abstract', sometimes explicitly mimetic of physical movement. As with Sterne, others (for example Claude Simon, Roche, Brooke-Rose, Barthelme) will insert visual symbols into the text (a hand pointing, the miniature drawing of a shirt regularly in place of the word "*chemise*": Simon, 1969); pages will be bordered, blank, or black. Where in Realism book illustrations were presented to support and substantiate the illusion communicated by the language, now language and visual presentation mechanically collaborate to envince each other's – and the fictional illusions' – fundamental non-substantiality.

c) The order of the narrative we read may be produced by rules that have nothing to do with the 'actions taking place within it' but rather with the actions that its maker went through in making it, its fabricational processes. Following early-twentieth-century procedures of *découpage*, a writer like William Burroughs (he tells us) may arrange his material according to a non-literary routine entailing, for example, the 'cutting-up' of a page of prose – his or someone else's – along predetermined folds (into halves, quarters and/or other mathematical sections), the destruction of pre-set percentages of such cut-up prose, and the pasting together of the remaining segments conforming to predeliberated geometrical sequences. What coherence the narrative may seem to have is a property not originally of its own but of a system expressly unrelated to it. We the readers, the writer of the words, and the composer of the text function in separate worlds, acting and thinking according to different notions of order.

d) A narrative may, in place of rules such as these, propose to operate according to a principle that is 'unformalized'. Works of fiction – such as Sanguineti's *Il giuoco dell'Oca*, Calvino's *Il castello dei destini incrociati*, Marc Saporta's *Composition 1*, Cortázar's *62: modelo para armar* [*62: A Model Kit*], and those others which come in the form of boxed sheets of printed paper – shuffle novels – claim in varying degrees to put the matter of arrangement (the sequence of reading) into the reader's hands. We're invited to 'read' each where, and hence how, we like.

Whether or not game-rules are present, as is often covertly the case, the customarily advertised 'randomness' of such texts is never total but relative (so long as any two symbols – even say "xb" or "A_{10}" – are juxtaposed in a fixed way on a page). The gesture is what counts. To the extent that the act of choosing is commended to us, to that extent narration is here put forward not as an expression of what 'always already is' in some totalized way, but rather as a challenge to us to recognize just how much we want to compose words in such a way – how we hunger to conceive of things as having, always and already, some stable and totalizable order.

If one response to the Realist posture – a 'neocosmic' response – is to put forward the uncustomary at the level of the story, and thereby perhaps to signal that new constructions of signification are in order, then another response is to institute the uncustomary at the level of discourse broadly speaking, to signal among other things that orderly signification itself is subject to question. If in neocosmic narrative departures from Realist norms are – with extraordinary freedom from inhibition in their choices of rationale – internally accounted for by the erection of alternative cosmically ordered fictional systems, there is an equally powerful movement in another direction, in which the possibility of a meaningfully complete integrating system is largely repulsed. I'm proposing that in anti-Realism alongside – or over against – the neocosmic there is an *anticosmic* urge.

Some real precision is wanted here. Certain potent narratives ahead that are plainly anticosmic seem to stop well short of denying the possibility of a totalizable universe outside the fiction. They may 'simply' build constructs that avert such considerations as to the nature of the 'actual' universe – for quite other, often divergent immediate reasons which must rest on their own intrinsic merit. The notions 'neocosmic' and 'anticosmic' bear not on different theories texts may hold concerning the nature of actuality, but rather on texts' different relations to *the convention that fiction gives a cosmic account of actuality*. However totalistic, the neocosmic posits a universe in essential features unlike the universe that the Realist reports to be the actual one. The anticosmic may frequently but does not necessarily assert that a cosmic actuality cannot be; like the neocosmic, it may merely decline the call to *report* a cosmic actuality. It – *both*, in fact – may be interested in other things.

Strange bedfellows. It would be sheer silliness to imply that these two, neocosmic fiction and anticosmic, had the same roots or could ever have been predicted until this moment in history to have anything much to do with each other. The first has been with us forever and has in the past (except when in the service of heretical mysticism) been a favoured idiom of conservative, orthodox ideologies as much as of programmes for reform. The second seeks to radicalize thinking (whatever its writers' worldly politics may be), and – as Robbe-Grillet pointed out early and we'll see later – had at its inception perfectly good reasons to stay away from 'neocosmism'.[37]

Nor would it be solid practice for us to build a book on the fact that the two happen to be the flourishing 'outsider' modes at the same moment in the present, if by 'flourish' we mean to refer to their popular reception. In the first days of their joint popularity, in this sense, they generally 'flourished', after all (think of Tolkien, then think of Beckett), for two quite different publics, ones we'd normally expect to have little to do with each other.[38]

What pulls these fictions together finally in the same book is, in fact, that it ceases to be feasible *by their own standards to keep them forever apart*. In ways perhaps unimaginable to Dante, Spenser and Milton on one side and Rabelais, Sterne and Diderot on another, it may turn out to be impossible to speak (as seems inevitably right) of Borges, Calvino, Nabokov, Barth, or Pinget as 'anticosmic writers', without saying that they are this by reason of their being equally essentially 'neocosmic writers'. They end up incapable of pleading one set of heterodox, anti-Realist imperatives without somewhere also pleading the other, as though the act of creation as they in their various ways conceive it may make this 'confluence' inevitable.[39] (Now that we spy hints of 'confluence', can it be only accidentally though pleasurably emblematic of this that when their names come out of the air they're the names of writers from what critics and teachers of an earlier generation thought to be cultures worlds apart, scarcely reconcilable as to ethos?) But that remains to be seen, and meantime what I've said only raises deeper questions we've not even broached.

We have a taste, then, in a 'global' way, of the kinds of things anti-Realist fiction may do. Yet the question persists: *Why*? Even our 'pure descriptions' refuse to remain pure; a compulsion to attribute motives keeps creeping in. Why departures from the Realistic conventions of 'Probability' should (to neocosmists) seem desirable, for example, is still unexplained. Why it should seem necessary (to anticosmists) for fiction to shun the totalistic mode, when fiction is only fiction after all, is still unresolved. What are their *reasons*, what ideas lie behind them?

2

IDEAS

Why play games?

We move now, heart in mouth, from the matter of narrative premisses to that of intentions. And we're immediately in trouble, or so it would seem.

I could flatly adopt the New Critical hedge, to say that whenever I speak of 'intentions' I mean, in fact, 'the text's intentionality'. That *is*, indeed, the bare bones of what I mean; I believe that what I say of a text's 'intentions' are to be found in the text's own instructions. But it's not quite as simple as that. If I sometimes speak of the potential motives of an author, the risk I'm undoubtedly taking is, I feel, not merely worth it – it is one that we can't in conscience sidestep.

When, in his novel *Lois*, Sollers' narrator says

> Students, don't let them grind you down. Now's no time for sitting. ... Reeducatize. Set up plans for study. Don't buy their cruddy junk. ... The bourgeois and the revisiono, hand in glove, in an elliptic concerted devious evolution, will shaft you. Fight back, counter-attack.
>
> (translated in Russell, 1981, 207)

I have reason to believe that Sollers designed it to be taken as part of an 'autonomous', 'self-reflexive' narrational context, but that Sollers, the man writing, also 'meant it'. I have overheard similar ideas expressed by him (among them ones which he gives no cause to doubt to be his own) 'outside' the medium of his 'fiction'.[1] And Sollers, as we'll later observe, has been one of the most passionately committed to the text's priority over any authorial presence. Anyone hoping this may be a preface to excursions into biography will be disappointed. It's only to say that unless we consciously face up to and scrutinize the deluge of discourse that invades our thinking with and without our assent, from within the text and from beyond it, on the topic of writers' motives, we'll never be in a position to begin to separate or discover the relation between these and their texts' intentions but will be swept away by their jumbled flood.[2] Once again, what follows is not in any way an historical account of the detailed aims of each writer or text I mention. It's a sketch (similar in style to that of the last chapter) of the *types* of intention that may be in operation in the main; an artificial schema by which we *may* in future understand – and at the same time against which we may test – individual anti-Realist works.[3]

Discussions in the past of a literature having an important element of 'the improbable' (of the 'fantastic', in other words) – as neocosmic fiction obviously does – have been perennially devoted to defining a class of such works *as* "fantasy" and to defending the meaningfulness of the term; and this seems fair enough. The label has the advantage of accuracy and the disadvantage that it would tell us little beyond its own definition, and for the latter reason in this book I'll continue to leave it for others to fight over, as an issue of meagre authentic interest. But in modern literary history two crucial (and in the end competing) conceptions have successively emerged out of efforts to explicate the operation of "fantasy", one in the nineteenth century and one in the twentieth. These – the notion of "imagination" and the notion of "equivocation" – in contrast to the unproductive epithet "fantasy" itself, call for some earnest thinking. While I take up the first of these shortly, the second is left for a later chapter where – because it's in effect an articulation of a movement on the part of anticosmic and neocosmic philosophies to unite – it becomes more strategically vital.

Neocosmic thinking

Passionate arguments for the creation of 'new worlds' in fiction abound in contemporary literary criticism. Depending on the theorist's particular leaning, appeals are made to various rationales put forward for their own narratives by a sequence of writers from Plato to

Thomas More to Tolkien and Borges, propounding successively the credentials of such fiction as metaphysical allegory, as escape, as utopian political polemic – and more. We need some kind of 'synthetic overview'.

It would be precious to find a fictionalist, a 'practitioner of the mode', whose own theory provided this. Or, failing that, that lends itself to some experiment by which we might find it ultimately within our reach. Of one leading 'neocosmic practitioner', a scholar and critic in his own right, it's been said that "No writer in our times has been more blessed with the gift of clarity. . . . His literary judgements, like those of the Dr Johnson whom he resembles in so many ways, are sometimes too rational, too clear-cut" (Walsh, 1979, 1, 11). This sounds encouraging. If I suggest that we take as the ground for such an experiment the propositions advanced by him, C. S. Lewis, as to why he wrote as he did, it's not in fact because they are rational or clearcut, but because – while they *are*, taken one by one, put with clarity – they (unlike those argued by or for a Tolkien or a Borges or others of their generation) actually turn out in sum to be so free of the unity we associate with personal predilection as to range *without* programmatic order over nearly the entire spectrum of others' theories combined.[4]

The background to the purposes Lewis may propose is a committed anti-Realist spirit. (We've already seen something of his thinking about 'serious fiction'). "There is death in the camera", he says (Lewis, 1966, 17); "one of the functions of art" is "to present what the narrow and desperately practical perspectives of real life exclude" (10). He frankly confesses to "an attack . . . on something which might be called 'scientism'" (76) whose field of view – what some "call 'real life'" – is "the groove . . . to which our senses and our biological, social, or economic interests confine us" (70). Realism, he suggests, is a prison; to those who would call the writer of his kind of fiction reactionary, inclined to escape from the realities of life, he offers the response Tolkien had once commended to him: "'What class of men would you expect to be most preoccupied with, and most hostile to, the idea of escape?'" and gives Tolkien's own answer: "jailers" (67).

Lewis proceeds, then, to set forth the terms of the alternative fiction he believes in. Within his lifelong Oxonian milieu, his explicit writing on the subject was specifically devoted to the defence of his work in what those around him would have called the 'low' genres, to which he at various times freely applied the terms "fairy story", "fantasy", "children's stories" and "science fiction". But in the end he unquestionably has always in mind (and continually refers to) what he considers the outcome of "an imaginative impulse as old as the human race" (67), the more massive pre-Realist tradition which he associates with Homer, Boiardo, Ariosto, Spenser, Shakespeare, Malory and the *Kalevala*.

The fictional fabrication of 'other-worlds' stories, Lewis tells us, can at the most primitive level produce in the reader a bracing and profoundly wholesome new sensation, not merely the adventurer's "excitement" – entailing the reader's imagined anxiety and its appeasement – but the experience of *otherness for its own sake*. Speaking of "what is said to be the most 'exciting' novel in the world, *The Three Musketeers*", he declares that it makes no appeal to him whatsoever, for the reason that "the total lack of atmosphere repels me. There is no country in the book" (7). What he seeks is "not the momentary suspense but that whole world to which it belonged" (5). The fairy tale, for example, "is accused of giving children a false impression of the world they live in"; but as a reader "I never expected the real world to be like the fairy tales" (28). Central to the value of *A Voyage to Arcturus* is for him "that idea of otherness which is what we are always trying to grasp" (12). Such works "are actual additions to life; they give, like certain rare dreams, sensations we never had before, and enlarge our conception of the range of possible experience" (70).

The sense of otherness has a psychological dimension. "'He who would bring home the wealth of the Indies must carry the wealth of the Indies with him'" (12–13). Otherness is not a manifestation of the material 'space' outside us but is latent *in us*, and is materialized in us by fictions's evocation of it. "Far from dulling or emptying the actual world," such fiction "gives it a new dimension of depth." The reader "does not despise real woods because he has read of enchanted woods: the reading makes all real woods a little enchanted" (29–30). It strengthens our relish for real life. This excursion into the preposterous sends us back with renewed pleasure to the actual.[5]

But in tandem with this revitalization of the direct imaginative perception of raw reality with which many neo- and anticosmists will thoroughly agree,[6] there is for Lewis the added possibility that 'new world' fiction may institute a language of an indirect metaphorical sort, illuminating otherwise ill-perceived aspects of the real world. A narrative about "beings other than human" may, for example, be "an admirable hieroglyphic" conveying "a knowledge of humanity" which standard "novelistic presentation could not yet reach", "certain profound experiences which are . . . not acceptable in any other form" (27, 16). We may see there, for one thing, aspects of human truth, creatively "isolated and fixed" (13). The traditional didactic uses of allegory for the promulgation of specific moral values needs no arguing here, and we know that Lewis is as professedly and professionally aware of them as any man in his time. Insofar as the work has some doubleness of meaning, some 'intimatory function' (as Stern would put it), 'the impossible" may be "a postulate" that will "usually point a moral" (70).

Yet, in addition to this, Lewis – with neocosmists to come – is persistent in arguing that this is 'illuminism' with a difference. "I doubt if it is as allegories that [such stories] arise in the author's mind' (69–70).

There are two sides to this. On the plane of the natural world, "it sets before us an image of what reality may well be like at some more central region" (15). And beyond that, "it can give us experiences we have never had and thus, instead of 'commenting on life', can add to it" (38). Alongside the allegorist's polemical life-commentary there comes a pair of positive intentions of a fresh kind. One has to do with the writer's own freedom to slough off the inherent limitations of the practice of Realism, and the other with the quality of the new experience for those reading a narrative in which this has been done. What characterizes Realism, above all, in his view, is that it is not merely myopic and trivial, but that it directs the individual's mind toward his/her own narrowly defined material self. "The dangerous fantasy is always superficially realistic".[7] It sets up reveries of wish-fulfilment on a plane at which 'the flattered ego' seeks gratifications of sorts that, in the ultimate, leave the human's larger being hungry and alone. "There are two kinds of longing. The one is an *askesis*, a spiritual exercise, and the other", the one solicited by Realism, "is a disease"(30). "We want to see with other eyes . . . to go out of the self, to correct its provincialism and heal its loneliness."[8] "The one picture that is utterly false is the supposed realistic fiction of the XIX century where all the real horrors and heavens are excluded".[9] It is not merely that "the world is made up not only of what is but what might be"[10]; it's that in actuality one "is born into a world of death, violence, wounds, adventure, heroism and cowardice, good and evil" (31); of "beauty, awe" and "terror" (68) – a fuller reality including "the mysteries, the intangibles, and the enigmas of man's deepest questions" (39) – which "quiet, realistic, 'slice-of-life'" writing is simply not efficiently adequate to cope with.[11] As Tolkien argues, "fairy" stories (and, by extension, his own) "have many more important and fundamental things to talk about" (1964, 55–6).

The potential for the writer, and for the reader in his experience of such narratives, in Lewis's view, has large implications. Lewis poses first a problem: "In real life, as in a story, something must happen. That is just the trouble. We grasp at a state and find only the succession of events in which the state is never quite embodied. . . . Can any such series quite embody the sheer state of being which was what we wanted?" His answer is that "it is sometimes done – or very, very nearly done" in a more essentialist, elemental fiction (Lewis, 1966, 20–1). By a process of evocation in some respects affined to what Janet (and subsequently Jung) called an *abaissement du niveau mentale*, where the rational function of consciousness is suppressed or attenuated and fantasy or dream comes forward, fiction can displace the stereotyped processes of cognition by which we habitually organize our perceptions along chronological, temporal lines, and we experience the pattern or essence of our being in a more fundamental, 'timeless' way. Very loosely paraphrasing Jung, he argues that narrative in this way "liberates the Archtypes [sic]"; it allows for the exploration of not only one's private vision but of more universal images springing from the realm of the suprapersonal human collective.

But Lewis declares a further aim. It is in the making of "stories" of this kind that man "most fully exercises his function as a 'subcreator'" (45). As it's put by Tolkien, from whom he derives the hypothesis, fantasy – "image-making . . . the perception of the image, the grasp of its implications, and the control" – is for this purpose. It "combines with its older and higher use as an equivalent of Imagination the derived notions of 'unreality' (that is, of unlikeness to the Primary World), of freedom from the domination of observed 'fact'". "To make a Secondary World inside which the green sun will be credible" is "narrative art, story-making in its primary and most potent mode", "indeed the most nearly pure form" of art (Tolkien, 1964, 44–5). "Starting out with an advantage: arresting strangeness", as Tolkien says (44), "by making, so far as possible, a subordinate world of his own" (Lewis, 1966, 27), the writer gives access to intuitions of the qualities of being that cannot be grasped by any number of representations of the familiar, no matter how mimetically probable, objective and exhaustive in detail. We can recognize in this the tone of Klee's oft-quoted notion that his was 'the intention . . . not to reflect the visible, but to make visible'.

In this conception of the text as the creation of a secondary reality (a notion shared in modern times by thinkers as divergent as Flaubert, Otto Rank, Robert Musil and Nabokov) there is a sustained urge towards the elimination of the welter of commonplace contingencies and assumptions for the sake of a more direct, face-to-face encounter with what may be some ultimate patterning of forces buried within them. Broad and brute matters (the nature of death, of chaos, of creation), it is hoped, may be articulated with austere and untrammeled, unrelenting clarity.[12] The idea is put forward as a doctrine by critics like Ziolkowski ("Fantasy ... represents not so much a flight from confrontation as, rather, a mode in which confrontation can be enacted in a realm of esthetic detachment, where clear ethical judgements are possible": 1982, ix) and in psychology by theorists such as Bettelheim (1976), whose view is that fundamental to human learning and development are the processes by which the crises inherent in the human condition – and the creative response to them – are encountered through the activity of fantasy.

Ziolkowski's – perhaps surprising – allusion to a "realm of esthetic detachment" lays the ground for our recognition of another motive in Lewis. "The impossible" in literature "may represent the intellect, almost completely free from emotion, at play" (Lewis, 1966, 69). The ramifications latent in this – as we'll eventually see – are enormous. If I assign to the domain of ideas it evokes the term "esthetic motive", it is merely for lack of a better heading for that wide province of literary motivation in which the text is claimed to have value for no reasons having to do with external utility but precisely because it 'serves no purpose' other than the provision of such pleasures as the act of the narration and the reading of it themselves offer. He has at least two different but equally capital values in mind for "impossible" fiction in this "esthetic" realm:

It may offer the pleasure – the intrigue, literally – of unalloyed cerebration, of ratiocination for its own sake: "the purest specimen would be Abbott's *Flatland*" (69) (a book routinely shelved in British libraries not under literature but among mathematics texts). Alternatively, it may bestow upon us – in the purer sense of the notion of the aesthetic, and we should watch the frequency with which he himself uses the word "pure" in this context – the pleasure of its own shapeliness and harmony; in other words its pure beauty. However much a reader may have been drawn by the apparent invitation to see Lewis's kind of fiction as the expression of psychological or metaphysical meanings, when we hear his description of the exact process underlying the making of his texts we are obliged to take this alternative earnestly indeed. In the beginning, there is the image. "I have never exactly 'made' a story. With me the process is much more like bird-watching than like either talking or building. I see pictures. ... Keep quiet and watch and they will begin joining themselves up" (32). "For me it invariably begins with mental pictures. ... Everything began with images." But that is merely the first half of the process:

"Then came the Form. As these images sorted themselves into events (i.e., became a story) they seemed to demand no love interest and no close psychology. But the Form which excludes these things is the fairy tale. And the moment I thought of that I fell in love with the Form itself: its brevity, its severe restraints on description, its flexible traditionalism, its inflexible hostility to all analysis, digression, reflections and 'gas'." "This ferment leads to nothing unless it is accompanied with the longing for a Form" (35–6). "There is one impulse in your mind of which, with all their psychology, [Lewis's critics] have never reckoned: the plastic impulse, the impulse to make a thing, a shape, to give unity, relief, contrast, pattern. But this ... is the impulse which chiefly caused the book to be written at all" (51).

This sequence of impulses will appear again and again in neocosmic writers' descriptions of their own writing processes. Calvino, for example, likens the act of narrative composition to that of "the tribal story-teller" who "assembles phrases and imagery ... making for the point at which something still unmentioned and only dimly anticipated materializes and sinks its ravenous teeth into us like some man-eating witch" (1967–8, 97–8). The admission into the writer's consciousness of these raw materials, Calvino says, this "pre-conscious matter" (101) is in direct response to "a typically human craving: the production of disorder ... as an inevitable reaction to a previous order" (95). But then "When I am faced with the giddy sensations of the innumerable, I get a feeling of reassurance from what is finite, systematized, 'discrete'." "Prompted by a kind of intellectual agoraphobia" (97) the "intellectual process is quite simply the revenge and triumph of all that is ... combinatory over continuous flux with its entire range of inter-related nuances" (95). "Eventually it is literature which salvages this domain and annexes it to the language of the conscious waking self" (98). For Calvino this conception (which he ascribes to E. H. Gombrich) of "the relationship between combinative play and the subconscious in artistic activity is the theme of one of the most persuasive theories of aestheticism you can find in print".[13]

Perhaps the most striking statement in this context – coming from Lewis – arises at the moment when he introduces his own 'aesthetic' intention. The paradox for him in *Flatland*, a 'book of paradoxes', is that – as an ascetically intellectual exploit – it arouses in us "emotion": "the sense (which it inculcates) of our own limitations – the consciousness that our own human awareness of the world is arbitrary and contingent" (1966, 69). We can feel the enigmatic tension implied in this, and it will be with us as we move through other texts. The narrative construction of a 'new order', then, for Lewis as for Calvino, is – according to this further theory – the enactment of the struggle not only between the actual world's teeming multiplicity and the ordering notion of *cosmos*,[14] but also between the artist's instinct for the imaginative proliferation of possibilities and his/her arbitrary gesture of aspiration toward order through pure form.

The idea of the uncustomary

Scholars interested in Lewis may not manage to find a synthesis for the multitude of motives he unfolds. What matters for us is that he *has* 'unfolded' them. For a neocosmist (let's say a Lewis at work, whether referential or even propositional in his intentions or not, the mode may appeal to his desire for liberation from the burdens of the materially banal and the ideologically immaterial that (to him) compulsively attach to the canons of Realism. It allows for a writing having a heterodox system – an 'economy' – of its own, whether this takes as its foundation some conception of natural law, some supernatural order, or some set of rules of narrative form itself. For us as his readers, the mode may seem to him to make for the intensification and amplification of our perceptions with regard to the universe beyond the text – whether for the purpose of quickening our sensibility of (1) the primal, innate and unanalysed texture of the natural world or of (2) a hitherto undiscerned order within the natural world, or to animate our intuition of (3) some inchoate unmediated plane of being behind the natural order, or of (4) some explicitly defined system beyond nature whether nature appears orderly or not. Or – without regard to actuality – the mode in his view may offer the reader an irreplaceable experience in the reading itself, by virtue of either (5) the sheer sensation of its raw, unresolved narrational matter and movement within the context of a fictive cosmos organized to sustain them, or by way of (6) the apprehension of some rewarding overriding formal pattern.

But plainly some assumption, some essential 'middle', has been left unexpressed. For while we may be argued at a momentary, 'local level' – in our roles as writer, as reader – to have something to gain from the abandonment of certain rules of expectation, nothing here yet explains on what grounds we as human beings in any more general way should be willing to make such a sacrifice. It's all very well to *say* that we may find our perceptions of the universe thus enhanced, for example, but might it not as easily be argued that as we read an unorthodox or 'improbable' narrative we are perhaps unhealthily and irreconcilably *severed* from actuality? What – in fiction of this sort or in us – can be believed, to the contrary, to encourage so *wholesome* a process as Lewis evidently feels it is?

Western tradition has in fact formulated an answer. Criticism has long been ready to consider those works of literature in which "the poet quite loses sight of nature", and in its place describes beings and events having "no existence, but what he bestows on them", to be – as Addison enthusiastically put it in the eighteenth century – both the product and the ultimate source of "the Pleasures of the Imagination". It's through the imagination, we're told, that "we are led, as it were, into a new creation" where poetry "has not only the whole circle of nature for its province, but makes new worlds of its own" (1712).

The history of the powerful and persistent effect in poetics of the conception of the imagination as the origin of – and as the basis of our *need* for – "heterocosmic" literature as Abrams calls it has been well chronicled and wants no elaboration here.[15] A random glance at references made to the imagination in a collection of essays by writers committed either broadly or quite specifically to what I've been calling *anticosmic* intentions in fiction reveals its compulsive attractions: "Le Clézio cast his lot squarely with those writers ... who recognize no valid reality external to that which exists within the individual imagination" (Cagnon and Smith); "Reality, whether approached imaginatively or empirically, remains a surface, hermetic. Imagination ... is exercised in vacuo and cannot tolerate the limits of the real" (Samuel Beckett); "The reality of imagination is more real than reality without imagination, and besides, reality as such has never really interested anyone" (Raymond Federman); "Exercising the imagination while at the same time apprehending its movement – such is the privilege that writing seems to enjoy" (Jean Ricardou 1967) (Federman, 1981, 215, 291, 266). We now recall that Alain Robbe-Grillet, a writer who boldly repudiates such literary desiderata as "character", "story", "nature", "commitment", "message", "allegory", "metaphor", and who praises the "clarity, the transparency" that in Roussel's fictional universe "exclude the existence of other worlds behind things", nevertheless proclaims that "our imagination is the organising force of our life, of *our* world" (1962, 102, 118).

The freedom of some such specialized, elemental 'imaginative faculty' in man from the contingencies of the natural world is a notion long voiced, even at moments when the defence of Aristotelian mimesis itself has been the ostensible goal. "Onely the Poet, disdeining to be tied to any such subjection" as may characterize all other disciplines is, as Sir Philip Sidney famously put it,

> lifted up with the vigor of his own invention, doth grow in effect into another nature: in making things either better than nature bringeth foorth, or quite a new, formes such as never were in nature: as the *Heroes, Demigods, Cyclops, Chymeras, Furies*, and such like; so as he goeth hand in hand with nature, not enclosed within the narrow warrant of her gifts, but freely raunging only within the Zodiac of his owne wit.
>
> (1595, 8)

As we've seen in Lewis, the writer may begin not with a doctrine or a discursive concept; wherever we look in the rationales offered for the instigation of neocosmic narrative, the process is explicit: literary creation starts with imagination, the activity of 'opening the doors' to the influx of images. "Everything began with images."[16]

We may wish to situate this view of mental activity comfortably within the limited context of Romantic thought. We recognize that context when Mary Shelley tells us in her preface to *Frankenstein* that with respect to "whatever moral tendencies exist in the sentiments or characters it contains ... my chief concern ... has been limited to avoiding the enervating effects of the novels of the present day" and that

> The event on which the interest of the story depends ... was recommended by the novelty of the situations which it developes; and, however impossible as physical fact, affords a point of view to the imagination for the delineation of human passions more comprehensive and commanding than any which the ordinary relations of existing events can yield ...
>
> (1818, 13–14)

The writer thus locates herself or himself – and consequently the reader – in an imaginational space which Hawthorne, in speaking of "Romance", describes as "a neutral territory, somewhere between the real world and fairy-land, where the Actual and Imaginary may meet, and each imbue itself with the nature of the other" (1850, 66). But appealing as the strictly Romantic attribution may be, matters are historically more complicated. Neo-classical theory, too, in its struggle to accommodate a unity of time/place/action in the service of universalized insight, has argued (as interpreted for example by Corneille) that as witnesses to the drama on stage we enter into a *lieu théatral*, a special world, an antechamber into which all chambers open, a median, unextended space where actors may pass in a step from realm to realm by virtue of the fluidity of meaning borne by the juxtaposition of images – events – discovered by the imagination. As it happens, prior to the formal onset of nineteenth-century Realism, in terms of the sheer number of their recitations, probably more fictional narratives in the history of culture have invoked this 'imaginational space' than all other narratives combined, by the bare utterance of some rubric analogous to "Once upon a time". Furthermore, at least since Bacon and Vico, and independent of the local vicissitudes of literary movements, in the guise of an account of 'primitive' or 'mythopoeic mentality', a quasi-anthropological theory of the operation within man of the narrative impulse has persisted in putting forward a similar view. Familiar permutations of this in recent times appear, for example (to explain how, say, a 'native' may in a multitude of different geographical locations declare positively that 'this very place is the centre of the earth'), in Lévy-Bruhl's notions of man's predisposition toward a "*participation mystique*" and Frankfort's and Cassirer's of the "coalescence" of time and place, where such rational rules as that of non-contradiction are supplanted by creative 'in-feeling' or intuitive vision. In each of these many and various traditions is a controlling intimation that there resides in human psychology an image-forming and image-fusing potential, activated by the displacement of the familiar, and by which naturalistic conceptual conventions are made to give way to fresh and fruitful perceptions of some paramount kind.

But propositions about the nature of literature that revolve around assumptions concerning the imagination – and around kindred notions similarly in vogue at various times in the past four centuries ('invention', 'wit', 'fancy' and 'originality') – pose very real problems. If the imagination is a human faculty – in an author, in a reader – where is it to be found? and do we in fact wish our fundamental conception of the qualities of a text to be dependent on any such notion of values resident in persons outside it? If the imagination is to be discerned, on the other hand, in terms of some special property of the external world of our experience which it discloses to us, how are we to define that property? Must we, for example, decide with each new bit of data, in every new text, whether it is imagined (or imaginary) or not? and if we were to set out to do so, how might we hope to do it short of testing it in each case against the totality of past human experience? The mind reels. We might conceivably hit upon some set of norms with respect to the *range* of 'experience' touched on in one text as against another. Texts whose *histoires* and/or *discours* are of a more 'limited' sort might be taken as having less appeal to the imagination than others, and this is often indeed the tacit basis underlying claims that one novel is 'more imaginative' than another. But can we really predict or wish to dictate in advance norms of 'scope' for a text – whether as to its 'subject matter' or 'treatment' – that will sensibly delimit all and nothing but what we feel to be imaginative? On the other hand, fiction (*l'ouvrage d'imagination*) is often addressed as imaginative in the sense that it deals with 'the imaginary' as distinguished from 'the factually true' Yet are we logically, empirically or even temperamentally so equipped as to find at hand rules of discrimination by which to separate and weigh up the 'imaginary' versus the 'true' within each work of fiction with enough efficiency to make the undertaking worthwhile? Whether in search of an accurate replica of actuality or in search of liberated invention – whether we take it as productive of truths or of hypotheses or even of 'mere signs' – do we wish to bind the activity of fiction to these distinctions in the name of a singleminded devotion to 'the imaginative'? *Or* in the name of a nervousness-after-truth which we know science itself (perhaps the set of disciplines most perpetually hard-pressed to make such distinctions) doesn't hesitate to confine to a very narrow and late stage of its own narrative-making-and-testing activity?[17]

It's possible to argue, as we'll find, that every linguistic utterance is figurative (that is, constituted by signs independent of an actuality to which it only appears to refer), or that all linguistic utterances indeed constitute actuality. Within the perspective of either of these views the 'imaginary/true' antithesis becomes senseless. And any conjecture propounding the imagination's effects that *may* eventually make sense would no doubt fall in some more shifty middle ground, and would persist in varying from context to context as our ideas of what was true and what was imagined altered. Even if we were right away to decide to our satisfaction what exactly the imagination does evoke, whether fictitious or real, it would seem that we'd remain bound to be making claims about qualities in authors and readers, and would have come no closer to observing what it was in texts themselves that let us know it was there. As a conception, for the purposes of literary understanding, imagination has intuitively much, and not enough in reason (given the present state of the art of reason), going for it.

Can this phenomenon be isolated in texts themselves? Efforts have long been made, and terms associated with the theories that have ensued – again 'originality' but now also 'novelty', 'the *insolite*', 'the romanesque', 'the arabesque', 'the baroque', 'the fantastic', 'the marvellous', 'the uncanny', 'the impossible', and, yes, 'the improbable' –

have each had some equivalent vogue. The difficulty remains clear. Once more, in seeking to define what we mean, whatever hypothesis we try, we seem instantly involved, by implication, in the necessity to assess the degree to which what appears in the text is *unfamiliar* – and our own tentative use of 'the improbable' is no exception – *in the total universe of our experiences*, with all the imponderables (and irrelevancies) that that may entail. In spite of endeavours to affirm the existence of a class of fictional events that are confined to what remains inexplicable within a specific text's own universe, conventional theory has unquestioningly maintained as given and not subject to further investigation (often *owing* ironically to the theorist's doctrinal stake in the appreciation of the text as a free and autonomous literary artefact) rules of explanation/inexplicability whose bases lie outside literature: to principles of causality, for example, belonging to conceptions of Natural Law. Contemporary theorists putting forward the case of a literature of 'the uncanny' have, valuably, wished not to stray into elaborate assertions about authorial imagination or external actuality but to stick within the bounds of the narrative's own conditions (for example Todorov, 1970, Jackson, 1981). But when it's proposed in such arguments that a given event remains unexplainable, the tacit or explicit assumption on which this is based is that the text itself first calls to mind (in order to put them into question) natural explanatory canons. Yet in fact, when looked at closely, these 'canons' turn out to be 'natural' only within the framework of *a certain kind of narrative*: specifically and virtually exclusively Realist narrative. If in considering those works which theorists have earnestly sought to find 'imaginative' on 'purely internal, textual' grounds, we were to set aside the textual expectations of Realism, the inexplicability of the 'inexplicable' event would itself become questionable.

Whether we do or don't wish to regard it as an outpouring of or an appeal to the imagination, when we seek to identify *on the page* what might be called the fantastic, the uncanny or the improbable, originality or novelty, what we're actually speaking of can more modestly and with greater clarity be considered an internally coherent incorporation, in the context of some definable repertoire of narrative conventions, of the uncustomary. We're thus in a position to respond with some intelligibility to the kind of question that leaves advocates of literary theories of imagination for the most part helpless: 'Where is it? Can you define it?' The *uncustomary* lies in the arrangement of words on the printed page, and it's to be defined empirically by the differences to be found between that and what is customary in the arrangement of words on the printed page in some stipulated body of texts.

'The 'modesty' of this – a displacement of emphasis from what we perceive as unfamiliar in the *totality of our experience* to what is more narrowly a matter of usage (what is most commonly done in a given corpus of literature and what is commonly not done) – may, considering the tone of high seriousness we like in literary theory, be off-putting. But it does appear (in the next few pages, I hope, in general outline) that of those features of neocosmic fiction and its intentions which theories of the past would have ascribed to the Imagination a competent working account may be given without quite such imposing appeals.

This modesty wants stressing. The suggestion in no way means to dismiss enquiries into the unfamiliar in life or into the operation of minds seeking to constellate it in fiction. Nor is it offered as any easy escape from our awareness of the immense diversity of sets of conventions around us and the nuanced overlapping among them that typifies the history of narrative, or from the sophisticated and stringent operations we need to go through in order to discover what is customary within any one of these. It is not an exposition of a systematic unified theory of what *produces* the uncustomary – whether in nature or in the nature of minds; speculations concerning the imagination, for one thing, will continue to be tested fruitfully, with or without that. Further, this is not a 'deviationist' theory – it's not a definition of what's 'good' in literature, to the effect, for example, that the deviation of a text from the norms of some standard language is the source of 'poetic quality' however much the fictionalist's own intentions may turn out to contain a premiss that there is a 'goodness' in 'deviation'.[18] But what's being said here does not have quite the sterile logical purity of a tautology, to the effect that what liberates a text from the strictures of other texts is that it's liberated from the strictures of other texts. It does make at least two essential special (synthetic) claims that the cautious reader may and should find demanding.

The first of these is that some clearsighted recognition, suitably refined, of the *données* of Realism such as I've indicated at length (though not at enough length to be anything more than provisional!) can provide a perfectly intelligible basis for the recognition of what constitutes the customary which the anti-Realist would take as his or her point of departure. The second claim is that the obvious complexity of our ascertaining norms does nothing to establish any logical impossibility of our doing so. If for example we think that this mode of distinction (the assessment in texts of the internally integrated customary *vis-à-vis* the internally integrated uncustomary) entails some new and extravagant form of 'statistical analysis' of texts, and if we've ever entertained the idea that we are not habituated in the most commonplace way in our reading to making extremely refined statistical analyses and arriving at positive decisions as to what is customary, we must think again. When in a narrative I write the three phrases "green grass", "green man", and "green sun", it takes the person who reads them (within the culture that we broadly share) but an instant to recognize he/she is confronted with radically different 'registers' with regard to what's customary in writing. Read from within the perspective of Realist custom, the first is unproblematical while the second and third provoke the mind reflexively to leap to some form of 'explaining away'; they must, for instance, be 'meant metaphorically' or they are 'the product of some character's aberrant thinking' (he is dreaming, drunk, drugged, hallucinating); they cannot be 'meant *really*'; if the context in which they appear insists integrally and consistently that they *are* 'real' in the world of the text, the text is ('Realistically') uncustomary.

I purposely choose three examples (green grass/man/sun) to make the point clear in a further, vital, respect. Observed within a wider perspective, the second ('green man') would be 'natural' (capable of being naturalized) as part of the customary repertoire of northern European narratives of the Middle Ages and the early Renaissance, and – like the 'Cyclops' customary in Classic Graeco-Roman narrative – has since (except metaphorically or by belletrist allusion) been substantively displaced from our conception of what is 'fitting' or 'canonical' in narrative. (The ways in which we now use phrases like 'jolly green giant' and 'little green man' confirm that the status of the image in narrative has so 'decayed' as to make it synonomous with the laughably uncustomary there.) The fact that we're prepared to recognize different registers of 'acceptability', and that for the 'green man' example we can find acceptability precisely only when we 'transpose our thinking' about it into another world of conventions than that of Realism, and that for the third ('green sun') we can find *no standing convention* under which it's acceptable (barring our removing it at least one step from the given 'reality' of any context in which we might find it – by saying it's a metaphor, a product of character hallucination, etc.), is good evidence of our readiness to discriminate with subtlety both the custom of a text – the repertoire to which it refers – and the occurrence of what may be uncustomary within it.[19]

The appearance in neocosmic fiction, then, of events which may seem thoroughly familiar in the context of the total range of our reading – e.g. of cyclopean men, of green men – yet that strikes us intuitively as uncustomary, presents no problem and requires no reference to what's probable in actuality. Neocosmic narrative is a local historical response specifically to Realism and here the adoption of givens resonant of say some Classic or Romantic extra-Realist convention only confirms a concerted movement towards what is uncustomary with respect to the norms of Realism.

One further thing stands out, now, that we may not have been in a position to realize before and that will bear watching. Against the background of Realistic norms, the 'serious', internally integrated presentation of a classical cyclops or a medieval green man in contemporary fiction might not be the only examples of the intentional use of the uncustomary for special, highly sophisticated reasons. So, for identical reasons, may be the emergence, for example, of such narrative phenomena – which it was *Realism*, after all, that persuaded us were 'naive' – as saints, villains, absolute mystery, absolute creation, treasure, apocalypse, glory, pure evil, final victory, universal annihilation, divinity, hell, and heroism.

It's possible, now, to take stock of neocosmic fiction's foreseeable intentions without assigning to it wildly vague undemonstrable properties, but rather in a fashion that can bring into reckoning both its own explicit distinguishing character and its writers' essential claims. This with the obvious – repeated – proviso that it's in no way self-evident that every narrative is or could logically be aimed at producing all the possible effects 'on offer'. Quite the opposite: by setting out the mode's whole range of intentional 'goods' side by side with all their mutual incompatibilities in full view, we're best placed to detect in future what may be the exact undertaking of each individual text.

(1) The combinative function The first possibility is so plainly simple that it can be expressed in a few words. Whether it's Sidney or Addison, Tolkien or Lewis, Borges or Calvino that we think of, we can readily expect that the evocation of the uncustomary will be appealed to as precisely that thing which fiction, by definition, ontologically or generically does. That it places in the mind combinations of data that were not established there before; that that is its sole warrantable contribution to human experience, and its *raison d'etre*. In Calvino's terms, "the *ars combinatoria* of a theorist like Ramon Lull", "a form of combinative play" (which he says is today "making quite a come-back"), is what literature is doing when it "charts out courses that skirt the barriers of interdictions and climb over them,

courses that bring you to say what you could not say before, that lead you to invent"; that "literature is constantly straining to slip free of this finite quantity" which we habitually take to be the limit of our knowing (1967–8, 95–8, 101). "Rather than serving as a mirror or redoubling on itself," as Ronald Sukenick puts it, "fiction adds itself to the world, creating a meaningful 'reality' that did not previously exist."[20]

(2) The play function But with this we've only begun. For – in view of our natural assumption that it's what *facts* (and not fictions) make us think about that's what matters – with all its rational power, the proposition that fiction makes us think what we'd not previously thought would seem quite reasonably to leave us asking 'what's the *use* of it? *Seriously*, now!' Neocosmists' sustained inclination to yoke together what it rejects in Realist literature with what it calls "serious" literature reflects more than merely a casual response to "serious criticism's" attitude of repugnance toward non-Realist fiction. From a certain – and increasingly prevalent – perspective, seriousness itself may not be all it's cracked up to be. As Calvino's and Lewis's references to 'play' hint, it may not be necessarily synonymous with positive value.

The uncustomary may invite us – indeed may challenge us – to play. By plying us to set to one side what we chronically regard as worth reading and thinking about, and by replacing given conventional preoccupations (social, economic, political, ethical) – particularly those heavily laden with theological moralism and dramatized in terms of perennial narrative *topoi* centring on standardized institutions – with ones instead to which we're initially unable to attach all that gravity which our Realist reading habits have encouraged us to hunt for in stories or to hang upon them by main force, it provokes us to find something else to do, something quite different, as we read. Sent on perilous journeys to find immortality, sprout limbs from the brain, or gather milk from the face of the moon, we *logically* (to keep reading) *must* take seriously what we *pragmatically can't*.[21] We – in this view of the operation of the uncustomary – find ourselves attributing significance (coherence) without significance (import).

In our individual lives we do this all the time – or did 'once upon a time', the argument goes, when we felt 'free enough' to. As happens in healthy childhood play: extreme tension and violent outbursts – with an awful intensity we'd normally expect only in moments of catastrophe – are to be found in 'adult' sport, in parlour games, in lovemaking, in celebration, in reunion, in carnival, in amusement park and circus and theatre. The uncustomary in fiction, as in play, may obliterate that earnest accord (life is real, life is earnest) we anxiously solicit in our daily affairs between the meaningfulness of activity and the energy we put into it, physical and intellectual; it would seem to call for a simultaneous doubleness of understanding. We appear to rejoice, for once, in anomaly. Our vocabulary reveals it: the play of ideas, the play of or upon the imagination, the play of or on words, a play on the stage, a play in a game, the playing of a rôle, of a position on the playing field, playing the field, making a play for, playing around, playing the game, playing fast and loose, playing fair or false or the fool; each entails some set of actions performed within a context set apart from that larger life-context in which similar behaviour might be awkward, inessential, dangerous, ridiculous and/or absurd, or not discoverably part of one's preferred definition of one's own nature, values or beliefs. Some rarefied *disponibilité* is entailed, and unaccountability (for perhaps the only and otherwise uncharted occasion in our lives) takes on peculiar value. One may move in and out of 'the action' at will – one plays the villain but with a certain inconsequentiality – one may play without having to pay. Seriousness is discharged. Should we want literature to do this to us?

Play is one of those things about which it's very hard to say exactly what one means without ending up saying the exact opposite. As its perplexed if not inimical relationship to seriousness shows, as soon as we've begun to define it in terms of what it's *for* (which is precisely what we want to know now) we seem to have moved into an area which is inherently not-play. Patently because it does seem so intractable to 'serious' rational pleading, claims for it of a mystical sort are inclined to arise in the intellectual climate that has engendered anti-Realist fiction, and it's easy to leap to these. We could do with a slightly more perspectived look, however brief, at just how and in what conditions play actually seems to 'come into play'.

In life, among the most common recurrent statements as to what we 'get out of' play are these. Play relieves the sense of monotony, of sameness, of boredom or ennui, and the sense of fatigue. People in and after play say that they feel 'refreshed'. Play relieves the anxiety that's associated with the sense that whatever one does ought to be meaningful and will have inevitably serious consequences. People in and after play say they feel 'how unimportant' things that had concerned them 'actually are'. Play dispels the sense of urgency in time and the urgency of the contingencies of place; of the sensation that time is of the essence, that action must be relevant, suitably swift, and appropriate to the total (not merely local) environment in which one may ever be held behaviourally responsible. People in and after play say that they have 'lost all track of time and place'; the memory of what has happened and the perception of the imminence of what is to happen are 'obliviated' in the present and the spatially immediate.

Taken one by one, a wide variety of anti-Realist tendencies selected almost at random may be read as appeals to impulses within us thus associated with play. As an answer to boredom or ennui fiction may not only deliberately avoid that 'subject matter' which is already 'probably' prevalent within literature, but also might be expected to repudiate the whole philosophical view which says that literature's proper function is to reproduce 'the same things' we commonly experience outside it. In response to anxiety, it may regularly remind us of the fictionality, of the book-ness of the book, of the fact that the experience we have in reading is separate from those that make us anxious, or may seek to instil in us the sense that the anxieties it causes us are by definition of an order confined to the period of our reading; or it may persistently relieve our obsession with consequentiality by resisting our habit of seeking import. To dissolve our compulsive regard for time and place, it may pretend to remove us from the sphere of temporal and spatial conditions in which such compulsions operate, or to disrupt the logical and chronological continuities to which they are bound.

But to suggest in this way (as both advocates and opponents of anti-Realism often do) that literature brings us into a 'state of play' *for the purpose* of retrieving us from ennui, fatigue, anxiety, the confines of time/space, is to do exactly what we don't want to do at this stage. Instead of proclaiming what it 'aims' to do, perhaps we can observe what we commonly say play may actually accomplish – what sentiments the sentiment of it may displace – and what consequently and more simply are its own conditions. (We may often best circumscribe a thing by locating the orbit of its antitheses). And here the essential effect of what we've been saying is manifest. In overcoming our sense of the exigent contingencies of time, place, appropriateness, consequentiality, play would seem to work by disengaging the habits of thinking by which we feel ourselves *bound to our context*. The clearest test of this lies in our experience of play against the background of 'work'. People, for example those involved in hobbies and sports of every imaginable sort, consider themselves to be playing (to the extent that they may even feel 'guilty') – and claim to experience all the effects we've seen associated with play – who to all outward appearances are working extremely, even irrationally hard. What's happening in such cases becomes especially plain when we think of those unmistakable situations of play in which one does the *same thing*, apparently, as when one is at work, but now in a *non-work context*: the busman's holiday. Any change, we say with some reason, is a holiday. Play does not require not working – unemployment may feel the furthest thing from play, and so may employment that is ostensibly 'easy' but laden with routine and monotony. Play – to be play – does necessitate or institute change. It's an answer to sameness, and can't be generated without the release of an event from its accustomed context. Here we're neither assigning a teleology to play nor (again) is our description of it an empty tautology. We're saying that the experience of the uncustomary is a necessary aspect of play, on empirical grounds, and *may* be offered as its primary benefit.

At least since Kant there has been a vital philosophical tradition to the effect that art, in its articulation of uncustomary alternative worlds, may be non-utilitarian in its intention and may indeed be positive yet without end-directedness. As we see when we read a popularly received simple modern restatement of this conception, the history of its application shows a chequered career. "In the late eighteenth and early nineteenth century", as M. H. Abrams describes it,

> some critics were undertaking to explore the concept of the poem as a heterocosm, a world of its own, independent of the world into which we are born, whose end is not to instruct or please but simply to exist. Certain critics, particularly in Germany, were expanding upon Kant's formula that a work of art exhibits *Zweckmässigkeit ohne Zweck* (purposiveness without purpose), together with his concept that the contemplation of beauty is disinterested and without regard to utility, while neglecting Kant's characteristic reference of an aesthetic product to the mental faculties of its creator and receptor. The aim to consider a poem, as Poe expressed it, as a poem '*per se* ... written solely for the poem's sake,' in isolation from external causes and ulterior ends, came to constitute one element of the diverse doctrines usually huddled together by historians under the heading 'Art for Art's Sake'.
>
> From Kant's writings, Schiller developed his own theory that art is the result of a 'play-impulse', a free play of the faculties without ulterior motive; that an appearance is aesthetic only in so far as it 'expressly renounces all claim to reality'; and that this appearance must be enjoyed without desire and without 'asking after its purpose'.[22]

Unquestionably that 'huddling together' has taken place in past historical accounts and we need to recognize that in the context of contemporary fiction, this would (as Abrams' own tone intimates though it's not in his brief to explore it) be misleading. Even giving due regard to Lewis's interest in form, there are few signs that nineteenth-century notions of art for art's sake (adding to the anti-utilitarian motive as they did the affirmation of the nobility of artifice and a quasi-religion of élitist aestheticism) give an apt formulation of what's primarily intended by anti-Realists. Seen in the light of what may be a new or revived 'pure-play' motive, nineteenth-century aestheticism arrogated to the authorial act of the craftsmanly shaping of the work (the artisan performance) a lofty gravity and histrionic bravura – a seriousness – which recent writers show little interest in ascribing to their own activity. Might sensation/experience for sensation/experiences's sake here be more correct?

Whether we take the invitation to play in this way or not – with or without a hedonist implication – it's clear that there lies within it an effort to interrupt the obsessive search for a rationalized product and to put in its place the experience of a process. The challenge laid to teleological seriousness is a challenge to what's felt to be a pathologically abortive straining toward closure, about which anticosmists will have a good deal more to say. When Tolkien argues that "creative fantasy" puts within our reach a "recovery (which includes return and renewal of health)" – that when by routine "appropriation" we've laid hands on the things "which once attracted us by their glitter, or their colour, or their shape . . . and then locked them in our hoard, acquired them, and acquiring ceased to look at them" (1964, 52) he only echoes Shelley's conception that the act of creation "makes us the inhabitants of a world to which the familiar world is a chaos. . . . It creates anew the universe, after it has been annihilated in our mind by the recurrence of impressions blunted by reiteration" (Abrams, 1953, 282). Paradoxically through the patterned 'aimlessess' of play we may, it's implied, rescue experience from the inanition wrought by habit. Far from lulling us into the oblivion of insensibility and indifference, it brings us to a state of "rapt, intransitive attention".[23]

We can't now mistake this particular appeal to the uncustomary for the more immediately familiar and more limited vision of social or political revolt. "Our distrust of convention", Gabriel Josipovici says, paraphrasing Northrop Frye, "is part of 'the tendency, marked from Romantic times on, to think of the individual as ideally prior to society'." Tempting as it may be, this restricted assumption that conventionality is only a social ill neglects the possibility, intimated in play theory as we've seen, that the hazards of stereotyped thinking may be more fundamental still. The distrust of convention may be directed finally not at society but at the inertia of *mind* itself, for its falling ever back (as Josipovici's own speculation in another context takes in) into "*habit and the failure of imagination*" (1973, 290, 296).

(3) The conditioning function But now of course we've slipped sideways. In this last stage of our thinking about the play motive as an antithetical counter to 'teleological seriousness' I've again begun to assign it a teleological end. I've let this happen for two reasons. First, to sharpen our awareness of just how easily this 'drift' can take place (and how lightly we must tread – a thing that play theory in its very seriousness is often indisposed to do – whenever in future we mean genuinely to address play-for-play's-sake and not something else that may closely resemble it). And, second, to show play's intimate connection with what is nevertheless a fresh, third literary motive. The uncustomary may be offered as *having* a purpose, a psychological one, yet still without any commitment – let alone prescription – as to 'what kind of *content*', in the outcome, the mind is to produce. Instead of a combinative function (one that is generically inherent in the operation of fiction) or a play function, 'pure and simple', the uncustomary may have a '*conditioning* function'.

The notion lies at the centre of statements like the following. "Abstractable content is not the meaning of a work of fiction"; yet that kind of fiction rooted in the uncustomary which Robert Scholes calls "fabulation" nonetheless "continues to look toward reality" (1979, 28, 8). The premiss on which this apparent contradiction (by Realist standards) is based is this: Fiction provides us "with an imaginative experience which is necessary to our imaginative well-being. And that is quite enough justification for it. We need all the imagination we have, and we need it exercised and in good condition"(24). Narrative, however fabulous, may *prepare* us for reality, without telling us anything 'about' it. "The overcoming or transcending of the world in art", says Susan Sontag, "is also a way of encountering the world, and of training or educating the will to be in the world"(1969, 39). "In art, 'content' is, as it were, the pretext, the goal, the lure which engages consciousness in essentially *formal* processes of transformation"(34). The 'purpose' of literature as art *may* be, for example, a 'moral' one without its communicating *a moral*, Sontag says; it carries out this purpose by the "enlivening of our sensibility and consciousness. For it is sensibility that nourishes our capacity for moral choice, and prompts our readiness to act". It's this activation of consciousness, "accompanied by voluptuousness', that "is the only valid end, and sole sufficient justification, of a work of art"(38).

This suggestion, that uncustomary literature (with or without the epithet 'imaginative') provides a kind of "training" or "exercise" for the mind, has about it at first contact the whiff of the undemonstrable that we're often ready to dismiss under the heading of 'mere' (and hence 'false'?) analogy, or metaphor. Whatever people say, we know that the brain is not correctly-speaking a muscle and we don't normally *see* it alter in the way that we unmistakably do see the body's muscles 'limber up' and take on strength, agility and precision of action following exercise. Yet without doubt the mind does perform differently after encounters with new experiences. It's a long-standing axiom in physiology, for which textbooks are filled with monotonously uncontested classic demonstrations, that skeletal and muscular functions not only benefit from but necessitate change (the subject's mere effort to stand motionless for as long a period as he or she might quite energetically move about proves unfeasible). And good evidence in experimental psychology suggests that, so far as it's been presently possible to ascertain, this is equally true of the nervous system, as anyone will know who has participated in experiments in sensory deprivation; the integrity of mental function appears to require the regular 'input' of fresh external stimuli. Whatever status we wish eventually to assign to such observations, where literature is concerned there are in fact several potential propositions contained within the notion that it engenders vital exercise for the reader. The first of these is that like other forms of exercise it contributes to the pool of experiences from which we derive our very sense of being. Human activities previously justified on the grounds that they were 'productive' in externally – for example socially – confirmed ways tend often in current Western culture to be sanctioned rather more on 'internal' grounds. Contraception, for instance, is endorsed on the basis that the prevention of the 'production' of children (previously an uncontested social good) makes room for the free exploration of one kind of play containing another value of its own; a 'product' is replaced by a 'process' whose benefit is often described as an enhanced awareness of otherness, of togetherness, and ultimately of one's own self. Under the same cultural influence, literature is now frequently spoken of as a kind of intercourse between writer and reader, by which the mere encounter with 'the other' (the outside, the unaccustomed, the alien), awakens a sense of the dimensionality of one's own being.

In addition to this, by 'stretching' the mind the uncustomary, it's implied, may generate a condition of *well*-being. It would have literally a tonic effect: by the analogy with physical exercise and bodily 'tone', by putting us through controlled conditions of stress, it contributes to the natural *tonus* – a healthful tension-at-rest, firmness, responsiveness, readiness to respond – of the mind. The value of this for the sense of self is clear. As one often hears the athlete or the dancer say, conditioned in this way one feels 'within oneself'. Not simply capable (in the face of what one may be called upon to *do*) but 'self-contained'. In a state of tone one actually experiences something approximating self-definition and a sense of commensurateness with one's own inward, often otherwise mutually crippling competing urgencies; the potentials and energies of which one's being may be composed *are composed*, poised in a state of alert equilibrium and competence.

In this notion of a condition of richly-felt 'fitness', it is as if one were defined not by one's utility or meaningfulness for the world outside but more directly by one's own autonomous ability and meaningfulness to oneself. There's no doubt that – as a feeling of euphoria – this sensation may seem delusory in the context of 'external reality'. The argument in its defence is that, first, without it one is in no adequate disposition to meet external reality, and second, that without the prospect of experiencing it, no amount of apparent 'coping' with or 'facing' external reality is meaningful, worth the effort, or – above all – anything but itself illusory. Not merely a pleasant and useful experience, it constitutes the absolute minimal basis for any perception of 'externality'; it is an ontologically essential *precondition* for the continuance of personal being and of any effort in the face of whatever may be external to personal being.

Our earlier reference to metaphor can help to make clear just how far this process might go in the dynamics of our thinking. The suggestion now is that the uncustomary may actually stimulate us to *generate* additional fresh perceptions. Recent research seeking to uncover the actual, deeply problematical operations by which we read metaphors, for example, tends (or has been interpreted as tending) to indicate that – far from leading us to reduce and confirm unexpected utterances by some lexical process of translation and definition into more literal, customary, orthodox, 'natural' concepts – uncustomary textual connections cause us to produce further and richer uncustomary connective 'texts'. Asked "simply ... to write out a description of the images or thoughts that came to mind when they read a sentence" of an uncommon (i.e. figurative) sort, those participating in experiments conducted by Robert Verbrugge responded (as might be predicted) in various terms, but in ways that were in general respects quite similar. The text "*Leaves are fingers*" produced, for example, the answer: "I see a tree with thousands of fingers growing as leaves. The wind blows them and they move and wave. Birds fly into the tree and the fingers grab them and hang on to them. But they soon let them go. At night the fingers curl up into fists. Sometimes they 'cup' together to hold bird nests" (Verbrugge, 1980, 114). "*Giraffes are skyscrapers*" produced: "I see a giraffe with a body like a building, running through the jungle telling how he's earthquake proof" (110). Such sequences of thought in our reading of metaphors are no doubt both intimately familiar to us and yet not at all reflections of a movement toward a simple more commonplace dictionary-like analysis or paraphrase. While an 'appropriation' has clearly taken place, it works not by 'explaining (away)' but by *developing* and *amplifying* the 'text', giving it 'meaning' by engendering connections (leaves that wave, grab, cup / earthquake-proof giraffes) of a further uncustomary sort. We may feel that the rubric under which subjects in this particular experiment were introduced to their task ("write out a description of the images and thoughts that come to mind") may have been taken by them to be asking for further images and/or for a narrative, at least a narrative of their mental activity. But while it's obviously extremely difficult to construct a rubric for such experiments that doesn't invite the subject to 'poeticize' – and I'm not wholly satisfied that this has been done in every such experiment – we may agree that the same rubric would not generate similarly uncustomary responses to more customary texts. The interpretation of this phenomenon, then, would be that a text of an uncustomary kind itself 'automatically puts the mind into' a fictionalizing, *new-connection-proliferating* 'frame'. Or – to express it in another way – *produces* just such an implicit rubric, as 'Once upon a time' may have done in the past. The argument here is that the very occurrence of textual events seeming unconfined by customary rules of relationship may actually have the effect of shifting the reader into a different 'mental gear' in which the sense-making endeavour is coupled with a new-relationship-making activity of his or her own. Thus primed, the reader is mobilized from the habitual passive mood of acceptance into an active and directed state of creative attention.

It should be clear from even the scant examples given that the text is not supposed here to open abruptly some nebulous floodgate to the reservoir of total possible conceptions. 'Giraffes are skyscrapers' does not appear to generate 'grasping trees' in the way that 'leaves are fingers' does, nor should we expect it to; it produces images along the track of associations analytically and empirically connected with the notion of 'height' by which giraffes and skyscrapers might be conceived to be linked. It works, in other words, by *informing*, by giving distinctive instructions as to the general *kind* of new connection-making that may now take place. This idea of a constraint on the function of fiction will become an embattled area in anti-Realist theory, and one that we must come back to.

(4) The prospective function Whether or not we view this in the traditional sense as a process in which an 'imaginative' (image-forming) faculty is aroused – perhaps now in a slightly more precisely specifiable way – we can readily sense the intimation that literature may thus 'tune' us to 'receive' and recognize subsequently a broader range of 'registers' of data and their possible connections (meanings?). We've broached, then, a further motive for the uncustomary in fiction. It may have not only a conditioning function, but a *'prospective'* function. Whether literature efficiently 'brings one to oneself' or not, however hesitant we may be about the body-training/mind-training analogy, it seems inescapable that there is no much better way than to adopt some such construct if we're to account for one irreducible mental phenomenon. Experience alters us; we learn. As psychologists are quick to say, a description of mind – impossible without some conception of a dimension of time – may be nothing more or less than a description of learning.

The argument, then, is that in its prospective function, the uncustomary opens and expands our awareness, both as to percept and concept, by 'showing what may be', with 'may be's' nice *double entendre* in regard to punctual time. It foreshadows, in other words, what presumably *is* and what in future is *possibly to be*; by its hitherto unforeseen rapports it may bridge the rifts in what is 'before' us. The turning here is that the uncustomary now is advanced as a means not merely to our feeling our 'readiness' but, further, our readiness *for* something. Importantly, while it claims it to be for a *purpose*, this view of fiction still retains a determined *disponibilité*, an open-endedness, with respect to what it is to be *about*. Eventuation (on the page) may precede utility (in life). A practical analogy might lie in the contrast between the respective prognoses for rigid single-crop economies (where new, even infinitesimally altered conditions such as a shift in environmental temperature of a degree or two may spell annihilation) and mixed, diversified economies (which tend far more predictively to flourish), or – more crucially still – in the case of biological variation generally, where 'mutant leaps', momentarily bizarre, seemingly senseless and non-viable mutational forms, prove in new conditions to be the salvation of the species. The uncustomary (through 'leaps of the imagination' in the traditional sense, through 'lateral thinking' in recent parlance) would have the effect of preparing us for conditions which the habits of standard reasoning may discover irretrievably too late. The argument is not intrinsically a defence of the irrational. For one thing, it says simply that the text throws up the uncustomary event, and lets reasoning and pragmatic experience decide in their own time whether it's reasonable or not. And for another thing, it offers the uncustomary as a mode of testing, of improving, reason itself.

This last, superficially surprising, suggestion needs clarification. A current and quite relevant attempt in physics to resolve apparent problems of indeterminism arising in quantum mechanics is the 'many-worlds interpretation' of events. Aiming in particular to cope with the relations between probabilities and the actual outcome of observations, it proposes that "there are infinitely many worlds" and that "there is no fundamental difference between the observed position of [a] particle and the other points to which the wave function assigned a nonzero probability. The particle exists at all the points. ... What happens during a measurement is that [only] one world is selected from among the infinite range of possibilities" (Gale, 1981, 118). It's not essential to our purpose here to defend this theory, though it's obvious that it's long been with us (Leibniz proposed three centuries ago the existence of infinitely many possible alternative worlds) and it's of interest that "although the many-worlds interpretation may seem bizarre, it cannot be ruled out on the basis of the physical evidence", as George Gale says; 'it is compatible with the results of all experiments". (Thus we find the novelist Raymond Federman putting forward what he calls "the pluralism of the world": "Reality (and I mean here daily social reality) is only one possibility among the millions of possibilities whose combinations of elements constitute the world. ... Today's literature refuses the idea of a single world, even if it means negating the real world" (1981, 309). What counts is that here an 'improbably' uncustomary image – by Realist standards – (a universe composed of an infinity of alternative worlds) is specifically put forward by some current philosophers in order to save the probabilistic assessment of experience. The practice of uncustomary thinking to serve a prospective function is actually widespread in western culture.

One of the most common devices in discourse on logic is the invention of the 'fantastic' instance. Just to keep faith with our first thoughts about the uncustomary (remember green grass/man/sun): we are customarily ready to assume that emeralds we see in future will be green since all those we've seen in the past were green. Readers in the philosophy of science, however, will recall the now famous postulation by Nelson Goodman of the predicate "grue". In his argument on the confirmability/non-confirmability of hypotheses based on induction, grue would seem to be a quality we might attribute to a thing such that we may be unable to avoid saying of it that it is both completely green and completely blue at the same time (1955, especially ch. 3). Once again, we don't need to explore the detailed applications and outcome of this uncustomary fictional artefact to understand when a theorist on physics such as N. R. Campbell says in a related context that "the fantastic example on which this discussion has been based was introduced in order that, in defining a theory and examining some features of its formal constitution, we might be free from associated ideas which would be sure to arise if the example were taken from actual theory" (1970, 256).

The implications are many. We've already noticed neocosmists writing of seeking in their 'uncustomary' worlds some way of avoiding "provincialism", "numbing minutiae", and of exploring something more essential and "true" through the medium of purer "form". But surely, we may say, for an idea to be true it mustn't be cut off from reality itself – these are 'only fictionalists' talking. Yet do such 'fantastical' departures from the norms of experience have a different status when performed by scientists? The suggestion is more than simply that we need to think up / think of 'grues' in order to think effectively both about 'greens' and 'blues' and about all gruelike events (for example some dread-wonderful 'bleen') that may spring upon us. What Goodman is doing and Campbell is saying has to do with the notion that in order to get a clearer look at reality we need constantly to 'examine our theories' formal constitution', to see whether *our way of thinking about things* itself makes sense.

This is different from saying that we must test our ideas against the material actuality to which they're meant to apply. We are frequently led by local contingencies to cobble together theories, because they seem in haste to fit the immediate evidence, without realizing that they don't fit our general ideas about how things happen and how we ought to form our ideas themselves. Superstition is entrenched in precisely such mental processes. Our ideas *as ideas* need regular testing, and we may often by unable to find ways until we construct models of our thinking – and check them against alternative models – that are, by the grace of their being uncustomary, released from the mesh of quotidian contingencies and expectations. This looks to be part of what writers of the uncustomary are saying when they speak of their fiction's displacing the probable to frame properly the essential; that it helps us the better to test the internal viability of our patterns of thought. It makes way for the 'epistemological break' that (in Lavers' paraphrase of Gaston Bachelard) "occurs when the definition of a new 'object' opens the passage from the empirical to the theoretical, in which, according to a witticism by another epistemologist, Alexandre Koyré, experiment has to be verified by theory" (Lavers, 1982, 19).

The uncustomary in the hands of a neocosmist, then, would entail not simply problem-solving (the principal appeal of Realism), but creative problem-generating. It has affinities with Keats' notion of negative capability, rationalized as it is, for example, by one of his interpreters in the common-enough assertion that "in our life of uncertainties, where no one system or formula can explain everything – where even a word is at best, in Bacon's phrase, a 'wager of thought' – what is needed is an imaginative openness of mind and heightened receptivity to reality in its full and diverse concreteness" (Bate, 1963, 208). It would, it's implied, put us in a position to find the adaptations imperatively required – with the boldness and deliberation that are needed and for which both our standardized rational procedures and our unconsciously determined proclivities often leave us unprepared – and to cope resourcefully with those increasingly rapid and unforeseeable alterations in circumstance that may remain beyond our direct control. To provide us, in the futurologist's idiom, with the commensurate diversity of 'blueprints', of 'scenarios' for change demanded if we're to be so placed as to be able to choose in any way where we're going. Its ambition would be to provide not 'the' answers but an adequate array of *possible* answers and – above all – with a spectrum of *tests*, with the hope in view of our apprehending where to look, how to look, what to look for, what *questions to ask*. It invokes the idea of an experimental novel, but in a sense not envisioned by Zola, for while from its perspective a Realist/Naturalist text constitutes a species of autopsy, of post-mortem, this fiction would be a conjectural, anticipatory mode making room for speculation before the fact: a simulation game, in other words, an exercise in the crucial philosophical problem of the relations between 'the known and the unknown' (cf. Kagle, 1977). The making of fictions of this particular sort is thus advanced as one of culture's primary means of achieving those 'paradigm shifts' in world-view by which the survival of *Homo sapiens* is made a continuing rather than a logically diminishing possibility.

Literary and philosophical theory abound with otherwise persuasive and illuminating descriptions of productive mental activity initiated by such fictional wagers (*paris*), positing it as self-evident that it's *metaphor* that is the source of innovation. This is palpably not the case, and we'll misapprehend much anti-Realist thinking until we've perceived why.

The following statements, for example, seem to – and in many ways do – express in another form the argument I've just described for the prospective function, with the term "noncanonical" standing in place, in important respects, of 'uncustomary':

> The noncanonical level of metaphoric comprehension [is] not based upon subsuming a manifold under some determinate concept, that is, [it does] not synthesize it according to some specific rule of the understanding. Instead, the act of reflection is a free "play" of the imagination and understanding. ... A metaphor asserts a formal unity between two particulars (individuals, classes, universals), yet the ground of this unity goes beyond any objective similarities between the two subject-things. ... Rather, an act of reflection is required that results in a new way of organizing our experience. Here imagination functions in what Kant calls ... its *productive* mode, when it spontaneously creates what is not present to sense. ... It is the 'free' or non-rule-governed reflective process that best characterizes the noncanonical aspect of metaphoric comprehension. That is, a metaphor may provide an organization of experience not anticipated by any set of fixed concepts one may possess. ... The new metaphor provides a basis for elaborating new concepts (or relations of concepts). ... Metaphors lead us to experience the world in novel ways. By causing a reorganization of our conceptual frameworks they institute new meaning. These foundational acts of insight are tied to truth claims because they alter the systems of fixed concepts with which we make truth claims. ... The primary role of metaphor is thus to establish those structures we *later* articulate by means of fixed, determinate concepts (and systems of concepts). ... As long as cognitivity is thought to be tied solely to

> determinate concepts, then metaphors will be condemned as dangerous frills wholly to be avoided, as Locke so harshly insisted, in any serious pursuit of truth. ... If metaphors are, on the other hand, indispensable for certain cognitive functions, this will only be acknowledged and explained as we develop a fuller understanding of human cognitive processes.
>
> (Johnson, 1980, 60–6)

This exposition, put by Mark Johnson in "A philosophical perspective on the problems of metaphor", does much to elucidate how, in the view at hand, fiction might work to 'open the mind' to future understandings. But it attaches to metaphor attributes which are not the property of metaphor *in se* but are rather the property of whatever *uncustomary* element that any utterance, whether metaphorical or not, may happen to possess. Its author confuses, as many do, the juxtapositional function of metaphor (which is universal and invariable, *a priori*) with a surprise-juxtapositional function of metaphor (which is contingent upon the reader's experience). As Johnson's very language makes explicit, metaphor is not inherently "noncanonical", it does not guarantee "an organization of experience not anticipated" or "novel relations and structures", until – by an arbitrary gesture whose justification Johnson has yet to demonstrate – he envelops it with just such qualifying terms; until, in other words, he classifies as a metaphor nothing that is not a "new metaphor". Metaphor-like utterances may be especially well adapted to the particular connection–formation process which the kinds of texts we have in mind may seek to instigate (though it's not, as we've seen, certain that these seek to be taken metaphorically). But it should be readily apparent that, contrary to common assertion, far from all metaphors could be claimed to have this same dynamic effect. We inherit, with our very ability to speak and read, a repertoire of metaphors – 'hot temper', 'tired saying' (this paragraph is full of them: "gesture", "envelops", "perspective") – that can as a matter of mindless routine be passed over as 'natural', as though their juxtaposed parts 'belong' together, almost as potential components of their separate definitions. It is true that they are 'noncanonical' in the narrow sense that they may continue to fail to abide by a 'system' of connections sanctioned by, for example, received theories of natural law, but they have *become* canonical within specifiable systems of verbal convention, and as such they cannot normally work in the way that Johnson suggests all metaphors work. It's not the figurative but, once again, the uncustomary aspect of utterances that would lend them that distinctive transformational force. If nothing else, this perception of the inadequacy of recent critical representations of metaphor (with metonymy) as the basis of literary innovation makes way for a better understanding of the thrust of anti-Realist fiction that turns out to be remarkably spare in its use of figurative constructions.

To put the notion of fiction's prospective function into the perspective of our actual, practical experience, no more than a word or so is needed to call to mind the accumulation of documented cases in which mathematical and scientific insights – of such importance as to have altered (so far as we can judge) the course of history – are recorded as having arisen from the discoverer's apparently unreasoned sudden juxtaposition (in play, in creative fantasy, in dreams and free association) of separate data having no customary or canonical relationship. 'It began' – comes the scientist's typical autobiographical report, couched in terms which we now well recognize from the vocabulary of fictionalists – 'with an image'.

(5) The instructive function But with this observation we've now come to the most extreme motive for fiction of this sort – and the most familiar, since we've ourselves been produced by a pragmatically orientated culture in which it would predictably have been given most weight and attention. The uncustomary in literature is proposed to have an *instructive* function. That is, by its unexpected relations it renders accessible to the conscious mind what had always been there but had hitherto been 'un-realized'. It can teach us not only processes but 'truths', actual facts.

It's of course by this ultimate utilitarian rationale – as writers from Lindsay, Cabell, Lovecraft, Tolkien, and Lewis to Sontag, Robbe-Grillet, Borges and Sollers angrily point out – that pre-twentieth-century nonrealistic literature has always conventionally defended its presence. The improbable utterance was 'merely allegory', 'merely metaphor', bearing within it some pretended truth more significant than itself. Some neocosmic fiction will not seek to abandon this appeal, and as an appeal (for those to whom it has special attraction) it stands so voluminously argued in the established dicta of literary history that it would be madcap to imagine a need to recap it here. Two particular conditions seem to attach, though, to the instructive intention where neocosmic fiction is concerned.

The first of these is that there may be two kinds of information on offer: useful information (of course) and (equally as a matter of course and startling only to those who might not know what we've come to know about neocosmic motives) 'useless' information, or what appears as such. It's conceivable – indeed, it should be obvious, only perhaps we're always looking in the other direction – that even didactic literature may have two aspects, two functions. We regularly assume, through a habit dating back to both Aristotle and Plato, that the aim to instruct is the irreducible (though sometimes companionable) utilitarian antithesis of an irreducibly non-utilitarian aim to 'please' or 'entertain'. There does seem little doubt that, as we've seen, while learning may be serious or non-serious business, the ineradicable insight behind every strictly utilitarian effort to *teach* – even, say, when it seeks to teach us that *play* is healthful – is that we must work to live. More than anything it's probably this ominous reminder built into didactic discourse that raises exasperation and that unmistakable feeling of tiredness when we hear a voice speaking in a conspicuously utilitarian mode. Do we have to be told, we exclaim, that life is a serious business?

But our experience suggests that there is also something in us that has always drawn us almost compulsively *toward* a whole host of uncustomary informational data to which no immediate utility can be readily assigned. This is the intense attraction we feel toward what can scarcely be called anything more grave than 'useless news'. (We recall the origins of the word 'novel' in the word 'novella'.) Name it what we will (and shall we call it something else when, as is so prolifically demonstrated, it manifests itself in other animals?) – native curiosity, desire for novelty or the unknown, a craving for disorder, as Calvino puts it – the appeal appears more universal and constant the closer we look. The flirtation on the part of literature students – of all ages – with matters of exotic anecdotal, 'incidental fact' (reflecting their genuine astonishment, anger, admiration, perplexity, nostalgia, anxiety, wonder, that such places, beings and ways of being might exist, that such events might take place) is something the literature teacher confronts every day. It is a fascination that he – particularly the complacent established male – typically feels himself institutionally responsible to pass mutely by with a tolerant smile, reflexively and unquestioningly considering it childishly undiscriminating, or immaterial. It strikes him, worst of all, as inconvenient, for reasons having to do, he believes, with 'the limitations of his teaching time' but that may largely be owing in actuality to the limitations of his theories and to his own obvious highminded ('serious') dedication to those as they stand. It's certainly open to us to say that no one has any business giving us 'information' that's not 'true' or 'relevant'. But the proposition will always (this argument for the uncustomary suggests) contain an element of the fatuous when it's fiction we're speaking of, since here everything told which we might argue to be 'truthful' is inevitably sustained by a structure of relationships that is by definition fictitious. When, in other words, a reader is found against all evident reason to 'like' reading descriptions of creation and of being that are offered as information yet that appear materially quite unreusable in any customary sense, we may be in the presence of an investment of interest in fiction that is both unserious and deep-seatedly authentic, both playful and experientially urgent.

The second quality belonging especially to neocosmic literature in this respect seems to be that where reusable information *is* proposed, the province of reality to which it often implicitly refers is what lies latent not in an already familiar external actuality nor necessarily in a metaphysical realm (such as a Lewis sometimes has in mind) but in the processes of the mind itself. This intention is made explicit, for example, in the epigraph to Doris Lessing's significantly entitled novel, *Briefing for a Descent into Hell* (1973, 9):

> *Category*:
> Inner-space fiction
> For there is never anywhere to go but in

Conventionally, the reader's only recourse, confronted with a fictional world that he/she finds positively uncustomary but whose intention seems nevertheless plainly mimetic, is to presume that it is to be regarded as a psychological 'inscape'. The premiss is that in some respect the text mimics the composition, the irrational yet (with adequate 'briefing') intelligible alternative order, of events that operates within what we're invited to call the unconscious. We're being referred to a repertoire of kinds of relationships which we both 'know' not to be 'true' by the standards of material natural law (the basis of Realistic custom) yet which we regularly recognize – on the grounds of our experience of the ways in which 'unconscious data' manifests itself to consciousness through dream, fantasy, hallucination, hypnosis, association, undeliberated behaviour – to be 'genuine'. The work of fiction proposes to act as either a direct representation of the unconscious, or as a 'neutral' word-list-like or ink-blot-like text through which – by building interpretive structures of meaning upon it – we elicit insights into our own individual 'truths' to which our customary habits of conscious thought, however powerful, can never have given us adequate access.

(6) The commutative function But one further intention may underlie the processes of neocosmic fiction. Its central conception is that

literature may institute a positive relation between the text and the world, yet one free of accustomed notions of referential intent, in the sense that it is not regarded as *telling* us something mimetically or instructively *about* the world. It appears perhaps most widely circulated in a theory of art articulated in a brief but important essay released in 1951 by E. H. Gombrich. Whether or not we find Gombrich's own view an ultimate solution to problems we've met in this domain, it exhibits a perspective whose vantage point is exactly that of the epoch of the development of anti-Realist activity and – as we might have guessed from the enthusiastic allusion made to him by contemporary fictionalists such as Calvino and critics such as Krieger[24] – one that's a product of the same broad historical-intellectual process.

In "Meditations on a hobby horse or the roots of artistic form", whose title makes plain the experimental spirit in which he wishes it to be read, Gombrich takes as his line of departure his extreme doubt as to whether our only choice in regarding a work of art is either to believe that it is "a faithful copy, in fact a complete replica, of the object represented or that [when it seems to fail to be this] it constitutes a degree of 'abstraction'" (1951, 210). In his view, when we see a work of 'primitive', modern primitivistic or 'abstract' art as purely an abstract representation either of some external reality or of the artist's inner world, we are in error. It is "an unwarranted assumption: that any image of this kind necessarily refers to something outside itself"(211); indeed, "any image will be in some way symptomatic of its maker, but to think of it as a photograph of a pre-existing reality is to misunderstand the whole process of image-making"(213). Actually, something quite different is happening. This is where the hobby horse comes in.

When a child is confronted with an artefact composed of a broomstick body and a "crudely carved head which just indicates the upper end and serves as a holder for" strings which it may or may not call reins, and when the child 'rides' it and calls it a 'horse', is he 'representing' or seeing its maker as having represented – as having sought to communicate to him some abstract truth about – horses? "We need only look at our hobby horse", Gombrich says, "to see that the very idea of abstraction as a complicated mental act lands us in curious absurdities". Should we say that, when a drunkard politely lifts his hat to every lamp-post he passes, "the liquor has so increased his power of abstraction that he is now able to isolate the formal quality of uprightness from both lamp-post and the human figure?"(209–10). By the logic of the reasoning that says that the artist who 'elevates his style' by disregarding the particular and by seeking to communicate the ultimate universal, the hobby horse's maker would have to be representing "the most generalized idea of horseness. But if the child calls a stick a horse it obviously means nothing of the kind. It does not think in terms of reference at all. The stick is neither a sign signifying the concept horse nor is it a portrait of an individual horse." Instead, "by its capacity of serving as a 'substitute' the stick becomes a horse in its own right"(210–11).

We've at this point entered into a different way of thinking about artefacts, in which substitution takes precedence over the representation of truths in the maker's – and the user's – intentions. "The clay horse or servant buried in the tomb of the mighty takes the place of the living. The idol takes the place of the God. The question whether it represents the 'external form' of the particular divinity or, for that matter, of a class of demons does not come in at all"(212). "The *tertium comparationis*, the common factor, [is] function rather than form. Or, more precisely, that formal aspect which fulfilled the minimum requirement for the performance of the function – for" in the case of the hobby horse, for instance, "any 'rideable' object could serve as a horse" in a context in which horse-rideability is the desired function in the child's playroom.

> The cat runs after the ball as if it were a mouse. The baby sucks its thumb as if it were the breast. ... The ball has nothing in common with the mouse except that it is chasable. The thumb nothing with the breast except that it is suckable. ... The child will reject a perfectly naturalistic doll in favour of some monstrously "abstract" dummy which is "cuddly". It may even dispose of the element of 'form' altogether and take to a blanket or an eiderdown as its favourite "comforter" – a substitute on which to bestow its love. ... The common denominator between the symbol and the thing symbolised is not the 'external form' but the function. ...
>
> (213–14).

An essential feature of this idea is that – because a sign may resemble any number of different objects (the child may use a stick equally for a horse, a sword, a sceptre – or, as Eco puts it, "everything resembles everything else") – anything we may call a sign's specific referent becomes that only by virtue of the sign's specific function.[25] This suggests that signs taken by themselves are indeterminate. Signs however never exist alone but always have functional relations with other things, and signs as functioning things can be determined.

Resemblance here, then, has a quite different status from the one that traditional (for instance Realist) ideas of referentiality would confer on it. As the 'comforter' example would suggest, the crucial relationship is not one between the created object (the idol, the hobby horse, the event in a story) and some other pre-existing object, but between it and a need in the mind of the user, which the creation's over-all composition (created or invoked context) engages. The word 'symbol' here, for example, means more simply 'image'. It is not, for instance, a metaphor. For metaphor is a device of communication; it is there to tell us something about something else, whereas a 'substitute' in this present sense is there at most to functon in the place of something else, with or without reminding us of that something. "Contrary to what is sometimes said, communication need not come into this process at all. ... We may sum up the moral of this 'Just So Story' by saying that substitution may precede portrayal, and creation communication" (Gombrich, 1951, 214).

It's not difficult to think of ways in which this conception – for all the difficulties it raises concerning "communication" – might help us to understand the operation of literature on our minds in a manner that would appeal to many anti-Realists. (For our purposes I suggest we call it a 'commutative' notion of fiction's operations for we are talking really not about the absolute and final replacement which 'substitution' so often implies but rather the eliciting of an event whose importance lies in the need it fulfils and not in some 'thing' that it deposes.) It could allow us to recognize more clearly, and cope with, the fact that we are so astonishingly ready to accept works that seem to set aside 'true-to-life' verisimilitude, and that we are prepared to accommodate (for example, to be 'moved' by) not only 'high' but also 'low' literature. And it might facilitate our practical handling of texts in ways that past distinctions concerning verisimilitude/non-verisimilitude and high/low quality have unquestionably and awkwardly obstructed. It would seek to permit us – where more intellectualist theories break down – to apprehend the *force* with which certain features of texts seem spontaneously to lay hold of us – features to which we commonly find applied vague and finally unhelpful terms such as 'the universal', 'mythical', 'primitive', 'archetypal', 'abstract' and 'fantastic'. It would also proffer means for dealing with certain aspects of textual indeterminacy, for perceiving more realistically the actual status in our minds of different kinds of fictional experiences, and for feeling more well-groundedly at ease (less intellectually 'guilty', infirm, defective or deficient) with what they actually do and do to us, when this seems to conflict with what texts – or their authors – claim to do. And, of special relevance to further issues we have yet to consider, the idea of a commutational function would seem to deepen our understanding of the gratification the artist can derive in working out of direct contact with the world at large, of one's slowness (notably in the case of 'alternative-world' builders from Lewis Carroll to Tolkien) in coming to seek to circulate one's work for a large-scale public, and of one's willingness to be 'uncommunicatively' obscure.[26]

In thinking about functionalist conceptions of how art works, we may hold in doubt Gombrich's proposition that, finally, "all art is 'image-making' and all image making is rooted in the creation of substitutes" (1951, 219). However, once we entertain the possibility that what is written in a text may be there to serve a function that is in some way distinct from representation, we may even imagine a sense in which it may be there not necessarily as a substitute but more purely to serve its particular intrinsic function. (The comforter to a child in care may be its *first* 'comfort' and any real mother may actually come along as a surrogate for *it* in her comforting capacity, more or less effectively. We may think in hindsight – or on the basis of some additional theory, say, of psychology – that the comforter 'had always been a substitute' for a mother which the child had missed though he/she had never beheld her, but that *is* another theory, though it's one to which Gombrich as a Freudian at this stage might have subscribed. Or, as Gombrich says of the hobby horse, "the greater the wish to ride, the fewer may be the features that will do for a horse"(218). The child may not even necessarily ever wish to 'have a horse' or have anything to do with a horse *per se*, any more than the monkey seizing a stone to hammer open a nut does so because it has ever seen and wishes it has a hammer, or any more than we make anything to serve a need. An event in a story may be there, in this view, as an implement with which to hammer out or mold or shape an otherwise unformed but pressing idea.)

The conception would seem to raise new problems. How, for example, can we reasonably receive a theory that appears so thoroughly to reject referentiality? Actually, as Gombrich too makes clear, referentiality is not at all dismissed as an intention. It is simply a different phase in the artist's relations with the thing he/she's making (Gombrich, like Sontag and many others, in fact regards it diachronically, as a product of a specific historical stage in a given culture's outlook), a different kind of response to the work of art on the part of its observer, accompanying the functional, commutative one. What's vital in this perspective is that in our referential mode of responding to art "a new context is created"(221), forming other expectations in us of the work – for instance accuracy, comprehensiveness, non-contradiction, compatibility with other external evidence: criteria surplus to our functional, commutational interests and expectations.

Historically, Gombrich's view is the product of a period in which he was himself particularly influenced by Freud, and readers having reservations about the latter will want to scrutinize it in the same way they may wish to do with the psychologist's theory of substitutive gratification. In a larger sense, the hypothesis brings to the surface the vast problem of desire itself – how we're to define and situate it in the spectrum of experience; an issue to which anti-Realists' contemporaries in literary philosophy (for example Foucault, Lacan, Barthes, Derrida) have devoted powerful and conflicting attention.

The point is that (while it is always further complicated by the fact of the tendency of signs – whether linguistic or other – to be entangled with referents outside themselves) the notion of a created object's having a functional effect in this sense, as well as a referential one, is so strong that it's possible to conceive of an 'event' in our reading as offering two kinds of 'value' at once: gratifying our wish to know some outside truth, and our wish to experience something here, at this moment, as we read, for its own sake. Here are two different, co-existing desiderata. This is particularly significant if, as it appears in this context, even the most non-referential text adds something new to the universe of our experience. In looking at a painted or sculpted image, in reading a passage, we are likely to be looking at *something* (words, say), and at *something other* (something ridable), at once. They are different from each other; they have a *complementary relationship* to one another. A text may in its fuller intention offer a world of signs that is not a replica of events outside it but that subsists as a discrete, differently functioning complement to external experiences and the signs we use seriously to express them. It takes what is outside it at most not as its subject but as its point of departure. It does not *stand for* but *stands in for* other events.

The uncustomary in fiction may well have all or some of these intended effects – a combinative function, a play function, a conditioning function, a prospective function, an instructive function, a commutative function – varying according to the text and to the reader. But we have uncovered the *possibility* of its retaining an orthodox referential motive founded on the assumption that determinate realities are there to be revealed through narrative. What's most certainly the problem at the heart of anti-Realism – conjuring the matter of referentiality, which a chapter ago I warned we must eventually face – stands ahead.

It's the question of 'aboutness', and it's the anticosmic mode that lays it full-scale before us.

Anticosmic thinking

"Realism", says J. P. Stern, "is, among other thing [*sic*], a *meaningful* mode of writing (and not the mindless 'objective' dummy of anti-realistic polemics)".[27] In this absolutely crucial matter, anti-Realist and Stern totally agree. As the former would put it, terms that we've perpetually used to express what we feel to be of value in fiction – 'idea', 'message', 'significance', 'theme', 'truth', 'rondeur', 'import', 'seriousness', 'depth' – all carry this assumption: that in every novel we expect there to be a declarative 'content', a coherent and cogent body of signification, which narration merely *serves* – which it acts in the service of and only serves up to us. That writing is nothing if it's not instrumental, that reading is nothing if it's not interpretation, and that the act of reading is the act of interpretatively 'unpacking' the contents – the immanent, always-already-there 'meaning' – of a text. That the text itself may be set aside as we might an empty vessel once this meaning has been drained from it, and that such meaning derives from the way in which it refers us to actuality outside it (whether as an 'objective representation' of, for example, nature, or as a 'subjective expression' of a state of mind however uncustomary) – or from its accord with some system of thinking by which we make sense of events outside it. But the notion of literature as offering a rëferentially meaningful product in this way will not now always be everyone's dish of tea.

The case is one that (so far as referentiality is concerned) had already received its standard statement in the graphic arts by the 1930s in declarations such as that of R. G. Collingwood in *The Principles of Art* (1938) to the effect that "today, the only tolerable view is that no art is representative".[28] Interpretation, as regarded by Todorov, is "any substitution of another text for the present text, any endeavor which seeks to discover through the apparent textual fabric a second more authentic text"; this projection of an 'immanent' meaning renders the text superfluous (1971, 238). The argument, in fact, moves to suggest that the hunt for meanings makes both the book *and* the world equally empty. "Today", says Susan Sontag, interpretation "is the revenge of the intellect upon art. Even more. It is the revenge of the intellect upon the world. To interpret is to impoverish, to deplete the world – in order to set up a shadow world of 'meanings'." "The idea of content is today mainly a hindrance, a nuisance, a subtle or not so subtle philistinism", she says. "A work of art is an experience, not a statement or an answer to a question. Art is not only about something; it is something" (1969, 17, 15, 30). As Robbe-Grillet puts it, "the function of art is never to illustrate a truth – or even a question – known beforehand"; "the world is neither meaningful or absurd. It quite simply *is*"; "we thought we had come to terms with [the world around us] by giving it a meaning, and the whole art of the novel, in particular, seemed dedicated to this task. But that was only an illusory simplification ... the world was gradually losing all its life in the process"; "the moment the writer starts worrying about conveying some meaning (exterior to the work of art), literature starts to retreat, to disappear" (1962, 48, 53, 56, 70).

"ROMANTICISM dealt with expression, REALISM with representation", asserts Raymond Federman; they are "two faces of the same coin. Both of them subordinate the text to an already established meaning, present in the world before the text is written" (1981, 293). "There are no innocent forms", says Philipe Sollers, "there is no degree zero of meaning. Thus, there is no 'true' or 'realistic' novel"; "the book which would be a real book, that is, a text, no longer informs, convinces, demonstrates, tells, or represents." (1968b, 65, 62). "The new fiction", Federman declares, "will not attempt to be meaningful, truthful, or realistic; nor will it attempt to serve as the vehicle of a ready-made meaning. On the contrary, it will be seemingly devoid of any meaning, it will be deliberately illogical, irrational, unrealistic, non sequitur, and incoherent" (1981, 13).

To be able to go forward from here it's essential that we remember in what sense it can be intelligible to say that a text – whose language, after all, is taken from the world of communication in which we use it to 'refer to things' – may ever *not* be referential. This view, we recall, is that there is no 'natural' inevitable connection between signifiers and events outside language but what we as language's users – for example as readers – assign to them in each individual case. To return to our test-word "green": think about it – *green*. I am willing to bet that just now you have thought of it as an adjective. Yet at the moment I have in mind the noun – as in "village green"! It's by my writing "the green" for instance, instead of "is green", that this would have been made obvious; but even when I'd thus particularized the apparent 'field of reference' for the word green, this argument says, that would have been only a *linguistic* act. I would in no way be actually 'making present' to you any 'green' that exists outside my text – I'd only have constellated in your mind a semantic relationship between the word green and other words in my text itself. We'll plainly have to reconsider, eventually, just how free words are of actuality – but you can see the *idea* of non-referentiality here, and it's in this way that we'll be understanding it in the present chapter.

The ideas of referentiality and systematicity

We seem to be confronted – and contemporary arguments on both sides on this crucial topic have perpetuated as a matter of course the assumption that this is so – with a single and unified radical conception: that we're on the wrong track when we ask what a book is about. But in point of fact – and this is vital – as the quotations we've just seen reveal, *even* to say with seriousness that a book is about something need not be to say that it means to be about something outside it. The writers before us are engaged simultaneously with two quite outstandingly different questions. Referentiality and meaningfulness are far from being the same things. Just as the rhythmic and tonal effects of a painting or a musical composition may be suggested to do, a text may propose (many writers will insist) a coherent systematic relationship between its parts without making claims about its relationship to the external world. And while we bring to the graphic or musical or verbal text associations (tonal or rhythmic or dictional ones, for example) from the outside world, we may finally hold the conviction that what gives it 'sense' is that its parts fit into a system (a grammatical one, for example), without our ever believing that it is 'telling us something' about that world. On the other hand, a text may appear to repudiate or discharge itself of commonly expected kinds of systematic meaningfulness, and may at the same time seem vividly to be addressing our attention afresh to aspects of the world at large. Questions of referentiality and systematicity may actually entail a considerably greater variety of conceivable textual intentions than our theories of literature so far have managed to disclose. What follows is a schematic view not of how texts are composed (of their actual performance), but of how they may be *regarded* as being composed. It's not, in other words, meant as some definitive classification of works of fiction, but as an idea about *theories* of fiction.[29]

The referentiality/non-referentiality of a text reflects a concern with the degree to which its data have a positive relationship to events outside it. The systematicity/non-systematicity of a text concerns the degree to which its data bid to sustain a stable, integrated and ordered organization of internal connections, whether of a grammatical/syntactical or other sort. It's the permutations of these possibilities that interest us.

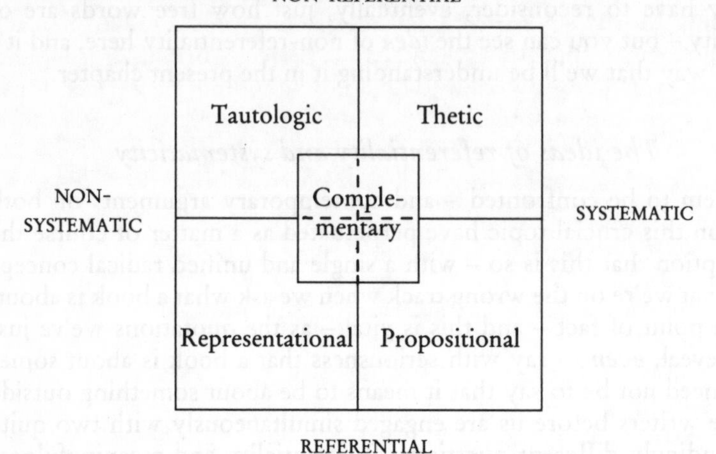

(1) The propositional intention A narrative that would be *propositional* is taken as directing our attention to the actual universe outside it (is referential) *and* as 'putting forward' some meaningfully consistent conception about it (is systematic). It offers a basis for interpretive paraphrase, which is to be reusable when we think – and declare things – about our actual experience. It's a notion of the function of fiction which is deeply familiar to us and it's the modality which anti-Realists would ascribe to all Realistic literature.

(2) The tautologic intention At another extreme, there are signs of a fiction about which it's asserted that it is *tautologic*. This doesn't mean that such a text would be 'tautologous' – 'only saying the same thing over (and over) again' – but that its intention is that it be taken as obeying rules ('logic') according to which an utterance says no more than itself: the same word, το αυτο λογος. When Sontag speaks of the necessity in art of our "experiencing the luminousness of the thing in itself", and reasons that "the function of criticism should be to show *how it is what it is*, even *that it is what it is*, rather than to show *what it means*" or when Ronald Sukenick says that "as artifice the work of art is a conscious tautology. . . . It is not an imitation but a new thing in its own right, an invention", each reflects a theme that has indeed a long tradition (Sontag, 1969, 23; Sukenick, 1976, 99). Coleridge argued for a notion of a literature that was 'tautegorical' ('expressing the same object but with a difference') as opposed to a literature that was allegorical ('expressing a different subject but with a resemblance'),

and Todorov assigns this perspective to Romanticism as a whole. In appraising Moritz's *Versuch einer deutschen Prosodie* (1786) he calls upon the logic of the latter's view that "a perfect work of art leaves no room for explanation: were it to do so, it would not be perfect, for it would depend upon something beyond itself, something external to itself"; "the work of art signifies itself, through the interplay of its parts; thus it constitutes its own description, the only one that can be adequate".[30]

This view interpenetrates the aesthetic philosophy of German thinkers to whom I've already referred, from Kant onwards, and is far from being confined to eighteenth- and nineteenth-century Romanticism alone.[31] Recent writers in other ways have been moving in the same direction, and if we use care in observing them before attributing tautologic motives to them we can find ourselves better placed to see – more clearly than theories have generally allowed us – that tautology is not at all the only alternative to propositionality.

(3) The representational intention When Robbe-Grillet rebels against "reducing the novel to a meaning that is exterior to itself" and when he says that "the work of art contains nothing, in the strict sense of the term ... it doesn't lean on any truth that may have existed before it, and ... it expresses nothing but itself" (1962, 71–3) we may think we're looking at a tautologist. Unquestionably he is committed to the 'itselfness' of things. "We are", he says, "in a *flat* and *discontinuous* universe where everything refers only to itself."[32] But there is a fundamental difference. Robbe-Grillet *believes in things*, and in a special relationship between his texts and these things. "There is in existence in the world something that is not man, that takes no notice of him, and has nothing in common with him", and which – while he must now never invest it with any "invidious network of feelings and thoughts" – he is responsible "to measure", to "describe"(77). Far from denying the relevance to his text of an exterior world, "to describe things, in fact, is deliberately to place oneself outside them, facing them. ... In describing this surface – to establish its exteriority and independence. ... to record the distance between the object and me. ... is tantamount to establishing the fact that things are there. ... These are the real, hard and brilliant things of the real world" (91–2, 118). Without doubt, Robbe-Grillet's massive procedures, of which we've noted examples, for the "destruction" of our conventional expectations (affecting time, plot, character, setting, metaphor, as well as theological, social, political and moral structures) pose a devotion to the rejection of systematicity. He frequently repulses the idea of

fiction as "merely reproducing, copying, transmitting" a "stable and secure universe"(144). Yet at the same time he makes it abundantly evident that by his "inventions" he answers our "need" to "return to the real in order to challenge the old formulae"; the aim in our abandoning "outworn forms" is "the discovery of reality" (154). This, then, is the third permutation: a fiction that would at one and the same time be anti-systematic and referential. A fiction appropriating in an intensified form the 'objectivist' (*chosiste*) orientation of realism; one whose intention is – in the somewhat less-diffuse-than-usual sense in which I use the word – *representational*.

The pattern of possibilities along these two axes now begins to take shape. Both propositional and representational fiction would entail positive relationships between themselves and actuality. While tautological fiction would decline to do that, it shares with representational fiction another feature. Each insists on what we've seen Robbe-Grillet call a "discontinuous universe". As it's phrased by Ihab Hassan, one must be "willing to entertain the notion that 'structure' is not always present or explicable in literary works". "A novel by Burroughs, a poem by Queneau, a painting by Johns, a film by Warhol, a sculpture by Oldenburg, a piece of music by Stockhausen may share another principle. The principle, as in Dada, is perhaps one of playful discontinuity. . . . If we need a literary theory at all, it is a theory of playful discontinuity. . . . It is a movement, beyond the control of the art object, toward the openness, and even the gratuitousness – gratuitous is free – of existence" (1975, 24, 27). This is what Federman is after when he says that the new fiction "will be deliberately illogical, irrational, unrealistic, non sequitur, and incoherent". In the representational view there is discontinuity among the raw data of actual experience, mimicked by discourse; in the tautological perspective, a discontinuity between discourse and actual experience.

(4) The thetic intention Yet the presence of an apparent systematicity in a work of fiction need not in principle mean that it's referential. As we know from longstanding conceptions of the psychological operation of creations in the visual and musical arts, the many signs and codes of which a work is composed may establish a context of organization outside, larger than, themselves taken individually yet not necessarily outside the composition as a whole. Tautologic texts disclaim this feature; the text is offered as a 'palimpsest' in which each layer of ostensibly meaningful notion cancels, obliterates, erases each previous layer (by procedures of which we've observed a number of examples in the previous chapter); when each utterance is solely itself

and no more, apparent relationships dissolve behind the words as we read along.[33]

All fiction is subject to the possibility of being regarded as tautologic. But the abandonment of *referentiality* does not inevitably entail such a process of tautologic dissolution. A narrative may, for example, be 'about' itself, in a variety of ways; its parts may 'inform' each other for us, they may communicate species of intelligibility and/or beauty with reference to each other and to the whole, as the whole may do with reference to its parts. In reading, "we must deal with a second-order language", says Jerome Klinkowitz, "divorced from the thing signified but living only insomuch as it points back to that thing. System replaces essence. ... Federman knows that literature fails when it claims to represent the other, so in his own novel he simply lets it represent itself. As such it is a system, an esthetic one" (1981, 178).

This is where '*theticity*' comes in. Unlike a tautologic utterance, which in principle can be restated in no form other than an exact repetition of its entire text, a thetic utterance 'puts forward' a thesis. (I've deliberately chosen a word etymologically denoting a function parallel to, though different from, the function of what I call a 'proposition'.) It 'lays down' a formulation or configuration, a programme of reading which – similar in this respect to that of a proposition – can be stated in terms other than and more compact than itself. This is so – it is systematic – because rules more abstract than itself can be extrapolated from the deployment of its data. Without referring to any actuality beyond that of the language in which it's framed, its events (its givens) may be described by statements less detailed than the text itself. We can do this, for example, in terms of those classes of distribution we've always had available for the interrogation of a work of art – regarding its 'data's' coordination and collocation (sequence, juxtaposition and counterposition, regularity, diversity and modulation of occurrence); relative quantity and proportion; homogeneity and heterogeneity, similarity and contrast; customariness (lexical, grammatical, syntactical or other) and uncustomariness. Every text gives us directions as to how to read it (as for instance 'Once upon a time' does) and we don't need to be told of such rubrics 'in so many words'. Simple redundancy for example (as I've noted in the Introduction) conveys to us powerful instructions – has a formative effect in ordering a text for us – which often no search for expository statements makes clear and which we come to recognize with real understanding only after close study. In a qualified way, a thetic text is thus, among other things, 'meaningful' because it's accessible to reconstructions according to many of the systems of enquiry by which meaning is ascribed to events generally.

Between thetic and propositional texts, only (this is a great 'only') the intended *context* differs. Propositionality would give shapeliness to our perception of the world's givens; theticality to our perception of the sum of the text's givens. Thus each is theoretically free, for one thing, to venture towards its own kind of extreme limits, though a thetic mode will hold special attraction to the anti-Realist partly because in its exploration of pattern its discourse is uninhibited by the literally 'common-sense' *bienséances*, the strictures of external verisimilitude to which propositional fiction has *conventionally* made its appeal. A simple 'metaplastic' play with typography, for instance – say, the mere omission of a single predicted letter – may without reference to 'common sense' modulate a rather tediously established verbal pattern into a fresh one in which the 'system' is not rendered defective but to the contrary appears almost to be 'doubled' or at least unexpectedly complicated, as in the delightful minimal text by Gerhard Rühm[34]:

leafleafleafleafleafleafleafleafleafleaflea

The difference becomes immediately clear when we look again at the three sentences I've quoted from Calvino's original Italian preface to *I nostri antenati*. Speaking of *II visconte dimezzato*, he says that he "had never thought even for a moment of good and evil ... I had used a well-known narrative contrast to give substance to what interested me, namely dimidiation". There could scarcely be a more explicit expression of the thetic intention. Beginning a new paragraph he then says "Contemporary man is divided, mutilated, incomplete, an enemy to himself." The entrance on the scene of this referential assertion turns Calvino's pattern of dimidiation toward a propositional end. Here is not the first time that the question of the admissibility of 'intentions' has reared its head – it's in the nature of this chapter, with all its risks. But there is nothing *in principle*, so far, against our conceiving, from this clear example, of there being two ways of taking a text – as thetic and as propositional – that are quite strikingly different. I'll have more to say about a literature that may be claimed to be thetic. It should be plain for the moment that any narrative that would be 'only itself' and nothing more is asking to be tautologic. But any fiction seriously described as *self-reflexive* (an idea much contemporary theory devotes itself to) – as addressing express attention to its own nature, for example, by raising questions in some part as to the function of some other part – *however* non-referential its orientation, cannot in effect be seen as anything but systematic, as anything less than thetic.

Leaving aside for the present the peculiar square I've placed in its middle and given the obvious waivers concerning the hazards of dichotomies, the uses of so rudimentary a 'diagram of possible intentions' as I've been referring to are limited; above all because it affects only two axes of intention and every text involves far more than these, however much the intersection of the two I've discussed may centre like the cross-hairs of a rangefinder on the crisis upon which anti-Realist focuses its main sights. But one help that it offers, beyond those I've mentioned and others that may yet arise, lies in the explanation it may provide, for example, as to how a work may appear deeply systematic yet claims to be non-referential; and how another may seem equally deeply hostile to systems yet disturbingly preoccupied with the outside world (including, specifically, how the world is unsystematic). The former seeks to function as a thetic text, the latter as a representational one. For once, in an elementary way, our strong intuitions regarding such pieces of fiction find accommodation without our violent imposition upon them of a surcharge of claims which the primitive distinction 'All books are disorderly and about nothing' has dragged along with it.

For anticosmic fiction, then, there is not simply one single possible radical response to the view that writing is systematically referential, but rather there is a network of distinct possible responses. Yet there's a profoundly pertinent issue that we've so far touched only tangentially.

The idea of indeterminacy

Though recent academic internecine disputes may have led some to think so, arguments against content, depth, truth, and the like are not always intrinsically arguments against determinacy. They may represent as problematical the idea of a fixed meaning behind the text, but indeterminist rationales have a distinct character of their own and the distinction is crucial to anticosmic thought.

The reactions to Realism we've considered up to this point have accented in one way or another the primacy of the text. Indeterminism stresses the primacy of the reader, or – more accurately – of the reading experience. That is, whereas Realism appears to propose that a narrative is in some important sense defined by what comes (exists) before it (for example, an 'idea'), indeterminism says that a narrative is to be described in terms of what comes after it (for example, a 'reading'). Peculiarly, unlike any 'pure' tautologic view of literature, indeterminism is as interested in taking referentiality seriously, in its own way, as Realism is. Indeterminist theory will sometimes seek to attach itself to tautologic ideology because the latter appealingly acclaims the liberation of writing from predetermined meanings. But ultimately, by contrast, it will welcome the fact that we do tend to make appeal to, to call upon, prior meanings as the ground from which our readings spring. For what is considered to be indeterminate is precisely that connectedness which we seek to establish between what is said and what the saying appears to be referring to. Without the conception that a signifier invites us to think of a signified – whether in terms now of external actuality or of some other kind of meaning – indeterminacy ceases to be a question. Tautologic thought will further attract the interest of indeterminists because insofar as literature is susceptible to an apparently infinite number of readings, from an indeterminist angle of view every text is just as indisposed to completeness and systematic *closure* as the tautologist would have it be. But once again, such indeterminacy is a product not of the text's non-referentiality but of its hyper-referentiality, its 'over-determination'.[35]

There are, then, two fundamental notions behind indeterminist theory which indeterminists themselves (as well as their critics) tend indiscriminately to treat, even in mid-sentence, as one. As variously adopted by fictionalists (such as Sollers, Pynchon or Brooke-Rose) and by critics (such as the later Barthes, early Kristeva or Derrida), they are certainly interrelated. But they don't logically or in practice aim towards the same horizons of expectation or generate the same kinds of 'stories' about what goes on when a writer writes or a reader reads, or indeed toward the same kinds of anti-Realist texts.

Intertextual indeterminacy pivots on the conception that all utterances, all signs, are texts whose meanings – produced by the reader – are merely 'nodes' in the total text, the network of the language of signs in operation in human experience. Books, traffic signals, advertisements, facial expressions, bottlecaps, thrown-clay pots and thrown stones, all belong to this *geno-texte* or *archi-écriture*. As such, they continually modify each other. According to a favourite idea of Pinget's, 'what is said is never said since it can always be said again differently'. As we write, as we read, what we do is not to find stable meaning in the act of finding relationships, but merely to unfold the seamless fabric of possible utterances which the text draws into the open. "The concept of *intertextuality* (Kristeva) here is essential", says Sollers in discussing his novels *Drame* and *Nombres*; "every text situates itself at the junction of several texts of which it is at once the rereading, the accentuation, the condensation, the displacement and the inwardness [*profondeur*]. In a certain way, the worth of a text's action amounts to its integration and destruction of other texts".[36]

What makes for indeterminacy – in this in-some-respects 'positive, constructive' notion of indeterminacy – is a function of the multiplicity of relations between signs. The crisis it seeks to evoke is that a text appears to 'give us' too many 'things', which melt into further signs, which signify other 'things', which in their turn ... ad infinitum; signs participate in a constant condition of flux, of becoming, their definitive individual identity forever displaced. The reader too, "this 'I' which approaches the text is already itself a plurality of other texts, of codes which are infinite or, more precisely, lost" (Barthes, 1970, 10). For this reason alone, if for no other, "the absence of an ultimate meaning opens an unbounded space for the play of signification".[37]

Extratextual indeterminacy (as we may for this occasion call it) incorporates an idea of a different kind. For all that recent articulations of it frequently rest (in Derrida for example) on a radical attack upon western culture's dualist habit of thought – right/wrong, serious/playful, reality/imitation, truth/fiction, nature/culture, soul/body – it revolves, itself, around a similar concept of its own of the distribution of our apperceptions. In this view (after Saussure) we discern what words signify in terms of (by contrasting them with) the latent 'traces' of what they do not signify; thus they actually call forth not the presence of such events but evoke their 'absence'. Texts perpetually 'defer' fixed integration and final meaning. Indeed, by this now famous process of the *différance* of any ultimate definition of differences between things, they generate only 'space' and move ever towards 'silence' – notions made popular in the early post-war years in literature by (for example) Beckett, and in literary theory by (for example) Blanchot. "Every trace hides an absence", as Jacques Ehrmann put it, "which is precisely why it exists as a trace" (1971, 240). No text – and no reading of any text – can logically be imagined to set before us any immanent truth, *not* merely because of the proliferation of possible 'given things' but because insofar as a sign would 'convey' something other than itself it is *by definition* only a signifier and is in no way the 'thing intended'. As soon as we look at anything as having meaning – even if what we say is that it means only itself (regarding a stone we name it meaningfully a stone, integrating it into a system of conceptual meaning) – we have opened a chasm between the thing and us, by the act of paraphrase. The 'thing' (the stone) is *always* outside the text, is extratextual, is always absent. The text gives us nothing but itself, not because it's tautologic in intention but *because* it 'makes reference' and reference does not 'put us in touch' with referents at all.[38] This in-some-sense 'negative', 'deconstructive' indeterminacy is a function of the relations (the chasms, in effect) between signifiers and signifieds, or – more accurately though more generally – between ('logocentric') cognitional and communicational acts, on one hand and, on the other, the actualities to which they (pretend to) address themselves.

Fictions informed by intertextually and extratextually indeterminist thought therefore will be marked by a deliberate ambiguity. But at deep levels they are different.[39] 'Intertextualist fiction' is genuinely pluralistic in its orientation, with reference to utterances outside it and to the material within it. The narrative at once would disintegrate previous texts (and previous parts of itself) and is rendered capable of doing so by its relationship to them; it draws both its transformational force and its indeterminacy from our experience of them. It moves toward plenitude, and through this toward the exhaustion of possibilities (as Barth would describe it) or through a growing anarchy of possibilities toward entropy (as Pynchon would say).

'Extratextualist fiction' is, logically at least, in a different position. In an early passage in his presentation of how writing must best function in the future (of which I've already quoted the first sentence) Jacques Ehrmann says "Every trace hides an absence, which is precisely why it exists as a trace. Instead of trying to go against nature by trying to force the signs to yield a presence which can only remain outside of them, why not opt in favour of the trace by attempting in *so far as possible* to efface all signs of a 'presence', knowing all the while that total success is impossible because it is contrary to the very nature of the trace?"(1971, 240). The absent from the text is made known by its trace in the sense not only that what is signified is absent but what is not uttered is made significant by each invocation of its antithesis or 'different'.

The emblem of intertextual thought is 'infinity'; the emblem of extratextual thought is 'impasse'. Through the confrontation of contrarieties the latter moves toward the anti-tragic, often playful observation not of (con)fusion but of nullity. As we would expect (as modelled by post-structural critical practices in dealing with anti-Realist and other texts, for example in Derrida and de Man), a fiction that looks toward extratextual indeterminacy will bear a heavier preponderance of data eliciting the sense not merely of the proliferation of possibilities but, particularly, of the mutual exclusivity – the internal *contra-diction* – of whole systems, of statement. The text seems to speak not only more and more, but against itself. The most fruitful activity we can engage in, it proposes, since we persist in writing, in uttering texts, is to produce utterances that act out this play of contradictions, in which assertion and its negative trace incessantly give birth and echo to one another. All texts in fact always do this very thing; no text exists but it destroys (deconstructs) itself. By this "subversive" activity, as Ehrmann put it, meaning "affects [*sic*] its own obliteration".[40]

Ideally a schema like that on p. 144 concerning textual intentions should in one sense make no sense to an indeterminist, since in his or her view it is the reader who produces the text and its intentions. Yet in spite of our taking pains to expunge the double contradiction it entails, we seem to be in the position to entertain the possibility that we can determine certain fiction to have been determinedly directed toward appearing indeterminate. While this is clearly a step in the direction of a sense of unity which we had no reason to hope for and which may give pleasure to some opponents of indeterminism, we must remember that it's an ill-gotten empirical – rather than absolutely logical – windfall, and that we still have more to say about where (in any scheme of intentions such as the one I've drawn) the indeterminist impulse may eventually be placed.

The idea of problematization

There are as many indeterminist programmes under the two main headings I've suggested as there are indeterminists. Among anticosmic texts taken as a group, the relative intentional emphasis shifts continually from work to work. But we can readily recognize how, with the principles of Realist narrative (outlined in the Introduction) as its jumping-off place, anticosmic fiction comes to produce a battery of unorthodox strategies such as those indicated in Chapter 1. Since anticosmic literature can be called fundamentally sceptical in its orientation, in any debate as to its viability the burden of proof falls to its opponents; its procedure is interrogatory. Each of the conventions/intentions I've attached to Realism becomes the immediate subject for a 'trial' in such narrative itself. What appears in each case to be an 'anticosmic statement' – characteristically a '*refus*' (we're dealing with what's sometimes called *l'école du refus*) – should in the first instance be taken in this way: the text asks a question by refusing to settle for a previously declared certainty.

The *referential* assurance – that a narrative refers 'naturally' to what's outside it – is replaced by the cross-examination of narrative language and its 'terms of reference': consistency of space, time, action, actors, and of narrative statement itself.

The *cosmic* and *illusionistic* assurances – that a complete and integrated system of causality may be described in terms that are rationally coherent and consistent with our systematic conceptualizations of actuality – is replaced by a counter: "today's literature", as Federman puts it, "refuses the idea of a single world".[41] In Hassan's idea of the new anti-art, then, "art orders itself loosely, even at random. Organic form becomes discontinuous, decentered, or aleatory form" (1975, 21).

The *exhaustive* and *declarative* assurance – that by skill and will the whole truth may be eventually ascertained and made clear, such that no truth inconsistent with the known truth may remain – are put in question by the claim that 'what is said is never said since it can always be said again differently', and are probed by narrations that both enact this inexhaustibility and seek to dramatize the complementary notion that what is said never in any case brings into immediate knowledge what it speaks of.

The *mimetic, probabilistic* and *objectivist* assurances – that the materialistically rationalized transcription of the data of the physical senses as determined by habits of consensus is the confirmed procedure for the communication of truth – encounter the response that probabilistic and objectivist mimesis is merely a form of rhetoric dependent upon culturally prescribed specious assumptions regarding the relations between perceiver and perceived. This rhetoric is now recirculated in such ways that it both is immediately 'received' and simultaneously displaces the possibility of attributing to it the kinds of truth which it's expected to report.

As we've seen, in neocosmic fiction deviations from Realist custom conventionally occur at the level of a text's *histoire*. Anticosmic fiction won't be outdone in this province. Story itself becomes one of its primary targets. The traditional novel, as Robbe-Grillet put it in 1957, "for most addicts – and for most critics – is primarily a 'story'. A real novelist is someone who can 'tell a story'." And with this there had always come fundamental assumptions. "All the technical elements of the narrative – the systematic use of the past definite tense and of the third person, the unconditional adoption of chronological development, linear plots, a regular graph of the emotions, the way each episode tended towards an end, etc. – everything aimed at imposing the image of a stable universe, coherent, continuous, univocal, and wholly decipherable." Story as such must be obliterated. With it must go that stable supportive Realist superstructure of what I've called 'parastory' and 'megastory', that quintessential strategy contributing to the referential viability of the narrative by which you "make what you write resemble the prefabricated synopses that people are used to ... to make it resemble their ready-made idea of reality" (63, 62).

Along with this comes an even more deeply searching radical programme. If it's become a commonplace to assert (with varying degrees of accuracy) that *Modernist* fiction may already have been a fiction in which story in that traditional sense had given way or lost its stability (in say *The Waves* or *The Sound and the Fury* or *Finnegans Wake*), nevertheless it was always on the cards that its speakers could be vividly characterized. For an anticosmic text, against that traditional background, "The novel that contains characters belongs well and truly to the past"(60). The psychological system for the focalization of events via the perspective of a named individualized human consciousness, as an anthropocentric culture's strategy for the projection of a bounded and integrated vision of existence, is to be eschewed. What distinguishes anticosmic fiction in this regard is that it denies that it is enough – as it was for Modernists – to say that the instability of character, and specifically the fluidity of private human subjectivity, is the Problem. The anticosmic text persists, for example, in refusing to refer to itself as the work of a narrator with a personal, psychologicial defect of perception as distinguished from any conceivable other narrator who might happen to have a better, clearer view. Insofar as it ever admits to psychology it wishes to accredit it with insight-value only at that moment – on that 'higher plane' – where it begins to say: our problem is a universal dilemma inherent in the nature of mind taken transpersonally, collectively. (It typically rests its logical plausibility on its being an anti-expressionist, anti-lyric mode.) In this respect, we must note, its immanent aim (insofar as it lays our troubles – and the source of its own narrative processes – at Mind's door) is broadly mimetic.[42]

Thus Ford Madox Ford is still proposing a Modernist view and not an anticosmic one when he rejects certain aspects of Realist character-plotting: "To get such a man in fiction you would not begin at his beginning and work his life chronologically to the end. You must first get him in with a strong impression, and then work backwards and forwards over his past."[43] The Modernist does still start with the 'strong impression' in the 'faithful-to-life' way; Joyce's *Ulysses*, we well recall, begins "Stately, plump Buck Mulligan ... ". The anticosmist typically drops Ford's phase-one altogether and proceeds with phase-two.

Here is a chance to see at work at least one example of the variability of emphasis in anticosmic fiction. Psychology, the cornerstone of Realist causality, meets different fates in different anti-Realist texts. If it's abandoned as the mode *par excellence* for the discrete differentiation of one personal mind from another, it may persist in another form. Nathalie Sarraute, one of the first to announce in full cry the demise of Realist conceptions of story and character, does so for her own special reasons. The contemporary reader, she says, "has watched the watertight partitions that used to separate characters from one another, give way, and the hero became an arbitrary limitation, a conventional figure cut from the common woof that each of us contains in its entirety, and which captures and holds within its meshes, the entire universe".[44] Sarraute has been, as many have rightly remarked, "one who was seeking to renovate the psychological novel" (Mercier, 1971, 128); what's at work in narratives of hers is not the idea that human nature is not psychologically characterizable, but that the Realist concept of *person* does not produce a useful model for its characterization. This is certainly a movement in the direction of the anticosmic. But it also points to a crucial difference between one branch of the movement (typical of the *nouveau roman*) and another (of which what's sometimes called the *nouveau nouveau roman*, sometimes *Tel Quel*, is an example).

The transition happens here. As Annette Lavers (paraphrasing the views, for a time, of Greimas, Rastier and Barthes) says, "character was now seen as either a 'figure' or a 'function'. ... Conceiving a character as the representation of a human person, having a consciousness and an identity manifested in its actions is an ideological, not a scientific concept" (1982, 178). Psychology, in other words, may be taken as merely one of those artificial, culture-based systems for the ordering of experience from which the writer may wish to free his or her text. Sarraute, as 'new novelist', eschewing 'characterizable person', nonetheless treats her texts as projects in the characterization of humanity. But now, in the 'new new' conception as Brooke-Rose retails it in her novel *Thru* (in part a parody of deconstructionism),

> The notions of subject and object correspond only to a place in the narrative proposition and not to a difference in nature hence no need to talk like Propp et al of hero villain lawbearer these are predicates. The agent is not the one who can accomplish this or that action but the one who can become subject of a predicate.
>
> (1975, 69)

We are here in fact witnessing the shift in the function of narrative data from the propositional to the thetic. The text is regarded as bound in no ways to laws of continuity outside itself; it is ruled by the rules of the language. Narrative is nothing more than a string of linguistic signs. When we read "he eats", there is for example no rule *in language* that says that the "he" of this string need be continuous with the "he" in any other string (however close, even in the same sentence), any more than that the "eating" in any two strings need be the same eating. It is only external rules of referentiality, cosmicity, probability and the like that insist on such continuity – rules governed in large part by purely customary expectations as to what texts in given contexts will do. And psychology – like history – is only a subsidiary one of those extraneous customs.

A profound attraction in this for an anti-Realist will lie in the immense fluidity it provides. No particular form of figuration – which is all that denotations of not only character but of time, place and action would now be – need logically control the text except a linguistic one. With a single blow, writing appears at once liberated from the vast congeries of laws of continuity which have made up the stability of the cosmos in a Realist fiction. The narrative, in principle, begins to lend itself to the notion that narration is here creating itself, out of itself. Whether we accept the implication that narration has some autonomous generative capacity of its own, independent of any still consistently characterizable volition, is another matter (and one that must be looked into). For the moment, the anthropocentric vision with all its constraints seems laid to rest. Starting by jettisoning character, more than by any other single gesture – by eliminating the 'module' upon which, more than any other thing, Realistic narrative causality is built – fiction seems to begin to find possible something like that infinite *disponibilité* it has long sought. It may truly 'play with figures'. Only: its essential premiss in doing so may be different according to different texts: old figurational dispositions (such as characterization) are unsuitable to present truths; or any figuration is acceptable since it need account to no authority (such as that of psychology) other than its own; or all figures are only signs (e.g. pronouns) without natural signification (such as 'people') and are hence equally entitled to unlimited 'free assembly'.

It follows that time and place too may now be regarded as released from their naturalistic constraints, as Robbe-Grillet reminded us in describing how he wished us to view the film *Dernière année à Marienbad*. "The universe in which the whole film takes place is ... that of a perpetual present. ... It is a world without a past, which at every instant is self-sufficient, and which obliterates itself as it goes along. ... The only 'character' who matters is the spectator. The whole story is happening *in his head*. . . . Time . . . isn't the agent for anything any more" (1962, 149–51). In the light of anticosmic theory in its extreme, 'maximal' form, the entire remaining repertoire of Realist conventions at the level of *histoire* can undergo similar treatment. Those human institutions, physical settings, moral and sentimental categories, together with their associated anecdotal and thematic *topoi* (as discussed in the Introduction) may now be subtly or violently displaced. Words like dislocation, *dépaysement*, disorientation, estrangement, hesitation and aporia (the self-cancellation of categories, value systems) come to fill the vocabulary of criticism in its attempt to describe such texts' psychological effects on the reader. The work may, for example, adopt the verisimilar portrayal of situations classically surcharged with sentimental affect, only to show them now empty of affect; or it may by its equivocal language leave them ultimately narratively non-functional or intractable to general paraphrase.

But it doesn't – as neocosmic fiction largely does – aim to complete its disruptive action within the framework of the *histoire*. Taking as another of its prime targets certain customary assumptions concerning the operation of language itself as a system of relations, an anticosmic text may play out its intentions in large part at the level of discourse. So the principle of comprehensiveness (with its commitment to informational, probabilistic and totalistic intentions) is supervened; the hope of closure is replaced by an openwork of seemingly infinite possibilities. The principle of the self-contained apparent infinitude of the text is supplanted by the conception of the text's utter dependence on and subjection to the infinite array of meanings of texts extending into infinity beyond it. The principles of equity and levelness of regard, of uniform and univocal discourse are overriden by an endless perturbation and equivocation of voice. The perspective of the middle distance which had assured a sense of "the purpose of the whole", of the consistent discreteness and integrity of entities (for example, of persons and definable actions) is abandoned in favour of movements away from or closer to events, to the point where their outlines become lost in the meaninglessly schematic, or in the contourless blur of unending minutiae. The principle of objectivity (with its concentration on objects, objectification of the subjective and of the abstract) is suspended; objects lose their status as fixed things and are perpetually transmuted into alternative things and/or become merely signs for further things which themselves dissolve continually in expanding pools of signification. The principle of the figuration of data is reappropriated to serve a contrary function; figure's positive metaphorical reference to more-or-less consolidated meanings is dispersed to leave a patterning of signs intricately, enigmatically "pure" of generalizable implication. The ironization of *histoire*, the defocalization of protagonist and of narrator, the narrative alibi, the demodalization and the detonalization of the text, instead of preserving thematic intimations from the charge of authorial prejudice and prescription, involve such intimations in an infinitely regressive chain of significations whose 'ultimate meaning' itself may remain undiscoverable. The principles of the familiarization of the exotic and the general disambiguation of discourse give way to a perpetual exoticization and ambiguation of the customarily most familiar.

A midcourse view

As within every 'insurgent movement' there will be different parties, we can expect neocosmic and anticosmic narratives to operate differently. Foreseeing its imminent vital attraction for radical fictionalists, recent criticism has commonly come to revalue and acclaim under the name of 'fantasy' much fiction soliciting the uncustomary of the sort we'd call neocosmic. Certain works (by Henry James, Lautréamont, Kafka) are chosen as 'pure' and worthwhile fantasy as opposed to others (by Tolkien, Lewis, Le Guin) that seem merely to advocate 'the marvellous', on the grounds that the former alone elicit estrangement, equivocation, hesitation. One of the central errors of criticism moving in this direction (inspired by Todorov's invaluable initial perception (1970) and exemplified by the arguments of, for example, Rosemary Jackson (1981)) is a haste on behalf of an essentially anticosmic theory to appropriate the neocosmic mode *where it suits it*, by attributing to it a teleology of shock. It would be tempting to assume, as such theories have, that because the unfamiliar is evoked in neocosmic fiction, this is its central and final *aim*. Yet this matches with only certain texts and not others, always resembles the *post hoc ergo propter hoc* argument (the zebra's stripes are what it lives for, are its *raison d'être*), and fails to account for the appearance of the unfamiliar (the uncustomary) in any usefully comprehensive way.

The fact is that even in those cases suiting 'hesitation' theories, the text availing itself of the uncustomary, as neocosmic fiction does, welcomes an intermediate illusion. The assembly of such fiction, all told, may finally be against shock, though each work's individual programme takes shock as its initiating strategy. It *wants* to make sense, in order to show how many perspectives *can* make sense, and to awaken us to the plenum of possible sense-making systems. Unlike anticosmic fiction, it's quick to relinquish for example the virtues and claims (or disclaimers) of irony, having foremost in mind not the *clash* of *inadequate* world-views but the thorough if *momentary establishment* of hitherto customarily unacceptable world-views. Anticosmic fiction seeks largely to contain its own (self-referential) critique; neocosmic does not, at the same levels at least. "Our self-referential mathematics and wiggly yardsticks got us to the moon", says Annie Dillard. "I think science works the way a tightrope walker works: by not looking at its feet. As soon as it looks at its feet, it realizes it is operating in midair."[45] By this process of inviting an intermediate illusion, analogous in certain ways to the Realist's 'middle distance' – by this tightrope-walk strategy – the neocosmist implies that the same ends as the anticosmist's may be reached: a less illusory perception may be hammered out on the anvil of illusion. Here intertextuality takes on a special meaning. While each anticosmic text may seek to engender *within itself* the perception of a multiplicity of exits, and each text tends to reinforce this by variations on a theme similar to its neighbour's, the community of neocosmic texts opens a multiplicity of new entrances, each with its often wittingly competing illusionistic closure.[46]

A further divergence lies in the problem of the *impurity* of neocosmic texts. As we see in the public statements of his intentions by, say, a C. S. Lewis – whose pronounced motives seem extravagantly diverse – there seems to linger around neocosmic aims a visceral, shoot-first-ask-questions-later attitude. There is often little visible effort to show that form and meaning are irreducibly ('organically' or 'logically') dependent on and shaped by each other. Yet the mode might pose a rationale of its own, external to each text but inherent in its controlling premisses, for such apparent disparities. Whereas in anticosmic narrative whatever the text does continually seeks to be seen to be embedded in its matrix assumption (about the limits, for example, of knowing or of signification), neocosmic literature may – insofar as it is propositional – vary by as many 'intimations' as can be constituted within the totality of conceivable cosmic universes. It may invoke a *disponibilité* (again that word, but I can't find another suggesting that positively searching and willing kind of disengagement), an openness of relationship between its 'form' and its 'information'. This raises a very large question indeed concerning 'analytic' versus 'synthetic' intentions and what I'll call the frequent 'homological claims' of literature, and we'll return to it.

There are other salient differences. When, for example, a neocosmic novel rejects character delineation of conventional sorts, it may do so because (as we've seen argued by neocosmists as divergent as Calvino and Lewis) it is looking to show suprapersonal processes at work.[47] An interest in such things may not be an interest in the transcendental (as hesitation theories are quick to presume) but rather, for instance, the collective. Nevertheless it *does* thus involve a concern for universals, and this is enough to repel the anticosmist. As was noted with some perplexity in Chapter 1 and reserved for review, in its texture anticosmic fiction typically gives the vast majority of its attention to – of all things – commonplace daily experience. "The objects of our novels", says Robbe-Grillet, "are objects which are comparable to those of our everyday life, objects like those upon which our attention is constantly fixed"; "our books are written", he says, "with everybody's everyday words and sentences" (1962, 138, 140). Where the neocosmist is inclined to design a book in the shape of a story and the anticosmist is disposed to reject story on the grounds that story (as Sartre had already argued strenuously in his fiction in the 1930s) gave transcendent shapeliness to experience which was illusory, so the anticosmist – paradoxically, we may think – feels often compelled to exclude from the text precisely what is initially shocking in a neocosmic story. The reason is far-reaching.

The dilemma was already there in Sartre's way of concluding *La Nausée* and provides another glimpse into the difference between anticosmic thought on one hand and not only neocosmic but also Modernist and Existentialist thought on the other. In the latter's leap to the absurd as with the neocosmist's normalization of the unnatural, "there is a risk for the writer", as Robbe-Grillet clearly foresaw in his attack on Sartre. "With the suspicion of absurdity, the metaphysical danger returns. Non-sense, a-causality and insubstantiality irresistibly attract other-worlds and super-natures. ... for *within* the immediate meaning we find the absurd, which is, theoretically, non-existent meaning, but which in fact immediately leads, by a well-known metaphysical recoupment, to a new transcendence. And the infinite fragmentation of the sense thus creates a new totality, which is equally dangerous and useless" (158, 160). What appears untowardly mysterious we swiftly turn into an all-resolving mystique – and by what rule (since it displaces standard rules) could we ever then deliver ourselves from that insubstantial dream? In an anticosmic perspective such as Robbe-Grillet's, the uncustomary around which neocosmic invention revolves would be an invitation to just such a 'disaster' and – except where it's encompassed as a phenomenon of narration itself – it must be repelled. The disparity that counts is not between customary and uncustomary visions of 'the world' but between *any* world and the language describing it, including the language of our normal systems of explanation. The more *customary* the *histoire* at some level, for the anticosmist, then, the more fruitfully manifest will be the language's trouble in coping with it.[48] This is only an aspect of a larger issue to which we must return: the conjecture that certain texts (for example neocosmic ones) may be ominously escapist in ways that others (for example anticosmic ones) may not.

But for the moment these two approaches to fiction have far more in common than we might first have conceived. Each endorses and celebrates the superordinate conception of the book as its own world – "cette ville (ce livre)", as one of Sollers' narrators puts it with characteristic condensation (1965, 138). *Both* appear to view narrative as having potentially combinative, play, conditioning, prospective and commutative functions. Each, above all, rebels with equal passion against the heaping of more and more weight, more gravity, on the side of the doctrine of consensus, of conformity of vision. For both – as indeed for Realists themselves (as we've seen Stern imply) – Realism's instatement of the banal is no mere casual matter of taste. When a certain writer speaks of "the grotesque fallacy of a realistic art" and expresses a contempt for the literature "that 'describes', for the realists and naturalists worshipping the offal of experience", and when he advocates in place of the Realist an artist who "is active, but negatively, shrinking from the nullity of extracircumferential phenomena, drawn in to the core of the eddy", it may seem equally likely that he's a neocosmist or an anticosmist (Tolkien? Lovecraft? Sollers? Federman?). The anguish of this writer – it's Beckett – is not due merely to the thought that Realism betrays life's truths by reporting some intrinsic banality in them. It is further because he feels, as do neocosmists and anticosmists at large, that the familiar serves that facile recuperation that in the anti-Realists' view renders us insensible to what truths there may be to be found (Beckett, 1931, 57, 59, 48).

Even at their greatest extremes there are unexpected signs of their affinity in matters of practice. Both, for example, frequently work to resist stereotypes and the etiolation of experiences by accentuating the raw nature of 'things as they are'. They join in an equal and overriding disinterest condemned universally by Realist critics (whether the writer concerned is Tolkien or Beckett, Le Guin or Borges, Lovecraft or Sollers, Beagle or Barth) in character, in psychological richness, variety, depth, rondeur.[49] Further, they invite an attitude in the reader that is qualitatively different from that encouraged by Realism. Instead of suggesting that in the book's world we 'see the world', they ask us – indeed, require us – to indulge in a 'perspectivist' process not unlike that described by Wittgenstein. We see an event in fiction as one thing, and then (or simultaneously) as another. Through this 'seeing-as' activity, in an anticosmic context we're challenged to regard the book's world as X but also as Y and as Z; if we view it as only one kind of system (whether X or Y or Z) we see dangerously both too much and too little. In a neocosmic frame we perceive the book's universe as *a* universe (of an X or Y or Z sort) but not as *our* universe; read thetically there is no danger in our contemplating this other universe, just because it's not ours; read propositionally, it may relate us to ours better, but only insofar as it places our former habits of mind into clearly apprehended perspective by its difference. By the standards of each mode, this continuous oscillation between our taking the text seriously and not seriously is not a flaw in the mode itself as it would be within the context of Realist illusionism but is a built-in and necessary aspect of its code.[50] The more 'embarrassed' we are by the text – by the recuperative hoops we're put through in order to feel comfortable (justified) in reading it, in our wishing for a 'normal' solution or in finding the text frivolous or tedious – the more stolidly or compulsively and unhealthily obsessed we discover ourselves to have been with the exclusivity of our pre-established modes of seriousness. In a way that unites them, in other words, and that separates them pre-eminently from what had come before, neocosmic and anticosmic fiction would replace Realism's and Modernism's 'euphoria of recognition' with what Tolkien called that equally elemental alternative, "arresting strangeness".

We can understand both how the respective admirers of each mode may have inclined to 'teach' them in separate books – and classrooms -- like denizens of galactically different mutually oblivious 'worlds', and how 'anticosmists' and 'neocosmists' themselves will have begun to regard each others' premisses and practices in a new, more open perspective – and to merge. Yet in this convergence, at each turn, anti-Realist fiction – in its appeal against 'serious' canons of form and signification – can be regarded as a medium for the displacement of customary notions of value. Is this then a literature without norms of its own? Will it never be found to 'declare itself'?

We need to look again more directly at the substance of texts.

3

SUBSTANCE

Game pieces and moves

There might be no specifiable, 'typically anti-Realist data'. Realist fiction undoubtedly does give priority of place, as we've seen, to certain delimited kinds of contexts of meaningfulness, narrative situations and events, and ideologems. If from these we can glean some sense of what it believes we ought to feel is 'what matters' and what channels of attention it would like our thinking to follow, we can logically imagine a different body of fiction that, by contrast, might include 'anything and everything' at the level of *histoire*, free of any apparent predisposition whatsoever. We need to ask where anti-Realist writing stands in this respect. Chapter 1 was fundamentally concerned with the *organization* of anti-Realist narrative givens, and not about what these 'givens' might be. A modestly down-to-earth experiment would be to enquire what if any substantive situations, motifs, 'signs' appear on the horizon when one enters the world of anti-Realist writing.[1]

To restore something of our initial openness of view, for a suggestively broad cross-sectional perspective, and for more crucial reasons that will emerge, I'm not going to attempt at this stage to draw lines between sub-classes of texts, neocosmic and anticosmic. In the main body of the discussion I'll be indicating a few sample cases by way of direct illustration. For suggestions as to where one might look for alternative, amplifying examples – and for some glimpse of the extent and persistence of their occurrence – a *selection* of further instances (the sample of parallel cases might easily be swelled far beyond the limits of space I'm allowed) appears in the notes to this chapter. Again, as Fredric Jameson says, "pure textual exemplifications of a single genre do not exist" (1982, 322), and – fortunately for those wishing to believe that each new book may offer something new – major differences occur from author to author, text to text.

Anti-Realist themes and motifs: definition and relation

In trying to think in some methodical way about what's 'given' in anti-Realist fiction, it will be obvious by now that we're unlikely to be prejudicing the case by interrogating texts in terms of the simple question: 'Outwardly and inwardly – in the narrative universe as a whole and in the internal worlds of its individuals – what is offered as certain or knowable and what is not?' It's in this primitive and open sense that I offer 'Knowing' and 'Uncertainty' as headings, as informal bases, to start.

Knowing

In every book, at whatever level we choose to take its codes and ultimate signification, there is some movement toward a differentiation between mental being and an impersonal world that contains it. (In the nature of language, I cannot say 'I' without implying also something other than 'I'.) This movement can be described in the context of anti-Realist fiction in terms of an indeed powerful fascination with the possibility/impossibility of the world's having integrity, continuity, stability, coherence and the capacity for progress – a progression in story form toward the interrogation of order if not toward 'a definition of a better order'. In narrative terms there is a word to accommodate this: the dramatization of the 'quest'; and it intimately suits a voluminous number of anti-Realist works. It's a no less dominant formal pattern in anticosmic fiction than in it is in neocosmic, so that we find the quest central not only to Lewis's 'Perelandra' series, Lindsay's *A Voyage to Arcturus*, Tolkien's *The Hobbit*, White's *The Once and Future King*, Beagle's *The Last Unicorn*, Le Guin's *The Left Hand of Darkness*, Landolfi's *Il Mar delle Blatte*, for example, but to Beckett's *Molloy*, O'Brien's *The Third Policeman*, Pinget's *Graal Flibuste* and *L'Inquisitoire*, Robbe-Grillet's *Le Voyeur* and *Les Gommes*, Cortázar's *Rayuela*, Vonnegut's

Slaughterhouse-5, Pynchon's *V*, Nabokov's *Pale Fire*, Fuentes' *Terra nostra*, Federman's *Double or Nothing*, Sollers' *Drame*, Calvino's *Se una notte d'inverno un viaggiatore* as well as, of course, numerous of his short stories and of those of Borges and Barth. In each of these, explicit adventures arise, frequently in the episodic picaresque mode, with the search for some specific entity (a person, a 'treasure', a meaning) as their *fil conducteur*.

Yet (*pace* Frye) far from all are covered by the quest. A parallel but different narrative *topos* equally haunts anti-Realist fiction's enactment of the struggle to take some orderly measure of reality: the story of *invasion* and its repulsion. Drawing much of its impulse from not merely the Gothic tradition but from turn-of-the-century regionalist fantasy (as exemplified in the French fiction of Ramuz, Arène, d'Arbaud, Alphonse de Chateaubriant, Pourrat, Giono, Dhôtel, Genevoix) and – above all – from myth-based Modernist psychologistic fiction, it's a mode in which culture becomes locked in combat with the abruptly intrusive forces of irrational nature or of what seem to be new values inimical to the survival of the existing order. With striking similarity to tales by Forster, Mary Webb, Lawrence and Faulkner, among English-language texts,[2] a disruptive force – most often in the form of some alien figure from another province of nature (a wild boar, a giant, a lion or serpent, a monster, a different race of 'men') comes as scourge to wreak havoc in the domestic world – in novels I've already mentioned by, for example, Lovecraft, Henri Bosco, Buzzati, Tolkien, Williams, Garner, Beagle, White, Golding and in Gardner's *Grendel*. The old order may or may not prevail; the hope that's most often offered is, rather, that chaos may be held at bay in the name of a new equilibrium.

Whichever variation operates, a whole range of local but central narrative motifs arises, as we might expect, out of what are finally dramatizations of the problem of limits, of the crisis of the 'dimensionality' of existence. Anti-Realist fiction becomes prepossessed with its own topology, with the arrangement – the definition and relation – of things in time and space, with its global geography and local topography as well as its 'history'. "Whereas in realistic fiction the setting 'tends to be primarily a context for the portrayal of character'", as Brooke-Rose says in paraphrasing another critic on the subject of science fiction, "'the phenomenon of *landscape as hero* is particularly common'" here, "'where the story is frequently neither character nor plot but the world the writer creates'".[3]

Whether in respect of movement outward (quest) or inward (invasion), the landscape of the text – its definition – takes on a terrible clarity. The principle of opposition comes to rule. The world is divided into *terrains*, distinct and mutually hostile. As with Modernists like Lawrence, Faulkner and Mann, in writers as diverse as Lindsay, Le Guin, Tolkien, Beckett, Bosco, Gardner, Calvino, Buzzati there is the *cultivated realm* over against the *wilderness*, the cities of the plain against the rarefied brute mystery of the mountain, the Old World against the New.[4] *Boundaries, borders, frontiers* now strike across the landscape, between the worlds of 'home' and of '*les autres*', frontiers with their timeless prohibitions, seething with eternal tensions.[5] They are boundaries plainly marked in texts by doors, gates, intervening rivers, deserts, seas, with custodial sentinels often on guard.[6]

The problem of frontiers is not confined to neocosmic fiction. The centre of the *histoire* of Sollers' *Drame*, as Stephen Heath neatly points out, "is exactly ... the problem of limits, images of which run through the text as a fundamental 'motif' (*bord, lisière, marge, mur, de l'autre coté, limite*, etc.). ... The problem is to be there on the edge turned out of oneself in the world of signs, to be there 'between', 'in the moment of limits'" (Heath, 1972, 232–4). So in anti-Realist texts of remarkably divergent sorts the protagonist finds him- or herself before some *ford*, some *bridge* to be crossed or not crossed, or in search of some *tunnel* from one land to another.[7]

Thus the temporal way of establishing order in things – through history – exercises its appeal but simultaneously finds its match (and often its replacment) in some spatial motif. If human-centred history was, as Flaubert thought, a post-theological 'nineteenth-century discovery' – even if it were, as nineteenth-century determinists themselves believed, the story of man being made in spite of himself – it called for faith in some causal system. If, instead, one begins to conceive of reality as the manifestation of some indifferent serial *happening* – the display of an aimless form-changing equilibrium, or of an a-teleological movement towards entropy, or of no movement at all – then temporal existence begins to give way once again (as it had in theocentric eras where a transcendent providence created a timeless 'design') to a vision in which events are flattened out into a 'timeless picture'.

So in Calvino or Borges, as much as Le Guin or Tolkien, the string of events is laid out simultaneously according to historical and geographical, 'geo-metrical' patterns, side by side, and continually shifting as to which is the figure, which is the ground. Stories are now not merely sequentially 'told' but charted, each plotted as on a graph. Calvino and Vittorini each compose a 'novel' whose main ordering principle is not that of a continuous narrative but that of a gazetteer of cities (*Le città invisibili* [*Invisible Cities*], *Le città del mondo*). Sanguineti and Calvino each compose a book whose multiple narratives are 'produced' by a deck of tarot cards or their semblance (*Il giuoco del l'Oca*, *Il castello dei destini incrociati*). Cortázar invites us to 'order' *Rayuela's* events according to a notion of an existence analogous to the chalked squares of a hopscotch grid. Calvino describes the narrative motion of characters in a story as corresponding to the curvature of printed letters in space ("La forma dello spazio"). Narratives begin to be conceived diagrammatically. Robbe-Grillet retails a protagonist's movements in terms of the route he takes around an island, which in turn follows the figure-of-eight design of the infinity sign (*Le Voyeur*); and a Claude Simon novel drifts from movement in time to movement in space corresponding to the outline of the ace of clubs (*La Route des Flandres* [*The Flanders Road*]). The relations between characters and events in Buzzati and Butor are arranged according to the floors they respectively occupy in a building (*Un caso clinico*, *Passage de Milan*), and in Claude Mauriac according to a table seating-plan (*Le Dîner en ville* [*Dinner in Town*]). *Maps* – sometimes actually given, sometimes verbally described – become standard objects essential to narratives.[8] *Inventories*, catalogues of objects, bulk large and take on special status of their own, not merely – as in *The Once and Future King* – to establish the special qualities of the world described or the ontological existence of things-in-themselves, but now, too, to confirm the power of the act of describing or naming (to which we'll return).[9]

The urge to define the shape and relations of things goes further still. Neocosmic narrative tends not only toward the horizontal unfolding of events in an orderly progression but toward developing its material vertically in terms of an organized *hierarchy* of figures within its story-world embodying an order of forces at work. The reader finds these arrayed in a different fashion characteristic of each text as he/she goes along. To display all such ways would fill a book on its own; by way of illustration I'll indicate one form they take with surprising frequency. Its (at first glance) extreme peculiarity combined with the astonishing frequency of its occurrence illuminates the potency such fiction can ascribe to the uncustomary as a source of integrative insight. Figures from the *animal kingdom* are given a narrative importance – that is, an indispensability in the determining of the story's sequence of events – that appears extraordinarily disproportionate to that which they have in shaping nineteenth-century Realist narratives (or indeed the 'narratives' of our external lives). For this there is a solid and persistent – if not often observed – Modernist tradition. But now, from the spectrum of animal figures and transformations (earlier mentioned) in Williams and Lindsay through the work of Lewis, Tolkien, White, Bosco, Arène, Giono, Gascar, Arévalo Martinez, Genevoix, Vittorini, Alvaro, Pedro Prado, Le Guin, Beagle, Saviane, Pinget, Buzzati and Calvino to the nearly obsessive narrative attribution of discrete individual powers to each of such creatures as the scorpion, mouse, butterfly, turtle, whale, swordfish, spider and hawk in Fuentes' *Terra nostra*, and the universe of creatures which are the learned subject of Borges's *El libro de los seres imaginarios* [*The Book of Imaginary Beings*] (from the griffin and dragon to the unicorn and uroboros) a vast congeries of beasts are typically not only ranged side by side, as they might be if their purpose were simply and vaguely to 'evoke nature's vitality'. They are ranked – as they are in medieval bestiaries and in the many works of the imagination informed by their systems down to the seventeenth century – in a configuration of conceptual horizons reflecting the entire cosmology of discrete energies implied to be at work in the universe of natural, cultural and metaphysical experience.[10] The codification of the phyla of living things appears to be taken as a model for the reconstruction and illumination of profound and otherwise enigmatically obscure aspects of the process of living. A trait of fiction of this sort – whether it adopts the 'bestiary' paradigm or some other among many – is not only that it resists interpretation of a Realist sort but that it baulks decipherment schooled by Romantic hermeneusis (which might at first seem more sympathetic) until such thematic readings as the conventionally simple Nature-against-Culture paraphrase are abandoned in favour of a far more text-sensitive, intricately differentiated and sophisticated hierarchical scheme of analysis.

It's not in the interests of anticosmic fiction, by contrast, to ignore the search for the definition and correlation of events. As it moves away from the constatation of already existent (for example biological) phenomena, it fiercely takes up a concern with fields affecting the activity of perception itself. It appropriates above all the shift of attention from 'object' to perceiving 'subject' that had been so gravely emphasized by Modernism. Crucially, ordering motifs begin to appear in which *sight* – so often described as 'the realistic sense', and logically the perceptual mode *par excellence* to be put to the test – comes to the fore.[11] What Hamon calls "the eternal naturalist *window*", that privileged object in Realist narrative, becomes a compulsive image in anticosmic fiction. It does so not simply as an emblem for the 'transparent medium' which the Realist saw fiction to be, now negatively subverted in its function as we might predict, but as a 'casement' for the positive organization of that which is 'observed'. Whereas in Modernist stories in which the window plays an important secondary – or primary but metaphorical – rôle,[12] now it is the protagonist's sole source of direct knowledge of 'the outside world', as in Beckett's *Malone Dies*, Mauriac's *La Marquise sortit à cinq heures* and *L'Agrandissement* (where the entire action takes place in a window), as well as – vitally – in McElroy's *Plus*. The 'jealous' husband in Robbe-Grillet's *La Jalousie* spies on A ... through the slats in a window-blind (*jalousie*); the narrator of Sollers' *Le Parc* obsessionally observes the people of the town in their windows opposite his own and 'observes himself' through his own window; events in Pinget's *Passacaille* [*Recurrent Melody*] are chronically separated from us by intervening windows; the narrator of *Pale Fire* devotes his days and nights to watching 'Shade's' windows from his own ("Let us turn to our poet's windows. I have no desire to twist and batter an unambiguous *apparatus criticus* into the monstrous semblance of a novel.... Windows, as well known, have been the solace of first-person literature throughout the ages") and, as the King of Zembla, in captivity he communicates with the world by mirror-flashing signals and calling aloud from his casement. In *The Third Policeman* the focus of the narrator's deranged attention in the two-dimensional house that dominates the last twenty pages is the window that "seemed to be in the centre of the house" (Nabokov, 1962, 71–2; O'Brien, 1939, 153ff.). The frontier fortress in which Drogo spends his stark life as sentinel has but one, interdicted, window onto the desert of the Tartars, and from the successive windows of the Starkness tower in *A Voyage to Arcturus* the protagonist is at the start shown his destination and, from a similar tower window at the end, the meaning – or meaninglessness – of his journey. Vital is the obvious fact that the window is actually a popular Romantic, Symbolist and Surrealist image as well as a Realist one, and that what characterizes its use is not *merely* the act of seeing but the act of framing what is seen from a single viewpoint – the real contrast to this usage lying in Classic/Neoclassical omniscience, where the essential organization is felt to lie not in the situation of the beholder but in the world beheld. *Frame-objects*, of many sorts then – objects that 'contain' images – photograph, painting, postcard, mirror, join the window as idiosyncratic 'props' of the narrative world of anti-Realism, as do such *specialized instruments of seeing* as lenses, spectacles, binoculars, the telescope, the kaleidoscope, the crystal and the crystal ball.[13]

Once again, as the titles above show, it is neither anticosmic nor neocosmic fiction but anti-Realism as a whole that is distinctively 'optically orientated'. And it's never more so than in its pre-eminent preoccupation with light. Or, more precisely, with *chiaroscuro*, with the opposition and interplay of *light-and-dark*, and with *colour*. A literature that's to become dedicatedly the most self-conscious in history will find perhaps the most elemental emblem of its own activity in the black/white 'dyad' from the *écriture/page blanche* of Mallarmé to the 'swarming, coagulating thread of ink' with which Calvino marks the closing page of *Il cavaliere inesistente*, the 'page-squares' with their 'blackened vortex of words' of which Sollers' *Nombres* are endlessly the explicit creation, and the large solid-black squares with which Barthelme, Sterne-style, intermittently fills the pages of his "Kierkegaard Unfair to Schlegel" (1970). We can by now easily conceive of a fiction in which reality is meant to be thought of as lying 'between the lines', in the space between the black that is writing and the white that is not, between the light of total perception and articulation and its total absence or impossibility, and this is a sphere of anti-Realist imagery to which criticism at large will happily give more space than we can afford here.[14] What serves best to disclose the special status of the 'optical spectrum' here is rather to point out a permutation of it whose persistent recent appearance would startle readers familiar only with pre-anti-Realist fiction. While the light/dark pattern may after all seem somehow thoroughly recognizable in the context of a conventional literature having clear moral intent – in the good/evil antithesis – now the intermediate 'spectrum', literally, takes on an unexpected importance (comparable with that of the taxonomy of beasts in the pseudo 'biological spectrum') in fiction's codification of *colour*.

Like many theorists of music, writers regarding literature as an expression of subjective and/or transcendental perceptions have at least since Goethe (an active early scientist in the field of chromatics), been drawn to the notion that written allusions to specific colours, like specific tonal effects in music, might be capable of inducing with precision specific feelings or ideas. Fictionalists having in addition (or by contrast) a vested interest in seeking effective textual modes that might bypass contingent mimetic referentiality are more often likely to be direct linear descendants of *symboliste* and early twentieth-century anti-representational theorists of art and music than has generally been remarked. Leaders among the latter – notably Kandinsky and Delauney – were also passionately committed to conceptions of a typology of colours as 'elementally pure' sensations, and of colours' differential effects in the organization of experience.[15]

Anti-Realism takes up the taxonomy of colours as though – for a moment at least – some 'prismatic' function in fiction might offer a mode (indeed, a 'direct, im-mediate' means) for the definition of things. The dogged recurrence of the colour red has long been remarked upon as a privileged *fil conducteur* (against the black-and-white theme of *page/écriture*) in Sollers' *Le Parc* and *Nombres*,[16] just as it has been common to talk at length of the 'colour symbolism' in the fiction of Tolkien, Lewis and Le Guin.[17] The light that falls on Nabokov's scenes passes with extraordinary frequency through windows of stained glass; his people are "coloured" ("we see the mineral blue of his jaw ... his magenta and mulberry insides"; "we, whites, are not white at all, we are mauve at birth, then tearose, and later all kinds of repulsive colors" (1962, 218, 173). Vonnegut's narrator in *Slaughterhouse-5* colour-codes his "main characters": "the blue line met the red line and then the yellow line, and the yellow line stopped because the character represented by the yellow line was dead. And so on ...", "death ... was violet light. ... Billy swung into life again, going backwards until he was in pre-birth, which was red light and bubbling sounds"; "the function of the novel might be in modern society ... one critic said, 'To provide touches of color in rooms with all-white walls'" (1969, 35, 137). Arcturus, in Lindsay's novel, is ruled by two suns, one producing "blue, yellow and red", the other "ulfire, blue, and jale"; its system generates new colours for new levels of reality; "blue is existence. It is darkness seen through light ... yellow is relation. ... red is feeling. ... ulfire is existence ... a different sort of existence"; the 'people' of this world are of new hues, their blood sometimes "milky, opalescent", their complexion "jale" or "gamboge" or perpetually changing (1920, 238, 49, 84, 71). In *The Third Policeman* the protagonist 'learns' that "the wind from the east is a deep purple, from the south a fine shining silver. The north wind is a hard black and the west is amber"; characters ask after one another's colours – "some of them, like purple, or maroon are very bad and always mean an early grave. Pink, however is excellent, and there is a lot to be said for certain shades of green and blue" (O'Brien, 1939, 28–31). Humour is only sporadically the 'medium' in which colour is expressed; it comes with compulsive thematic (if not always propositional) seriousness. In McElroy's *Plus* 200 words occur to evoke an omnipresent green, appropriately the conventional colour of the process – befitting the notion of photosynthesis which is central to this narrative – of self-contained living growth, whereas the next most frequent colour, red, appears 107 times, according to a study by Brooke-Rose.[18] But if the "green idea" (a persistent phrase) lies close to the centre of this book's thematics, as a mode of definition, we can see coming the deeper problem to which all such references are allied.

"Fundamentally", as Brooke-Rose says, "*Plus* is about cognition, and cognition is a paradox". For "colour is an idea. But [the beholder's] sight is also an idea" (1981, 286, 281). No system is more resistant to definition – for all its on-the-page efficiency as a mode of definitions and relations – than the 'colour scheme'. Thus we see now one of its main attractions. On one hand, a feature of anti-Realist fiction's references to colours is its insistence on the 'primary' ones (for example in the world of Arcturus, where there are not three but five). Now, of "turquoise" we may say that it's "between blue and green", but what do we say of "blue" or of "green"? We begin to lose touch. Writers can declare that when they say blue they mean 'in the wavelength range of 575–500 nanometres' – and we may expect anti-Realists to adopt just such language for the exact purpose of showing that the more precise the visual reference (the very stuff of Realism), the more empty it is. On the other hand, moving *away* from the 'pure colours' – indeed from the ultimate purity of black and white – there is an increasingly tormenting welter of intermediate possibilities. "The juxtaposition of the phrases 'a white' and 'a colored man' always reminded my poet", says *Pale Fire*'s narrator, "of those outlines one longed to fill with their lawful colors – the green and purple of an exotic plant, the solid blue of plumage, the geranium bar of a scalloped wing" (Nabokov, 1962, 173). The idea of colour now becomes a direct *challenge* to the mind's will to distinguish, to define. Robbe-Grillet, whose texts are revealingly bare of references to colour for all their obsession with visual description, says it early: "it is almost always the sight of an ill-defined colour", he says of Sartre's Roquentin, "that brings on his fits of malaise.... Colours ... constitute an ambiguous sort of contact accompanied by innumerable impressions; it demands, and at the same time refuses, his acceptance.... Colour is susceptible of change, and therefore *alive*".[19]

So it is that in the very texts we've just referred to, the yearning for a 'lawfulness' of colours is perpetually rebuffed by the 'liveliness' of experience. In Arcturus, in the region of Matterplay where forms endlessly proliferate, "all the different combinations of the five primary colors of Tormance seemed to be represented, and the result, for Maskull, was a sort of eye chaos" (Lindsay, 1920, 190). On Le Guin's planet Winter, as the narrator moves from the land of Karhide to that of the people of the Orgota, he finds to his relief that the latter "were colourless, steady, subdued. I liked them. I had had two years of colour.... A change was welcome" (1969, 101). In

O'Brien's novel, Fox, the mysterious third policeman himself, is "crazy": "'It was the colour'", the protagonist is told. "' ... It was not one of the colours a man carries inside his head.... It was ... different'". "This new colour" – the narrator muses – "apparently its newness was now enough to blast a man's brain" (1939, 133–4). The very existence of a spectrum of colours becomes the basis for the dramatization of the tension between proliferation and order in, for example, Calvino's story "Senza colori" ["Without colours", 1965]. "*Before forming its atmosphere and its oceans*", the tale begins, "*the Earth must have resembled a gray ball revolving in space*". All the narrator can see at the start is "gray upon gray". The narrator's lover, the female Ayl, lies "colorless, overcome with sleep, in the colorless sand". Markedly reminiscent of the rigidly stable and ordered civilization of the ants in *The Once and Future King*, whose language of discrimination is based on mere binary formulae such as "done/not-done", "We didn't have many concepts at our disposal"; he and Ayl converse in terms of "sand. Not sand ... Rock. Not-Rock". Then "all of a sudden the world was immersed in a light never seen before. Purple chasms gaped at the foot of orange cliffs, and my violet hands pointed to the flaming green meteor.... The world was testing the forms it was later to assume". Rapidly the two figures come to a parting of the ways: "I was seeking a new world", while for Ayl "anything that looked likely to break the absolute visual neutrality was a harsh discord". Ayl seeks to hide, "to slip off among the crevices of the mosaic", and plunges "'down down into the bowels of the Earth'"; in losing her the narrator realizes "that I would never again be able to escape those gilded and silvered gleams, those little clouds that turned from pale to pink, those green leaves that yellowed every autumn, and that Ayl's perfect world was lost forever" (Calvino, 1965, 59–70). As in *Plus*, where the narrative movement away from green is not merely a movement towards the red end of the spectrum but towards the multiplicity of colours generally – a 'red shift' towards sleep and death – now the colour-coded experience of the infinity of possibilities carries with it the death of stability and order.[20]

Uncertainty

If anti-Realist fiction focuses our thinking on what we 'can' – what we can do and can know, what is and is not within our 'ken' – neocosmic stories in particular tend to dramatize the possibility of cunning and the successes of the canny. And antiscosmic stories, contrarily, tend to dramatize the imminent triumph – in spite of all our efforts – of the 'uncanny'.[21] Yet both modes are equally logically committed to the 'perturbation' of our sense of the knowable. Ranging our minds over texts as divergent as ones by Tolkien, Lindsay, Le Guin, Buzzati, Bosco, Calvino, Borges, Barth, O'Brien, Nabokov, Robbe-Grillet and Sollers, it's impossible to miss the urgent recurrence at the level of *histoire* of *riddles, mysteries*, the *emphemerality* (and not simply the Realist's unreliability) *of appearances*, and the predication of *the invisible* and *the unknown*. In contrast to the readily recuperable, common, 'domesticated' settings and situations of Realism, here the *topos* of the *wilderness* is brought into the foreground – whether in the form of the forest, the labyrinth, the wasteland – with its sensations of disorientation, loss-of-way, and *vertige*.[22]

The quasi-heroism of the sort often called up in neocosmic (as in traditional 'pre-Realist') narrative is in a sense constituted by the conquest of that wilderness. But the wilderness-crisis recurs in the hero-less world of anticosmic fiction. New 'anti-heroic' figures emerge to confront and disclose the enigmatic nature of experience, and are identified by their struggle to penetrate through the apparent limits of the known into the as-yet unknown. We discover the *spy*,[23] the *detective*,[24] and the *voyeur*.[25] Stories here are beset by the appearance, unprecedented in Realism, of *seers*, quasi-prophetic figures invoking the possibility of transcending the bounds of the known. Ready examples appear obviously in Williams, Tolkien, Lewis, Buzzati, Beagle, Le Guin and – archetypically, perhaps – in White's beneficent Merlyn and Lindsay's maleficent Krag: sur-human figures displaying a *maîtrise* of those laws operative in 'strongly cosmic' worlds only. But in even the most propositionally affirmative fiction, such as *The Once and Future King*, the soothsayer's efficacy is often highly provisional; Merlyn is helpless to alter events, and is explicitly at bottom a well-intentioned blunderer. And in fiction making claims of an at least latently *anti*cosmic sort, nearly identical types appear with only the most superficial modifications. Like *The Third Policeman* with its protagonist's idol "De Selby" whose metaphysical pontifications form an ironic counterpoint to the story, the majority of Borges' *histoires* and Calvino's 'cosmicomic' tales are organized around the 'meta-historical' speculations and predictions of superior visionaries – some nominally 'historical', but all expressly (re)invented for the purposes of the narrative.[26]

This can be subtle business. Anti-Realism's intrigue with the overstepping of perceptual and conceptual thresholds may show it to be both promising and ominous. First because it represents, after all, a form of trespass, or transgression. And second because – even in the absence of moral limits – in inviting the fusion of irreconcilables it points towards *in*definition and the terror of *con*fusion. As it is in Renaissance and Romantic tradition (in its various Promethean permutations – the liberating pact with the devil, the attainment of the philosopher's stone), transcendent unity here is finally an equivocal good. Both neocosmic and anticosmic fiction, then, include an array of settings and objects embodying the *topos* of the yin/yang or of the syzygy, or union-in-opposition or – in fuller terms – of the dissolution of distinction in some emblem of totality.

Thus, as in both romance and in Modernist fiction – where those magicians, visionaries, seekers (aiming to gain a footing in some two worlds at once, that of earthly ego and that of extranatural forces) habitually cling to and identify their efficacy with certain tools – *mediating instruments* abound. Like the traditional 'seaweed' token found at the foot of the bed of the dreamer of mermaids (of which there are so many permutations in romance) or the Princess's box in Borge's "Tlön" ("the first intrusion of this fantastic world into the world of reality": 1964, 16), objects persist as links between one plane of knowing and another. Containing the codes for the understanding of alien realities, *books* become crucial (René's book in *Le Sanglier*, the so-called *Necronomicon or The Book of Dead Names* that recurs throughout Lovecraft's fiction, the manuscript-in-a-bottle of *Terra nostra*). Through Krag's enigmatic lens in *Arcturus* Maskull sees the worlds beyond. The ring is the source of the power to move freely from one realm to another in *The Lord of the Rings*, as are the sword Excalibur in *The Once and Future King* and the clock in *The Last Unicorn*. Calvino's nonexistent knight takes his place in the real world by virtue of his armour and quits it when he leaves the armour seaweed-like behind. But it goes further. The medium becomes the message. As Barth, calling on the archetype among mediating objects, the key, famously reminds us in *Chimera*: "the key to the treasure *was* the treasure".[27] The flying carpet and the memory machine in Márquez's *Cien años de soledad* [*One Hundred Years of Solitude*], translating men from place to place and from one time into another, become the people's ultimate treasures. The Zahir and the Aleph, the precious coin and sphere in Borges' stories, become symbols of "man's free will", of "'the Rending of the Veil'", the "sphere whose center is everywhere and circumference ... nowhere", "one of the points in space that contains all points".[28] The treasure box sought by the protagonist of *The Third Policeman*, containing the bomb that "explodes him from life into death", becomes the box of omnium, capable of generating all colours, sounds and forms, "the essential inherent interior essence which is hidden inside the root of the kernel of everything and ... is always the same" (O'Brien, 1939, 95).

Failing to provide some instrument by which to move its characters beyond the confines of the imperfect here-and-now, a text may put in their minds a *place* that performs the same miracle. As Rosemary Jackson says of 'the hollow land' in the arrestingly prefigurative novel of that name by William Morris, the "protagonist seeks this hollow region as being a realm before time, before separation into self and other, before the establishment of distinct identities or genders, before the 'fall' into difference and a consciousness of ego ... a realm of integration" (1981, 46). As a *topos* to be *tried*, such a space becomes a 'common place' throughout anti-Realist fiction. In Vonnegut's *The Sirens of Titan*, a "chrono-synclastic infundibulum", central to the narrative, is a place "where all the different kinds of truths fit together" and where one perceives "that everything that ever has been always will be, and everything that ever will be has always been" (1959, 12, 19–20). Borges's Library of Babel "is total"; "its shelves register all that it is given to express, in all languages. Everything" – including the refutation of everything to be said (1964, 54, 57). In Calvino's "Tutto in un punto" ["All at one point", 1965], "neither before nor after existed" and "all the universe's matter was concentrated in a single point" such that "every point of each of us coincided with every point of each of the others in a single point, which was where we all were".[29] In *Le Parc*, Sollers' narrator listens "to a night that became only the night, to a bedroom that opened on to all bedrooms, to a body, mine, that became every body. ... Reduced to a mental frontier where everything loses its form. ... Trying to reduce himself to one moment: and one place, whereas one is every moment and every place" (1961, 42–4). In *Terra nostra* the prophet Ludovico tells the king:

> We will ... transform this place into a space that truly contains all spaces, into a time which truly embodies all time: a theater in which we occupy a stage where your altar stands today, and the world will unfold before our eyes, express itself in all its symbols, relations, strategems, and mutations. ... We shall know the truth of the order of things. ... We shall know everything ... in the single instant which is all times, and in the one space which contains all spaces. ... All things being converted into all men, all men into all things, external multiplicity nourishing eternal unity, which in turn simultaneously and eternally nourishes multiplicity.
>
> (Fuentes, 1975, 705–6)

Both *Terra nostra* and Saviane's *Il mare verticale* – narratively constructed along the 'lines' (literally) of evolutionary and historical progression – ultimately thus owe their extraordinary formats to the principle that a book itself may be a locus conflating all time and space into a single text, ostensibly extending in finite linear language the infinitesimal non-extended nature of being, to present a synchronic (ontological) vision in diachronic (narrative) terms. Thus, too, *Slaughterhouse-5* purports in its epigraph to be "a novel somewhat in the telegraphic schizophrenic manner of tales of the planet Tralfamadore", where "there isn't any particular relationship between all the messages. ... There is no beginning, no middle, no end, no suspense, no moral, no causes, no effects".[30]

But, as the Tralfamadorians say, in such a vision there is no room for free will, for without "warnings or explanations. ... We are all ... bugs in amber" (Vonnegut, 1969, 61). This is 'the (Fearful) Sphere of Pascal' of Borges' essay of that title. It is the *lieu théatral* to which Fuentes clearly refers. A perfect setting for 'esemplastic' harmony in the eyes of a nineteenth-century Romantic and of certain neocosmists (for example Williams, Le Guin), the *lieu théatral* can also to many anti-Realists be an arena for the enactment of chaos. As in Borges' conception, where "the contact and the habit of Tlön have disintegrated this world" (1964, 18) by the creation of an ideal universe in which 'realistic' differentiation is extinguished, so the invention and propagation of signs, of *language itself* – the last (or first?) locus and implement of mediation, between mind and thing and between mind and mind – may become the source of a universe where, at the conclusion of Calvino's "Un segno nello spazio" ["A Sign in Space", 1965] for example, there is

> no longer a container and a thing contained, but only a general thickness of signs ... occupying the whole volume of space. ... There was no longer any way to establish a point of reference ... because it was clear that, independent of signs, space didn't exist and perhaps never had existed.
>
> (1965, 47–8)

"The discovery of the chrono-synclastic infundibula" in *The Sirens of Titan* "said to mankind in effect: '*What makes you think you're going anywhere?*'" (Vonnegut, 1959, 23).

As individuals we are going, of course, toward death – and this proves to turn up another motif of a like sort. The *coniunctio* of life and death is a further pivotal point – expressed often as a cipher, a void – around which narrative lines converge. "... Between obverse and reverse", as Ricardou says of *Le Parc*, "there occurs that supreme interstice around which the entire book *revolves* without its ever being named: the exact instant of death" which occurs in that "large blank" between the two parts into which the book is divided at p.51 (Ricardou, 1967, 276–7). This is the blank that occurs, too, between sections of *Le Voyeur*, where the unseen murder is committed, and the unspecified event ("something happened") appearing in an early scene of *The Third Policeman* which we discover only on page 170 to have been the death of the narrator. Just as in this book and in *A Voyage to Arcturus* and *The Once and Future King* (whose title refers to precisely this 'turn around'), where all events bend inevitably toward that point where the annihilation of the present terrestrial and temporal being of the protagonist occurs and the eternal round begins again, so *Pale Fire* comically yet remorselessly reminds us that it is tracing the threads of "the web of the world, and the warp and the weft of that web" by which events, from one country to another and from calendared and clocked instant to instant, converge upon the killing of Shade "in the clash between the two figments", and upon the final-page initiation of the new round in which the narrator himself will die (Nabokov, 1962, 227, 236).

The alternative to death would seem to lie in the conventional – but not *Realistically* conventional – hope of *immortality*, a further motif persistent throughout the work of Williams, Lewis, O'Brien, Barth, Márquez, Fuentes, and Borges. Yet, once again, as Borges for one puts it, the 'situation is the same'. At the close of "Los teólogos" ["The Theologians", 1964] Aurelian learns that in the eternity of their lives in Paradise "he and John of Pannonia", his perpetual opponent, "formed one single person". In "El inmortal" ["The Immortal", 1964], if he is to die, the narrator says, "I shall be all men; I shall be dead"; if one were to be an Immortal, by the same token one would have discovered that "all our acts are just, but they are also indifferent. There are no moral or intellectual merits. ... No one is anyone, one single immortal man is all men" (Borges, 1964, 126, 118, 114–15). To aspire toward – or even actively to conceive of – some unity transcending the contingencies of a differentiated reality, whether in death or immortality, is to entertain the peril of the dissolution of that personal (Realistic) identity by which conception and aspiration are defined.

So fiction, drawn not merely toward enigma but toward paradox or some semblance of it, now searches out narrative images for the articulation of *anomaly*. Events happen 'where they shouldn't' or 'when they shouldn't'.[31] Time moves backward, sideways, or stops.[32] Space is reduced, enlarged, 'displaced' or 'evacuated'.[33] Dimensionality, as we'll see, is distorted or described as illusory. And forms and actions 'go wrong'; heteromorphism and 'monstrosity', 'deviation' and transgression, will come into play.

We note here that perhaps one of the most fundamental – and most frequently cited – topoi associated with the manifestation of uncertainty will be the generation within the *histoire* itself of 'information without reason' – the anarchic 'spray of phenomena', the formless 'muck' or 'drek' of experience as unassimilable experience – to which I've referred before and which calls for fuller treatment in Chapter 4.

But already the scene has begun to shift. The sphere of 'personal identity' may be the very centre of knowing and the focus of uncertainty. The *topos*, supported with energy by contemporary Lacanian, Foucauldian, phenomenological and Marxist arguments for the decentring of the subject, yields vital, distinctive motifs (cf. Lacan, 1949; Foucault, 1969; Dallmayr, 1981; Althusser, 1969). Uncertainty appears in several modes.[34] *Fusion* may set in; a person may merge with, lose him- or herself in, another person or thing. *Pale Fire*'s narrator from start to finish identifies himself with (and protests against his identification with) John Shade, with Hazel Shade, with Gradus and others. In "Axolotl", Cortázar's narrator becomes the caged salamander he adores; in "Cockroaches" Bruno Schulz's narrator becomes the roach he abhors.[35] Calvino's Gurdulù imagines he is a duck, leaves, earth, soup, in a world "in which all things dissolved and tinged all else with itself". For the narrator of *Le Parc* "in the cinema, I find myself at one among the characters before me on the screen. . . . I became that wall. A crack in that wall. I was that leaf-strewn path; that stretch of stagnant water by which an invading army passed. I was the queen's comb; the ship's flag" (Sollers, 1981, 35–6). In Le Clézio's *Le Procès-verbal* the protagonist "*is*, variously, a vegetable, moss or lichen, the sea, an oyster"; in his *La Guerre* [*War*] the only 'clear character', Bea B., becomes "at various moments a mechanized doll, a kind of car, a tower, a manatee, a thought, the sun, or even herself".[36]

But, often largely to evade this physical/metaphysical 'confusion', the mind may retreat into *isolation*, unable to sustain – or determined to repel – the identities imposed on it from without. Murphy, Molloy, Malone and the host of Beckett's 'unnamables' seek constant redefinition of themselves (as do Pinget's and Sollers' numerous recluse figures), and ultimate obliteration, in absolute seclusion. Márquez builds a novel on the "private and terrible solitude" of the shifting existence of persons within public history (Márquez, 1967, 60). The central figures in Barth's "Echo", "Life-Story", "Title" and *Lost in the Funhouse* (1968) are perpetually in flight from the unstable external 'identities' of which they're composed and cry for escape into the artificial act of private creation or into death itself. McElroy's protagonist in *Plus* chooses to shed not only his social identity but his very body in his solitary flight into space.

It is in isolation that the most vertiginously harrowing aspects of the indefinition of self are disclosed. For here, in the confrontation with oneself, one faces the elemental nature of *otherness*. Befitting the very word and as Lewis has already told us,[37] it has its positive as well as its negative side. "*Light is the left hand of darkness/and darkness the right hand of light*", as Le Guin's novel says; "'Duality is an essential, isn't it? So long as there is *myself* and *the other*'" (1969, 199). To know 'I', I must know 'not-I'. If, as Oliveira in *Rayuela* believes, love is "a giver of being", it is so by the grace of the conception of difference; if in truth one is always alone, let this truth reveal itself where it reveals itself best, in the society of others. "That's how, paradoxically, solitude would lead to the heights of sociability, to the great illusion of the company of others, to the solitary man in a maze of mirrors and echoes" (Cortázar, 1963, 99; cf. 222–3). The dilemma, now, lies not in the mere possibility that in actuality 'no one is out there', that one is *only* in a world of mirrors, but in this possibility *plus* the possibility that – alone or in company – one's very self is something other.[38] By electing solitude we may elude that corruptive "*regard d'autrui*" that threatened – in Sartre's view, foreshadowed in fiction in Gombrowicz's early and incipiently anti-Realist novel *Ferdydurke* – to force false fixed identities upon us. But what if by the very nature of consciousness (in the form of rational modern Western consciousness, as Fuentes or the Symboliste might argue) "*je est un autre*"? Here the deepest trouble begins.

Shade's poem "Pale Fire" says "A syllogism: *other men die; but I / Am not another; therefore I'll not die*." Kinbote's answer is: "This may please a boy. Later in life we learn that we *are* those 'others'" (Nabokov, 1962, 35, 132). One's sense of oneself – that one *is* at least one's self – is not the safe conduct one thought. The portent steals upon us that whatever one thinks one perceives – even one's own being (that one in the mirror who enquires after our existence with such solicitude) – it is always outside, beyond reach and out of control. The fragmentation of personal identity is an old narrative figure, but in its traditional forms there was always something safe about it, for there it was framed within a stable moral context: Hyde is sundered from Jekyll by reason of the evil within himself, characters in *Dracula* taking on new personalities do so by reason of the force of external evil drawing them 'out of themselves'; repulse evil and integrity is preserved. For those with conventional faith in reason, ethical order or spiritual salvation, the sense of otherness is a difficult but undeniable good. It's the basis for rational systems of discernment and (in the belief of many such as Buber, Cassirer) an essential aspect of positive religious aspiration by virtue of the experience of wonder and the intuition of the presence of divinity it conveys. Now it becomes a source of "Terror", as the title of a Nabokov story makes plain. The narrator one morning encounters his face in "the looking glass" and fails to recognize it as his own:

> ... The more insistently I told myself 'This is I' ... the harder I found it to make the face in the mirror merge with that 'I' whose identity I failed to grasp. ... You see, we find comfort in telling ourselves that the world could not exist without us, that it exists only inasmuch as we ourselves exist, inasmuch as we can represent it to ourselves. ... My line of communication with the world snapped, I was on my own and the world was on *its* own, and *that* world was devoid of sense. ... I understood the horror of a human face. Anatomy, sexual distinctions, the notion of 'legs,' 'arms,' 'clothes' – all that was abolished, and there remained in front of me a mere *something*. ... And I know [the story concludes] that my brain is doomed, that the terror I experienced once, the helpless fear of existing, will sometime overtake me again, and that then there will be no salvation.[39]

There will spring from this a startling display of unexpected and seemingly eccentric images in fiction, of which the two most excessive examples may be Nabokov's and Barth's stories of siamese twins ("Scenes from the life of a double monster", "Petition"), in whom contrary wills and sets of self-perception are simultaneously joined and stalled by their perpetual conjunction, with the narrator of the second of these 'in love' with a woman who is herself two people in one (Nabokov, 1959; Barth, 1968). In *Se una notte d'inverno un viaggiatore* the narrator turns a wrestling match into an ontological *agon*:

> In the tangle of male limbs opposing and identical, I try ... to strike myself, perhaps the other self that is about to take my place in the house or else the self most mine that I want to snatch away from

> that other, but which I feel pressing against me and which is only the alienness of the other, as if that other had already taken my place and any other place, and I were erased from the world.[40]

In a way that was only dimly foreshadowed by what may once have been thought its ultimate expressions in Modernism – in, say, *Der Steppenwolf* [*Steppenwolf*] – the motif of *the double* presently takes on more far-reaching permutations and implications. "I know she's Talita", thinks the protagonist in *Rayuela*, "but a while ago she was La Maga. She's two people, just like us"; "'... this dirty game of substitutions that occupies us for fifty or sixty years. ... It wouldn't seem strange to me at all if you and I were the same, one on each side. ... You're my *Doppelgänger*, because all the time I'm coming and going from your territory to mine ... you're my form staying there looking at me. ... '" (Cortázar: 1963, 346, 345). In the single image of the *doppelgänger* a double anguish may now be invoked. The Realistic struggle for objectivity, even about oneself – and the struggle to get out of, to be free of oneself (an urgent theme throughout, for example, Beckett and Barth) – meets the thwarted yearning for oneness which for some is the very motive impulse behind traditional fantasy.[41] Federman's novel isn't called *Double or Nothing* for nothing. For the narrator of *Thru*, utterances themselves dwell in this crisis. "All discourse is the return of a discourse by the Other, without whom I am not, but to whom I am more attached than to myself"; "mimesis inevitably produces a double of the thing, the double being nothing a non-being which nevertheless is added to the thing" (Brooke-Rose, 1975, 64–5, 106). The radical erosion of the sense of identity, of 'the unity of subject' (where not only in English but in other languages 'I' appears so often cognate with the integer '1') in favour of plurality, begins to make way for the dismemberment of credence in all those further organizations of perception which it inevitably subtends.[42]

And so we come to that pre-eminent mediating instrument of vision, the motif of *the mirror*. The capital emblem of mimesis, already for centuries a literary cliché before Stendhal appropriated it for modern Realism's 'first phase' as George Eliot and Henry James did for its 'second' and 'third', the type-image for self-knowledge and the exact and compelling counterpart to the window as type-image for one's knowledge of the external world, the mirror now becomes its own counter-reflection – the sign of the inadequacy of mimesis itself.[43] It would be a mere nuisance to recite all the possible illustrations here; we can do best simply to scan in a broad way its fundamental appeals. Like the window – and like a book – the mirror is an object to be regarded in itself yet that is ostensibly 'transparent', giving a neutral view onto a world beyond and on which it has no influence of its own – when actually it is absolutely opaque, showing only the viewer's self and the world that he/she already inhabits. Like a window – and again like a book – it frames and thus organizes what it shows and excludes beyond its margins all but what it selects, this committing the viewer to some deception which he can circumvent only be endlessly shifting his own 'angle of view'. As a thing that distorts (because no 'glass' is perfect and because as a mirror it is furthermore a perennial contrivance for the deliberate production of optical illusions, as it is in Barth's 'funhouse'), it can persuasively show 'things that aren't there'.[44] Crucially, *un*like the window and *perhaps* like a book, as a source of knowledge it is only and totally 'reflective'. Astonishingly, mirrors and mirror-like objects are the sole means by which we can directly 'know' our image, our face and specifically our eyes, the express sill of our vision, that faculty by which we not only read a thing but by which we think we most realistically know anything, including our very selves. The mirror is the instrument of self-regard.[45] Yet in the very act of so 'seeing directly' ourselves, we see not our self but our *double*; someone outside this someone we are. And someone who is the *reverse* of ourself; a negative double whom we shall never 'positively' see in the form that is actually us unless we once again double our mirror, looking through mirror to mirror, ever distancing ourselves from ourselves.[46]

Thus the mirror brings both replication and contradiction, in infinite multiplication and an unremitting displacement and alienation, estrangement.[47] Even if the visible universe is not taken to be an illusion such that, as the narrator of "Tlön" says, "mirrors and fatherhood are abominable because they multiply and disseminate that universe" (Borges, 1964, 4), what it then 'really is' – indeed, what its perceiver really is – will again and again (in for example Barth, Fuentes, Biraghi, Federman, Saviane) be subjected to that phantasmogorically nightmarish "sensation of estrangedness" that the narrator in "Terror" so early described (Nabokov, cf. n. 39). Seeing may be believing, but it's no longer seen to be knowing.

There is a further conjunction of hope and deception associated with mirrors which the anti-Realist won't fail to make use of. As we know from fiction extending from MacDonald's *Lilith* and *Phantastes* through *Alice Through the Looking Glass* (which Nabokov for one translated) to Cocteau's *Le Sang d'un poète* [*The Blood of a Poet*] and *Orphée* [*Orpheus*], the mirror may be offered as a *door*, a portal to some ultimate truth, a way into the Beyond. "I receive from the mirrors", says the narrator of a portion of *Se una notte d'inverno un viaggiatore*, "images that direct sight cannot embrace. From mirror to mirror . . . the totality of things, the whole, the entire universe, divine wisdom could concentrate their luminous rays into a single mirror. . . . A system of mirrors that would multiply my image to infinity and reflect its essence in a single image would then reveal to me the soul of the universe, which is hidden in mine".[48] As invoked by Cortázar, O'Brien and Fuentes, among others, the looking-glass may seem to enable the transcendence of time.[49] So a 'world' – or a book – may be suggested to be a 'labyrinth of mirrors' (a set phrase ever repeated by fictionalists now from Mauriac to Fuentes), a total enclosed environment like that of the "catatropic instrument" to which *Se una notte d'inverno un viaggiatore*'s 'seventh novel' is devoted – a version of the kaleidoscope in which the bits of coloured glass are omitted and the mirrors reflect instead the shifting multiform patterns of 'reality' itself beyond the glass. But, as each of these fictionalists makes clear, there is here finally terror too. As with the prison room of mirrors ordered by the king in *Terra nostra* for the endless mating of Don Juan and his 'lover' – where walls, floors, doors, ceilings, windows, "every inch must be reflection", a room where "the day will come . . . when they will not recognise themselves in these mirrors", "condemned to see themselves . . . in a world consisting solely of mirrors" (Fuentes, 1975, 691–2, 709, 770) – so in Calvino's "catatropic room" of mirrors the narrator, imprisoned with the woman with whom he'd make love, at last discovers that "I can distinguish no longer what belongs to one and what belongs to the other, I am lost, I seem to have lost myself, I cannot see my reflection but only theirs" (Calvino, 1979, 168). Some sense of unity may be here; "it seems to me", Calvino's narrator concludes, "that everything that surrounds me is a part of me". But self now has nothing to do with any inward sense of identity. To be 'identical' only with what is outside is to submit to the instruments of – to sacrifice knowing on the evanescent altar of – appearances. The anti-Realist, above all, 'reflects' upon the irony of this.

Anti-Realist themes and motifs: causation

The last section was about knowing; this one is about doing. If there's any area of human concern that narrative literature makes generically its special province, it's that of causality. Of what events can be 'made to happen'; of what events in our experience can in turn be taken as *effective* (productive of other events); and, most precisely, of what human beings might be described as capable of doing and incapable of doing.

Efficacy

It would be mere sophistry at this stage in the game to pretend that in anti-Realist narrative customary optimistic assumptions about what the human mind and human action can accomplish are held to be securely, unequivocally true. What remains in question is 'What, in an anti-Realist perspective, *can* be done? What room is left for activity, for volition, for freedom?'

Actually, there are many answers given of an apparently affirmative, optimistic sort, scarcely one of which hasn't something fundamentally to do with the making of some 'new truth'. In place of the 'discovery' of the 'always-already-there', the text 'produces' the never-previously-there. With the accent on 'production'.

Neocosmic fiction in particular is a mode in which *heteromorphism* plays a powerful rôle. Uncustomary and anomalous forms appear everywhere. Distinctions between male and female, human and non-human, and between animal, vegetable and mineral are disrupted; 'natural laws' are broken. Giantism, dwarfism, monstrosity and deformity (teratism) become crucial.[50] Plots are often largely controlled by the presence of figures alien to Realism – the unicorn, the hobbit, the nonexistent knight, the two-dimensional building, the androgyne, the man-tree and fish-tree, the tree of glass and the three-armed human, the six-toed hero and the plumed serpent, the giant sea-roach and the hero with worms crawling from his veins, the goat-boy, the alligator in the sewer, the poetry-reciting birds.[51] Yet what is consumingly idiosyncratic of anti-Realist fiction is not the non-Realistic unique shapes it presents *ab initio*, but that a critical phase in the narrative consists of the generation *within the story* of new forms. What matters in *The Last Unicorn* is not the existence of the unicorn but the narration of its transformation into a woman; what's important in the realm of Arcturus is not that creatures exist there with heart-tentacles springing from their heads but that it is a place where the human protagonist grows the same organs. This is a fiction in which *metamorphosis* and, specifically, *transubstantiation* and *transpeciation*, take effect. A character *becomes* invisible, a character *becomes* another beast, a dinosaur becomes a man, a man becomes two men, a sea-creature invents its own shell, characters in space create their own bodies or create space before them as they go.[52] The shapeshifter comes into his own. In writers as diverse as Williams, Barth, Buzzati and Nabokov emblems of transformation and polymorphism (butterfly, chameleon, chimera, Pan) become literally 'pivotal', along with the impedimenta of scientific and occult theories of evolution and – with little authentic partisan intent – of political revolution.[53] In striking contrast to nineteenth-century Realism, *transexuality* – so elaborately and relevantly now explored by Barthes in *S/Z* – comes remarkably to the fore. Sexual ambiguity – in the forms of transvestism, bisexuality, hermaphroditism, transsexuality, and sexual oscillation and indeterminacy – figures boldly throughout the spectrum of anti-Realism from *The Left Hand of Darkness, A Voyage to Arcturus, Il cavaliere inesistente, Thru, Rayuela, Pale Fire, Ada, Il Mar delle Blatte* to *Terra nostra*. Along with the narrative *topos* of biological and ethical reversion to 'the animals that we are' that generated such at-once satisfying and scandalous *frissons* in pre-Victorian and Victorian audiences from the time of Mary Shelley to Stevenson, here one of the conventionally most provocative expressions of social and psychological instability serves the theme of the transcendence of those polarities by which identity was traditionally defined. Once again unity, fusion, becomes both a promise and a threat.

The dark side of efficacy, of power, begins to show – and by no accident. The dissolution of boundaries and constraints takes on an urgent new status. The sanctity specifically of the licit human sentiments which we saw to be sheltered by Realism – associated for example with sincerity, good works, caritas, simplicity, solidarity, personal dignity, the innocent and the underdog – may now encounter violence on a new scale. There becomes frequent the fantasy and performance of incest, masochism and sadism, bestiality, vampirism, cannibalism, pedophilia, pederasty, sodomy and arabesque fetishism.[54] Not just crime, not just murder (constant trappings, after all, of Realism) but mass murder and murder treated with gratuitous indifference become commonplace. Accidie and anomie find a new structural and thematic function. Examples have been richly catalogued and annotated in criticism devoted to black humour and need no detailed inventory here. What's most important in this context is that (while a major literature exists that is intent on showing in deadly earnest the cruelties of the contemporary world) where anti-Realism is concerned, a species of narrative 'humour' or impassivity does persistently accompany such transgressions of conventional limits – as though it's not the gravity of the event's local implications but the very transgressive quality of it that counts.

One kind of case may be taken as an illustration. Black-humouristic anti-Realism inverts/subverts Realism's morally-directed stylistic decorum in the description of the common life, and specifically, for instance, its discreet reverence of humans' 'natural bodily functions'. Texts contain a multitude of situations of the type in which, for example, a hospitalized character is endlessly nourished by tube with his own urine (Heller), a character mauls or/and makes love to another's deformed hump (Southern and others), and a narrator–character subjects the human genitalia by turns to ecstatic mystical adoration and nonchalant mutilation (Burroughs and others). Feeling may run deep, as it certainly does in *Slaughterhouse-5* and *Catch-22*, but (as these titles show in their apposition of moral traps and a-moral cold numbers) what we're meant to look at is the possibility that the frontier of values *may be crossed* without feeling, with 'absurd' facility. There are many dimensions to this.[55] But a primary one has to do with more than simply the obvious fact that the special diversion (in several senses) of black humour, as well as of the uniquely humourless *nouveau roman*, derives from some character's effort to normalize an abnormal situation and some narrator's effort to denaturalize, to 'abnormalize' the 'normal'. The attack on customary boundaries is paramount, but what is more: the 'normalization' of the abnormal can momentarily represent the nullity of all customary forms of decorum, all norms. Basically two kinds of scenes occur. Characters feel Realistic pleasure while performing acts violating the terms of Realistic sentiment, or characters do Realistically (un)pleasurable things but feel nothing. In this regard, it can easily be argued that anti-Realism's repeated obliteration of clear plot lines itself has a forceful thematic effect to this end. We are hardly aware (and the immense volume of Beckett criticism scarcely notes) that in the 'story' of *Molloy*, both Molloy and Moran – purportedly so 'inert' as 'characters' – happen to bludgeon other characters to death. By means of the verisimilitudinous representation of classically high-affect situations as empty of affect, or by means of the ambiguation of affect to such an extent as to leave it narratively non-functional or intractable to general paraphrase, the absence of recognizable meaning becomes the salient 'feeling'. Something new has certainly been created; but it momentarily seems in some sense a void. The narrative, like those characters in Calvino's story, creates space before it as it goes, and part of the story is its telling us – by shocking our customary sensibilities – it's doing it. It may be inherent in anti-Realist fiction in which the dissolution of the foundations of accepted sensibility is at a crisis that, for manifest reasons, few are spared, every 'character' is in some respect a victim, and that a kind of muscular (if nervous) extravagance, or a sinewy restraint, on the part of the *narrator* is often the clearest token of 'efficacy' to be found.

But the narrator isn't the only one with the power to create fictions. Characters may manipulate the truth, they may become first and foremost dealers in dissemblance. Mimesis as an external intention calls forth mimicry as an internal *topos*; within the *histoire* itself, simulation merges into *dissimulation*. Persons may assume personae not their own. Over against the search for truth, falsification may be hypostatized. From *A Voyage to Arcturus* – where the grinning mask that individuals reveal at the moment of their death becomes the mask of Crystalman, emblematic of the world of false appearances – through the false stories Gregorovius gives of himself in *Rayuela*, to the endlessly discussed manifold series of impostors in Borges and Barth, *masks, disguises, 'im-personations'* abound in anti-Realism.[56] 'Mistaken' and 'double' identity – so common throughout Robbe-Grillet, Calvino, Fuentes and Pynchon – assume a new meaning. A paradigm is *Pale Fire*, a study in counterfeiting, charlatanry, camouflage and hoax, with its cast of "clowns", "masqueraders", actors and non-actors in makeup, wigs and false moustaches, where we're told of its central figure Shade at the start that "His whole being constituted a mask" and at the finish that his foil Kinbote "may assume other disguises, other forms, but" that he will "try to exist" – and we're left to wonder just exactly what manner of 'existing' this would be.[57] So within fiction people make further fictive 'people'. Toys and particularly toy versions of real places and things flourish, and dolls, manikins and dummies take the place of humans and humans uncannily replace dolls.[58] The very creation of whole pseudo-realities will be the principal act of certain characters. Following Pirandello's lead, like *Rayuela*'s Gregorovius but now at the very focus of events, in Beckett's *Malone Dies*, Pinget's *Baga* and *Mahu*, and in stories in Lem's *A Perfect Vacuum*, 'persons' will invent their own lives and the lives of other 'persons' – who may be simultaneously inventing *them* in their own ways.[59] What is 'put forward' or 'proposed' in a book bodes not to be some propositional truth but a 'pose' in itself.

The process of 'embedding' texts, one in another, is reciprocal. Beyond the hope latent in reality created by characters within the fiction that contains them, there is the alternative hope of their breaking out of that fiction into the reality that had seemed to contain it – into the world that their readers know or thought they knew. *Pale Fire* is a book told by a narrator who claims to be the editor of a previous book written by someone else – a poem called "Pale Fire".

He then gives us that book in its entirety: "Pale Fire" (thirty pages) is completely contained within *Pale Fire*, and in spite of the latter's plausible editorial machinery we can readily decide that *both* are fictions. Slightly more disturbing is our experience when in reading *Pale Fire* or *Molloy* we find references to people who never appear here (Pnin, Lolita, Murphy, Malone) – yet who do appear in other books by these authors; the very flat, 'matter-of-fact' quality of the allusions confers a kind of 'objective, external' existence on the central figures of those other works of fiction *Pnin, Lolita, Murphy, Malone Dies*. Still we're on fairly secure ground: since Balzac, at least, this has been a standard Realist game. Now, though, things become more complex. In a story by Tolkien, Lovecraft, Borges, Calvino, Lem or O'Brien we'll be told of people informed or governed by the rules of some 'real book' whose existence seems free of the fictionality of the story itself, a text not merely of their world but one to be found – if we trouble to search – in our own. In the second edition of *The Hobbit* the narrator 'reveals' that his narrative is based on the Red Book of Westmarch, a history of which he is only the editor; and so forth.[60] Mauriac (as we've seen) gives us whole novels 'written' by 'people' who are characters in other novels of his. This latter seems all right – for it's Mauriac who signs these novels, and 'Mauriac' breaks in from time to time (in *La Marquise*, for example) to clear the air: "thus", he says, "Bertrand Carnéjoux records his novel, and I record in the novel in which I have given life and speech to Bernard Carnéjoux, that ... [et cetera]. A triple character, this Bertrand Carnéjoux, since he's supposed to write the books in which he plays a hero's part. A novelist animated by a novelist whom I (myself a novelist) have put into a novel in which, however, nothing was invented, a labyrinth of mirrors".[61] But who is this 'I myself' if not another character, and what is the status of these 'uninvented' truths if not that of yet another invention?

Now we're in for real trouble. In *The Necronomicon*, edited by George Hay, well-known contemporary scholars have published detailed theses arguing that the Necronomicon of Lovecraft's fictions has really existed or exists in some library somewhere.[62] In *Slaughterhouse-5* Billy Pilgrim, we're told, "re-invents" his world with the help of his reading of science fiction. That's fair enough (and – often missed by critics – it's philosophically crucial); it's an eccentricity of his own character.[63] His favourite science fiction *author* is Kilgore Trout, and that's all right too: Kilgore Trout is another fictional character in the book. It needn't even trouble us that he's a character in other novels by Vonnegut – we're used to that now. But I can presently go into a bookshop and buy a book which I am told is *by Kilgore Trout*. When a 'real writer', Philip José Farmer, composes and publishes *Venus on the Half-Shell* 'by Kilgore Trout', this comes not merely unopposed but perforce welcomed (as a fact if not as a novel) by Vonnegut, for whose own Kilgore Trout the whole of human history including no doubt P. J. Farmer is a contrivance of other characters (the Tralfamadorians)[64] within novels which Vonnegut has invented.

How 'potent' a fiction may be thus reverberates through reality itself. Indeed, the more assertions we produce about reality, it may seem, the more we equivocate. And efficacy becomes a dilemma. Out of touch with a definitive Creator, the vast 'intertextual' network of other 'creations' – of human powers at work – becomes a tangle that may as much paralyse as liberate us.[65]

Inefficacy

Whether in Beckett or Tolkien, Borges or Sollers – it appears virtually impossible to discover any character who has any conventionally Realistic vocation (unless it be writing), any clear estate or place in human society, or who has any abiding interest in any of these things. What can conceivably be the meaning or relevance of 'efficacy' or 'inefficacy', then, for characters so free of 'real' aspirations? This produces one of the most difficult questions an anti-Realist text has to answer, and the unpersuasiveness of its response for people reared largely on 'realistic' precepts is one of the principal obstacles to its own success among a wider readership. For the figures in such fiction are without question deeply 'interested' in *making progress*, yet, characteristically, without having an unequivocally pragmatic end in view. Even in the case of a novel like *The Lord of the Rings*, where the *action* is the most clear, it is hard indeed for the natural pragmatist to imagine it judicious to read 1500 pages about a group of creatures seeking to get rid of a ring, all the more if it's as wondrously effective as this supposed ring. It is the *notion* of progress and its obstructions and diversions, not its objections or objectives, that anti-Realist fiction more often than not takes as its *intrigue*, its Ariadnean thread. The least radical Tolkien himself would have a phrase for it: not the winning of the game but the taking part. The question of progress and, in the act of its testing, the progression of mind (and sometimes spirit) as it processes the procession of events, of words and ideas.

We recognize where this must lead. How straight, determinate, progressive is the course of a life or the thread of a narrative? The ubiquitous *topos* of *the labyrinth*, for which Modernism has well prepared the way, is now upon us. As to any dream we may have of making palpable headway in the world or in a book, both of these are labyrinths, as Borges will tell us again and again.

As a motif the labyrinth may prefigure the inchoate mystery of nature itself, as it does in the Gollum's cave (*The Hobbit*), the mines of Moria (*The Lord of the Rings*), and the underworld of Threal (*Voyage to Arcturus*). But now, as in the tradition of the original labyrinth of Minos–Theseus–Ariadne, it becomes the quintessential *artefact*, fashioned (as Joyce reminds us) by that demiurgic tutelary house-god of the builder of fictions, the artificer Daedalus. Whether in the shape of an enigmatic formal garden (*L'Année dernière à Marienbad*,[66] "El jardín de senderos que se bifurcan" ["The Garden of Forking Paths", 1964]), a palace (*The Last Unicorn*, "La casa de Asterión" ["The House of Asterion", 1964], *Gormenghast*, "Abenjacán el Bojari, muerto en su laberinto", *Pale Fire*) or a fortress (*Il Deserto dei Tartari* [*The Tartar Steppe*]), a 'funhouse' (*Lost in the Funhouse*[67]), a city (Robbe-Grillet's *Dans le labyrinth*, Butor's *L'Emploi du temps*, Pynchon's *V*), an entire culture ("Tlön"[68]), or an idea, an intricate scheme ("La muerte y la brújala" ["Death and the Compass", 1964]), not only may art lie at the heart of the labyrinth but the labyrinth may stand for the totality of creation. The chalked squares of the hopscotch ground (and on which the book *Rayuela* [*Hopscotch*] is patterned) form a "labyrinth" containing everything from "Earth to Heaven" (Cortázar, 1963, 214–16). But if totality is here, it is – as we might now expect – a polarized, duplicitous whole. As a game ("funhouse", "hopscotch") it may articulate the issuelessly frivolous; yet it is also a death-trap ("Death and the compass"); it's at once a game and the theatre of the most mortal ordeal. It contains unity in contrariety – one is free to move through its straitened corridors, but only in one of two opposite directions, outward or inward. As such it expresses that ineluctable confinement from which no writer may escape: the *linearity* of linguistic action.[69] And it doubles inanely upon itself – one may be forced to pass in the opposite direction the very point one has already reached even when one follows a 'correct' single path towards the desired end. For it to be operative, *choice* is the labyrinth's whole significance; choice and the seeming indistinguishability (indeterminacy) of the bases for decision.[70] And if inwardness–outwardness (which way are we going? which way do we *wish* to go?) is its constitutive dilemma, the labyrinth is always in another sense an *interior*, and suggests the ultimate interior that is the *mind*.[71] As such, it's both a retreat and a prison, a tomb.[72] Yet if it's a genuine (Thesean) labyrinth, it has a way out – it's not, in a word, perfectly, neatly 'closed'. The real treasure may lie at its dark centre, but this may be its central deception. For the centre – the Realist interpreter's goal, the meaning buried in the 'depths' of a work of art – is the antithesis of enlightenment and resolution; at the centre one is furthest from the light of conscious, material or rational 'reality'. One has still the whole about-face retreat journey outwards to bring such treasure to light; one does not clearly see the prize in the obscurity of the labyrinth – or one leaves it behind as one departs. As in life, or in a book, the labyrinth's corridors glint in a kind of 'black-light' (note the recurrence of this image among anti-Realists) with eternal surprises – startling dead-ends, turnings, meetings, and intrinsic wonder, a-maze-ment – yet it is finally the very precinct of spiritual *ennui*, for without some 'sense of direction' which it's the wanderer's own task to bring to it, it is an inert, inchoate, aimless, senseless shadow-world. Thus not only does a reader submit himself or herself to the labyrinth of a text to *make* of it what he/she can, but the writer creates in the labyrinth of his or her story an empty structure until some reader enters it.

Anti-Realism finds more in this reciprocity of action than previous literary movements ever dreamed of. Progression may begin to seem inextricably bound to regression. The *topos* of *regressus ad infinitum* looms. At the close of Borges' "La busca de Averroes" ["Averroes' search", 1964] the narrator says "I felt, on the last page, that my narration was a symbol of the man I was as I wrote it and that, in order to compose that narration, I had to be that man and, in order to be that man, I had to compose that narration, and so on to infinity". The anti-Realist may now hold with any or all of the following conceptions: In the labyrinth of human experience, in literature, every utterance is the beginning of an infinite search for its own origins; there is no story that does not commence with all the stories that the reader knows and all the stories that the writer knows, and each of these is in turn the product of all the stories that have ever been told and lived. All objects (in space) and all events (in time) have meaning only – at best – in the context of some greater/smaller, earlier/later space or time. All 'things' are infinitely duplicitous in that a thing perceived is never only itself but is – from the instant it's perceived – also the representation of something other, the thought or word which it evokes and which it is not. When we speak, when we write, we do 'make something new', but it is always only another container whose contents were put there before us, and is itself within a further container among whose contents we are, together with all that that made us make what we've made and which we can never, literally, comprehend, and this in turn is further contained ... into infinity. If the effort to capture a meaning contains its failure since within each inner story there must remain a story yet to be told, every class of experience – every box into which we put experience – is spurious, its own 'definition' being incomplete. So in much anti-Realist fiction the illusion of closure, of accomplishment – the ultimate test of efficacy – will be repulsed. As Lem phrases it:

> What, then, is consciousness? An expedient, a dodge. ... In the language of physics and information theory, it is a function that, once begun, will not admit of any closure – i.e., any definitive completion. It is, then, only a *plan* for such a closure, for a total 'reconciliation' of the stubborn contradictions of the brain. It is, one might say, a mirror whose task it is to reflect other mirrors, which in turn reflect still others, and so on to infinity. ... So the *regressus ad infinitum* represents a kind of pit over which soars and flutters the phenomenon of human consciousness.
>
> (1971, 500)

A further form of embedding thus appears: that of the *mise-en-abîme*, of *nesting* images, Russian dolls, Chinese boxes, boxes within boxes. Openness is fervidly acclaimed, put into action by the creation of stories in which strategies of illusionistic regression compel the reader to accept a multiplicity of stories without which any one of them is incomplete, and strategies of anti-illusionistic metalepsis oblige us to '*jootse*' from illusion to illusion, leap recursively from one story-system to another. We're compelled to think how artificial must be the completeness of any datum, since some other (such as the narrator's own 'story') contains it.[73] So dolls-within-dolls, people-within-people, spring forth.[74] From O'Brien (1940) and Peake (*c.* 1950) to Robbe-Grillet and Nabokov, chests-within-chests, houses-within-houses, come in an appropriately endless succession.[75] And regressive and recursive–metaleptic narration appears everywhere, following Pirandello: Barth's nine-tiered sets of tellings-within-tellings in "Menelaiad"; the 'novels-within-novels' and fictitious critiques-within-critiques of *Se una notte d'inverno, A Perfect Vacuum* and Borges and Bioy-Casares' *Crónicas de Bustos Domecq* [*Chronicles of Bustos Domecq*][76]; the unbroken stream of narratives composed of undifferentiated transitions between levels in the *nouveaux romans*, in Barth and Calvino; the problematization of the narrator's and reader's own status in Brooke-Rose's *Thru*,

> Larissa is producing a text. But which text? . . . this one and not, as previously appeared, Armel, or Armel disguised as narrator or the narrator I disguised as Armel. . . . Larissa has . . . usurped my place as narrator

Barth's "Life-Story",

> in the corpus of fiction as far as he knew no fictional character had become convinced as had he that he was a character in a work of fiction

and Calvino's conclusion to *Se una notte d'inverno*,

> Now you are man and wife, Reader and Reader. A great double bed receives your parallel readings. . . . And you say, "Just a moment, I've almost finished *If on a winter's night a traveler* by Italo Calvino".[77]

Thus an infinitely creative process is the demonstration of its own inefficacy by reason of the infinity of remaining possibilities of which it unreservedly reminds us. Only in the mind of a God can there be final efficacy in this sense (as Borges' "La escritura del Dios" ["The God's script", 1964] is designed to make clear); and if the creative power of the writer is its symbolic correspondence, this is the mere shadow of something whose sufficient existence to cast a shadow is itself an uncertainty which only a complete acquaintance with the infinite could resolve.

It's important to take note of the fact, with its implications – as contemporary criticism has been disinclined to do – that infinite regress *never appears* in a text or anywhere else. We can at most only allude to it, by means of emblems of which nesting motifs provide the most common examples. Thus *nesting*, and not infinite regress, is the larger, generic *topos*. (This could scarcely be more obvious than it is in the many cases where nesting may actually invite us to consider the possibility of *finite* regression. That is, that events at one level may be contained within some greater sphere of experience that's definitive, where some 'ultimate – merely humanly imperceptible – truth' may prevail. Neocosmic literature informed by religious intentions – as in Williams, Lewis – will plainly be meant to work according to this strategy.)

Writers will from this point be ready to conceive that the only progress lies, as we've heard before, not in the end but in the process.

Yet if the key to the treasure is the treasure, then the way to the treasure is a *circle*. "The common end of all *narrative*, nay, of *all*, Poems", Coleridge wrote, "is to convert a *series* into a *Whole*: to make those events, which in real or imagined History move on in a *strait* Line, assume to our Understandings a *circular* motion – the snake with it's Tail in it's Mouth."[78] With this literary tradition behind it, with its positive one-making/whole-making ('esemplastic') intention, there should be no surprise in uncovering the motif with extraordinary frequency in cosmically-orientated (neocosmic) fiction. "Most modern fantasy involves the notion of a return to a starting point so that one ends where one began. This motif of circularity is an image of the preservation of things as they are."[79] We may find Manlove's blanket assessment useful in some cases. But these 'strange bedfellows' will discover many reasons for playing the same 'circle game'. As we're told in Borges' "Los Teólogos", "the mirror and the obolus [the circular coin] were the new schismatics' emblem" (1964, 122).

When we seek, for a start – on a blackboard, on the ground, on a piece of paper – to represent the enclosure of everything that is our subject, we seem inevitably to draw a 'ring' around it. As has been abundantly argued in detail by Jung and his successors, especially in their elucidation of the mandala, the circle is throughout the range of cultures a persistent unitary emblem for *totality*. Even where duplicity arises, traditions find a way of embracing it in this form – in, for example, the famous occult yin–yang. Should he/she wish to 'describe' a truth (the traditional task) yet relinquish the ambition to 'define' in a to-the-point fashion, the writer may find the circle as the very emblem of his or her particular *kind of process*: the writing 'circumscribes'; it doesn't tell a thing but 'draws a line' around it. The foremost hope may be for a 'perfect circle' – a conventional image for perfection itself – all its points equidistant from its centre, its central meaning.[80] If writing must be linear, then the perfect written text may have as its eidolon the sole possible line without 'loose ends', the circle again. But further still, if literature must be linear and the protagonist or the work is taken to be engaged in a 'quest', the circle above all things is the sign of 'getting nowhere'. It may be that zero-sum, that cipher, the ejaculation 'O', that connotes nothingness, nullity, the void.[81] Activity itself may appear to be emptied of effect. The circle may intimate change yet simultaneously stand as a fixed totality within which all action is dissolved in the action of fate – the cycle of nature, the roulette wheel, the spinning-wheel of destiny, the wheel of fortune – that deals out an ultimately "incessant and circular" reality, "relentlessly returning to the same exhausted point of departure while they believe they have reached a new shore".[82] There may for the writer be the compensating gratification that, if the work forms a circle (or a sphere), it is a closed world, tautologically pure, autonomously perfect. It may thus, however, become the circular *prison* of Borges' "La escritura del Dios", with its coterminous "feelings of oppression and vastness" (1964, 169). Or, to 'turn this around', it may hence merge into that perennial and not merely Pascalian "fearful sphere, whose center is everywhere and whose circumference is nowhere".[83] In this way, in even its most affirmative sense, where the universe or the text may be taken as signifying something positive and real, what it englobes is *too total*. The world or the work may be conceived as a compass, a windrose, encompassing or 'clocking' at once all possible directions and spaces, just as the face of a clock indicates at once all possible times. All specifications as to truth in the circle of a perfect work must simultaneously be accompanied by their opposites and contain their own negation.

For some one of (or cluster from among) these reasons we therefore find – as Manlove easily documents – overall narratives by Williams, Lindsay, Lewis, Tolkien, Peake, Le Guin and T. H. White whose unifying feature is that they are circular. The protagonist returns to the place and the status from which he/she had started out. This is not, however, a feature merely of such 'clearcut' neocosmic cases as *The Lord of the Rings*. It extends to the stories of Molloy and Moran and the protagonist of *The Third Policeman, Se una notte d'inverno un viaggatore, Il mare verticale*, and *Le Voyeur* among many others. So Calvino's "Giochi senza fine" ["Games without end", 1965] concludes with its 'characters' pursuing themselves endlessly, and the pilgrim in *Terra nostra* foresees that "at the end of this voyage we'll have returned to our point of departure and everything will have been in vain" (Calvino, 1965; Fuentes, 1975, 414). So in *aria da capo* a number of Pinget's novels repeat in mid-stream the passages with which they had commenced, Nabokov's "The Circle" – the last story in the collection in which we have it – ends with the "sentence existing implicitly before its first one",[84] and *The Once and Future King* closes with the phrase "THE BEGINNING". So O'Brien says of *The Third Policeman* "In shape it is circular and by nature it is interminable, repetitive and very nearly unbearable",[85] and for Sollers "writing would be linked to a space in which time had somehow *turned*, being only the circular operative movement", with reading being "the deciphering act which can never be definitive and global but which manifests itself as circular metamorphosis", just as we are "each of us" the world's "hidden, irreducible cipher" (Sollers, 1968b, 69–70).

The compositional circularity of stories is matched by a wide variety of complementary images. "*Circular labyrinths*" fill Borges' pages, where the facets of a man's life, history and "worlds" and "heavens", too, are described in the same way (e.g. Borges, 1964, 73, 119, 120–1). The obvious motif of the *ring* in Tolkien is matched in more than one text by the figure of the *uroborus*, made famous by Jung and Neumann.[86] The *wheel*, a favourite of Borges, and the *bicycle* – perhaps mind-boggling in the frequency and unmistakable narratorial mystique with which it recurs together with *pairs of spectacles*, until we've recognized the image's patent and not always comic iconic kinship with the infinity sign – take on a 'character' role in *Molloy*, *Le Voyeur* and *The Third Policeman* as well as in Gadda's Modernist *Cognizione del dolore* [*Acquainted with Grief*], in the notoriously 'phantasmagoric' writer Pieyre de Mandiargues's perhaps least anti-Realist story *La Motocyclette* and Pirsig's *Zen and the Art of Motorcycle Maintenance*. *Coins* and *enigmatic spheres* come to rival the status of conventional science-fiction's flying saucers.[87] *Clocks* and *watches* crowd the texts.[88] Special attention should also be given to the *spiral* motif.[89] *Word-circles* appear whose status is expressly obscure; is it a 'pure discourse-level' event when throughout *Cosmicomiche*, for example, 'characters'' proper names – Qfwfq, Pfwfp, Kgwgk – form palindromes readily read as sets of concentric orbits with 'voids' or 'black holes' ('nonexistent letters' in Italian) instead of suns at their centres?[90]

And ultimately the verbal palindrome, literally a 'running back again', a 'feedback loop', is only a local articulation of the wild-goose chase expressed in texts on a more global plane by the *topos* of the *red herring* (and it *is* a *topos*; we must not be misled into imagining that it bears some supra-textual virtue or ontological indeterminacy). Stories recount quests for entities that are never to be found within their 'present worlds': Pynchon's *V* (the 'person' 'V' her/him/itself); *Molloy* (mother/Molloy); *Arcturus* (Surtur); *Il deserto dei Tartari* (the Tartars); *Pale Fire, The Once and Future King, Terra nostra* (the crown of definitive sovereignty); *The Third Policeman* (the watch, the bicycle, the treasure); "Night-Sea Journey" ('You'). *Pale Fire* and *Thru* end with 'indexes' giving entries whose relevance to the text is fictitious or undiscoverable.[91]

It's no accident that in *Catch-22* anti-Realist fiction has contributed to Western languages the catch-phrase by which the twentieth century encapsulates its perception of the 'infinitely regressive loop'. But questing itself now contains special new perils, and – with these – obsessive new motifs.

In texts whose events – from neocosmic adventure to reflexive anticosmic search – are virtually built upon, strung upon the connective thread of the image of the *road*, the *path* or *trail*, there's scarcely a work in which *immobility* and *waiting* aren't central narrative situations. Vehicles are stolen, lost, or fail or crash, or are explicitly remarked for their absence or are halted in time.[92] *L'attente* and hesitation, vital motifs in a positive sense in Modernism (where in the act of waiting, for example in Lawrence, Mann, Faulkner, one finds an illuminating contact with nature, or a kind of *tapas*, a state of brooding preliminary to revelation), may be posed as equally fruitful in writers such as Bosco, Buzzati, Le Guin. But they may now also become the initiating tokens of inefficacy – in Beckett, Borges, Barth, Mauriac and Sollers from *Waiting for Godot* onward, in the guise of aporia. And *lameness, mutilation, impotence* and *paralysis* become unequivocal narrative crises in fiction I've mentioned by writers from Beckett and Burroughs to Lindsay, Landolfi, Pinget, Gardner, O'Brien, Heller and Fuentes.[93]

As one waits, so one may play *games* – one 'tries one's hand' against fate. In the stories of White, Tolkien, Lewis, Garner, Beagle, Le Guin, in the interludes between heroic acts – and in heroic acts themselves – play slides by sleight of hand or wager of will from 'gambol' to 'gamble'. In Roussel, Beckett, Sollers, Nabokov and Borges, chess – its pieces, pauses and moves – becomes a pervasive idiom. Cards, dice and lotteries become self-evident even in the titles of Federman's *Double of Nothing* and *Take It or Leave It*, Sanguineti's *Il giuoco dell'Oca*, and *Il giuoco del Satiricon*, and Borges' "La lotería en Babilonia" ["The Lottery in Babylon", 1964]. Characters make what they can of 'the Chain of Chance'. This 'making' is crucial. The *jeu de hasard* that operated in the creation of Surrealist texts becomes an express 'subject matter' in anti-Realist narrative. While from their different viewpoints a Burroughs, a Calvino and a Sollers argue for a 'writing machine' or 'word-dicing machine' run by the 'rules' of chance,[94] a sect within "La biblioteca de Babel" suggests "that all men should juggle letters and symbols until they constructed, by an improbable gift of chance, these canonical books" (Borges, 1965, 56). So Calvino's *Il castello dei destini incrociati*, Sanguineti's *Il giuoco dell'Oca* and *Il giuoco del Satiricon* and Lem's "U-Write-It" place the gaming with life-stories before us, within their stories. A 'new order' is the dream.[95] The "word games", "word golf", "game of worlds" of *Pale Fire* have their 'intellectually passionate' aspect; as Kinbote puts it, "The poet's plan is to display in the very texture of his text the intricacies of the 'game' in which he seeks the key to life and death" (Nabokov, 1962, 200).

But the 'endgame', the culminating risk – as those antipathetic to anti-Realist gaming itself will inevitably remind us – is not that one may stake one's life on some wrong number but that, as "Giochi senza fine" concludes: "We had lost all pleasure in this game of chase, and we weren't children any more for that matter, but now there was nothing else we could do" (Calvino, 1965, 80). As "El Zahir" exhibits (and indeed as stories of gambling have argued), one may become ruled by the game and the objects (in place of 'the object') of the game. The perplexity yawns wide: is it the thing that obsesses the mind, or the mind that is obsessed with things? The *topos* of *automatism* takes shape. Word-gaming itself becomes likened to *babble* (as we'll see further later), and characters repeatedly display *compulsions* and *tics, empty verbal doodling* and *physical order-making rituals* of which the classic example is Molloy's mute but eloquent ceaseless arithmetical shifting from hand to pocket to mouth of his numbered 'sucking stones'.

The eighteenth-century *topoi* of the *man-machine* (after La Mettrie and D'Holbach) and of the *book-machine*, both explicitly foretokened in Sterne, come into the foreground with more sinister implications. Resounding now simultaneously, equivocally with both the optimistic associations of the deist's clock and the terrors broached by Gothic romance, both *man* (as a half-mechanical god-monster in Vonnegut, Heller, Pynchon, Barthelme, McElroy) and *book* are assigned the capacity to produce out of determinate initial laws the infinite unforeseeable. Each may generate an endless stream of possibilities, and each may in its automaton way – like some Tinguely machine – perhaps inevitably utterly 'destroy itself'. Power and powerlessness become potentially synonymous.

More problems unfold. If you lose in the Lottery of Babylon you go to prison. As the motif of the labyrinth has already foreshadowed, *confinement, captivity*, becomes a perpetual hazard of life. From *Flatland, The Once and Future King* and innumerable texts by Beckett to *Deserto dei Tartari, Cien años de soledad, Pale Fire, The Third Policeman, Catch-22, Slaughterhouse-5*, "Il conte di Monte Cristo", *The Last Unicorn, Terra nostra* and *Plus*, protagonists find themselves enclosed in some cell, some dungeon, some cage, confronted with the possibility of an eternal deadlock. The double-bind, the dead-end, the game's stalemate takes on the grim proportions of a far more encompassing impasse.

Now the cul-de-sac, one discovers, may be a snare of one's own nature; one may be immured within oneself. *Insentience* becomes a *topos*. Paralysis was one thing – "crippledness affords its own heroisms, does it not", as Barth's narrator in "Autobiography" says – but there is still more. "Are you there? If so I'm blind and deaf to you." The 'halt' become the 'blind'.[96] As in Gadda's *Cognizione del dolore*, so in increasingly more stories ("Autobiography", Beckett's trilogy and *Texts for Nothing*, Pinget's *Passacaille* and *L'Inquisitoire*) blindness and deafness become critical motifs, only now without their Modernist Tiresian promise of compensating in-sight. And with anaesthesia comes amnesia – not merely in *Briefing for a Descent into Hell* but in *The Sirens of Titan* and *Slaughterhouse-5* and throughout Beckett's trilogy as well as Robbe-Grillet's, Barth's and Pinget's stories – such that past and present sensations are portrayed as dissolving together into indiscriminable fictions.

The committed humanist reader (whom so many anticosmist writers repel) may think that these are representations of lamentable misfortunes. But ambivalence is here. Barthelme's "Paraguay" takes up 'white noise' – the technological emblem and instrument of sensory deprivation – as a positive option, the narrator placing it in satiric perspective (1970, 36). *Plus* presents a protagonist whose own physical machinery of sensation is surgically removed; but the brain grows its new senses. Pynchon's protagonist perceives that should he find V, "where else would there be to go but back into half-consciousness? ... Approach and avoid". "He didn't know which he was most afraid of; V [whom he sought] or sleep. Or whether they were two versions of the same thing" (Pynchon, 1963, 53, 341). Approach and avoid; the very language of classic stimulus/response theory in the experimental production of ambivalent behaviour in the subject by sensory manipulation. In response to the metaphysical ambi-valence of possibilities such as now appears, there seem to be but two alternatives, and the neocosmic protagonist inclines toward the first, the anticosmic toward the second. Pynchon's Stencil "tried not to think, therefore, about any end to the search".[97] Either one chooses not to contemplate essential features of the game (its peril or its pointlessness) and goes on, or one surrenders to accidie. Contrary to some critics' correctly hesitant suggestions, the outlets of dream and madness play only a limited role in anti-Realist fiction.[98] Motifs reflecting *abandonment in life* take over – expressing either *irrationally precipitous action* or *loss of purpose*, *involition*, and *indifference*. "So it goes"; the phrase we so persistently associate with its threnodic refrain in *Slaughterhouse-5* springs forth equally in *Grendel*, on one hand, and *Pale Fire* on the other.[99]

The puzzle of our coming into material existence – from the indifferent's viewpoint as from the mystic's – is not merely that nothing may be gained but that, in sharp paradox, '*nothing*' is lost. That is, in life we lose the neo-Platonists' imagined perfection of a non-contingent, pre-existential void. The disintegration of value may thus now become a value in itself. The process of degeneration – not progress but regress – may be a way towards recovering that primordial nothingness. Both Molloy and Moran deteriorate 'before our eyes'. "The most you can hope is to be a little less, in the end, the creature you were in the beginning, and the middle", says Molloy, "... it is in the tranquility of decomposition that I remember the long confused emotion that was my life". And Moran at the close of the book echoes this inversion of the Wordsworthian sentiment: "physically speaking ... I was now becoming rapidly unrecognizable"; "almost elated, enchanted with my performance. ... I shall soon lose consciousness altogether" (Beckett, 1951, 38, 29, 231, 221). "For to know nothing is nothing, not to want to want to know anything likewise, but to be beyond knowing anything, to know you are beyond knowing anything", says Molloy, "that is when peace enters in"(83). Like so many of Beckett's voices, Barth's "basket case" in "Autobiography" intones the theme: "I haven't a proper name. ... Contentless form, interestless principle; blind eye blinking at nothing" (Barth, 1968, 33). Not simply insentience but *nescience*, now, is offered. The reaching after *vacuity*, and *oblivion*.

An ultimate aspiration along this course emerges for the writer: *silence*. "To restore silence", says Molloy, "is the role of objects" (Beckett, 1951, 12). It is the ostensible purpose of Barthelme's and Lem's narrators' notions of "white noise" and the "Perfect Vacuum". It's what Sollers' narrator writes of when he says in *Le Parc* "that this whole complacent, numbing succession of words must be destroyed. ... Silence that closes up without leaving traces. ... The liberated silence of someone who has succeeded, by depriving himself of one of his functions or senses, in finding a way out of himself."[100] We detect in this call to silence the now further familiar appeal to the fantasy – or intuition – of *absence*. Nor can we make out that in anti-Realism these are the province only of the anticosmic. 'To restore silence' – the "vasto silenzio", when the storm-winds have died away – is the 'natural' role of things at the end of Buzzati's *Segreto del Bosco Vecchio* and a multitude of other neocosmic closed-world narratives. It's the silence with which *Voyage to Arcturus* finishes, the silence through which the protagonist of *Deserto dei Tartari* has lived and in which he dies, the essence of the '"Che non c'è"' and the birds' incoherent "'Poo-tee-weet?'" that end *Il mare verticale* and *Slaughterhouse-5*, the disappearances with which Calvino's three novels in *I nostri antenati* [*Our Ancestors*] conclude, the 'beyond' – "which opens . . . in the darkness of the pupils, the mirrored hall of the retinas, in our true element which extends without shores, without boundaries" – that forms the last lines of *Cosmicomiche*, and the "flashing" through which the last character in *The Inheritors*' closing sentence "could not see if the line of darkness had an ending". Nor does the anticosmic retain sole access to the *angst* accompanying the palpable 'presence' of absence. T. H. White, driven by a "life-long concern for the sheer identity of created things", early in his Arthurian cycle writes:

> The place in which he found himself was absolutely flat. . . . Here, in the belly of the night . . . there lived one element – the wind. . . . It was a dimension, a power of darkness . . . it . . . came from nowhere. It was going through the flatness of nowhere, to no place. . . . [Arthur], facing into this wind, felt that he was uncreated. . . . He was living in nothing – a solid nothing, like chaos.
>
> (1958, 162–3)

Of this passage a scholar not remarked for extravagant or radically pretentious readings has more than once noted that "this is a picture of identity totally lost: it is White's *le néant* to his *l'être*". This "mad black wind" returns to propel the last chapter of *The Once and Future King* to its fatal conclusion.[101] Unmistakable is the analogy with *The Third Policeman*'s "hard black wind" and "black air", to which is owing the 'hallucination of night' contained within the 'hallucination of human existence'.

In such a context, we must not omit this: it is an identifying trait of anti-Realism that, by contrast with Realism – where it figures as one of the consummate 'ways out' – throughout its narratives scarcely an example occurs of suicide. It's in fact the only significant body of fiction since the eighteenth century of which this can be said. While many protagonists contemplate it, they do not *leap* to their death. There is clear confirmation in this that it is the *trial* of effort and anguish, the *process*, that is the anti-Realist's *métier* and matière. The protagonist may 'go blind', but by staring fixedly into the sun.[102]

We can say something substantial now about the 'substance' of such fiction.

In sheer 'physical story', the Realist psychological middle ground between exotic material exploit and acute meditative stasis seems to disappear. With that, in the seventy- or eighty-odd novels and stories to which I've so far most regularly referred as 'specimens' of anti-Realist fiction it's difficult to find narratively significant examples, let alone any continuous exposition, of those experiential concerns (such as the institutions of marriage, family, church, government, commerce, law) and antithetical thematic *topoi* with their immanent synthetic solutions (affecting social, sexual, and economic power, materialism / idealism, public solidarity / private authenticity, innocence / corruption, aspiration / self-effacement) that were central to the texts forming the nineteenth- and twentieth-century Realist background.

Set over against this, among the same anti-Realist samples one is scarcely able to find a case that does *not* make constitutional narrative use of a conspicuous number of substantive motifs and thematic *topoi* of a significantly different variety – among which we can readily cite ideational and textural preoccupations with: spatial order as against temporal order; mediation, transgression or dissolution of limits; radical transformation, heteromorphism, transpeciation, transsexuality; otherness; involition, anomie, insentience, nescience; anachronism, anatopism; the *lieu théatral; the mise-en-abîme*, infinite regress; *l'attente*; gaming; dissimulation and disguise; impotence and paralysis; taxonomic formulae (optical, zoological...); mirrors; labyrinths; circles, spheres; process and procession against product and progression; timelessness; absence; silence. Narrational data, that is, of which Realist cases are nearly wholly devoid unless it be to function in a fashion which anti-Realist usage is manifestly designed to invert or subvert.[103]

We have in anti-Realism, then, a *custom*. As with Realism, though often seemingly now selected for the impression of the 'fluidity' which they 'produce', anti-Realism is replete with an iconography and a set of 'regulatory mechanisms' operating not only along narrational lines such as those described in Chapter 1 (multiplicity, ambiguation and equivocation, assertion/revocation, mutual exclusion, parataxis, metalepsis, circularity, regression/recursion, and so forth) but within the discourse, at the level of story. These are *thoroughly comparable* in their structural and textural status with those of 'classic' fictions and are not dependent for our observation of them on the recognition of some unique new plane of actual or reading experience. They establish standard formulaic conventions of their own, and many – on both levels – have achieved the comfortable standing in our time of the cliché.

As I intimated at the start of this chapter, while the array of such 'codes' is undoubtedly complex but nevertheless highly specialized and idiosyncratically distinctive when we size it up against the perhaps equally complex but plainly different system of Realistic formulae, every time I've begun to differentiate *within* anti-Realism between anticosmic and neocosmic thematic *topoi*, I've had finally to uncover some resistance to that effort. Distinctions on this plane between the strategies of the two groups are not merely not so readily made as superficially seemed (and as critics would have argued who are up to the present temperamentally smitten with only one group or the other), but sometimes prove downright wrong. Others will work toward fine-tuned discriminations, if only to justify their own predilections, and this will be of value. What does vary most will be the usage from work to work, neocosmic or anticosmic; and for the discrimination of that, well-grounded but close-textual comparative studies will in future, as always, prove best.

Does this mean that in the context of our own discussion we must persist, as I've done throughout this chapter, in declining to say that any one book is 'about' some one of the issues I've mentioned? Definitely I've been talking of internal thematic *topoi*, not of any all-embracing 'theme' beyond which the text as a whole may not in some sense 'escape'.[104] And there is no question but that a neocosmic text (for example *The Once and Future King*) may intend to elude contamination by various of its internal working *topoi* (for example that of the dissolution of identity), just as much as an anticosmic text (for example *Le Parc*) may intend to evade the attribution of overriding propositionality to one of *its* internal working *topoi* (for example any apparent intimation that it is useful to see 'life' as 'black and white'). This kind of demurral (*différance*) is indeed a general feature distinguishing much anti-Realist literature as a whole from most Realist fiction.[105]

We can, however – *without* leaping to assumptions about what such books *propose* – discover at least one configuration that appears to embrace many if not all of the patterns we've seen. One that may nevertheless – exactly as James's phrase would have it – 'take on the dignity of a prime idea'. It has two aspects, bound together in ways now familiar to us by the logic of such fictions: the narrative enactment of the overturning or failure of fixed customary systems of understanding, and – in the face of that – the narrative invocation of wonder and/or perplexity. If we wished to discern in this some pre-eminent metatextual stance, we should reasonably describe it (the more we think about it) as the rhetorical *posture of astonishment*.

This last has large implications – to which we'll return.

4

SHAPE VERSUS SUBSTANCE

What are the stakes?

Let's not pretend that an elephant lives for the sake of its trunk. A dismal mistake we often commit in theoretical discussions is to assume that the product of a movement in art exists solely in order to be the thing that makes it different from the products of other movements. We're particularly inclined in recent times to overlook the fact that works that thwart easy understanding may not always be there to defeat all connections between themselves and other actualities. It's plain by now that any account of fiction whose repulsion of Realist models is vigorous and concerted would be naive, to say the least, if it sought to exclude a multitude of works that are nevertheless, like Realist fiction, frankly referential in their intention.

Referential anti-Realism

The 'substance' *of* an anti-Realist text (as I spoke of it in the last chapter) may be offered as referring to a substantive reality *beyond* the text. While both neocosmic and anticosmic narratives reflect a concern for process, both may sometimes be 'transitive' in intention; the work may be viewed as bearing a 'message' within its 'medium'. We sense intuitively that while it rejects verisimilitude as a stable and abiding good, it is nonetheless *veristic* in its aims. Neocosmic fiction might come first to mind in this respect. We may be more readily disposed to think of its adoption of the uncustomary as not simply for shock (hesitation, estrangement) as an end in itself, but because it appeals to the writer as the best way to oblige the reader to think along new lines towards some positive truth.

But it doesn't end here. A peculiarity of the public assertions of those innovators moving toward the *anti*cosmic is that they persistently adduce 'veristic' rationales for what they do. Beckett, Robbe-Grillet, Barth, Federman, Sukenick, Barthelme, Pinget, Sanguineti, Sollers: their utterances are charged with the phraseology – alluding to the 'obsolescence' or 'exhaustion' or 'death' of Realism, to the 'present' needs of 'contemporary' or 'post-modern man', and to the conviction that 'the novel is the way this society speaks to itself' – of an empirically-rationalized outlook whose capital presumption is that there exists an external, circumstantial, historical truth to which it is the burden of literature to respond and which literature 'inscribes'. (It makes no difference whether or not the writer's view is that, by reason of the nature of language, he or she has no choice in the matter. Once one has – as these writers have – expressly declined to deny the influence of history in one's utterances, one's commitment to the idea of its responsiveness to some veritable truth becomes a constitutive part of one's writing activity). When Calvino declares (1967–8, 98–101) that the fictionalist brings forward "pre-conscious matter" and its otherwise unknowable pre-linguistic "meaning" – or when theorists intellectually pledged (as say Rosemary Jackson is) to the concept of the function of hesitation in fiction argue that "the literature of fantasy ... is all that is not said, all that is unsayable, through realistic forms" (1981, 25–6) – we recognize faith in referentiality. Whether as a visionary or an autocritical mode, the anti-Realist text is commended to us as one that can communicate, even more efficiently or accurately then Realism, some further truth.

This would appear to be a deeply contentious 'overview', since it might seem to attribute to all fiction a propositionality which anticosmic thought seeks to dislocate; we'll return to that problem. For the moment we can certainly agree that the latter at a metatextual level does intimate that thinking is a process intractable to definitive (for example cosmic) assertion. In this perspective, what genuinely separates the body of anticosmic from the body of neocosmic fiction is not so much a propositional emptiness in the one and a propositional fullness in the other, but rather a tendency toward propositional uniformity in the one and a propositional diversity in the other. For while neocosmic fiction cannot *enact* at the level of discourse the *topos* of the instability of meaning or value as anticosmic fiction often hopes to do, it is fully capable of expounding it (as *A Voyage to Arcturus* does) within its *histoire* – and in addition to this it may on the other hand expound a seemingly infinite variety of alternative 'themes'. Evidence of this lies in *topoi* that we've by now readily perceived (and that the professed commentators on writers from Abbott and Williams to Fuentes and McElroy amply recite in detail elsewhere), such as the urgency within the human condition of rational thought, of creative action, of the relinquishment of ego, of political freedom, of wholeness of psychic being, of social solidarity, of reconciliation with mortality, of the quest for beauty or harmony, of personal dignity, of attunement to nature or deity. That we can't in a single discussion such as this hope to encompass the array of propositional *topoi* in neocosmic fiction is not a testimony on its own that neocosmic fiction is propositional and anticosmic is not. It points instead to a unitary aspect of what may be propositional in anticosmic fiction on the whole – where a harmony of *discours* and *histoire* tends consumingly to be regarded as obligatory *a priori* – and a licence of divergence within neocosmic fiction between the respective implications of *discours* and *histoire* which the writer may not only accept but may prize.

The perplexed issue of the integration/non-integration of the 'form and substance' of a text is one of the crucial problems with which this chapter is concerned, and we must take it slowly, *pian piano*. What counts for the moment is that, quite plainly, insofar as a text may *offer* external information, an anti-Realist one (as we've seen) may 'choose' to put it forward as something to be taken not propositionally but representationally, free of any ordering, controlling system. As we've already found in writers from Tolkien, Lewis and White to Robbe-Grillet (and, in other ways, in Sollers), things-as-they-are (*tels quels*) may sometimes be regarded as the matter that matters most. But can our relation to 'things' come to a rest at this point?

There may be in things-in-themselves gratification and wonder for the perceiver. The text may, as Manlove extensively maintains in his analysis of the work of White, Lovecraft, Tolkien, Williams, Peake, Beagle, Lewis and Le Guin, institute "the praise of the identity of things". "In the opinion of Tolkien", for example, "human perception itself can be an evil, in that it enslaves its objects by making them familiar to the point where their identity ceases to be noticed", whereas, as Tolkien himself says, "creative fantasy . . . may open your hoard and let all the locked things fly away like cage-birds. . . . no more yours than they were you" (Manlove, 1983, 155–6). Carpenter's biography of Tolkien as noted by Rogers "stresses Tolkien's attitude of the explorer rather than the inventor: he *finds out* what his new words and strange references mean, as if his material had 'a real extra-mental existence'" (Carpenter, 1977, 72: Rogers, 1980, 65); there are powerful suggestions of this same process in different guises in Pinget, Sollers, Nabokov, Calvino, Robbe-Grillet, Barth and Borges. An anticosmist among these may vehemently reject any association with notions of the marvellous. A neocosmist may with equal conviction reply that the 'magic' of a thing would *be* the capacity it has to assert its uncaptured essence, even aggressively. The very paralysis immanent in wonder – the way it has of arresting the mind – forestalls masterful naturalization whether ponderous or breezy, and leaves the thing unemptied of its intrinsicality, true to its way of being. The neocosmist might therefore argue that when we thus 'let things be' they don't blur into indefinition and thus invalidate our judgement (as the anticosmist may suggest) but instead gain definition by lending substance to our sense of 'difference', and thereby actually reinvigorate our powers of judgement. What's less clear – a question foreshadowed by the language of transcendent experience the neocosmist may invoke (wonder, the marvellous, magic) – is how his/her 'representation' of things-as-they-are can escape the larger implications of his/her cosmic intention. Can 'things be let be' in an authentically representational way, when they are nevertheless deemed to be finally inseparable from some larger, unifying system – from, for example, the cosmos of a Middle Earth, where the central and triumphant intelligence is to be a hobbit? The anticosmist would say: no chance; no way.

But to test the rightness of this we must ask: does the evident orderliness of a story itself inescapably preclude the free transmission of information, of 'things as they are'?

The seemingly excessive, redundant 'circulation of information' typical of Realist fiction is a recurrent issue in contemporary criticism. As we've seen, it serves several intentions at once, and one of these is certainly the Realist text's appearance of referential reliability. Thus Christine Brooke-Rose, writing as a critic, takes a neocosmic work, *The Lord of the Rings* (since we've reopened the case of Tolkien), to task for "the heavy over-determination of the referential and symbolic codes" where the information given "is too clear, over-encoded, recurring beyond purely informational need" (1981, 123, 106). There is a "reduplication of adjuvants" who in turn have no function except "to reveal information" (237–8). She lists a variety of Tolkien's "'hypertrophic' redundancies" – such as his long appendices full of genealogies and the like – which "playfully reflect the author's private professional interest in this particular slice of knowledge, rather than narrative necessity" (247). Though these are not "in the least necessary to the narrative", she points out acerbically, "they have given much infantile happiness to the Tolkien clubs and societies, whose members apparently write to each other in Elvish. . . . Indeed the very maps are over-saturated, with ranges, rivers, regions and sites not mentioned in the narrative" (247–8). Brooke-Rose's thesis is that this 'serious flaw' in Tolkien's trilogy is "used by Tolkien for expansion in the direction of 'realism'" (238). The text is grossly overburdened with "naive and gratuitous intrusions" (terms she uses repeatedly) "from the realistic novel". These she lists at great length: "attempts at the psychology of minor characters", descriptions of "dwarf and elvish characteristics", events that are "so completely unmotivated (marvellous), except by these *a posteriori* political–genealogical considerations, that the reader is uninvolved" (250, 249, 252). The "reduplication of adjuvants" not part of the story's quest "in my opinion . . . seriously weakens the structure"; "the real quest starts at Bree (chapter 10!)" following "much padding"; and "digressions" constituting "megatextual information" are presented throughout "*so that*" the quest may be "delayed" (237, 236, 244–5).

Now a characteristic of Brooke-Rose's position is that she must – and properly does – show that these features extend to other recent fiction. "The circulation of information about the invented world seems to be a real and unsolved problem in SF"; "'cognitive' science fiction . . . has run, if not into a rut, certainly into" similar "difficulties" (101, 256). We're clearly confronted with an aspect of current fiction ('delay', 'digression', 'gratuitous padding') springing from a commitment to an apparent superfluity of information – which, in view of what we're so ceaselessly told is an obsessively efficiency-and-haste-minded reading public, should make it highly unpopular in a way that's massively belied by publishers' figures, as Brooke-Rose's own reference to the Tolkien societies shows. Something else must be going on here.

The nature of the confusion is revealed by Brooke-Rose when she startlingly adduces 'classic' Realist criteria – in her persistent remonstrations that Tolkien blunders in his 'psychology' of 'characters', that he obstructs his quest-story, that the reader is left 'uninvolved' – as the basis for an attack on what she characterizes precisely as the Realist qualities of the work. That she should choose a text statedly "belonging to the marvellous" (245) as an exemplar of Realist procedure is unusual; that she should then express displeasure that this 'Realist' procedure does not in her view work here throws the mind into a spin. Can it be that Tolkien does Realist things "*so that*" (as she says) his Realism will fail? It takes no profound insight to recognize that the bases for the 'failure' (for example of 'involvement') to which she attests are the bases for the text's success for other readers, since she has made the point herself. There are plainly different bases for success in such fiction, one having to do with story (Brooke-Rose's startling criterion) and another having to do with information itself.

In fact, anti-Realist fiction displays – in writers from Calvino and Fuentes to Pynchon – a remarkable fascination with the proliferation of esoteric information. Contemporary readers seem willing to undergo all manner of narrative 'barbarisms' (such as those Brooke-Rose points out in science fiction) for the sake, exactly, of just such exotic amplitude. Why?

Brooke-Rose, elsewhere fiercely astute, is exactly right in that – inasmuch as the quest is the central narrative 'line' in *The Lord of the Rings* – what *The Lord of the Rings* demonstrates is that this adventure is a 'thread' in a fabric whose fuller substance 'overweaves' or 'superscribes' it. The intensive story of a hero and his 'singular' adventures are regularly folded into the progressively expansive network of data making up his world. This is not an argument for any great, subtle or ironic sophistication in Tolkien's fiction (though Brooke-Rose probably too easily – especially as an anti-Realist herself – leaves unassimilated her own observation of his "playful" intent). It is merely a suggestion in favour of what he and our own perception of his work have told us all along and that we oughtn't let our own other kinds of sophistication obscure: that he offers information in support of the "marvellous" composition ("subcreation") of a world. It's not (only) the need for Realistic plausibility (Brooke-Rose's word) that the plenum of information is meant to gratify, but another need. It proposes to amplify and consolidate the text's *cosmic* intention – our sense of the coherent strength of the world-*system* described. The more 'substance' it can 'contain', the more powerful its total superstructure – this argument would say – however 'weakened' the local narrative's structure may be. This cosmic intention is one that neocosmic fiction shares with Realism. What Brooke-Rose fails to note is that it is a *different* one from the intention – the Realist story intention – which she feels is defeated, and one that (as Tolkien's devotees evidently feel) does not conflict with but is necessarily built upon a burden of 'non-narrative' information.[1] (Here is where the word *histoire* as opposed to simply *story* shows its special value.) The book is in this sense an expression of faith in system-seeing beyond storytelling.

But another school of texts will insist on posing 'system-seeing' and the 'pure representation of things as they are' as mutually inimical. Naked representationality can reveal its insensate, rampant side in a deluge of textual manifestations we've not yet considered as a kind, and which by their very nature and intent one is unfitted to recount in any comprehensive detail but can only circumscribe in sum, in a generalized way, as a conflux of strategies and *topoi*.

Sartre has long since announced it, in *Nausée*'s protagonist's remorseless awareness of the 'viscous puddle of existence' that 'floods over', sweeping beyond the rational grasp of consciousness.[2] It remains for anti-Realism to make of it a capital theme. "The blood drains from my head", Molloy thinks, "the noise of things bursting, merging, avoiding one another, assails me on all sides, my eyes search in vain for two things alike, each pinpoint of skin screams a different message, I drown in the spray of phenomena" (Beckett, 1951, 148). "Very likely I have lost my senses", says "Night-Sea Journey's" narrator; "the carnage at our setting out; our decimation by whirlpool, poisoned cataract, sea-convulsion; the panic stampedes, mutinies, slaughters, mass suicides" (Barth, 1968, 9). To remain in life, says the narrator of *Il mare verticale*, "is to walk the smog-streets ... it is the cyclone, the torrent, the cancer that wastes the blood.... Is there a way to stem this whirlpool of facts?"[3] In the face of the plenitude of things-as-they-are, wonder now turns to consternation or panic dismay, to some form of terror.

The issue centres not in the fullness of the information with which experience confronts us, but in the nature of the particular relationship that we establish with it. The crisis is shadowily foretokened in the simple resumé we might put forward for any of several *nouveaux romans*. "Or if there is a cause, it is the whole atmosphere of the ten days, not any specific event or emotion", says Mercier in describing the outcome of Simon's *L'Herbe* [*The Grass*]; "Butor's protagonist", Mercier writes of *La Modification* [*Second Thoughts/A Change of Heart*], "similarly renounces his mistress and decides to stay with his wife, not for any one specific reason, but because of the whole complex of experiences – fatigue included – which makes up his overnight train journey to Rome" (1971, 297–8). Everything, in other words, nothing less than the totality of events, is the cause. There is a deep initial affinity in this with the strategy of Naturalism. If any one trait marks (or mars, as some say) the Naturalist novel, it's our sense of the relentlessness with which it cumulatively heaps the full weight of actuality's data onto the scales on the side of its narrative outcome; *everything* contributes, deterministically, to the heroine's downfall, the hero's suicide. The difference now is that the text's givens seem not 'of a piece' as they so clearly are in the socio-political novel of Naturalism. On the contrary, we can't feel that *anything* in particular is a-building to this clear and inevitable end, for the necessary 'law' or principle (on which determinism rests) is missing; only the sheer weight of pullulating eventuality, the whirling 'vortex of facts' remains, unresolved. Meaning, we too often forget (as critics as much as 'lay humans'), is not merely a product of our integration of data. It is equally a product of our rejection, our suppression of data. Quotidianly, for our very sanity, we ignore as insignificant – as if it weren't there – the vast array of sensations with which we're perpetually bombarded by the bedding, the clothing that wraps us round; it's thanks to this *selective* awareness that we start into violent action at the sensation of a minute insect moving there. The story of the princess and the pea is as much a story of 'normal insentience' as it is of hypersensitivity. Meaning-producing is limit-setting. Our reductive habits of systematic auto-anaesthesia, of partial oblivion in the interests of meaning, is something anti-Realism will actively resist. If it frequently enacts the catastrophe of the 'systems breakdown', it will often do so by invoking that nemesis of systems, the 'informational overload'. Neocosmic fiction is unremitting in developing this as a *topos* at the story level. As early as *A Voyage to Arcturus* it was to emerge as a central motif in the vision of the world of Matterplay, where "every square foot of space was a tangle of struggling wills, both animal and vegetable.... Nature was precipitating its shapes into the world"; its streams have their "source in Faceny", who "eternally contemplates Nothingness" (Lindsay, 1920, 192, 194, 203). In *Grendel*, "the world was nothing: a mechanical chaos of casual, brute enmity"; "the world is all pointless accident" composed of "meaningless objectness ... universal bruteness" (Gardner, 1972, 12, 17). 'Characters' are evolved whose mental states encompass the dilemma. Before a certain afternoon, Borges' anamnesiac Funes "had been what all humans are: blind, deaf, addlebrained, absent-minded.... The truth is that we live our lives putting off all that can be put off"; but now "the present was almost intolerable.... Funes remembered not only every leaf of every tree of every wood, but also every one of the times he had perceived or imagined it. He decided to reduce each of his past days to some seventy thousand memories" only to surrender to his "awareness that the task was interminable" and useless; "he was the solitary and lucid spectator of a multiform, instantaneous" world; "to think is to forget differences, generalize, make abstractions"; Funes succumbs to the "heat and pressure" of this "teeming" reality (Borges, 1964, 63–6). The child–protagonist of Nabokov's story entitled (significantly)

"Signs and Symbols" is the endless prey of "referential mania" who

> imagines that everything happening around him is a veiled reference to his personality and existence.... Phenomenal nature shadows him wherever he goes.... Pebbles or stains or sun flecks form patterns representing in some awful way messages which he must intercept. Everything is a cipher and of everything he is the theme.... He must be always on his guard and devote every minute and module of life to the decoding of the undulation of things.... With distance the torrents of wild scandal increase in volume;... What he really wanted to do was to tear a hole in his world and escape
>
> (Nabokov, 1959, 64–5)

just as Funes, yearning for the peace of sleep, imagines "himself at the bottom of the river, rocked and annihilated by the current". Nescience now finds its counterpart, its consort – not merely its antithesis – in 'total sentience'.

Thus matter, the object of the senses and the 'natural referent' of psychological Realistic literature, becomes the essence of 'what's the matter'. In Calvino's story "La molle luna" the substance of the moon falls to form the substance of continental earth, "a mud of acid mucus which penetrated into the terrestrial strata, or rather a kind of vegetal parasite that absorbed everything it touched, incorporating it into its own gluey pulp, or else like a serum in which colonies of whirling and ravenous micro-organisms were agglomerated, or else ... or else ..."; for an "incalculable amount of time we will be condemned to sink into the lunar discharge, rotten with chlorophyll and gastric juices and dew and nitrogenous gases and cream and tears" (1967, 17–18). At the close of his "Quanto scommettiamo", "now events come flowing down without interruption, like cement being poured ... a doughy mass of events without form or direction, which surrounds, submerges, crushes all reasoning" (1965, 109). But, as Nabokov's "Signs and Symbols" foreshadows and as will come more and more to the fore as the neocosmic vision merges into the anticosmic, 'matter' will begin steadily to lose that very differentiable character by which it had asserted its precedence and prepotent dominion over the 'signs' of which it may seem to have been the progenitor. As Calvino's "Il guidatore notturno" concludes, the 'characters' become a "transformation of ourselves into the messages of ourselves.... Freed finally from the awkward thickness of our persons and voices and moods, reduced to luminous signals.... Each with his meaning that remains hidden and undecipherable because outside of here there is no one capable of receiving us now and understanding us" (1967, 143–4) "In the universe now there was no longer a container and a thing contained", says the narrator of "Un segno nello spazio" at the end, "but only a general thickness of signs superimposed and coagulated, occupying the whole volume of space" (Calvino, 1965, 47–8). The *undifferentiated mass, the sea, the whirlpool, the flood, the morass*, the image of drowning in the '*spray of phenomena*' become urgent motifs. Distinctions between phenomena themselves – 'primary' and 'secondary', 'signified' and 'signifier' – come to be seen as vain and senseless, and what is sometimes referred to as the living or reading experience of 'hypertrophy' (which we might only half-laughingly render here by the pun 'phenomenal growth') becomes an elemental *topos*.

The 'information explosion', then, takes on an essential role at all levels of narrative. 'Copia', that salient strategy of medieval and Renaissance rhetoric – hypostatized by writers in the lineage of Rabelais, Sterne, Melville and Joyce – with its logically 'interminable' catalogues and inventories mimicking the infinite abundance of Creation, now reasserts the complex indissoluble relation between mimesis (copy) and proliferation (copiousness). "Our exemplary fictions", writes Philip Stevick of contemporary 'post-Realist' narrative, "extend themselves in ways that are more additive than dramatic or progressive" (1981, 39). Thus Barth in his defence of his famous 1967 essay on "The literature of exhaustion" can ten years later redefine its subject without hesitation as a "literature of replenishment" (1980); 'exhaustion' had always for him been not only the description of a literary condition but also, simultaneously, the prescription of a literary activity. From the most minute story-moments (Beckett's Watt in his room moves or attempts to move in all the possible directions: 1953a, 203–4) to the global procedures of the writer composing his work ("I was tempted by the diabolical idea", says Calvino of *Il castello dei destini incrociati*, "of conjuring up all the stories that could be contained in a tarot deck"),[4] fiction may seek to 'instantiate' the inordinate nature of experience by the (*nota bene*) systematic production of an avalanche of data. This is the "maximalist" impulse Hassan speaks of when he contrasts the fiction of Nabokov and Pynchon with the "minimalist" texts of Beckett and Borges (Hassan, 1975, 93).

That contrast is relevant, but there's yet another way of seeing the situation, and here the vital word is 'inordinate'. Just as one counter to Realism is to answer its amplitude with parsimony (minimal fiction), another may well be to outdo that amplitude – as Pynchon does – by means not of enigmatic or comic brevity but of supersaturation and ironic *longueur*. But as Joyce reminds us when he lays before us his "allincluding farraginous chronicle", or as Mann does when he tells us that "only the exhaustive is truly interesting", it would be peculiarly hard to say at what point the plenitude of Realism and Modernism stops and that of anti-Realism begins. The real antithesis lies not in the *fact* of fullness of detail on one side or the other, but in the degree of its order/disorder. Realist fiction places itself (or attempts to) between the extreme profusion and the extreme schematization of what's told (the latter as it appears, for example, in fairy tale, parable, the *récit* of a Voltaire or the perfectly *long* but highly allegorically schematic narrative of, say, *The Pilgrim's Progress*). Anti-Realism may thus move toward the latter, as indeed Calvino's tales in *Castello* actually do, or toward the former as Pynchon's *V* does. What *distinguishes V* from a Realist novel in this regard is not merely that it is densely 'informational' (John Stark subtitles his book on Pynchon "The Literature of Information") but that its information seeks to remain unresolved, devoid of systematic closure. As Tanner says of *V*'s two protagonists, Stencil's project is "to find his way through the labyrinth, but in the process he transforms the labyrinth into a useless plethora of clues" and "for Benny Profane there are more signals than significances; he detects no clues anywhere and is a motiveless wanderer ... going nowhere and seeing only separate objects in a disintegrating world" (Tanner, 1982, 42). In principle in the fiction now before us the substance, the 'subject-matter', is offered as raw 'hyle' without (informative) 'entelechy'. As *all substance and no shape*.

In this sense, then, the 'genuine article' of faith (or un-faith), the irreducible *topos*, is not the plenum of data but the *anarchy* of data. Terminology recently in use has to be watched in this light. 'Overdetermination' – an excess of 'solutions', of 'meanings' for a given event – is a favoured strategy in fiction of this sort, in Pynchon and others; but it's only one among many. And 'redundancy' may well seem just the thing we'd expect in what is after all a pleonastic fiction; but in fact here is a literature one of whose fundamental devices is the deliberate *reduction* of redundancy. For the special quality of redundancy, insofar as it's a philosophically useful notion, is that by the iteration in different guises of the same conception aspects of a work's structure can be inferred from other aspects; a schema begins to emerge. The less data is redundant, the *more* it remains unresolved. As Leonard Meyer says, "If a complex structure is completely unredundant – if no aspect of its structure can be inferred from any other – then it is its own simplest description. We can exhibit it but we cannot describe it by a simpler structure". It "'is not to be understood *but only to be demonstrated*'".[5] Without redundancy, every event remains 'novel', a 'foreign particle' literally 'unassimilated' by the body of the text or by external custom; the reader's 'channelling capacity' becomes overloaded, and his/her 'reading matter' spills over in confusion.

Here 'entropy' – a rich associated motif borrowed from thermodynamics, integrated into mathematics and information theory and made popular by criticism following Pynchon, a theory of *processes* whereby the transmission of energy or of data becomes predictably disordered and chaos inevitably ensues – is only one further model within the wider area of thought at hand.[6] As a specifically dynamic and frankly (if 'paradoxically') systematic narrative construct, it poses in fact a scenario, an apocalyptic progressive drama, as both the various technical denotations of the term and the *V* passages cited above readily reveal. While as such it is eminently suited to fiction and unquestionably has its resonance in readings of stories such as those of Calvino mentioned earlier, as well as of Beckett's novels of the 'decomposition' of identity, entropy does not (as many assume) 'mean' chaos and holds no uncontested cachet in the catholic world of anti-cosmic fiction, for instance, where the vision of a more directionless infinite state without beginning or end makes its special appeals.

These considerations nevertheless prepare the way in post-war narrative for the onset of a movement that is instinctively anti-Realist yet whose orientation is in fundamental ways different from those we've discussed so far. It proposes a literature that is nothing if it's not unconditionally and resoundingly referential in its intentions. In its view the welter of the world is too much with us to be a matter for 'pure fiction'; the motif of the wilderness as a fictional place gives way to the *topos* of bewilderment as a mental condition from which no conception of the limits of our reading can save us. With the obliteration of stable distinctions, the narrative writer may now evoke that most central crisis, the disintegration of the boundary between fiction and fact itself. In a universe of spreading crime, mass suicide and mass murder, of the "perplexing fictionality of the 'real'" (Zavarzadeh, 1976, 24) where scientific and technological revolutions appear to burst the seams of everyday probability – this new argument goes – the mere presentation of the plethora of 'facts as they stand' can make of every reader a Funes: a spectator (like the child in Nabokov's "Signs and Symbols" and the narrator of his "Terror") face-to-face with the otherness, the unassimilable alienness of actuality. Open representationality, *chosisme* even, is revitalized. Under a variety of names ("the nonfiction novel", "transfiction", "faction"), narrative now seeks – as described by Zavarzadeh, the critic perhaps most methodically committed to giving it conceptual authority – to be plainly (in the classic, pre-Husserlian sense) "phenomenalistic". Unneedful of radical manipulation at the level of discourse, the text's 'natural referent' – the swarming, unaccustomable incoherence of reality itself – supplies the very substance (and all that the human mind can endure) of estrangement. The reader's attention is 'simply', forcibly riveted upon the 'raw', 'brute' givens of existence, and on the inadequacy of established intellectual and fictional conventions to the task of redeeming them. That writing may be unable to accommodate, to *comprehend* reality becomes the text's most ultimate 'fact', the fact of which the text constitutes its own irrefutable documentary demonstration.

Referentiality now comes on with a vengeance. Where in Realism fictionality had been justified by virtue of the amplificative support it lent to fact, and fact had been adduced to amplify and support the fiction, now fiction and fact are so thrown together as to smother the reader's confidence in either. In texts famous in this respect by writers ranging from Mailer, Tom Wolfe, Oscar Lewis, Castaneda to Barthelme, Barth and Federman – and often borrowing strategies from earlier models as diverse as Breton and Dos Passos – the intention is frankly expressed. Starting often openly with the publicly 'known facts' of his/her own biography (deliberately and irreducibly so imbedded in the fiction of the narrative that their authenticity becomes imbued with an unexpected uncertainty), the explicit 'author' moves progressively outward to embrace concertedly 'stranger-than-fiction facts', above all, which the Realist would have felt most compelled to omit because they'd have undermined the very plausibility and order of his/her *histoire*. Not only 'external *histoires*' but 'external *discours*' (cut-and-pasted '*objets trouvés*', for example, from newspapers, matchboxes, labels) become part of the fabric of the text; the book's discourse merges with the discourse of 'the world at large'; as a 'work of reference', the text asserts that it is not merely an index to reality but a metonymic fragment of it, a collage that is part of the hectic collage of actuality. As a collage, "as Barthelme illustrates" (Stevick tells us), the text "expands so as to seem to include almost everything. New York is a collage. Fiction is a collage" (Stevick, 1981, 20). If the work can no longer be thought capable of 'totalizing' experience by representing it, it may in the avalanche of its information represent that anarchic aspect of totality which makes it untotalizable.

With meaning, value is now called into question. The text may be likened, as it is by Barthelme, to "Harold Rosenberg's 'anxious object,' which does not know whether it's a work of art or a pile of junk" (Bellamy, 1974, 52). *'Junk'*, *'muck'*, *'drek'*, *'excrement'*, *'waste'* – the detritus of culture's frenetic efforts to make sense (and where value is missing, *all* effort lies 'waste') – becomes a compulsive *topos*. The aesthetic underpinnings of Realism – in the systematic scientist's or mathematician's joy over an 'elegant proof' and his or her frankly expressed search for an intuitively 'beautiful solution' – are now overturned: "The real world that science reveals to us is by far superior to the fantastic world created by the imagination", wrote Ernest Renan at the high noon of positivist hopes.

> It is futile to inflate our ideas, to sacrifice the reality of things for the mere fragments we have brought forth.... If the marvels of fiction have always seemed necessary to poetry, the marvels of nature, when revealed in all their splendour, will constitute a poetry a thousand times more sublime, a poetry which will be reality itself, which will be at the same time science and philosophy.[7]

By apparent fiat, by what is superficially nothing more than a reversal of taste (though in truth it contains the rejection of the deeper systematic theory underlying the positivist's 'tastes'), what was potentially comely to the Realist is (also) garbage to the new referentialist. Experience may contain provisional charms. But the cumulative representation of 'nature' and its signs, of 'the reality of things' whether attractive or repugnant by any intermediate standards, constitutes now an accretion of 'refuse' and borders logically always on an act of *refus*.

Two observations seem indispensable at this point concerning exactly how we are to read, where we are to 'situate' such texts in the continuum between 'fiction' and 'reality'.

One is often reminded – both by the apparent tonality of 'inordinately referential' fiction (particularly when written by Americans, perhaps by reason of the especially pragmatic intentionality they affect or we attribute to them) and by those writing *about* such fiction – that its strategies have marked affinities with those in the great western tradition of parody and satire. Inconsistencies, contradictions, irreconcilables within culture itself are perennially drawn into the foreground by the exoticization of the normal and the normalization of the exotic.[8] But we need to keep alert to the fact that both satire and parody may be seen by the anti-Realist precisely as the easy and perhaps exhausted conventions of philosophically more optimistic and credulous times. And that, when they now arise, the devices of a Voltaire or a Swift cannot be taken as prima facie evidence that – as with Voltaire and Swift – reorientations in ethical or political attitudes, for example, are offered as solutions to the kinds of crises the writer has in mind. Satiric and parodic modes as traditionally structured (with their routine and often mechanical rhetoric of inversion, hyperbole, litotes and so forth) are themselves likely to become increasingly the eminently vulnerable targets of attack for a literature whose endemic enemies are just such routinely complacent and mechanistic patterns of thought. There are few sharper examples of the utility of the distinction we now make between 'motivation' as a formative principle organizing the utterances within a text and the more traditional 'motivation' as some finalistic intentional impulse behind a text. For all his or her apparent laughter, the anti-Realist may be whispering 'Beware!'

A second caveat is that, if even satire may not be the unifying 'metatextual' intention of such seemingly radical representationalist narratives, it's possible that the latter may not always seek – or hope – to 'lose itself' so thoroughly in the undifferentiated maelstrom of data that assails us as might have been thought. "The phenomenalistic use of fact in narrative", Zavarzadeh persistently insists, is "transcriptive, anti-symbolic, and purely literal.... The nonfiction novelist merely registers facts without the accompaniment of an interpretive pattern". "The nonfiction novel replaces 'interpretation' with a 'transcription' of naked facts" (1976, 65–6, 224). We know the neocosmist's and anticosmist's answer to this: the text's act of accretion itself, if nothing else, produces something that is none of those things which it pretends to 'transcribe'. Thus *whatever* it is, the text interposes something new between us and our other apprehensions of reality; and this may indeed be one of its latent aims. Recent transatlantic fiction in English of an avowedly representational ('phenomenalistic') sort may pose not so much a description as a *counter-description* – an answer to life, not in the sense of a solution but in the sense of a substitution, a reply in kind whose inescapable restatement of things-as-they-are sets the scene, an invented locus, a 'buffer-zone', for a new transaction with life.[9] The burden of this remark is not so much to celebrate the mode as to indicate that the limitations attaching inevitably to referential claims put it closer to Realism than its advocates would make out. And that, oddly enough, from an anticosmic perspective at least, it shares in a backward way something of the aspect of neocosmic narrative, where *symbolism* appears often on offer as the mediating nexus between the publicly assumed-to-be-known and the privately conceived-to-be-known. Put another way, the anticosmist might regard each of these modes as just a bit too much to the left or the right of the ideal: the 'phenomenalist' ensnared on the fictitious side of its referents, the neocosmist on the referential side of pure fiction.

With 'substance-centred' phenomenalist fiction, where the 'matter' of existence significantly resembles Calvino's 'gurduluvian soup' (as if smelted into some 'fourth state' of 'plasmic' in-difference – to borrow the physicist's metaphor – in the crucible of everyday actuality), we are in one of the several borderlands between anti-Realism and Realism. In the most literal sense, in its repugnance for (or nostalgic farewell to) systems, it would be anticosmic. What divides it from both much neocosmic and most anticosmic fiction are these: at the level of *histoire*, here what is 'given' is (all too) evident; it is in the technical but crucial sense always already there. What is not evident about the 'given' is only what to make of it. While the mode is clearly anti-positivist, the acceptance of the empirical modality is essential to it. The sense data of the phenomenal world are – far from being less or more than we can know or be sure of – all that we can know. And at the level of discourse, for it to perform its very function it is incumbent upon its language to make clear – declaratively transparent – that these apocalyptic givens are authentic and 'real'. As even its most complicated virtuosi – a Pynchon, a Barthelme – go to great lengths to make it seem, it is not the fault of the writer but of natural ('entropic', say) actuality that the human mind is under threat. The gestures on the part of a Barthelme, for example, in the direction of the uncustomary perturbation of *discourse* have regularly a desultory quality, like Lem's, suggesting that the writer has already ruminated and now lyric-sardonically regurgitates its strategies as but another permutation of liberal-chicultural dreck.

This last mentioned, sophisticated, not merely metatextual but essentially ethological, 'metaliterary' perspective has much to be said for it, and the texts it engenders find strong favour among many followers of narrative innovation. Yet while traces of its procedures show up in the work of, for instance, Federman, Barth and Sollers, it serves as evidence that not all innovative fiction is guaranteed to be welcomed in the 'inner circles' of anti-Realist 'Theory', for reasons that are plain. Narrative whose accent is on the inundative welter of information external to it can be entertaining and often deeply 'moving' – so long as it keeps one step ahead of its readers' capacity for synthesis. But, as anti-Realists try to show in a multiplicity of ways, we become swiftly innured to merely pragmatic diversity and glut. In this regard, such literature is prone to being viewed as – literally – unchallenging. So long as our faith in our *senses* and in *language* are left thus undisturbed, our powers of recuperation and 'accustomization' are quick and powerful indeed. Too much so, the sustained anti-Realist may say.

'Non-referential' anti-Realism

Against the view that narrative means to tell us of the world outside it, theories persist with equal vigour to assert that it does not – that literature neither describes always-already-there facts, nor expresses some constant paraphrasable attitude on the part of its author, nor figuratively intimates systems of meaning beyond the text. What I'm going to suggest is that behind this there lies yet another larger conception, a perennial and more all-embracing bipolar model in western culture for distinguishing between the ways in which we organize our understanding. More than simply asking us to consider whether any particular utterance 'actually refers outward' or not, it poses the questions: when we look for truth, do we ever look outward, beyond the limits of language itself? and should any text ever even *invite or entertain* the activity of looking outward beyond itself?

Here is one of the most suspicious areas within this book – if not in literature itself. The distinction I have in mind comes as a functional notion and as a set of fixed categories of texts; as a description not of absolute textual achievements but of an ideational predisposition informing the way texts behave and are talked about. If we need some useful prop to keep our minds open for the moment, this would be that such a model is demonstrably irresistible to many anti-Realist writers and their respective supporters, though it may but rarely be put succinctly before us by them in the same terms.

Referential fiction can in a special but philosophically essential sense be called 'synthetic', as opposed to a fiction that may be 'analytic', in its attitude. I'm not now speaking of synthesis as we commonly use the word when we talk of say a 'cultural synthesis' or of the synthesis of ideas; nor am I speaking of (vaguely) 'examination' or 'dissection' or 'interpretation', as we frequently do when we use the word analysis. Freely put, synthesis does not now mean 'unifying' or 'homogenizing' but means literally 'bringing together' information (which *may* eventually form a 'truth') from diverse realms of experience – from the spheres not only of deductive reasoning but also from material observation, psychological intuition, ethical apprehension, metaphysical revelation, aesthetic perception, and so forth.[10] Analysis, in this view, works contrarily to gain information by interrogating the 'intrinsic' meaning and 'meaningfulness' – independent of the contingencies of external experience – of ideas, of the formal properties of a given language. A feeling for this discrimination can be had from traditional expressions such as the following, put forward by C. S. Peirce, a scientist and logician forcefully resurrected for other but closely related reasons by contemporary linguistic and literary theorists whose ideas are central to anti-Realist programmes we've been discussing: "All our reasonings are of two kinds: 1. *Explicative, analytic*, or *deductive*; 2. *Amplificative, synthetic*, or (loosely speaking) *inductive*."[11]

This needs some illustration. A statement classically advanced as an example of an analytic utterance is: 'All men are mortal.' Its truth seems inherent in the customary meaning of its terms (men are *by definition* mortal), and when one says 'All men are mortal, Socrates is a man, therefore Socrates is mortal' one has learned something about Socrates by a process of reasoning that is, we traditionally say, purely analytical. In contrast, examples of synthetic utterances of the classic sort would be 'All men are idealists' or 'All men are androgynous.' The customary definitions of their terms do not provide a warranty for the truth of these statements, and to establish their truth one would have to make use of evidence from outside these definitions, by reference to experience in the (given) world.

Now, we can *read* the analytic statement as synthetic. We can say that by the evidence of our experience 'Christ' is 'immortal', or 'Shakespeare' or 'Kilroy' – and so 'all men are mortal' loses what we had thought was analytic proof of its truth. That is, we can set aside the customary definition of 'mortality' (which depended on our taking a materialist – for example, biological – view), by interpreting the statement *metaphorically* or in some other 'non-standard' (for example metaphysical or aesthetic) way. By like token, we can *read* a synthetic statement as an analytic one. All men are 'idealists', we may say, in their insistence on living as though they weren't mortal, all men are androgynous in the complexity of their physiques or their behaviour. We – again – have carried this out by interpreting a statement metaphorically or according to some more uncustomary (for example, some special philosophical or psychological) frame of reference. There is no doubt but that as readers we have a great deal of power in these ways, and we're frequently predisposed to use it, in our compulsive search for some 'recuperation' of the text that will bring it comfortably into line with our own most normal habits of thought. And why not? What harm can there be in our doing so?

It's not my purpose to argue the long philosophical history or present validity or invalidity of the analytic/synthetic paradigm. It's simply to say that different strains within anti-Realist fiction will tend to make appeal to one or the other of these reading norms and we'll miss much of what's being attempted – what's going on – if we don't see it. Two things emerged in the preceding paragraph. First, that the distinction between analysis and synthesis is potentially an unstable, 'unreal' one. And second, that the fictionalist may find a deep vested interest in preserving its stability, its 'reality' in our minds, just as – when the corresponding radicalization of music was taking place – it was of concern to the composer Stravinsky (as musicologists will describe) to organize his perception of his own work's operation in terms of that of composers whom he viewed as "analytic" (Webern) and "synthetic" (Berg).[12].

There's no question but that 'representational' fiction of the sort we've considered in the previous section depends massively on our apprehension that it is synthetic. On our momentary belief, that is, that the terms by which we've until now defined our reality are set at odds by the 'new evidence' which it 'brings in' of the nature of the external world. That either the text is senseless double-talk judged by our customary terms of signification, or it is bringing to light experiential information which could not have been predicted by simple analysis of those terms as we customarily use them. But this is far from being a feature only of fiction whose intention is explicitly representational. We find that the synthetic premiss is fundamental to much if not all neocosmic narrative. Calvino's story "La distanza dell Luna" ["The Distance of the moon", 1965] *becomes* neo-cosmic at the moment its narrator – borrowing the entirely customary form of utterance 'I swam furiously through the water' – says instead "I swam furiously through the sky" (15). Without claiming in any immediately discernible way to be referential, the text has produced 'seriously' a piece of 'information' which no definition of "I", "swam furiously", or "sky" could analytically have provided – that is, that here is an 'already there (prior to the utterance) world' in which 'early terrestrial beings' can swim in space. This is of decisive importance. Neocosmic fiction insists that it is not to be read in the first instance according to any procedure that might remove it from the realm of standard, customary interpretation. We are free 'later' to take it metaphorically or in any other manner we like, but in the 'first reading' it means to be taken *prima facie*, literally, *au pied de la lettre*. Its 'first order' assertions are to be 'taken as read'. Borges's "El inmortal", if we do not take it in that way, stands as gibberish from the outset; as soon as we found the terms "men" and "immortals" applied to the same entities in the story, we'd be in no position to be able to make sense of the events that take place in it at the literal *or* at any metaphorical/ allegorical level. (No allegory concerning 'men who live forever' can begin to operate until we have accepted that in the narrative where it's to operate men do live forever.) The same applies to Borges' "Tlön", to Le Guin's *Left Hand of Darkness* – where 'characters' deny time or procreate with others of their own sex because they are constitutionally 'idealists' or 'androgynes' – and to a vast number of other neocosmic fictions. If in any way we 'stop too soon' and say with any 'seriousness' that analytically, by definition, men simply cannot live forever or be *really* idealists or androgynes, we call a halt to thinking about the narrative as a narrative altogether, figuratively or in any other concerted way. Such texts *function* narratively by virtue of their requiring us to 'take seriously' data – as if it had empirically-confirmed truth in its given 'world' – which customary analytic definitions of the language used would not include.[13]

Mightn't we argue, to the contrary, that this information has been offered as a set of new 'analytic' definitions, befitting the new world described? The point is that in such narratives data is expounded as if it were part of a description of a world that has these features not because the text by linguistic fiat wills it to do so, but because for the duration of our reading it 'really exists', in exactly the way that the world of a representational text is expounded as existing, prior to the text's description of it. The discourse is in the mimetic mode, and the *histoire* is characterized by its iteration of scenes of exploration and discovery belonging to the language of empirical (synthetic) disclosure. The rhetoric of analytic fiction, on the other side (as we'll see), habitually implies 'If you look more closely you'll find that word X also really means Y (and perhaps also Z)', whereas in the stories just mentioned it implies 'If you visited world X you would find that it contained Y and Z.' In the terms of synthetically-disposed fiction, during its course the attributes of the world described may be recounted by the narrator (or indeed by us) in a variety of ways linguistically without this discourse's altering the world's 'substantive nature'. Its posture is not that of reiteration or clarification or redefinition of what we say but of addition to what we 'know'.

Thus many narratives of different kinds, both referential and far from explicitly referential, adopt the synthetic posture for reasons having to do with the individual natures of their enterprises, just as others will eventually adopt an analytic posture for their own special reasons.[14]

But what kinds of intentions might lie behind such postures? Where we speak of 'synthetically-inclined' fiction, the notion 'given world' as phrased above – as contrasted with 'the world' outside the text – is of vital importance. With regard to neocosmic fiction, what's happening is that the text *mimics* – it *uses the devices* of – referentiality to delineate *some* world without necessarily intending actual referentiality. Here is where it becomes plain that questions of referentiality/non-referentiality and questions of syntheticity/analyticity are not the same and will be viewed as such only at considerable cost to our understanding. In the former pair the concern is to make use/not make use visibly of data external to the text, on the *assumption* that such data reveal useful truths about the world/do not usefully reveal truths about the world. Referential texts profess positively to be giving such truths, while non-referential ones do not. When, on the other hand, writers (or their texts) evince a concern with the difference between synthesis and analysis (which is actually a concern for the problem of truth value), they are in fact not merely (or not even) *giving truths* but are engaging with the question as to *what function* fiction is to perform *in relation to truth*.

In Calvino's "Il conte de Monte Cristo" this question is joined and illustrated with striking though artful directness. Edmond Dantès and the abbé Faria are imprisoned in the Chateau d'If. Faria tunnels ceaselessly in infinite directions throughout the fortress, pragmatically, empirically feeling for an exit; Dantès sits still in his cell constructing hypotheses as to what the ideal fortress's design logically would be, which – when finally conceived – would by contrast yield the real fortress's inbuilt 'way out'. There are copious variations on this *topos* by Calvino, Barth, Borges, Nabokov and others. The difference between 'deductive' and 'inductive' modes of thinking becomes the basis for an elemental distinction between kinds of narrative and their respective intentions. This distinction we can now see when we compare, for example, Rühm's text:

leafleafleafleafleafleafleafleafleaflea

with those, say, of Lindsay's *Arcturus* or McElroy's *Plus* where the protagonist in each case grows a new limb. In the Rühm (enacting Dantès' mode), a flea grows out of a leaf by a transformation of the language itself. In the Lindsay and McElroy (Faria's mode), the transformation is the product of *other*, *outside* principles altogether (and a different one in each text, we note), ones belonging to the nature of the worlds which the language only 'neutrally' describes and which no analysis of language – of the 'logical nature of fortresses' – might have predicted or explained. Neither the Lindsay nor the McElroy need be taken as giving us information about *the actual world*, but both are *dramatizing the process* (their protagonists' uncovering the forces at work in their worlds) of gleaning and assembling such information. A text that evokes a synthetic stance may thus be arguing that the *activity* of 'bringing in' external phenomena is powerfully relevent and worthwhile, *whether the text itself brings in 'real phenomena' or not*. To 'read' a text with synthetic 'motivation' as an analytic text – to allege that its assertions are not telling us something about 'a world' but are simply respecifying, redefining the meanings of ideas, of words – may be to mistake the most vital recommendation the text has to make and for which the text itself means to be a model: That while an analytic statement ('All men are mortal') may have the unmistakable advantage of containing, as the philosopher may say, a logically 'necessary' truth and a synthetic one may not ('Water boils at 100° centigrade', 'Men die in war'), the latter's information often nevertheless appears true, not to say useful. Our survival would be impossible were we to ignore all such 'non-analytically-necessary', non-self-evident sources of information. The synthetic approach would seem to suggest that the most fruitful human thinking activity may be the one that is *heterogeneous* (or, more accurately, heterogenous) *in its reference*, and *'amplificative' in its aim*. That, put another way, the best part of human awareness resides not in the reassessment of what its discourse contains but in the discovery of what, if anything, is other than it and that lies beyond it.

Peculiarly, seen in this light it is neocosmic literature that opens the possibility of indeterminism – of our being persuaded, if we're not careful, of the truth of everything and anything. It may be that its very tendency, further, towards systematicity is its spontaneous pragmatic response to our nervous intuition of this. (The freer the paradigmatic axis, the more rigid the syntagmatic.)

But even without or before its calling forth our sense of the indeterminacy of experience an energetic alternative tradition exists whose argument is that the attitude we've described is naive. And that (to look at matters from the other side) to attribute *synthetic* intentions to a literary work – for example, to assign it either actual referential meaning *or* pro-referential motivation – is to dismiss literature's whole rationale and *raison d'être*.

It's indispensable here that, from the start, we see that while the conception of the analytic/synthetic dichotomy springs historically from a search for ways of coming to grips with truth, now (again as a historical phenomenon) it is appropriated by many for purposes that may leave questions of truth to one side. We'll find anti-Realist writers vigorously echoing the philosophical tenet that "truth remains essentially a property of linguistic expressions – sentences and theories".[15] But, while the synthetic attitude at some point necessitates the inclusion of analytic understandings in its effort towards truth, the adoption of the paradigm by *analytically*-predisposed writers is by its very nature likely to disavow an explicit interest in matters of truth, since these seem perpetually to engage us in just those preoccupations from which they may wish to dissociate themselves. Truth is 'about' what 'life is like', and the artist may desire to convince us that the essential definition of art is that (as philosophers themselves, from Kant and Hegel to Kierkegaard, seem often to say) it makes no claims on us as life does, that it is in some way free of life's standards of judgement with values of its own. Hassan (borrowing from Elizabeth Sewell) describes mid-century avant-garde literature as falling into two categories: the 'language of nightmare', "that of confusion and multiple reference; it creates a world in which all is necessary, all significant; everything is there at once", and the 'language of number', which "empties the mind of reference; it creates a world of pure and arbitrary order; nothing there is out of place".[16] Whether or not one accepts wholeheartedly these descriptions, there are aspects in the first that coincide with a conception of synthetic fiction. It's no accident that the second alludes to a kinship between, on one hand, a kind of fictional intention which we can readily redescribe as analytic, and, on another, 'number' which we normally associate with a mathematical intention. "Mathematical creation", as classically depicted by Poincaré, a 'role-model' for generations of mathematicians, "is the activity in which the human mind seems to take least from the outside world, in which it acts or seems to act only of itself and on itself".[17]

We have seen this latter strain of thought running through anti-Realist theory from the beginning, whether it's Robbe-Grillet's or Borges' or Sollers' uses of geometrical and arithmetical patterns of discourse that we look to or Lewis's or Calvino's or Nabokov's fascination with autonomous literary design as a whole. The problem of the analytic attitude lies before us. One can as a matter of course imagine that fiction with a synthetic orientation – acting, say, neocosmically – may work toward new, uncustomary conjunctions of 'data' to facilitate and extend some one of the functions of mind (combinative, play, conditioning, prospective, instructive, commutative) to encompass experiences before which 'natural language' is inadequate. And that an analytic fiction – particularly in the guise of anticosmic narrative – may seek to put that same 'natural language' to the test of internal analysis. But the matter goes well beyond this. Synthetic fiction may place much the kind of value we traditionally do on our experience of the 'extra-linguistic' world and the heterogeneous bases for our knowledge of it. But any literature of radical analytical disposition will tend to attribute a priority to the utterance itself that far exceeds our habit (whatever our actual life-style). In supreme contrast to representational fiction, the text may wish to become '*all shape and no substance*'.

Arising now with the analytic conception of literature as utterance first and foremost, there are at least two consuming prospects that come to prepossess many anti-Realist fictionalists. One is the idea of narrative as an autonomous voice, a seamless narration, something approaching pure language. The other is the idea of narrative as an autonomous artefact, semantically silent, something approaching pure form.

It's plain that for the time being we've shifted our angle of perspective. In past discussions we've seen anti-Realist fiction as clustering around two fairly distinct notions of what is 'right' in the way of *narrative structure* (analogous in important ways to parallel 'world-views' or notions of the structure of human experience), the one systematic, neocosmic, the other non-systematic, anticosmic. We're now obliged to consider that when it comes to how anti-Realist texts *wish to be read*, to be 'taken', for synthetic or for analytic value, in principle either kind of *structure* may at the start be regarded as equally viable. As the diversity of the preceding examples shows, anticosmic fiction may be largely synthetically *or* analytically motivated, and the same can be said of neocosmic fiction. The radicalization of attitudes toward narrative as a systematic thing has come to coincide with the radicalization of standard attitudes toward narrative as a source of non-literary, non-linguistic information. Out of this conflux of different but related concerns the rapid evolution of anticosmic fiction has provoked fresh, vigorous and stark conceptions of reading and writing as analytic activities, as we'll see.

The idea of pure narration

It's become a commonplace observation in discussions of myth and folklore as the 'primordial' forms of narrative that one of their most prevalent motifs is the dramatization of the power of "the word" itself as a – if not *the* – source of creation. In the beginning was the Word. The evidence for the near-'universality' of the mythological *topos* of the Logos as formative principle, of the *act of naming* as an act of creating, is stunning. The gods bring about the ordered array of the celestial and terrestrial bodies and their respective powers by uttering their names, and the people of the earth partake of these forces, in the recitation of their myths and genealogies, by the ritual repetition of those names. When in Genesis, at Babel, humans hubristically conceive that "nothing will be restrained from them, which they have imagined to do", they say "let us make us a name"; and the punishment for their presumption is that their language will be confounded (Genesis, 11:4–7). The notion of the power of the word doesn't die with the emergence of Christianity,[18] and is by no means relegated in historical times solely to the dark corner of the necromancer's incantation or of horror movies. A reasonable proportion of Western civilization's repeated attributions of incantive, talismanic or prophetic powers specifically to writers – to the Poet – contains unmistakable and eloquent traces of this residual, or continuing belief.

The striking thing for the rationalist will be that where in fiction explicit supernaturalism may seem to have abandoned the field, the dream of the potency of utterance fails to relinquish its ground. We might well expect that Williams' *The Place of the Lion* could come to its resolution in a closing chapter called "The naming of the beasts" –

> She was aware then that the forest all around was in movement; living creatures showed themselves on its edge. . . . By the names that were the Ideas he called them, and the Ideas who are the Principle of everlasting creation heard him. . . .
>
> They were returning, summoned by the authority of man from their incursion into the world of man. . . .
>
> The sound of her name still echoed through her spirit when . . . she looked again upon the glade of the garden where the image of Adam named the beasts, and naming ruled them.[19]

– for Williams is avowedly a theological fictionalist. We may even think that there lies within Le Guin's *The Wizard of Earthsea* some mystical impulse – though she might declare it to express a *psychological* insight – when we find that the story of the protagonist's growth and achievement of mastery is in large part the story of his coming to perceive that each person, place and thing has 'a true name distinct from its name in ordinary human language', and of his learning these names.[20] But if the case of Le Guin isn't already problematical, further difficulties arise when we consider Gardner's *Grendel*, where the promise of a metaphysical order is expressly denied, and where the 'Destroyer's' antagonist is not Beowulf (who appears, anonymously, only at the last moment) but – once again – the poet, the harper, significantly called the Shaper: "the pride of creation", who "built [Hrothgar's] hall by the power of his songs: created with casual words its grave mor(t)ality", and who "had changed the world, had torn up the past by its thick, gnarled roots and transmuted it" (Gardner, 1972, 28–30). A superficial irony of literary history is that the further fiction 'advances' – so long as it's taken as an advance (as it is by anti-Realists) that it moves away from Naturalism (just as Naturalism had moved away from 'supernaturalism') and towards the idea of narrative as a 'self-begetting' thing – the more it's inclined to acclaim the supra-natural puissance of words.[21] The account given by Tolkien of the moment of inception of his mammoth neocosmic work on 'Middle-Earth' would seem astonishingly offhand and out-of-joint if we didn't know of his (like many recent writers') obsessive proclivities along these lines. As an examiner he encountered a student's page left blank "and I wrote on it; '*In a hole in the ground there lived a hobbit.*' Names always generate a story in my mind. Eventually I thought I'd better find out what hobbits were like".[22] Fictions by Borges, Calvino, Nabokov and Lem are littered with candidly 'word-centred universes'.[23] On the other side, Pinget's transitionally neocosmic *Graal Flibuste* is a 'free' demonstration of the process at work within the text itself, concertedly giving over much of its bulk to the *loci classici* of myths of creation, such as its vast newly-coined genealogies and inventories of flora and fauna springing into being on the page, as we've already noted, by means of linguistic transformations. The process expands until in *Mahu* we find a fiction composed of a collecton of set-pieces in which, for example, a chapter is actually the 'story' of a name as if it were a 'character' (17), a chapter that's the story of an adjective (12), a chapter that's the story of an idiom (13). . . .[24] "A book", says Sollers, "is a Name – in capitals – in the act of naming" (1981b, 204). As the logical negative counterpart to the positive *topos* of creative naming, the *terror* of 'the *un*namable' is not an invention of Pinget's mentor Beckett, but only reaches one of its climaxes – foreshadowed by MacDonald, Bulwer-Lytton, Poe, Maupassant and others – in his work, just as it strains towards another climax in the work of Lovecraft.[25]

As in no other literature before Modernism, and in quantifiably marked and new ways unmanifested in Modernism, in anti-Realist fiction the act of writing and the *interaction between written texts* (as though these constituted the primary reality) are tenacious *topoi*. Not only do narrators or central figures persistently appear (as they indeed do in Modernist fiction) as writers or storytellers – in for example Mauriac, Barth, Sollers, Pinget, Calvino, Borges, Federman, Nabokov, Vonnegut, Saviane, Biraghi – but the actions and impedimenta of the business of narrating become intrinsic narrative furniture. (We recall, for a start, the incessant attention given to the manipulation of paper, ink, tape-recording, and so forth, in texts by Sollers, Barth, Federman, Cortázar, Calvino, Brooke-Rose.) But this is only the beginning. The emphasis on actively 'scriptive' as distinguished from the 'passively descriptive' experience leads to the notion of the '*textual*' aspect of experience itself. The oscillation of focus between 'this' written text and 'those outside, pre-existent realities' that turn out only to be *other written texts* – between present creations and the nomination of earlier creations – becomes a tireless *topos* far exceeding the traditional limits of mere literary allusion. (Seemingly extreme cases in stories by, say, Borges, Calvino and Fuentes, where principal 'characters' are 'in fact' Don Juan or Don Quixote, give way to determinedly intertextual narratives by, for example, Sollers, where it is deliberately made difficult to discover what is *not* an appropriation from some other piece of writing.) And, more provocatively still, forming a further *topos*, narratives explicitly vacillate between 'representations' of events and '*representations' of the representation of events* – so that, for instance (and perhaps only the simplest illustrations of the practice), the magus in *Terra nostra* "was paper. Always he was paper, either a hero or an author of paper", while the writer Brother Julian declares that "only what is written is real" (Fuentes, 1975, 771), and in the "dough of the void" of Calvino's "La forma dello spazio" ["The form of space", 1965] 'characters' ('people') are made pliant to the 'characters' ('letters') of the text, so that the narrator "could seize" Ursula H'x "by the hair and bend her against a *d* or *t* just as I write them now, in haste, bent, so you can recline against them".[26]

We are, of course, talking about language as a centre of human experience. It's not enough now even to say that for an anti-Realist, whether it be a Pinget or a Nabokov or a Tolkien – as critics have often said of the latter – "language was his field of interest: languages and language" (Rogers, 1980, 41). The premiss is that the matter exceeds the bounds of personal predilection. "How can you escape from language . . . how can you escape, even if only for a single time, even if only from the word KNIFE?" says Le Clézio; "our knowledge is perfected only by language" (Cagnon, 1981, 218–19). Nabokov, his exegetes often point out, "argues again and again that reality is purely linguistic" (Stark, 1974, 101). Anticosmists will have a deep-seated modern philosophical tradition to appeal to for authority, as Federman in a typical passage shows: "*The limits of my world*, writes Wittgenstein, are the limits of my language. what [*sic*] cannot be said cannot have meaning".[27] The idea, contrary to current opinion, is not a new one. "If I must sum up on the subject, we shall find that nothing done with intelligence is done without speech, but speech is the marshal of all actions and of thoughts", Isocrates wrote.[28] For him, speech was the basis of civilization. To master utterance via rhetoric was to engage in the promulgation of harmony and order, and to control all learning. There are important practical historical reasons for citizens of fourth-century Athens to have held to such a conception. When recent arguments closely affined to those of anti-Realism insist that western culture ever since has erroneously persisted in logocentrism (where Logos is tacitly held at some level to be the rational principle behind the shaping of reality – with the very modes by which reality was approached themselves called '-ologies'), they appear not less but further to accentuate in their own right the power of language to sweep away its own errors. It may be no matter of chance that recent literary and philosophical thought – inundating library shelves with texts in which efforts towards human understanding are offered under the headings 'A Grammar of', 'A Rhetoric of' – should have resurrected the conviction that who can discover a systematic means for the comprehension of the operations of language might be best placed to regain some governance of the human condition.

When anti-Realist theorists make appeal, as they tirelessly do, to the Wittgensteinian 'The limits of my world are the limits of my language, what cannot be said cannot have meaning', on the surface at least this is done not in a spirit of faith but typically, rather, in an attitude of often anguished scepticism. The thrust of it is clear. In analysing cultural codes affecting clothing and food, Barthes argues that these – appearing in language as "signifiers (in the form of nomenclature)" – in fact name "their signifieds (in the forms of usages or reasons)"; "it appears increasingly more difficult to conceive of a system of images and objects whose *signifieds* can exist independently of language" (1964a, 10). That the notion of the priority of language raises – if it does not beg – serious questions is a problem buried within the more obvious and unquestionable fact that it is indeed difficult to *talk* about thought(s) without using language.[29] "'To think'", says Sollers, quoting Mallarmé, "'is to write without accessories'. . . . In the last analysis, we are only our system of reading/writing" (1968b, 72). The effects of this postulate will be enormous.

If all human thought is manipulated by or contained within language, then – since language is a system of conventions – we are all caught in our very thinking within the trap, the web, of the received perceptions of some society. ("THE NOVEL IS THE WAY THIS SOCIETY SPEAKS TO ITSELF", Sollers reminds us.) The more 'transparent' we think our language to be, the more this is so.[30] A vital correlative of this outlook is foreseeable. As with most literary movements-in-revolt, anti-Realist theory approaches its problem (this time the problem of language) with a language of its own that seems deeply tinged by the rhetoric we associate with phobias of domination. Culture uses language to advance the tyranny of the elite,[31] the tyranny of fixed attitudes,[32] the tyranny of history,[33] the tyranny of meaning.[34] It is indeed difficult to find language-centred anti-Realist argument that is free of *this* vocabulary.

Here is actually a fundamental article on which Realism founds its own distinctive status as against its opponents'. In his attack on the *nouveau roman*, J. P. Stern categorically declares that "a realism composed of nothing but language-conscious fictions is an impossibility, albeit a fashionable one" (1973, 85). But the opposition remains equally uncompromising: "Realism, here", says Barthes, "cannot be the copy of things, therefore, but the knowledge of language; the most 'realistic' work will not be the one which 'paints' reality, but which . . . will explore as profoundly as possible the *unreal reality* of language" (1964b, 160). Language becomes the 'subject' of literature. The novel of the future, as Federman sees it, 'will create a kind of writing, a kind of discourse whose shape will be an interrogation, an endless interrogation of what it is doing while it is doing it" (1981, 11). Writing's project now "is not the mirroring of some 'Reality'," as Stephen Heath puts it, "but an attention to the forms of intelligibility in which the real is produced, a dramatization of possibilities of language, forms of articulation, limitations, of its own horizon" (1972, 22).

But if the vision is to hold, narrative must now operate in a different, new way. If the effort to disclose a pre-existing reality behind the text's language is to be laid aside, so must be the effort to disclose a pre-existing author. The work is not the 'product' of a characterizable person – whose personal nature and intentions it is for us to discover if we're to 'understand' the work – but the product of language itself, and of our reading of it. "Once the Author is gone", writes Barthes, "the claim to 'decipher' a text becomes quite useless. To give an Author to a text is to impose upon the text a stop clause, to furnish it with a final signification, to close the writing".[35] "An author", Sollers tells us, "is not really the cause of what he writes but its product" (1968b, 66).

We can see this coming, in Beckett's *The Unnamable*: "All these Murphys, Molloys and Malones do not fool me. They have made me waste my time, suffer for nothing, speak of them when, in order to stop speaking, I should have spoken of me and me alone. . . . The tittle I thought I could put from me, in order to witness it. Let them be gone now. . . . There, now there is no one here but me . . . these creatures have never been, only I and this black void have ever been" (1953a, 421). Such passages at first seem essentially lyric expressions, verging on the solipsistic yet personally characterizable in the Modernist vein, expressions to be interpreted by means of those specialized critical skills of *psychological* reconstruction brought historically (and significantly) to the fore simultaneously with Modernism itself. Indeed, we find Sollers' narrative voice in *Lois* saying of its discourse: "It's an instantaneous association"; and we may well feel that we recognize here the appeal to psychologically-based rules of verbal production to which Joyce was so committed. But (in spite of the impact we know Joyce to have had on Sollers) we would in this view be wrong; Sollers means precisely to have left that Modernism behind. If the character of 'real characters' is to be renounced, so must be that of 'narrators'. The Sollers narrative goes on immediately to say, "I have as a base only my own nullity", and it is the nullity that Beckett's voice, too, seeks.[36] The idea of a narrat*or*, understood in a psychological mode, is itself refused, and the 'associational' process referred to is increasingly to be that of the continuous unfolding of 'impersonal' language alone.

Seen in the context of time, then, a narrative considered in this way suspends all interest in the external past and the external future. That is, it repels our thinking about it 'genetically' – our looking into its 'depths' to discern its 'real sources', its before-the-writing, prior truths – and it repels our thinking about it 'teleologically'. Unable to acquit Realism of the duplicity it congenitally enacts by its will to be an *instrumental* medium – pretending to give things-as-they-are and ending up using things to 'make out' something else – narrative now abjures after-the-writing, prospective truth. Further, in its notion of place as well as of time, it aims to be pure. If in some classic view of the status of fiction (to steal a Platonic analogy) there were (1) an ideal world, (2) a world of earthly appearances, and (3) a poetic world, a fictional '*lieu théatral*' in which these might be synthesized, according to the poet's vision, as Sidney would have it (the St Petersburg of Tolstoy, the Arcturus of Lindsay): for the writer now there is a fourth 'space'. One in which fiction-making itself takes place (at the hands of the writer, at the hands of reader), and where those other three worlds are obliterated, lost, in fact come continually into question but never into being. "It is from itself", Federman writes, "from its own substance that the fictitious discourse will proliferate" (1981, 11). "It is Narration that speaks", as Barthes proclaims in discussing Sollers' *Drame*. "The voice is not here the instrument, even depersonalized, of a *secret*": the essence attained is not that of a person, it is "that of literature".[37]

Thus Narration is All. Analytic rules of linguistic generation become the sole 'causality'; the narrative is a narration of itself. "The entire interest of the pages of description", as the case was put early by Robbe-Grillet, "no longer lies in the thing described, but in the actual movement of the description".[38] "'What takes place' in a narrative is from the referential (reality) point of view literally *nothing*", wrote Barthes, "'what happens' is language alone, the adventure of language, the unceasing celebration of its coming" (1975a, 124). The time and space that govern are not those of what is *narrated* but those occupied by the narration itself, and its reading. The text ('*parole*', or '*écriture*') is the performance of '*langue*'; it makes pure language perform.

In the first instance – as we've already seen – the figure of the writer writing, creating, "imagining pen in hand" (as Ricardou puts it: 1967, 265) shadows the page. But this 'writer' may now be a metaphor for the text. Rapidly, in this order of things, we may find before us a "floating narrator and floating narrative" (1971, 124). The stability of distinction between 'writing' (as an object) and 'writing' (as an act) disintegrates, and the writer-figure and the configuration of what is written emerge out of and dissolve into one another. "The title 'Autobiography' means 'self-composition'", Barth tells us; "the antecedent of the first-person pronoun is not I, but the story, speaking of itself"; "I see I see myself as a halt narrative. ... contentless form. ... I must compose myself. / Look, I'm writing. No, listen, I'm nothing but talk" (1968, x, 33). "He awakens one morning in what he has written", says Sollers' *Drame*. "Literally: without transition, opening his eyes, the story continuing, reciting itself. ... He issues naturally in fact out of the text, he's freshly touched its autonomous existence".[39]

It's in such moments as these that the way lies open for language to commence to 'act on its own', for the process of signification-shift – of 'autonomous transformation' – to take over. This, to borrow a phrase from the title of a fiction by Friederike Mayröcker, is the beginning of "Narrating of a Narration" (Russell, 1981, 61). (For major – and diverse – explorations of discourse operating according to the principles considered here, recourse should be had to, for example, Pinget's *Mahu*, *Le Libera*, *Passacaille*, Baudry's *Personnes*, Sollers' *Le Parc*, *Drame*, *Nombres*, *Lois*, *H*, Porta's *Partita*, Federman's *Double or Nothing* and *Take It or Leave It*, and Brooke-Rose's *Between* and *Thru*; for obvious reasons having to do with the very nature of the language, where quotations are concerned I'll keep here to samples in English.) In Brooke-Rose's *Thru* we see this crucial event both described and simultaneously performed:

> sudden isolation
> of seeing nothing whatever in the
> rear
> of
> the
> mind
> and
> no
> narrator at all though this is only a
> manner of speaking since the text has
> somehow come into existence but with
> varying degrees of presence either bent
> or gazing into diasynchronic space or[40]

A typical passage taken at random now – "A dompna soisebuda composed of femme-reine, femme-enfant, femme-fatale, grey eminence Cleopatra's nose Musset's Muse a bit of Heloise old and new" – shows at work the activity whose fundamental process the text displays with dour precision in the last line of the following:

> and if you lose the thread of the texture you lose your head your paradise your utterance your pygmalion-skinned hero creature that slips out of your grasp and becomes a line in its own rewrite rule going forth to multiply the multiplicator of books and looks within books like a function of narrative
>
> $f(\text{bo (lo (bo (lo (books) oks) oks) oks})^{n}$

As the superscript ^{n} is designed to imply, the 'number' of permutations admitted by narrative operating analytically may hope to be unlimited. Thus in "The Voice in the Closet", Raymond Federman's text interrogates the status of Federman:

suppose he gives up dies one morning among millions of unfinished moments in the middle of a word will I remain suspended from his blood lifeless voice within a voice without a story to tell my beginning postponed by federman's absence . .

. . . .

space of future reinstated in stories only from past images presumed shape reverse of farness stifling faces federman now confront much moinous wordshit start there to provide single voice long dodge closet yet a single word failed logos draws map of journey to chaos evoked a bird here where namredef renders speech burnt out to better question. . . .[41]

And as the phrases "future reinstated in stories only from past images", "word failed logos", and "renders speech burnt out to better question" reveal, the text will seek to refuse to 'settle' for the language it receives from the external world, and instead strives to 'suspend' it by – to cite a recurrent locution – 'putting it back into circulation', by continually retracing and remodelling customary significations.[42] This theme is roughed out in, for example, Barthelme's ten-page "Sentence" ("this infected sentence") which begins:

Or a long sentence moving at a certain pace down the page aiming for the bottom – if not the bottom of this page then of some other page – where it can rest, or stop for a moment to think about the questions raised by its own (temporary) existence

. . . .

that in our young manhood we were taught that short, punchy sentences were best (but what did he mean? doesn't 'punchy' mean punch-drunk? . . .) . . . we are mature enough now to stand the shock of learning that much of what we were taught in our youth was wrong, or improperly understood by those who were teaching it. . . .[43]

The sheer textural, perceptual difficulties for the Realistic reader of such texts as Brooke-Rose's and Federman's – even when their language is quite clear – are self-evident. For one thing, as we might have predicted in the case of so strong a programme of discourse, there is the disturbing sense of an *absence (or 'weakness') of process* at the level of *histoire*. The utterance itself is proffered as the sole, necessary and sufficient cause, just as in the case of a dream we sometimes tell ourselves that its being a dream is the defining, enabling cause for what happens in it.[44] In the face of the narrative fiat, the accustomed 'normal forces of nature' guaranteed in Realism put up no struggle. Deliberately, 'natural' process and 'natural' constraints are dissolved, and the reader looking for a (Realistic) 'narrative' in this narration may feel 'lost' as in a dream.

Equally disconcerting here is a kind of '*flatness*' of discourse which it's often hard to differentiate from monotony. In its movement towards the extinction of illusion at the level of *histoire*, the narrative inclines to suppress the 'heights and depths' associated with the hierarchical norms of thematic (for example, psychological or moral) interpretation and evaluation. The text, both physically and linguistically, is a 'pure surface', no more and no less. This is undoubtedly part of the import of Beckett's frequent instruction, during rehearsals of his own plays, to the actors: "No colour! no colour!"[45] It is the '*production' of the words* on stage (to which he gives meticulous attention), and not their interpretative evaluation, that counts.

A third snare for the Realist reader is, of course, that such narration can by his/her standards be obscure. While 'experimental' fiction perennially falls to that charge, there are again special reasons in this case extending beyond the writer's desire – so diligently advertised by well-wishing contemporary criticism – to disrupt the natural attitude and challenge the transparent and '*lisible*'. If the text aims to *maximize* the sense of *process at the level of discourse*, this reason follows directly, with or without the presence of any radical intent. Not surprisingly, 'narratologists' or 'diegeticists' – as writers of narration-centred anti-mimetic texts – frequently refer to their activity as a calligraphic one (for instance Sollers, a follower of American letters as assuredly aware of Pound as he is of Roussel). The idea can be easier to follow if we explore our experience of different physical writing systems. Let us think of Realist fiction as analogous to the consistent use of 'Roman' or 'capital' letters, each letter free-standing and clear, in which a large part of the actual movement of the pen – called the *ductus* – is invisible. (The clarity thus produced makes this system the one in which children are taught to read.) Modernist fiction, with its relinquishment of the 'invisibility' of authorial action in favour of some accent on the subjectivity of the narrator, might then be momentarily thought of as analogous to *cursive* calligraphy (or 'handwriting'), where a larger part of the pen's movement is actually inscribed on the paper. Discourse-stressed narration, then, moving as far as it can in this sense from the Realist mode, may find its analogue in a writing in which the ductus is massively if not entirely inscribed. The text, incorporating all the swirling vortices and re-tracings and 'semantically irrelevant' hesitations of the writing 'hand', becomes highly '*scriptible*', deeply 'writerly', and at the same time it threatens at every moment (which parts of the onflowing line constitute the 'meaningful word'? which parts are 'merely' expressions of the activity of writing the word?) to become '*illisible*', 'unreaderly' – that is, literally, 'illegible'. We'll need to come back to the problem of the ostensible meaninglessness of the narrative 'ductus'. But in the logic of the theory we're obliged to accept that – as against our experience of other forms of 'experiment' – we're not to imagine that this impression of the text's obscurity is only temporary, that with increased understanding we will clear it away. This comes forcefully home to us when we recall that whereas the Modernist invites us to make sense of his or her script (however initially obscure) by interpreting it as the eventually comprehensible outpouring of the mind of a finally characterizable 'writer', that particular hope is here rebuffed.

But all is not lost in obscurity. Narration-centred texts make very explicit appeals to the reader seeking to recover referentiality, meaning, and a wide variety of 'sensuous gratifications' from them. There's good evidence that from an early age we seek and enjoy the frissons linked to the 'senseless' play-of-words in narrative for its own sake.[46] But beyond even this, and often with real sophistication, the text contains a diversified orchestration of illusionistic lures, including sensationalistic evocations of moments of sexual activity and material violence.[47] This may not be solely the outcome of a cynical strategy designed to keep the reader reading, to play 'upon' us. But the rationale can be a further one. Now a major impulse within fiction is one in which narration calls for an interest in itself and in the 'play of differences' between levels of signification itself. In place of 'communication' it proffers 'non-directive fullness'.[48] In place of 'meaningful depth' it offers '*thickness*' ('*épaisseur*', '*spessore*') – a richness of relationality within the text, and of processive experience for writer and for reader.

This play of differences – and the play of all signs, of which the narrative is finally an inseparable part – can of course remain 'purely' play only so long as differences remain non-definitive, in perpetual suspense. More than any other mode, narration-centred fiction formally courts the coalescence of 'content' and 'form', 'fact' and 'fiction', 'fiction' and its 'criticism', and does so especially by seeking to dispel readers' confidence in the first element in each of these antitheses ('fact', say, before 'fiction') to which, as the deconstructionist proclaims, cultures have industriously given priority.[49] (Thus, now, 'literature' and 'theory' are inevitably to be regarded by some of their ultimate practitioners as inextricable aspects of a single continuous discourse.) The text would become an edgeless and untenanted, seamless serial happening without atmosphere, setting, character, story or theme and without terminus, ceaselessly differentiating between signs but undifferentiated as a sign of anything final beyond it.

Our notion of the *lieu théatral* now takes on a new meaning. Discussing with Sollers the thrust of his writing, David Hayman says "There's then a constant mutation, a chaos, ultimately. But having in view a kind of homogeneous *lieu absolu*?" Sollers' accord with this vision of his intention appears complete. "An indescribable homogeneity!" Sollers replies.[50]

The abiding traits, on the page, of such texts are thus strongly determined by the precautious apprehension that as soon as discourse were to 'come down on the side of something', some content to which it attributed intrinsic 'seriousness', it would become merely instrumental and relinquish its own pre-eminence. Thus hesitation, aporia, is vital for deeper reasons than simply for the reduction of the illusion of transparency or of cosmic systematicity. We've seen over and again anticosmic fiction's exercise of strategems for the dismemberment of our expectations of narrative: its perturbation of the convention of unmixed discourse (via, for example, metalepsis), of stability of object (via, for example, what we might call a tactic of 'a-nonymity', the attack on the fixity of the names for things and even on the continuity of pronouns[51]), of stability of subject (via, for example, the fluctuation of narrative voice to the point where all that appears to remain is the 'totality of voices' of which the whole text is composed). These are certainly everywhere evident in 'pure narrational' fiction. Further, we're familiar now with ways in which discourse may accentuate its primacy by calling attention to itself by self-reflexive strategies, whose particular popularity among post-war American writers is a signature of their work. Of Flaubert's dictum 'God everywhere felt, nowhere seen', Realism took up the second clause and anti-Realism falls upon the first.

But for 'analytic, pure narrational' fiction, there are disquieting limits to the efficacy of such ploys. Self-reflexivity, for instance, can only make a fool of itself – as writers are often now aware and as the *topos* of infinite regress shows – since for a text properly to 'demonstrate', to point to, itself it must stand outside itself, and this no text could accomplish however much it 'wished'. "For anti-representation, self-representation is still too representative".[52] Something yet more radical is wanted, whether it's to be found in discourse itself or not. A profound irony inherent in the logic of narratology is that, on two scores at least, narrative, as a thing, must work against its own enterprise.

First, it must strive to be dynamic when it appears to depend for its substance on a constituent that is static. Narrative has always been taken to operate by the fabrication of images. The image, that very axis upon which poetics sempiternally turned, may conceivably have always been the totally wrong object of attention when the mind sought to grapple with the nature of narrative, a mode of discourse whose whole essence was the progressive disclosure of movement, of action, of change. It's this that Barthes partially perceives when he describes the project of what he calls "*l'oscillation*" in writing: "One is witness to a mad combat between the 'inconclusion' of attitudes... of which the con-sequence [*succession*] is always open ... and the weight of the Image, which tends irresistibly to solidify; for the destiny of the Image is immobility". The "scandal" of Sollers is that he "attacks the Image"; that he seems to desire to "forestall the formation and stabilization of each and every Image".[53] It is hard to conceive how narration could purge itself of images – particularly since all signs (as the very word we use for 'signs' shows) risk changing places with images. And even when it puts images into oscillation, a narrative *in toto* falls prey to being regarded as constituting 'an image', as we know from our experience of everyday criticism. It must wrestle, then, with its own nature, and be seen to be doing so.

As if this were not enough, along with its opposition to the static quality of the image, 'pure narration' must at once also repel the dynamic, progressive implications of its very narrativity. We've seen anti-Realism's restive response to the linearity of language, coupled with its persistent efforts to render eventuation in some 'simultaneous' way, as though narration might be made a static object. It now becomes still clearer why. It's no accident that two modalities of understanding that many anti-Realists reject are those two that Flaubert had called the great twin discovery of his century, science and history. For both systems share the same progressivist, fundamentally evolutionary mythos. The unfolding of objective external reality in each case is a *story* (*histoire*, *storia*). The activity of science is equally bound to an historical theory of truth: truth is the object of a narrative, temporally-defined *process of finding out*. The 'classic' novel – whether the picaresque, the *bildungsroman*, the *roman expérimental*

– is a dramatization of faith in this process of progressive unveiling. Discard credence in history, in science, in synthetic referential paths to truth – in favour of an intrinsic, pure, analytic mode of apprehension – and you stand challenged to create a kind of writing that is anything but narrative. Post-war criticism's own turning away from traditional diachronic and toward synchronic readings of fiction is heavy further evidence of this same attitude in contemporary thought about how writing should be seen to function. Narrative must try not to be taken narratively.

As these near-paradoxical crises reveal, if this is not a case where literature is against itself (*pace* Graff, 1969), it is one in which narration is. We've arrived, in fact, at another thematic *topos*. A theme, that is, that runs throughout narratological fiction and its commentaries and that may be different from all others in that while it is concerned expressly with what such discourse is said to 'do', it comes to us *as* a theme, in didactic expository form, and not (we may dare to say) as the outcome of anything discourse ever actually does. The *topos* appears, actually, in two seemingly opposed guises, and ones we've already glimpsed in another context: copia and vacuity.

To start with, we know that this is a fiction aiming to defy closure. Its reader may in addition feel – even after the briefest examples on the previous pages – that it tends to be a fiction that actually 'rattles on' as if *ad infinitum*, just as 'plethoric' representational fiction does. Yet this is *not* representational fiction, and another logic lies behind it. Rabelais' eternal device "*et cetera*" ('*and other* (unuttered thing)'), the very emblem of the narratological text, is the one sign it can never admit into its discourse – the text *must* in theory go on 'in so many words' – there can be no exhaustion of the subject while *anything* remains unuttered.[54] A recent critic speaks of "the new torrential style of writing" (Lavers, 1982, 23) as a response to the breakdown of the hope of a totalizing vision of existence. This may be true in part. The writer knows it to be absurd to 'give information' but cannot resist the almost kinesthetic bitter pleasure of writing 'as if' the activity made sense, or offers the torrent of verbiage as an ironic surrogate for the naive effort to represent the torrential spray of external phenomena. It doesn't hurt here to remember that etymologically the 'author' is literally the 'augmentor'. The *topos* involved, in the first of its two aspects, is *babble*. It can be seen as the awesomely inescapable end result of a kind of positive feedback inherent in the logic of uttering, of which the 'narratologist' is deeply aware: the more that's to be said in favour of not speaking, the more will be spoken. There is no corrective to language which language can contain – unless it is, somehow, more language. The tower of babble is its own retribution.

The reader finding such *longueurs* so rebarbative that no internal logic seems sufficient to justify them may exclaim that here is really a case of logorrhoea produced by some *horror vacui* of metaphysical proportions. That is correct; the intuition of the void is the other side of the same coin. We've returned by the back door to the motif of *silence*. As two influential anti-Realist theorists devoted to the "Literature" or "Aesthetics" of "Silence" have put it, "in an era of widespread advocacy of art's silence, an increasing number of works of art babble. Verbosity and repetitiveness are particularly noticeable in the temporal arts of prose fiction, music, film and dance" (Sontag, 1969, 26–7); "*l'ère sans parole*" (as Blanchot termed it) can produce a literary movement towards silence or, simultaneously, "a form of writing that is incessant sound" (Hassan).[55] Generating words may – as the title *Graal Flibuste* hints (perhaps without Pinget's full awareness) – become a mode of metaphysical filibustering. Beckett's Moran expresses the case: you can "detect, beyond the fatuous clamor, the silence of which the universe is made".[56]

This passage of Beckett's reveals yet another striking 'doubleness'. Because, first, it appears to be *descriptive* (of the universe's ultimate silence). And second, it appears also to be *prescriptive*, for the following sentence reads: "I desired this advantage for my son." (We recall Molloy's saying that "to restore silence is the role of objects".) It works something like this:

Silence *is*, descriptively, the abyss between the sign and its referent, between word and reality. This is the insistent theme of 'absence'.[57] Even infinite regress itself, as we've noted, never appears in a text but can only be alluded to by means of an emblem, some "clamor", some form of babble. It's the condition Lem's fictitious critic describes when he says "sentences mean nothing *in themselves*". Yet Lem's own text discloses the conundrum. For this 'critic' is writing of a fictitious work of fiction called *Nothing at all, or the Consequence* in which "there is no narrator; he is replaced by the language, that which itself speaks", "a surface that, eaten away ... by that all-consuming cancerlike Nothing, has ceased to exist *even as a negation*"; the 'narrator', his 'narration', their 'critic' and his 'critique' all dissolve in a book by Lem entitled *A Perfect Vacuum* which its preface describes as "a book 'about nothing'".[58] As Beckett suggests, the babble/silence conception, Janus-faced (like the Barthian conception of 'exhaustion'), will not only describe but will prescribe what writing is to do. Narration 'traces', 'circumscribes' what it cannot describe, and the more that it plays at describing what it cannot describe, the more it contains silence, the ultimate 'truth'. That then, in this view, may be narration's aim. The rôle of 'the dismantler', the 'world-destroyer' – which at the beginning we saw as some part of the intention of 'anticosmic' fiction – is carried to its logical end.

So theoretical discourse associated with narration-centred writing abounds with the rhetoric of destruction; narration exists to 'extinguish', to 'abolish', to 'obliterate' itself. "One writes", says Sollers, "to keep quiet and to attain the written silence of memory, which paradoxically returns the world to us in ciphered movements, the world whose hidden, irreducible cipher each of us is" (1968a, 69). As John Cage says in his book *Silence*, "there are silences and the words make help [*sic*] make the silences. I have nothing to say and I am saying it and that is poetry as I need it" (1961, 109). "I want to write a novel", says Federman's narrative *Take It or Leave It*, "that cancels itself as it goes along",[59] Perhaps, Hassan writes, putting the case in its most optimistic form, "the function of literature, after all, is not to clarify the world but to create a world in which literature" in its declarative function "becomes superfluous" (1975, 9–10). Unfolded to its furthest point: in this recirculation and ultimate devalorization of literature, narration may perform the yet more trenchant function of depotentiating, of emptying language itself of its power over the mind.[60] Narration as pure language at last will triumph when it becomes not only 'seamless' but 'seme-less'.

This leads to an issue whose purport is so pervasive as to make it a concern underlying anti-Realist activity at almost every turn. One whose central intuition can be readily expressed in a few words, while the complexity of the evidence customarily brought to bear to establish its centrality to literary enterprise fills volumes.[61] Where does semantic 'meaning' takes place? Where, exactly, can a text be said at all to 'exist'?

Writers shifting toward pure narrationality have played in many ways with the generation on the page of 'semeless', 'meaningless' signs. Here is one oft-cited example. In the midst of several texts written in his own language, Sollers introduces Chinese characters; the ideogram, for example, that in Chinese stands for the number 4. The French (or English) reader may be expected to be stymied. What is one to make of this 'shock'? Sollers is not 'fudging' – he's unmistakably using 'real language'; the only problem is that here is a language that is meaningless to his text's anticipated reader. In the case of the experience offered to the reader of a Modernist text (by, say, Eliot or

Joyce), as Edmund Wilson saw, there was certainly 'shock'; but it was of a kind fairly called the 'shock of recognition'. What we 'went through' was the process of discovering that what we at first thought we could not 'naturalize' was actually 'natural' – but simply not until this moment 'realized'. The difference with Sollers' Chinese characters is that we know immediately that they *are for someone* 'natural' – only they are *not* naturalizable for the 'natural' reader.[62] By this literally stunning reversal, by playing with the very notion of *language* as a mode of *communication*, by giving us 'perfectly good information' that informs us of nothing, the text would stir in us instantly the sense that the necessary information is not *its* property – the failure of the text to inform us is not *its* fault – but ours. The text is truly 'analytically pure' until it's satisfactorily synthesized for the reader *by the reader*. In the idiom of this programme, (if the writer 'creates' it) it is the reader who finally 'produces' the text. This is actually what Lem's text speaks of when it says that sentences "mean nothing *in themselves*"; it is the reader in his own context that "fills every sentence with meanings" (1971, 410).

We are not now dealing with the always-at-any-rate-debatable cliché that the text by its complexity or obscurity may better stimulate its reader into 'participating' in its 'creation', which even today some essentially Modernist theorists claim to be the aim of anti-Realist experiment. More: the conception is that this is *always* all that ever happens when we read. A book exists only insofar as a reading of it takes place, making it what it 'is'. " ... A text consists of multiple writings", says Barthes, "issuing from several cultures and entering into dialogue with each other, into parody, into contextualization; but there is one place where this multiplicity is collected, united, and this place is not the author, as we have hitherto said it was, but the reader".[63] That dreamt-of *lieu théatral* that haunts the anti-Realist text is a reader on the stage of whose mind it will be produced.

But the formidable import of this becomes obvious when we realize that I should have said not 'the reader' but 'readers'. If "an author is not the cause of what he writes but its product", as Sollers argues, then "a work exists for itself only potentially, and its actualization or production depends on its readings and the moments when these readings are actively accomplished" (1968b, 66). Thus "the presence of a reader", as Ehrmann declares, "is no more explicit nor implied than is that of an author. This presence is just as indeterminate"(1971, 241). Finally, a narrative in this view would be no more or less than the indefinably infinite composite of all its possible readings.

It should be said now that the notion of an analytic literature is in this way brought most under fire by the logic of many of those who most believe in it. For from the standpoint of any who seek to advance it as pure language, insofar as language is a product of its users, it must be as analytically *impure* – that is, as contingent on extra-linguistic conditions – as there are instrumental uses for language itself. Narration-centred fiction will be known by the purity not of its language (as some eternal and universally constant thing) but by the purity of its commitment to language, of which contingency is now taken to be an ontological property. That thing 'indeterminacy', always hovering in the background, has now descended fully upon us. Nor need we turn to an anticosmic text to find the crisis of the indeterminate reader spelled out. "I began to write the story of a hidalgo from La Mancha who continued to adhere to the codes of certainty", says an unnamed character in *Terra nostra*:

> That faith, I said to myself, would originate in reading. And that reading would be madness. The knight … would attempt to transmit that reading to a reality that had become multiple, equivocal, and ambiguous. He would fail time and again, but every time he would again take refuge in reading: born of reading, he would remain faithful to it because for him there was no other licit reading. … This hero of mockery and hoax … would be the first hero, furthermore, to know he was read. At the very time he was living his adventures, they would be written, published, and read by others. A double victim of reading, the knight would twice lose his senses: first, as he read; second, upon being read. … But as object of reading, he begins to conquer reality, to infect it with his insane reading of himself. And this new reading transforms the world. … The world disguises itself: the enchanted knight ends by enchanting the world. But. … reality delivers him to death. The knight will continue to live only in the book … there will be no other recourse to prove his own existence, it will not be found in the unique reading life gave him, but in the multiple readings life took from him in reality. … I shall create an open book where the reader will know he is read and the author will know he is written.
>
> (Fuentes, 1975, 767)

This 'writing of the author' is only partly performed by Fuentes' narrator when he tells the story of this 'author', since it is we who are left to supply the name of "Cervantes" and, with it, our own diverse readings of the man who used that (itself biographically dissembling) name – and with this, our readings of ourselves as readers. Thus Lem's 'critic', in drawing to a close his 'reading' of that nonexistent novel to which we've referred, can write "*horror vacui* smites us, at the same time entices; the reading turns out to be not so much the destruction of the world of lies of the novel as the form of annihilation of the reader himself as the psychic being!" (Lem, 1971, 413–14). Just exactly how incapable we are of arresting this terrible process it remains to be seen.

But as I've suggested, there is another way of thinking of narration as an autonomous analytic experience.

The idea of pure form

One of the tacit, unquestioned first principles of contemporary criticism[64] has been that the new generation of extraordinarily form-conscious fictionalists think of 'form' – synonymous in the past with the concern for non-instrumental, 'content-free' beauty – as in fact a Trojan horse by which ideological content was always conventionally smuggled into the reader's consciousness. And that they adopt formal strategies invariably as an iconoclastic procedure for the liberation of the reader from such manipulations. That, in genuine radical spirit, they feel that that form governs best that governs least; and that the more concerted their attention to form the more it displays a search for authentic formlessness. This set of assumptions *needs*, however, to be 'questioned'.

The popular identification of radical literary action with literary 'formlessness' is actually uniquely deepseated where narrative is concerned. Coherence of eventuation at the level of story and coherence of form have been assumed implicitly to be indissoluble; impair the one and you disabled the other. Modernism, particularly in its exploration of interior monologue, would at first seem to have made way for the dissolution of form in its having released narrative from the constraints of rules other than those of psychological association. But, as the necessity here of a *psychological* rationale makes clear (a rationale that had in any case already 'liberated' fiction in this respect as early as *Tristram Shandy* if not *Gargantua et Pantagruel*), Modernism's challenging gesture in this direction had always been bound to the postulation of a pre-existing 'character', a personified mentality that was subject to the material laws of a formally stable Realistic model of existence. This alternative rule continued to hold fiction at least at one long step's remove from the 'transformational revolution' – ushered in by innovations in linguistic theory following Peirce and Saussure[65] and supported by the premisses, for example, of both structuralist and post-structuralist argument[66] – that has become one of the key features of recent contributions to fictional activity. It took post-war anti-Realism to engender the powerful perception – only foreshadowed in fiction by such as Roussel, Queneau and earlier Surrealist experiment – that, in narrative, not merely textural permutations but whole series of 'story-events' may be given as engendered entirely by transformations within the language of an utterance itself. With this concept of the fluidity of narrative eventuation, one of the first things commonly thought to be 'on the way out' is form in the traditional sense expressed, for example, by C. S. Lewis.

An intrinsic and seemingly form-threatening aspect of this insurgent conception of transformational processes has been that while the narrative events they bring forth may well be taken as 'revealing unexpected truths' about external reality, they are in their inception, and may be in their intention, *free* of such Realistic connections. A leading objection launched by many to whom anti-Realism is repugnant is that by *reason* of its analytic rather than synthetic 'origins' – its willed suspension of the strictures of reality – it threatens to be 'free' of *all* constraints, all kinds of verifiable order: that it inevitably invokes anarchy. Certainly we've seen among anti-Realists (precisely those questioning extra-textual systems) the allure of the image of chaos. It should be hard to imagine, in other words, how a literature of this radical sort could dream of anything like that orderliness we conventionally associate with an aspiration toward purity of 'form'. Nothing in it would logically, anyway, entail such a thing.

As soon as we begin to consider texts making appeal to our sense of their intrinsic value, however – as perhaps illustrative of life, perhaps not, but having a worth of their own as fabrications – a new feature emerges. Nabokov's poet Shade, interpreted by Kinbote, discloses the theme. "... We too might wish to cut short a reader's or bedfellow's questions by sinking back into oblivion's bliss – had not a diabolical force urged us to seek a secret design in the abracadabra".[67] His impulse is to "plunge back into his chaos and drag out of it, with all its wet stars, his cosmos", "the Daedalian plan simplified by a look from above – smeared out as it were by the splotch of some master thumb that made the whole involuted, boggling thing one beautiful straight line" (Nabokov, 1962, 204, 206).

> ... *this*
> Was the real point, the contrapuntal theme;
> Just this: not text, but texture; not the dream
> But topsy-turvical coincidence,

Not flimsy nonsense, but a web of sense.
Yes! It sufficed that I in life could find
Some kind of link-and-bobolink, some kind
Of correlated pattern in the game,
Plexed artistry, and something of the same
Pleasure in it as they who played it found.

(53)

We recognize easily by now this *topos* of *design*, a constitutional theme running throughout the work of Nabokov, of Calvino (whose description we've already noted of his own trilogy *I nostri antenati* as essentially the appropriation of synthetic conventions for analytic formal purposes), of Borges, and of others central to anti-Realism. We can readily conceive from all that we've seen down to this point that anti-Realist texts – *particularly* those of an anticosmic inclination, whose fascination with the Flaubertian eidolon of a 'book about nothing' is unmistakable – may well become susceptible in ways that fiction rarely has been to the vision of the meaning-purged artefact as imbued with the properties of autonomous form. And that – as Kinbote's allusion to beauty intimates (and as is conventionally said of Flaubert's disposition when discussions of his *livre sur rien* arise) – we may be face-to-face with an overture toward what in other times has freely been called the realm of aesthetic experience.[68] " . . . A work of fiction exists", we hear from Nabokov, "only insofar as it affords me what I shall bluntly call aesthetic bliss, that is a sense of being somehow, somewhere, connected with other states of being where art . . . is the norm" (1955, 286). But Nabokov might certainly be a special, eccentric case. We need to look into this very closely.

As a reader in such 'other times' might have said, the familiar utterance 'Able was I ere I saw Elba' offers two kinds of satisfaction, one of which is in some way missing from the utterance 'Napoleon lost his power when he was returned again to an island prison, one this time called Elba.' While both utterances communicate much the same informational sense, the first – in its form as a palindrome – offers a playful pleasure that the second does not, by virtue of its added visual 'graphic perfection' (or near-perfection). This would be a kind of perfection that – in its compactness, rhythmic regularity and symmetry – stands above and is 'free of meaning', even while it reinforces in its formal 'circularity' the very propositional meaning it 'contains'. (Calvino's "Il conte di Monte Cristo" explicitly explores this formal, 'palindromic' quality of Napoleon's story and in a certain way is an extended permutation of the palindrome I've quoted, though there's no sign that he was aware of the English utterance itself.) Much of the theoretical – and, in traditional terms, aesthetic – interest in such word-play lies in the tension that can thus be produced between these two levels of experience. Between, that is, language experienced as having a 'natural', semantic, communicational function and language experienced as having a function as artifice, manipulated to satisfy rules of relationship over and above the incidental exigencies of the artefact's sheer functional (linguistic, semantic) operation as a specific, unique set of communicative signifiers. Every text has a form. The question is, while much fiction now appears to query the validity of organized perceptions of experience, just to what extent does it (as we might expect) actually forswear the formal organization of its own utterances?[69]

As it happens, notions of the value of 'analytic purity of form' are far from being as eccentric to our culture as we may tend to think. To put it in what's perhaps an odd way, 'emptiness' has always had made out for it a very real appeal at certain levels of our experience of the work of art. In the western world, those who 'do' the non-performative arts have been perpetually predisposed to fashion even their most determined representations of actuality out of *one material* or *another*. This is so simple and taken-for-granted that it needs stating – because we forget what an astonishing thing it is to wish so relentlessly to do.

Classically, the sculptor made not only the figure of the man but the grass 'he' stood on, the sword 'he' grasped, the clothes 'he' wore, *everything*, out of *stone* (or out of wood, say, or clay); when it was needful to supplement this with some other material vast pains were taken to conceal the fact. In this 'great tradition' the painter made his or her world of paint on some surface, covered this surface entirely with paint, and displayed vigour and wit in finding ways of gaining the effect with nothing but paint. In the same tradition the composer of music felt subject to violent attack when he or she called for not merely 'pure musical instruments' but, say, a cannon to secure the sound desired – *especially* if the sound to be evoked was that of a cannon. When movements in art have emerged in which other 'resources' – for example, *objets trouvés* – are imported from realms outside that strictly defined by the medium concerned, with conspicuous frequency they've been accompanied by propositions precisely to the effect that the idea of art as pure (as not mixed with life) is a delusion. The essential precept behind this anti-cannon canon of art appears to be (logicians must forgive us for momentarily pinching their word) a 'parsimony' of materiality. A fundamental function of art, it's presumed, is that it uses as little as 'humanly' possible of the materials of actuality in its representation of reality. That what remains – what would remain in the *livre sur rien* – is the form. That, in other words, the special gratification we owe to art *is* the tension we feel in perceiving how the work is not made of – *is not* – what it directs our mind toward. A gratification stirred by our perception of the *difference* between the artefact and 'actual things', and crystallized by our perception of its own formal properties.

This conception inevitably arises as one of the central themes of the philosophy of aesthetics, whenever art is regarded (as it has been in traditional philosophy) as pre-eminently belonging to an aesthetic sphere. In general terms, it raises as many questions as it resolves. But we see its drift, and it strikes a familiar chord as we reconsider some of the favoured preoccupations of anti-Realist literature. When we think of the sculptor as saying through the work 'Here, this is not grass – it is stone – stone only, stone forever, never grass', we can't help but recognize in it the idiom of analytic fiction when it says *This is language and nothing but language*. As a mode of art, literature of course, being made of language – where one must first *see* the word 'grass' *as* the meaningful thing 'grass' before one can begin to consider much of its formal relationship with the words around it – would be quintessentially a medium enacting that tension I've mentioned, since language is always both something itself and referring to something else which it is not. There is now the possibility that the increased insistence in anti-Realist narrative and anti-Realist theory on the theme of 'absence' – the absence from the text of the substance which is its subject – may in some sense have as part of its burden the even more complicated notion not merely of 'fiction' as indeterminist illusion but 'fiction' as determined artifice – as an art object. Whether it's the promise of some tension (or resonance) between substance and form that it offers or some further promise of value in its very form on its own, the reader may have real difficulty in discovering unequivocal reasons not to suspect – in recent narrative making analytic claims for itself – a hint of some aesthetic intention.

In the vast assemblage of anti-Realist discourse, statements can be found expressing objections to aesthetics as a consideration. Jacques Ehrmann disputes the "religion of beauty" ("this stupid 'goddess', mute as a dream in stone; the justification for so much fanaticism and the pretext for so much cowardice") on the grounds that in separating the poet from others ("as the high priest of his cult") culture not only asserts a linguistic power-elitism but divides discourse itself into categories that are false. Ehrmann himself, however, then falls back to devote his anti-aesthetic forces only to the attack on the notion of 'poetic language', as if this were the sole manifestation in literature of the effort toward 'beauty' or formal gratification (Ehrmann, 1971, 242–3). When Sollers advances his idea of a book working in another new "dimension" he describes this not only as a book that "no longer informs, convinces, demonstrates, tells, or represents" but as one that is "opposed to the idea of power, to aesthetic values", which – in their encouragement of easy and sensually gratifying *lisibilité* – constitute a kind of opiate for the masses.[70] But once again the threat of the aesthetic comes to be identified by the writer with the "author's 'style'" or with "a complete, definitive repertoire of beautiful language" (Sollers, 1968b, 62). In such 'arguments', the limitations of what is said by contrast with what might conceivably be said about 'form' – whether for or against it – can't escape our attention. Since the beginning of serious speculation in critical circles on anti-Realist writing as a resolute activity, that reticence has persisted. Why?

The phenomenon of anti-Realism's present response to the problem of aesthetics is peculiar in the history of literature. Intimately associated theorists from Barthes to Sontag speak with passion for writing as a thing aesthetically experienced, for both writer and reader.[71] Yet their reluctance to name express textual criteria for aesthetic judgement (other than which philosophical enquiries into aesthetics themselves have no more primary business to consider) is openly avowed. As to the fictionalist speaking of fiction's aims, by comparison with writers in every other major literary movement in the past several centuries with the possible (and possibly significant) exception of Naturalism, the anti-Realist – while he or she has much to say about pleasure associated with *play* – is the one who has most perennially and strikingly kept silent, or kept his/her own counsel, with regard to questions of beauty, specifically, and with regard to the entire sphere of human aesthetic experience generally. There are, in fact, very 'serious' reasons indeed for anti-Realists of several sorts to stand clear of the area, as we'll see. And their hesitance when they do touch on the question makes evident their awareness of their having let themselves in for more than they've bargained for or – to put it with slightly greater precision – more than they wish to bargain for.[72]

What a literature does or intends, though, may often be different from what it talks about doing or leaves to be presumed about what it's doing by its public silence. The matter of 'poetic language' is a case in point. Quite apart from the fact that there's plenty of such stuff in anti-Realist fiction (as passages quoted throughout the past pages will have revealed), to look to poetic language as the only possible evidence of aesthetic concerns in a text would be poignantly naive. Even an educated guess as to what's actually going on in fiction in this domain must require the casting of a far wider net. How should this net be designed?

In western tradition, aesthetics has by general convention been regarded as the business of considering the nature of things – and decisions and assertions about things – viewed as having values in themselves as opposed to things viewed as instrumental means to other ends (ends such as the giving of information, the promulgation of ethical, politicial, metaphysical conceptions and the like). In the same broad tradition, most aesthetic theories, however else they may disagree, tend in some way or other to go on to identify such values with those formal features of objects which invoke in the spectator some apperception of contrast or tension between opposed sensations, often (in many theories) inducing an accompanying sensation of reconciliating proportion, or equilibrium, coherence, harmony or wholeness. Furthermore, when there has been an endeavour to single out 'objectively' the *formal properties themselves* by which objects bring about such sensations, it's been a widespread custom *in this tradition* to point to specific 'qualities' in objects in a similar, binary fashion. Whether or not grouped under the general heading of equipoise between the antipodes of 'monotony' and 'confusion' as Santayana saw it, common examples of these proffered pairs of formal properties in objects are readily recognized: unity v. multiplicity; uniformity v. diversity; orderliness v. chaoticity; moderation, consolidation v. proliferation, exuberance; symmetry v. asymmetry; restraint v. liberation; rhythmicality, periodicity v. sporadicity, erraticity; accordance v. discordance; judiciousness v. convulsiveness.[73]

A particular species of bifocal vision is needed here. While it's essential to remember that such a tradition maintains that the formally pleasing is a product of the presence of and interplay between *both* elements in any of these 'pairs', in another perspective those elements on the 'lefthand side' – as spelled out above – have conventionally on their own a special relationship to 'form'. That is, they ('orderliness', 'symmetry', 'rhythmicality' and so on) are specifically identified by their promotion of 'shapeliness', of '*formliness*'. By 'formliness' I mean not merely the unique and unrepeatable formal properties of some particular object in view, but rather, beyond those: formal regularity. This is to say that an object appearing to have formliness appears to respond to or correspond with 'rules', literally, 'regulations' of form which are repeatable, 'transportable', transposable to or able to operate with similar effect in other cases. (One may find the same pattern in two fabrics woven of different materials.) What is 'formly' in an object is not made inevitable by the object's specific materials (or semantic 'meanings'), or by the rules of the medium (graphic, say, or linguistic) in which the object is manifested, or by merely the conditions of a stochastic system (that is, by chance or probability).

Once again we may seem to be begging questions now, for we can conceive of differences between cultures or individuals, for example, such that 'rules' holding for one may be insensible to another. But this is entirely suited to our present purpose. It's the web of contemporary culture's conventional perceptions of form that will provide the most testing 'net' for 'catching' the data of a contemporary literature seeking to break with convention in its relation to form. Anti-Realist fiction's pressing preoccupation with the properties indicated at the 'righthand side' of each of those pairs – with multiplicity, discord, disorder, proliferation and the like – we need recount no further. On that evidence, such literature should seem to have no interest in traditional formal canons. There should be no significant sign of effort towards unequivocal achievement on the 'lefthand side', either for the sake of the assertion of unity, order, symmetry, rhythmicality (et cetera) on their own or for the sake of their bringing about any equilibrium with their antitheses. On the other hand, even if texts didn't in some different quarter express some interest on the part of analytic fiction in form-in-itself, should *conventional* tests disclose it in such radical writing we should already have learned more than we'd anticipated, and would have to think again about the whole anti-Realist enterprise.

This is a critical juncture. Whatever one decides, there is as I've said no question of imagining that any text has no 'form'. Nor need one, in speaking of finding there the operation of any traditional aesthetic standards (were it come to that), be assumed to be expressing some article of faith of one's own in such standards, let alone assigning 'beauty' on the basis of them to the works in which they are found – though of course the reader *having* faith in them would be free to do so. What this book is itself seeking largely to do is to consider what such texts' *decisions* may be, and on what grounds, in advance of any fierce debate about the relative merits of those decisions.[74] The job is simply to recall that the appearance in a text of shapeliness or formliness has in the past been *customarily* thought to show a discrete and powerful aesthetic concern for form in itself, and to ask whether anti-Realist fiction, in assaulting custom as we generally expect it to do, in some way eludes that kind of characterization.

* * *

To start with, it would be blinkered of us not to remark the persistence of the *topos* of design itself (which extends all the way to Brooke-Rose's 'transformationally free' *Thru* with its repeated theme of the "very subtly planned chaos" with its "odd, beautiful coherence"). Without having scrutinized every individual text one might wish not to attribute irony-free faith to such passages in fiction, across the board. But as we know, when we observe a painting – whether it be 'deeply (semantically) meaningful' in the Realist sense commonly ascribed to a Da Vinci or a Rembrandt, or ironically troubled in the way that a Magritte or an Escher may be, or 'free of meaning' in the sense many may wish to assign to a Mondrian or a Pollock – we can be constantly aware that we're in the presence of a highly organized formal order, produced by the frequency and distribution of colour, line, mass, texture. And if one disclaims the possibility of enquiring as to the *distribution and frequency of linguistic events* in a written text, one is trapped: there would in fact be no way intelligently to discover the text's relation to the question of form at all. As we'll soon find, it's the declared wish among the most insurgent writers that their work be proved by this very test. What may seem to be an irksomely 'technical' way of talking about writing is actually essential not only for this historical reason but because reading is continually under the influence of just this aspect of what we read, and no attempt to understand what's happening as we read could hope to be genuine without some sharp effort to trace it. The few cases I outline here are meant to serve only as the most cursory illustration of *some of the kinds* of textual events which a thoroughgoing project of this sort would disclose in voluminous detail.

Among the things for which all that we've said about anti-Realist theory has left us most unforewarned is that, unlike those conventions that it seeks to devalorize, the emblems by which the 'putting-into-question' activity is invoked – the labyrinth, the circle, nesting, the *lieu théatral*, frame-objects such as the window and the mirror, the all-encompassing library, palace, city, book, mandala-like images such as the coin and the die, the recursive or palindromic utterance – are used with extraordinarily repetitive regularity and stability of reference. They are never 'emptied' of their positive signification *nor* are they depotentiated by overdetermination, but are retained with remarkable consistency as dynamically effective events (that is, as narratively portentous in precisely the way that discarded 'classic' motifs such as the transfer of money, the wedding, the pursuits of labour, the discovery of 'hard facts' had been) from beginning to end, and are not submitted in the way we should have expected to parody or irony. More than this: as the examples I've just mentioned reveal, while such favoured figures do indeed consistently represent 'infinitude' or proliferation, with equally striking consistency they are also emblems of *containment*.

But let's not rush into things. What of texts at the 'microtextual' level? Perhaps here there are, formally – on the plane of 'pure lexical' usage, say, if we look closely – no such 'containments', no constraints, compositionally. We know that in anticosmic narrative generally, and in narratological fiction specifically, *time* as a system of orderly relations is under rigorous attack. Is this equally true of all possible fields of perception?

We can argue by now, with real assurance, the 'cause' of narration-centred fiction in its struggle against 'story-time'. Where causality at the level of story is to be displaced by the causality of narration itself, and where 'presence' is to be the 'present' of the narration (or of the reading), time – a field in which causality operates – must be surrendered into the arbitrary custody of the narrator (or of the reader). There is nothing capricious or casual, in other words, in this 'prejudice' against fixed standard notions of temporality; it is of the essence. In vivid contrast, however, spatial arrangement may turn out to retain – or even gain – immense strength as an organizational conception. The recognition of the *extensionality* of a written text – the text as a *surface* – may come to obsess the writer. The apparent antithesis between the linear temporal experience of literature (as language) and the experience of the work of visual art, with its imagined appeal of spontaneous total apprehension, will serve as a continual provocation to the narratologist. (So not only do narrators in neo-cosmic contexts – in Nabokov, Borges and Calvino – describe living figures as moving in de-scribed arcs and parabolas in space, but in Sollers and others the articulation of their 'telling' is portrayed as a material movement over a page.) And further: the 'surface', the 'superficiality' of the text, its two-dimensionality as opposed to 'depth' and even as opposed to 'layeredness' (that conception so favoured by Modernist-inspired criticism of the mid-twentieth century as it began to perceive the illusory nature of notions of 'depth') comes into its own. Even 'thickness' will be rejected by a Sollers, for there are no such things as layers or thickness in narration, there is only continuity. All at once, whereas for the Modernist duration had been a challenge, now the idea of extension in space itself becomes a greater one, and the writer explores the real and the illusory 'dimensions' of this 'ground' of which – or on which – his or her fiction is com-posed, 'inscribed', 'traced'. Time itself becomes only one of the flat signs analytically 'nominated' on the page and it is circumscribed by far more prolific notations, designs, of customarily spatial sorts.[75]

At the level, then, of its election of lexical signs, the diction of narration-centred fiction – however 'confused' its *temporal* signs may be – is characterized by the overwhelmingly rich deployment, for a start, of a language denoting spatial (for example visual) relations, following patterns of *ordination* with metronomic regularity. We've noted the force with which events in Sollers, Brooke-Rose and others are associated in strikingly methodical ways with balanced contrasts between black and white or dark and light, and with an equally formalized order of colours arranged spectrally. Far from being stochastically random (or formally 'open' and unpredetermined as Realist description strives to appear), narrational attention is focused on data arranged in 'matching sets', governed by starkly simple principles of *complementarity* and/or *reciprocity*. Just as geometrically regular configurations become central to its arsenal of imagery – circles, squares, triangles, figure-eights, crosses, parallel lines and right-angle intersections, chessboards and chequered street-plans – so perpetual allusions to *orientational relations* are constellated everywhere with a symmetricality unprecedented in fiction. As Federman's "Dashing from Don to Tioli" begins,

> this story will now tell itself alone without the support of the person (pronominal or otherwise) which gave it movement composure and identity (HERE) it will move therefore without efforts by a simple horizontal accumulation – but vertical also – of signs and facts which by process of surcharging upon one another will decipher themselves left to right but also top to bottom because to come back (retrace) to the place or space where closed was the story upon the threshold. . . .
>
> (1973, 260)

Interior is placed in punctual rhythmic counterpoise against exterior (a pattern on which the carefully alternating movement of the whole of the narration of Sollers' *Le Parc* is founded), vertical against horizontal, north against south and east against west, parallel against convergence or divergence, curvature against angularity or straightness, progresssion against recession, ingress against egress, up against down, left against right, back against front, top against bottom, right side up against upside down, in and out. Contemporary anti-Realists' enchantment with 'pure prepositional' titles – Brooke-Rose's *Between*, *Out* and *Thru*, Sukenick's *Out* and *Up*, McElroy's *Plus* – reflects more than just a coarse rejection of the predication of fixed objects and events. It manifests a sophisticated positive concern with patterns of position and of movement, with relationality, and with situations of language in which 'the action is (tenselessly) frozen' to allow the contemplation of the empty shapes of those customary utterances by which we make objects and events transitive – by which we 'express' them into fluid and ephemeral motion. The way *Thru* plays with the permutations of its title's own letters displays neatly this formal fascination with the internal relations composing what is itself a hollow, purely relational utterance.

Processes like these spread far and wide. Relations of every sort are subjected (for example in *Plus*, in *The Third Policeman*, in Sollers' *Le Parc, Drame, Nombres, H, Lois*) to the same painstakingly austere parallelistic treatment. Leaving probabilistic accountability behind, tactile for instance, (like visual ones) are posed in close reciprocal tension within the same passages and within alternating passages of narration: rough with smooth, hot with cold, wet with dry, hard with soft, light with heavy, blunt with sharp. In like fashion – just to vary our field of observation with an example from an area we'd customarily expect to be intractable to such manipulations – while 'depth of character' is dissolved, 'persons' are denoted in terms of schematically clearcut attributes in reciprocal pairs or triads: male/female/hermaphrodite, old/young, fat/thin, tall/short, ugly/beautiful, and so on.[76] Such procedures can be adequately imputed neither to any faith in the binarist theories of cognition, say, of a Lévi-Strauss nor to the 'universal' psychological processes which such theories claim to elucidate (since – if for no other reason – other kinds of literature, presumably produced by equally 'universal' processes, do not behave in this precisionist way). What we begin to conceive, if we're not to elaborate explanations far more baroque and fanciful than the simple evidence would warrant, is that the text now invokes some fundamental taste for the balanced interplay of antitheses independent of discrete circumstantial meanings, and the experience of equipoise, itself, that it instigates.

Here, on its own, is a field of formal narrational preoccupation crying for interrogation of a sort that criticism has so far failed to provide. But what if a text eschews – as we may expect such narrations to do – the in-built orderliness which its terms bring with them by their *signification* (since, after all, 'up' and 'down' are patterned in their relation by virtue solely of their having standard semantic connections)? Keeping still to the observation of narration-centred texts at the level of the minute operation of 'lexia', we find in fact that other kinds of order persist with equivalent strength. Independent of semantic signification, such narratives repeatedly work by the *clustering* of identical or *parallel parts of speech* and *'phonic' or orthographic data*, including the iterations of assonance, consonance, alliteration and rhyme. *Thru* is now surcharged with cases of the sort, as the following random samples show : "Now and then the mosaic of bent heads breaks and the boulevards which were originally promenades constructed out of demolished bulwarks are bouleversed back into bulwarks again"; "Books within books, looks within looks, looks within books, books within looks. Another idyll then, or semiotic idylls";

heads I win tails you lose   the trace
the scar
the scare
the scream
the scram
the marks
the skermish[77]

It is difficult to discern by exactly what principles we might conclude that such utterances differ from the usage of "poetic language". We may well consider the processes to be those described by Kinbote when he attributes the play of Shade's poem's language to the "spell of misleading euphony" (Nabokov, 1962, 110). The discovery of them in the text, however, does not depend on any genetic psychological theory such as Kinbote's. The point is that it's impossible to pretend that no constraint operates. The movement is not away from order but towards an order engaged by the rhythmic, echoic appeal of a 'periodicity of return' of certain phonemes or literal characters, out of which both semantic confusion and new semantic connections *may* (often via the mediation of punning) or may *not* arise. The prospect of profusion may lie ahead – the text has the potential to 'roam' into areas prohibited by customary programmes of narrative discourse. But the very sense of the *possibility* of profusion is produced by our recognition not of the abandonment of (semantic) rules but of the introduction of *new rules* into narrative of a formal (aural or literal) sort, with which our knowledge of even the most commonplace norms of aesthetically-orientated poetic activity has made us familiar since childhood. "My matter is form in itself", says Sollers' narrator in *Lois*.[78] Such activity cannot be covered by saying simply that it was produced 'merely by verbal association', since everything of importance would remain to be understood. Why, for instance, should formal patterning exercise such force in linguistic association in the first place? And why do we find no instructions in such texts not to respond to them as we do to identical configurations in other, explicitly aesthetically motivated literature?

Formal parallelism among 'semantically empty' utterances now extends far beyond the local clustering of like signs. Examples abound; the following are simply two of the most rudimentary, if pervasive, cases; ones with which units of narration close and ones with which they open. Throughout narration-centred fiction, in a way for which there is no precedent in Realist narrative, utterances are terminally punctuated with great regularity by question marks ('?') or by ellipses ('...').[79] The thematic potential of such devices for anti-Realist fiction is obvious – the idea of there *being* a terminus is thereby repelled. What is marked, on another level, however, is the frequency and evenness of distribution with which this happens throughout such texts, independent of any dynamic of certainty/uncertainty at the level of *histoire* or propositional argument. We are in fact dealing with the phenomenon of what by any standard can be correctly called a narrational *refrain*. That is, with cases in which the *ostensibly* primary narrative is 'broken up' (we note the etymology of 'refrain'), but in which – as in poetic convention and in music – the element interrupting the continuity of the 'story' *generates* continuity at another level. Perennially missed by current criticism but evident everywhere from *Lost in the Funhouse* and *Se una notte d'inverno un viaggatore* to most of the fiction of Pinget, Brooke-Rose, Federman, Sollers and Roche, the consistent text-long reiteration of the same limited number of discrete literal locutions and (typo)graphic signs guarantees a formal stability and rhythmicality that transcends any indeterminacy of *meaning* which the narrative as semantic object may appear to suggest.[80] Here, for instance – balancing the common periodic 'closure' of sentences or sections just mentioned – is a repeated device punctuating their beginnings. In narrative after narrative (Sollers' *Nombres* and Pinget's *Le Libera* are classic illustrations) upwards of 40 per cent of the text's paragraphs start with a conjunction, the same conjunction – with few exceptions "and" or "or" – appearing again and again.[81] (The comparable statistic in typical works by Flaubert, Balzac, Eliot or Tolstoy is well below 2 per cent.) What is compellingly clear about the 'narratologist's' persistence in this usage is that he/she does so in a way that is transparently *not* conjunctive in any semantic sense. The passages so 'joined' *have* typically no direct bearing on each other at a propositional level. The word's recurrence cannot be accounted for by either 'the grammar of the story' *or* by any 'transformational' process arising from the language of the surrounding text. It is a pleonastic, purely syntactic (semantically nonfunctional) refrain; what is left, what prevails, is actually the gesture alone, standing emblematically for the steady momentum of the rhythmic narrational form itself. The narrator returns to this sign – so quickly discarded as a woodenly mechanical and sophomoric-semaphoric gimmick by the traditional writer experimenting in parataxis, however anxious he or she is to persuade us of the text's genuine continuity – for exactly the reason that "*it's time*" for it to reappear. (Sollers, we'll find later, proposes exactly this rationale.) It's no accident that the closest one can come to a useful analogy in explaining this arbitrary 'gesture' may lie in the example of the 'impulse' given by a conductor prior to the orchestra's actual first-played notes – a sign forming no part of the 'content' of the musical text yet essential to the *proper rhythm* of its performance.

Still within the domain of local utterances, such procedures extend further. Even when a text is taken semantically, but now as proposing the meaninglessness of semantic utterances, it may in and by the very nature of the acts it performs propound a yet more remarkable orderliness. Once again, a single example that pervades anticosmic fiction, and one deserving a full-scale study on its own: Derrida in his long and acclaimed analysis of Sollers' *Nombres* declares that the only way to (re)present the book would be by measuring, through "a statistical accumulation of 'quotations', the well-calculated, rhythmically regulated effects of a recurrence", and that its themes are "*illisibles*" unless seen within "a deliberately distributed chromatic system" (Derrida, 1969, 294–5). He swiftly and relentlessly then moves to demonstrate the dominance throughout the text of a particular systematic 'effect'; one that is in fact one of the two or three controlling – if not universal – features of anticosmic procedure and discourse. Every established conviction or certainty resting upon "the oppositions between value and nonvalue, respectable and nonrespectable, true and false, high and low, inside and outside, whole and part" is undone by a process of conjoint "reversals", of "mirroring".[82] So prevalent is this form of discourse in anticosmic fiction, as we've seen from early on, that it's become one of the normal operations of anti-Realist literature. "It was night. It was also an imitation of night", says the protagonist of *Terra nostra* (Fuentes, 1975, 553); we've seen Beckett's and Robbe-Grillet's analogous evocation/revocation play with the same motif (pp. 86–7). We are free to take such operations as intending the 'undoing' of certain established habits of thought. But there is no reason why a polaristic model, such as this is, should necessarily be the only way to accomplish that effect. Any 'stochastic' or 'chaotic' model might do as well.[83] The sole 'assurance' the procedure attacks is the reader's faith in the rule of non-contradiction. Any full explanation of its privileged place in such fiction must include some acknowledgement that it *is* offered as a privileged one – that such narrations are *taken in*, at some level, by the polaristic patterning of thought which they work on another level to override – for some reason extending beyond its thus limited thematic, polemic utility. We perceive swiftly then that there is another potential attraction in the evocation/revocation mode of discourse. Consistent "dialectic also offers the assurance of structure".[84] Under the sway of the statistical experience of texts (an aspect of reading which, as I've argued, is *always* our habit and which a Derrida would only have us conscious of) we are once again 'touched' and played upon by the enticement of the rhythmically symmetrical composition of utterances. Such redundant symmetricality in fiction can be wholly accounted for only when we observe its residual, beyond-the-utilitarian, formal allure.

With this possibility in view, when we look to the global ("macro") organization of anti-Realist narration we find further surprises. That predisposition toward circularity, for example: We're obliged to realize certain new (or very old) things about the mental processes it elicits. We may easily – under the influence of recent theory – *thematically interpret* the evocation of the circle as the invocation of 'openness' or 'infinitude' (the linearity of narration is endless). But if we follow the instructions of a text, or a theory about texts, that tells us to relinquish the temptation to interpret, we're suddenly confronted with a 'shape', in the circle, that is literally the most complete and closed structure conceivable. The linearity of the narrative (whether it be that of *Molloy*, "Las ruinas circulares", *Le Voyeur, The Third Policeman, Se una notte d'inverno un viaggatore, Mahu* or *Le Parc*) is self-sufficingly, tidily 'shut' in a particular way that Realist narrative never approaches and categorically seeks to reject. Whatever its thematic, propositional intention, anti-Realist fiction's allegiance to circularity of organization, wherever it's to be found, is the articulation of formal unity, consolidation, restraint, economy and simplicity, resolution and designed composure. The same can be said of such fiction's almost equal prepossession with narrative patterns (for example, in *Pale Fire, V, Molloy, The Third Policeman, Le Parc*) making express show of the inevitable *convergence* of persons, places, and events.[85]

We may, here again, keep faith with what we feel to be the fiction's intentions by setting aside such 'naive' examples – in which what happens at the level of *histoire* is the basis of judgement – and look only at the global arrangement of textual discourse itself. But at this level, too, what we may call '*tabular constraints*' play a forceful part, as a selection of kinds of cases from among many reveals:

In anti-Realism, whether it's Cortázar's *Rayuela* (with its 'two books', one essential, one 'dispensable'), Pinget's *Le Fiston* or *Mahu*, Calvino's *Il castello dei destini incrociati, Le città invisibili* or *Se una notte d'inverno un viaggatore*, Sanguineti's *Il giuoco dell'Oca*, or Cage's "Where Are We Going? and What Are We Doing?' (1961), with their alternative or parallel narratives, there is an energetic and relentless effort to present – in successive parts or even on the same page – a mathematically regular, strictly rhythmed and symmetrically arrayed deployment of 'contradictory' narrations that are finely balanced in quantity, diction, and level of discourse. We may well recognize here the operation of the instincts that impelled the construction of Browning's twelve-part *The Ring and the Book*. In both situations it's as though the writer were working to a 'table of measures'. Browning's 'instinctive' taste for measure is twofold: he plays the rôles of both the objective and scientifically judicious advocate presenting a balanced argument, *and* of the poet presenting a felicitous, aesthetically-balanced work of art. While Browning is culturally and fundamentally committed to a Realist system in the framing of his *argument*, the writers at hand are not, and the element of 'balance' in their inventions is positively in excess of the mere exigencies of propositional overdetermination. Their texts are designed as deeply contrived freestanding artefacts (free of the presumptions of objectivist dogma) whose appeal is more to the unmixed pleasure of formal composition even than Browning's.

As we begin at this stage to witness the full extent to which narration-centred fiction may be frankly, mechanically artificial, we risk a quite crucial misapprehension. Surely the contemplation of the machine-like cannot be a source of gratification, an object of pleasure, we may say. Apart from the fact that in thinking so we would be ignoring much of what we know of Renaissance and eighteenth-century metaphysical and aesthetic thinking and would be showing the colours of our own narrowly post-Romantic heritage, there is a more general problem in such an unreflecting stock response. We should be seriously confused if we thought, as some anti-Realists themselves have affected in their condemnation of 'poetic language', that any 'pure form' toward which humans (or writers) might aspire must always or even largely be characterizable as decorative. What human beings – not to mention such bizarrely sophisticated human beings as writers – sometimes seek in the way of the 'pure' or 'absolute' or even 'beautiful' is rarely concerned with the pretty. So it happens that a text may now advance an absolute regularity far in excess of that which even the most standard aesthetically-orientated (prettiness-seeking) critical analysis might uncover. It becomes no longer sufficient to note the fixed periodicity of recurrence of certain motifs (not only of light-and-dark, of window-and-mirror but of 'squares', blood, 'burning', 'red', 'dice', 'pen', 'knife', as documented in Sollers by Kristeva, Ricardou, Barthes and Derrida in their different ways). Nor do we adequately encompass the practice when we cite, as Derrida does, the steady emergence of even more extreme but still local procedures such as the one by which, in *Nombres*, "all the sequences that begin with the number 4", their headings appearing between parentheses, are written in the present tense, and are addressed to "you".[86] The concerted activity of 'graphic' tabular composition now extends to englobe the entire work. "It is these weights and measures", as Derrida quotes, discussing *Nombres*, "these frames, these meridians, and these artificial horizons which, in their very construction, possess a kind of rigor that is absolute and general, mathematical" (Derrida, 1969, 296). As Derrida puts it, *Nombres* "have no present or signified content. And, *a fortiori*, no absolute referent. . . . They don't show anything, don't tell anything, don't represent anything, aren't trying to say anything. . . . The transformations of meaning no longer hinge on any enrichment of 'history' and 'language' but only on a certain squaring [*quadrature*] of the text" – that feature which he calls *Nombres*' 'tetralogical configuration'. (I point out *quadrature* from Derrida's French original because it would particularly appeal to Sollers, for reasons we'll see.)[87] Thus Baudry's *Personnes* and Sollers' *Nombres* and *Drame* as well as Brooke-Rose's *Thru* will be numbered (and sometimes decimally sub-numbered) section by section, and/or will contain actual tables (not only in *Personnes* but in *Thru*, where a 'timetable' sets forth, *à la* Stuart Gilbert's recapitulation of *Ulysses*, the book's succession of themes) expressing the formulary composition of the text as an object occupying, as Sollers has told us, a "predetermined, arbitrary, numerical space".[88]

But surely the attraction to 'pure form', particularly if we associate it with aesthetic intention, has little to do with numbers and/or mathematics? The answer is of course that, in the context of western culture's habits of mind, the two are extremely difficult to *separate*. The world of written works as a whole is of course replete with books divided into numbered sections without, we commonly imagine, any aesthetic concern whatsoever; that is, the universe of 'text-books'. But the textbook/fiction book distinction is not a simple one. 'Non-fiction' books, widely governed by rules of mathematical and scientific discourse largely concerned with how to build a narrative (for instance, how correctly to order the stages of a logical proof or how to build and how subsequently to write up an experiment), are congenitally arranged according to some more or less explicit system of ordinational numbering which Sollers' novels, for example, straightforwardly emulate.[89] In the non-fiction texts what is wanted above all, we believe, is that statements be made to conform to an external, transportable, previously agreed framework of 'constants' – of steps taken by the narrator, demonstrating that his/her discourse is a pure untainted container whose contents are uncontaminated by his or her action but merely transparently displayed by it. The objective, it's popularly assumed, is only to implement the discovery of some practically useful information. What, then, are we to do with the scientist's and the mathematician's ceaseless allusions to good narratives (experiments, proofs) as 'sweet', 'elegant', 'beautiful'? As a central figure in twentieth-century mathematics declares, the mathematician's "criteria of selection, and also those of success, are mainly aesthetical"; they "are clearly those of any creative art", "akin to the atmosphere of art pure and simple"; "the mathematical criteria of success ... are almost entirely aesthetical" (von Neumann, 1947, 7–9).

This seems a classic case of an anomaly, if not an outright contradiction – the attribution to an instrumental activity of aesthetic properties. Yet actually it divulges a vital insight: that the *virtue* of the activity the mathematician describes lies (or would lie) in its adherence to autonomous and transposable formal rules, in its independence from the 'meaning' it communicates and in fact from any utility which that meaning might eventually possess. When, on the other hand, we turn the situation around to regard the attitude of *writers* making no pretension to mathematical or scientific utility, we find them joining their endeavour to that of the 'pure mathematician'. In composing *Drame*, *Lois* and *Nombres*, Sollers says, "I wanted there to be the most extreme geometric certitude. ... I passed days, months, imagining I was in the process of really writing a cube. ... I have the impression of touching, as I trace the words, a geometric, algebraic substratum".[90] We might easily go on to recall the intense similarity of the connection so often recorded between the activities of those involved in mathematics and that other linear, 'narrative' aesthetic medium, music. Sollers' narrator in *Lois* writes "Music at this point is much closer to me than you perhaps will ever be"; asked to describe the meaning of music to him and of its rôle in his fiction *Paradis* he says "Oh! Music is everything. . . . I take music like logic".[91] Thus many of Sollers' titles refer to processes of regulation: *Logiques, Lois, L'Intermédiaire, Nombres* and, as its epigraph has made clear, *Le Parc.* As the composer John Cage – acclaimed among literary theorists specifically for his advocacy (and demonstration) of indeterminacy and his rejection of systematic meaning – makes explicit in his "Lecture on Nothing", "form" and "structure" for him have "no point" and are consequently good, in exactly the way that rational disciplines such as mathematics are. "The technique of handling materials is, on the sense level what structure as a discipline is on the rational level: a means of experiencing nothing."[92] What is paramount is that where the writer or the composer consistently a-scribes mathematical properties to his or her text and where the mathematician consistently claims aesthetic properties for his/her 'text', assigning its affective power to its orderliness and shapeliness of form, it will be awkward if not impossible to establish that there is any difference between their intentions in these respects. Formliness begins to assert itself in identical ways as the warrant – the 'criterion' – of the work's 'success'.[93]

A startling feature setting language-centred texts apart from other fictional modes in the past half-century – a feature long ago abandoned by Realism – is that they are more often than not littered with non-linguistic visual illustrations. Riffling through the pages of Brooke-Rose, early Sollers, Roche, Federman, one is obliged to realize that their writers, *as writers*, feel that language is *not* autonomous, not sufficient to 'tell itself'. The reasons for such apparent breaks with their own theories are many, including the prepossession with the notion of writing as 'graphic' and with the inadequacy of language to its ostensible task. But two traits stand out. Unlike the illustrations in nineteenth-century Realist texts (which were equally prone to the criticism that their authors were ultimately unable to put all their faith in their words), they are persistently not mimetically referential but analytically abstract. And they are almost universally, seemingly obsessively, symmetrical – circles, squares, radial forms, triangles, axial grids, four-square box graphs, equilateral directional diagrams.[94] In scientific (and associated, for example literary structuralist) usage, the construction and illustration of hypotheses in symmetrical form is conventionally rationalized according to some concept of symmetricality in nature, but in science itself the validity of such a concept is the subject of heated debate, and the narratologist has in any case, as we know, potent cause to reject such appeals to nature. It is as if the symmetry of presentation of data so enclosed were here again offered as some unreasoned, intuitive guarantee of the worth of the relations proposed. This is all the more striking when we perceive that a vast number of such designs are offered as representations in various forms of the procedures and shapes of the very works, as wholes, in which they appear.

It doesn't stop here. Reappropriating the earlier tactics of Cubist and Futurist 'writing', the pages of discourse-centred fiction (Brooke-Rose, Federman, Roche) are full of examples of *typo*graphic dis-play. Letters, words, sentences are modelled to form suns, trees, human shapes, faces and a wide array of highly regular abstract patterns. What's more: where no 'thing' is 'pictured', both semantically 'thick' and 'thin' texts are typographically 'perfected' on the paper. Lines are – in the printer's jargon – by conspicuously unorthodox spacing 'justified' to all four margins in ways overtly exceeding the printing compositor's conventions, to make perfect rectangles of text with lines of often precisely equal character-quantity, such that what is most pronounced of all to the reader *is* their optical 'perfection'.[95] The bases for our frequent resistance to such material may be most revealing of its intentions. At its best as *mimesis* (of which the most successful examples may have been produced long ago by Futurism, in for instance the fold-out "Carta Sincrona" in Marinetti's *Zang Tumb Tumb*, 1912) it has the liabilities of the crudely clever, perfectly conical Christmas-tree composed on a typewriter; it is intrinsically impoverished in its representational capacity. As a mode for the *parody* of mimesis, it inevitably cannot contain or confront head-on and thus inescapably fails to rebut – either by irony or mockery – what most characterizes and, some would say, justifies mimesis: the sense of material precision and detailed textural richness. Though we may sometimes wearily feel otherwise, we know that the contemporary writer is too sophisticated in other respects not to be aware of the deficiencies in such a set of strategems *as a mimetic or anti-mimetic* gambit. What we recognize to be more plausibly hoped for in them is exactly their potential for schematic, abstractive effect. This effect might be taken on its own as a mode of pastiche (playing on the follies of systematic thinking), were it not for the fact of its own clockwork recurrence, far beyond the limits of our laughter or of telling surprise; had corrective insight been its aim, one instance in a long text would have more than exhausted its slim reward. Once more it's clear that the writer is drawn to a series of devices by the awareness they may arouse of the activity of the generalized representation of forms and of formal relations, and of form's tension with the particular and unique utterance (the letters, words) which it 'composes'.

An acute peculiarity, then, of recent fiction that is claimed to be analytically pure is that it's inclined to be highly patterned, and that one can reject this movement toward shapeliness as evidence of formalist motivation only if one acknowledges instead that it is systematically propositional. We *may* take its reiterated motifs (circles, dice, labyrinths) as something *other* than neutral formal notations denoting, in their global recurrence, order-and-pattern-making. But we can do so only by reverting to a reading of them not as indeterminate but as emblems of determined semantic conceptions – emblems *signifying* 'indeterminacy', for example, by externally agreed standard convention.

The one way out of this would be to declare that we see formal order-making (rhythm, for instance) in the first place only because that's what we're looking for. That *we're* producing such forms. This would appear to be a strong and appropriate argument. The real problem is that it fails to coincide with what the writers actually say. The case of Sollers, so widely put forward as a most extreme and powerful example of the indeterminist at work, deserves to be considered as a primary illustration on this score. Speaking of Robbe-Grillet's fiction, he writes:

> Everything takes place as if the matter of his books were composed of raw elements of reality, *rhythmically disposed* in a *durée* arising from their juxtaposition. Now this association is not irrational, though it most often escapes chronology. It seems that certain elements 'call' one another forth by a *structural necessity* (visible at the hub of their junction) or because, abruptly, '*it is time*' again to encounter this room, this tableau.[96]

Sollers has been critical of Robbe-Grillet, and we can expect an analytically-inclined thinker to object to the latter's representationality. But the *formal* aspects (indicated by my italics) he finds in Robbe-Grillet are identical to ones that Sollers' own writing shows itself in ardent search of, as – if we were ever before in doubt – we now see. In *Le Parc*, among a multitude of similar passages in his work, the narrator speaks of "a co-existence of disparate elements . . . *connected* in some way" where

> one could live for ever between that plate and that vase, or simply between these two formless areas of colour: a concerted interval

> that *links* them, a luminous place without thickness or depth, liberated from space and time ... the subject of the picture hanging on the wall here, opposite me, is a *more compact*, more obvious – or enigmatic – *resumé*, of this room and that table. And replaces it, occupies it *proportionally, detached, cut off, homogeneous*....[97]

Or of the park itself – at whose entrance is an inscription giving "the *regulations* governing conduct in the park that no one has ever read, but which everyone obeys" (Sollers, 1961, 90):

> I walk among varied and contradictory essences, where one passes without transition ... from one time to another time. As if, a trace having been made in the middle of the town, ... *a whole has been organized here*, in spite of everything, in *one complicated design*.
> ... I can become the complete opening through which I at last see what I wish to see ... *composing, ordering* in spite of myself. ...
> (90, 43)

So, in reviewing his work in *Drame, Nombres* and *Lois*, Sollers makes it plain: As he wrote them, he had come gradually to understand that "it would be necessary completely to recast *la rythmique*".[98] (The *rythmique* of Dante had fallen upon him "like a mystical experience"[99]). "You've mentioned", he says to his interviewer, "the very deliberated use of rhythm. I try to integrate different metric traditions. ... The essential aspects. ... are metrics and rhythmics".[100] When asked whether we mightn't be lost without some "structure" in a literary work, he answers "Listen, the essential is the perception the writer has of repetition. What does he think of repetition; how does he use it; and how does he place himself in relation to his own repetitions?"[101] Of his *Paradis* he says, "there is at the same time the rhythm, the dance, the roll-on of syllables and the rendering of events. The continuous roll-on of the words corresponds to a kind of maximal immobility. ... The idea is to make the subject seem to be something whose circumference is everywhere and whose centre is nowhere".[102] "Is it truth you're seeking?" "Yes", he responds, "the beauty and splendour of truth, certainly. ... 'Beauty', 'splendour', these are no longer values but a radiance, an abstract force".[103]

In *Rayuela*, Cortázar's writer Morelli too speaks of beauty. He "thirsts for the absolute"; and "there is only one beauty which can still give me that access: the one that is an end and not a means, and which is so because its creator has identified in himself his sense of the human condition with his sense of the artist's condition". It would be perverse to insist that when a writer such as Sollers attributes intrinsic force to beauty as distinct from truth (it's ill-mannered to ask at this point where this 'truth' fits in) he must be saying that he feels (as a character says of Morelli) that "'his work won't have any other value except aesthetic'" (Cortázar, 1963, 446, 474–5). Yet there's no question but that, like Morelli, the figure Sollers lays before us 'thirsts for' some absolute to which, *conventionally*, the aesthetic aspiration was there to give form. In the next chapter we'll find foreshadowed what may be another way of looking at this.

The cases cursorily hinted in the preceding pages are only a coarse sampling of some of the most radical anti-Realist fiction's clear flirtation with the vision of pure form.[104] But we can begin to generalize. We're not questioning here that an accent on form can serve anti-mimetic purposes. Theorists devoted to promulgating discourse-centred narrative, such as Sollers', freely describe its processes as the "Formalization of the Fiction". That is, as Ricardou goes on to define it, "the tendency whereby the activity of these formal principles ... is intensified, and even made the object of an undeniable ostentation. ... Beneath the profuse variety of variables, more general patterns begin to emerge. ... The systematic application of a pattern", the "alignment of the disparate along the coordinating axis of a small number of basic schemas certainly removes us from the everyday world, and plays a decisive anti-naturalist role" (1971, 119, 121). "The narration is allowed to materialize only in obedience to a rigorous system of fragmentation", Ricardou says of *Personnes* and *Nombres*. "Since the order of the very different sequences is determined by the requirement that the combinatorial grid be covered methodically, all attempts to subsume the narrative movement's diversity under a unitary principle are blocked a priori" (125–7). While we now readily recognize the truth of the description Ricardou offers, we can rapidly see the rift between it and the construction he places on it in the last phrase. By such formal grids the narration is "distributed mechanically and with periodic, violent switches", he accurately reports. But having thus violated mimesis, how are the 'methodical', 'systematic', 'rigorous' 'formal principles' by which this alternative autarchy is thrust forward not subsumed under some unitary principle?[105] With critical brilliance Ricardou and other narratologists demonstrate their rectitude in speaking unswervingly of formal principles as 'determining' such texts' utterances. The theory would be unintelligible without precisely that lemma. Categorically for them, a privilege inheres in formalization itself such that it – in the place of 'naturalistic' rules – is accorded equally unconditional 'aprioristic' jurisdiction. The writer is thus in the peculiar position that while a mode – a numerological or other ostensibly semantically purged 'system' – has surely been discovered by which to shake the foundations of the conventional propositional recuperability of his or her text's signs, nevertheless, as the example of Ricardou's argument shows: this clean, 'detached' meta-system cannot *work* in this way unless it is itself assumed to have semantically for the reader, as it has for Ricardou, an integral formal orderliness. (We assume that the signs '1', '2', '4.15' have this clean quality, but only by what is itself a semantic convention, just as others in the past have assigned 'purity' to such numerical systems as the notion of the golden section, by a semantically agreed aesthetic tradition.) Though a Ricardou, in his further essay on *Le Parc*, discloses in detail the omnipresence of "regulatory mechanisms" there, he abandons to our imagination on what *grounds* Sollers should have decided that the *reglé* rather than the *déreglé* should have been the most satisfying mode for the generation of his text. The *formal basis* of the discourse's enunciation is accounted for, but not its *formliness*. The theorist would answer that the pleasure lies in the unsettling apparent paradox of the activity.[106] But there is of course no actual paradox here – there are no two irreconcilable truths, but rather there is merely a contrast and resonance between two levels of information or of 'reading' (between, say, the uncustomarily 'irregular', disorderly *histoire* and the uncustomarily regular activity of order-making 'external' to it). Much recent theory, caught up in its own weightily 'serious' interpretation of fictional texts as philosophical and even polemic exercises, avers that such fiction makes use of formal regularity (to point up semantic irregularities) on purely *pragmatic* grounds, without being in any way committed to form as a good on its own. But, as the example of Sollers shows, this often turns out not to be what the writer actually, ultimately believes. On philosophical grounds which relevant theorists (following Gödel, for example) are compelled to maintain, it is likely that no conceptual *rationale* for the voluntary effort toward formliness can exist that does not depend on the postulation of a higher system that is at least as formly – that is, cosmic. The anticosmic writer showing formliness is thus logically bound to confess – if he is to remain anticosmic – that he does so because he purely and simply (without pragmatically warrantable argument) likes formliness. This is no more or less than what we had recognized by other, empirical means to be an essentially aesthetic attitude. As Sollers and

Brooke-Rose, as much as Lewis and Borges and Nabokov, indeed do identify it when they speak of "beauty".

Here then is a conception that a literary work may hope primarily to be a syntactic rather than a sematic achievement. 'High' in syntactic value, in other words, and 'low' in semantic. The text is 'meant' to provide (just enough) semantic 'competence' to evoke the sense of *difference* necessary for us to discern and draw gratification from its syntactic 'performance', rather than (just enough) syntactic performance for us to perceive its semantic content, as in the case of Realism. The syntactic arrangement of Rühm's "leaflea ... " gives a semantic surprise, but its main effect would be to throw our attention back to the satisfying recognition of the power of even minimal syntactic action. There are indeed many ways of conceiving of the exact appeal of such qualities in texts, all of which cry to be explored. We may, for example, think of them as 'geometrical' systems – a notion not only suited to the conceit of the book as a 'world' (*geo-*) to be 'measured', but clearly of documented appeal to writers we know, from Robbe-Grillet and Nabokov to Brooke-Rose and Sollers. As in geometry, quantities (semantic values) may change, may move toward indeterminacy, while configurations and proportional rapports remain constant, just as Sollers suggests in his references to 'immobility' and to the Pascalian sphere.[107] Or we may consider the possibility that in the place of cosmic systems fiction may turn toward the construction of 'sets', 'groups', or 'sequences' – shapely suites of procedure – in the mathematicians's sense. Making appeal not to our understanding but to our sensuous pleasure – a pleasure in concerted sequentiality without 'consequence', or sequentiality in tension with the aspiration toward consequence.

As one of Sollers' narrators says, "everything has a form" (1961, 43); and one might expect any anticosmic text to acclaim and seek to engender a unique form (one 'unconformable' to other texts) every time. No literature has ever worked more strenuously to persuade its readership that it is free of everyone else's canons of orderliness. Signs that such fictions, instead, support and transport conventionally recognized formal traits from work to work suggest that their writers view form as a superordinate good transcending the benefits of total freedom.

But when we say that transformational narrative renders itself at many levels subject to what are in some sense '*algorithmic*' *constraints*, we've not denied the importance of the act of narration. Consider cases of creations at opposite ends of the spectrum of 'aporic', ambiguous, perturbational objects classically produced in art and with which anti-Realism has historically deep affinities, however uncomfortable the current 'serious' innovator may feel about them: the *trompe l'oeil* (the 'ultra-artificial') and the collage of *objets trouvés* (the 'ultra-natural'). The 'bowl of fruits', the 'books', 'musical instruments' and 'household implements' that line the 'shelves' of the Renaissance nobleman's study which are in reality only a marquetry illusion created in a smooth plane of wood on a flat otherwise featureless wall; the 'face of a nobleman' astonishingly and convincingly composed on a wall (by say the Baroque or Surrealist artist) of actual fruits, cutlery, jewels. Rarely if ever does the thoughtful observer in either case believe the object beautiful, yet he or she may feel that nowhere in art has there been any 'work' more 'beautifully' conceived (as an enterprise) and executed. (He/she senses behind it, for example, the *marqueteur*'s masterly selection and juxtaposition of colours and grains from his 'palette' of timbers, his hands shaving whisper-thin curls from satinwood and box to form their invisible joins, or the Surrealist stylist's weirdly effective sense of the correspondence in colour, mass, texture and line between the objects (of one class) used and the objects (of another class) mimicked. It's in the activity of the 'joiner' that the observer takes pleasure; it's not *something beautiful* that the artefact makes manifest, but the *beauty of its making*. The persistent ambiguity in our response to 'artistic objects' – objects perceived as 'things' versus objects as predications of the manner of their coming into being – doesn't stop with such habitual expressions as 'oeuvre', 'work' 'building' but extends to the word 'art' – *ars*, craftsmanship – itself. Peculiarly, a kind of empathic, *kin*-aesthetic delight is called for; the action of the maker fashioning the object becomes 'the object'. In this view, formalist narration – coinciding with the upsurge of the 'happening' in other media – becomes a performative art. In 'tracing' (what we think to be) the narration's movements we enact that performance. It's in this sense that Barthes, in his late and most indeterminist phase, can freely say and repeat unequivocally that his "friend" Sollers' novel *H* is "beautiful" and possesses "a *material* plenitude of pleasures".[108]

There may be a further way of accounting for the shapeliness found in discourse-centred narrative. One might say that anticosmic fiction as a whole is *compelled* to be patterned at the level of discourse – being anti-systematic at the level of *histoire* – by the rule mentioned before of the inverse relation of paradigmatic and syntagmatic functions. (We want chaotic 'contents' to be compensated by orderly 'presentation'.) But such a 'rule' is not an inevitable ontological – for example, linguistic – law. In neocosmic fiction, embodying a further, supralinguistic premiss, the appearance of systematicity represents an *active choice* on the part of the narrator. On what principle might the anticosmist base *his* or *her* unmistakable *decision* that system is good at the level of discourse when it's not good at the level of *histoire*? (Indeed, we shall have to ask eventually whether, once a system has been chosen to operate on one level, it can be prevented from operating on another.) Once again, the upsurgence of formliness exceeds the theoretical limits overtly posited by or for the text in other respects.

It's a problem. We can see, of course, why much anti-Realist thought must have real philosophical difficulty in openly and fully addressing the matter of aesthetic value which so manifestly preoccupies a surprising number of its practitioners in fiction.[109] The analytic theorist cannot claim utility for the narrative; yet he/she is restrained from appealing to 'pure pleasure' in the way that a Gautier or a Pater might have done. The fictionalist perceives clearly the charge that may be levelled against him or her as it has been against those in kindred criticism: "the key value terms of poststructuralism as they are expressed by Derrida ... (and pursued with erotic zeal by recent Barthes) are practical and affective, not cognitive" writes Lentricchia. "... A new hedonism is suggested. Terms like 'joy' and 'activity', and their variants, are fundamental. They recall the overt preoccupations of the nineteenth-century aesthetes with a *telos* of 'pleasure' and a quest for 'freedom'".[110] Often moved by reason or temperament to precisianist – if not puritan – self-scrutiny, the anti-Realist is further aware of the external socio-historical spirit of apocalypticism on which his or her very insurgency so often depends with its appeal to his/her contemporaries' sense of anguish, in the face of which anything resembling frivolous hedonism would seem a profound embarrassment.

The situation is made vividly clear by the fact that in nearly every place where it might open an enquiry into its position on aesthetics anti-Realist argument instead acclaims '*play*'. The difference between play and aesthetic pleasure is exactly that aesthetics, the business of finding beauty, is constitutionally associated with the activity of defining values and their associated rules. It is a form of seriousness, while the pleasure of play is by definition not-serious and even anti-serious.[111] The embarrassment entailed by the notion of aesthetic interest in this context is extreme, on at least two counts. Because looking for rules is on its own ideologically inadmissible. And because taking such interests seriously means taking seriously some conception of oneself (I am partly defined by my definition of what I like or desire), which is for the same – and perhaps other – reasons inadmissible. Beyond this, many will declare, thinking aesthetically is inescapably thinking referentially ("beauty is merely a referential code sending us back to beauty as statue painting or goddess"[112]) and is thinking in terms of categories; once discard categories of experience, as we've seen many like Ehrmann argue, and aesthetics must disappear.

Whether or not we come to take radical writers' silence on this subject – coupled with theorists' outspoken espousal of play for which manifold examples and oddly vague definitions are given – as eloquent, it will have important and perhaps further surprising repercussions for the logic of anti-Realist gestures all told.[113]

I've treated ideas of the text as 'pure narration' and as 'pure form' separately, dreaming to give something like a momentarily clear and unobstructed view of each in its 'ideal' aspect. But this artificial way of proceeding can't go on indefinitely. The more closely we look the more we seem likely to see the former in practice move ever toward the latter. They share the fundamental predisposition toward analyticity. It will be further argued by some of those believing in 'pure narration' that their traits are logically bound up with one another.[114] And clearly it's not *incompatible* with free narrationality *per se* that it may enunciate utterances in a balanced and patterned way. The only deep problem is that when it does so, a choice at the disposal of the writer has been selected for which a theory of pure narration doesn't alone give account.[115] Comprehensible motivations have been brought to bear in support of this kind of choice. Above all, the apparent formation of a text is called upon as the means by which its apparent information is dissolved. But now, the *implications* for the *reader* of the many texts built upon such a supererogatory formalist decision – particularly if it's meant to be the reader and not the writer who forms or produces the text – may be other than had been bargained for. Confusion is brewing for anti-Realism which must be reckoned with elsewhere.[116]

CONCLUSION
The anti-Realist tradition

"My hope ... was to construct a self-perpetuating movement, the book in process of becoming a world."[1] In these few words the radical anti-Realist – Sollers, describing his motives in composing *Lois* – returns us to the world/book *topos* with which we began. And alerts us to the fact that fundamentally, inasmuch as anticosmic theory's critique of neocosmic fiction would be valid, its own narration may fail to evade the same liabilities. The two modes are equally subject to systematic ("construct"), referential and determinate ("book") readings – readings elicited by authors who are accountable ("my") for the instigation of these effects – and can even in their most radical states only *declare* that they are not, or metaphorically represent texts that are not. In another place I try to make clear in detail why this is so, and will not burden with that speculative and controversial argument an essay which, while always open to debate, has taken description as the main model for its way of proceeding.[2] In the meantime, we can recognize that each anti-Realist text has its way of protecting its reader from its own influence – from the hazards of our utterly confounding its 'world' with some 'real world'; the neocosmic by the assertive 'uncustomariness' of its *histoire*, the anticosmic by its persistent allusion to the multiplicity of 'customs' on which its *discours* depends. But we can go further than this.

There are many kinds of distinctions we might now begin to draw, to gain a perspective on anti-Realist fiction as a whole, at one extreme, and on any individual anti-Realist text, at the other. (Contrasting the literature's stance with that of other radical movements, for example, we might say that *futurismo* was more highly mimetic in its impulse and confident in the efficacy of a single coherent 'I'; that *surrealisme* saw a continuity of a higher order behind it all; that *dada* was more programmatic in its belief in the utility of direct action; and so forth. Contrasting a text by say Vonnegut with one by Brooke-Rose or Sollers, we might find them not unrepresentative of a difference between American and European anticosmic writing, with the latter laying seige to Realism's *having* declarative intentions and the former assaulting the *specific* declarative intentions – the ethos – it associates with Realism; and so on.) There is plenty for others to be getting on with. The best we can hope to do here is to round out (frame) the particular – always artificial – kind of picture with which we started.

One might well endorse some or all of neocosmic fiction's various aspirations – its notions of narrative as performing some 'pure fictional', combinative, playful, conditioning, prospective, instructive or commutative function – and see still that it may be accused of treacherous oversimplification. Actually, while anticosmic narrative is typically *equivocal*, narrative can be both explicitly univocal in its discourse and deeply *ambiguous* in its over-all signification, and studies of neocosmic fiction (by storytellers as diverse as Buzzati, Borges, Calvino, Bosco, Lindsay, Le Guin and Fuentes) repeatedly insist on this quality in it, to the point of arguing rather persuasively that texts in this mode are both unitary in motive and inherently ambiguous.[3]

Beyond this, though, there lies the charge that neocosmic narrative is unwarrantably simplistic by reason of its very proclivity towards storytelling. It should now be admitted that, far from being an invention of anticosmic theory, this suspicion of 'story' has not only always been a principle behind *Realist* narrative theory (hence the cult of *slice-of-life*) but – in the view that the poetic/histrionic play of feelings over events could be of use only in primitive cultures and must fall away as civilizations advance – is intrinsic to the philosophy of Vico, Herder, Hegel, J. S. Mill and was already a hotly contested issue at the time of Shelley's attack on Peacock. But when Flaubert intimated that history was with science his century's real muse, he made way for an insight central to the anti-Realist movement. The *virement* of attention in our times toward *discours* and away from *histoire* (history), like the relinquishment of diachronic in favour of synchronic studies, expresses the essential decision that a positivistic faith in the systematic reconstruction of experience by storytelling means is unsuitably naive. There seem to be (at least) two parts to any reasonable answer neocosmic thinking might give.

The first has to do with the fact that while storytelling may be an inadequate form of *representation* of reality, the doctrine that simplification or systematization is incompatible with our effort to treat reality with truth is itself only a local, post-eighteenth-century cultural one and is not a logically inevitable one.[4] There appears to be no correlation between systematic thinking and any decline in our observation of 'the facts of nature', nor has complexity of thinking been a guarantee of 'truthfulness', as our experience of intricate late medieval theories of the natural universe shows. What has been 'dangerous' in the past ideological systems has been their exclusivity – their concerted effect in repelling alternative systems. What's proved critical has had little to do with any risk of oversimplification, but has rather had to do with our ability/inability to make room for *diversity* of often equally simple interpretations of events, which might be tested logically against one another and against the evidence of our senses. (Complexity does not itself repulse systematicity but is actually a notion of diversity made to conform to a system. A complex construction placed upon data may really not offer freedom but may foreclose it, entangling our thinking in its web.) This argument would suggest that what we need from art is that diversity. Within the range of anticosmic fiction, where its rejection of cosmic attitudes rests largely on the notion of indeterminacy alone, variety of outlook can readily seem quite limited. A problem in the writing of this book, in fact, has been that while no one neocosmic text guarantees an infinite multiplicity of perspectives (of views concerning what 'matters'), the *possibility* of neocosmic fiction *provides* for it to such an extent that there has been no chance for us to embrace or examine in detail the array of premisses it offers – beyond the mere citation of general 'contexts for premisses' sketched in Chapter 1.

A second part of an answer to the anti-story theory relates – beyond the question of what the universe of neocosmic texts might tender – to what each individual text may have to offer. Both anticosmic and neocosmic fictions are devoted to alternative perspectives on the art of experiencing, itself. The difference is basically a matter of at what juncture and at what level the greatest insight is to be produced. Anticosmic thinking says that it happens at the point when we realize that we must defer closure (and, often, that this is a problem of – happens at the level of – language). Neocosmic thinking seems to say that insight arises when we perceive *that we are closing* – 'closing in on' a decision, whether linguistic or not – and *how this resolution comes about*. We know that in the neocosmic view, the storytelling mode may not be one that 'covers up' truths as opponents of 'decidable' or 'readerly' texts maintain, but rather one that uncovers, 'draws up from the deep', uncustomary and hitherto unperceived options, as a Philip Sidney or a C. S. Lewis or a Fuentes would maintain. And these would be radical options, this time, for which neither Realist nor anticosmic narratives can make room or provide an adequate proving ground: to test (as Golding, Saviane and Calvino do) the strength and resolving power of our ideas of progress and evolution, or (as Abbott does) ideas of the limits of perception, or (as Lindsay and McElroy do) ideas of the relations between material and pure being or non-being, or (as Nabokov and Borges do) ideas of design in human transactions, or (as Borges and Calvino do) ideas of phenomenal-versus-ideal representations of experience, or (as Fuentes does) ideas of historical-versus-essential being, or (as Williams, Le Guin and Calvino do) ideas of personal-versus-archetypal being. But more: neocosmic narrative, it would be said, sees value in soliciting its reader to engage with these possibilities – to play them out – in the continuous, developing ways that we believe we experience the customary. Story, then, in this perspective, would be the unique medium in which humans can hope to bring discourse into touch with the experience we have of the *eventuation* of the data of our lives. For those believing experience is more than 'just language', a neocosmic story may thus have a dimensionality exceeding the 'purely linguistic' developmental values claimed for an anticosmic 'transformational' narration.

Oddly enough, neocosmic narrative also finds itself taken to task for being too complicatedly ambiguous. It appears often unable or even unwilling to avoid seeming not merely metaphorical or allegorical but – following the distinction made by late-eighteenth/nineteenth-century Romantic and twentieth-century dynamic psychological theory – obscurely symbolic. (It does not re-present the already known but, via the symbol, would provide a nexus – a '*lieu*' – between the already perceived and the otherwise unperceivable.) This conception of fiction, as we know, anticosmists such as Robbe-Grillet vehemently reject, on the grounds that it opens the way to interpretations of reality that would transcend the stark material substantiality of things-as-they-are. Here comes an elemental aspect of the anti-Realist movement to which little space has so far been given here. The anti-Realist impulse in the arts has always, in fact, had not one but two divergent and equally urgent inner motives: the formalist and the symbolist. Neocosmic writing shows the depth of its roots in the latter. Historically, in the period prior to the 1930s, the *élan* of avant-garde 'abstract' painting springs not from a formalist but from a symbolist attitude; like *symbolisme* in poetry and the drama, it seeks to oppose bourgeois naturalism by an appeal to a realm of trans-material apperception. Neocosmic fiction shows positive signs of interest – from Lindsay, Williams and Lewis to Bosco, Buzzati and Le Guin – in this approach to truth. A striking feature of the account of literature given by J. P. Stern to which we can return now from a different angle, is that the one distinct and valid alternative to Realism he foresees is this one.

> Realism allows for symbolical meanings, but it limits their range, to the point where a break occurs between '*is*' and '*stands for*', where shared knowledge gives way to intimation; symbolism begins where intimation ceases to be subordinated to a realistic purpose and becomes dominant, an open-ended vision. ...

In this last phrase Stern reveals the intuition of an unexpected, 'modern' (or 'post-modern') potential for symbolic literature – the problematization of Realist thinking – which Robbe-Grillet, and much sceptical formalist theory in general, has been disinclined to recognize. For Stern, Realism

> may require historical information. But once that has been provided, it establishes a self-explaining continuity – whereas symbolism insists on the enigmatic break – between the common norm *given* in the language and a contingent, *created* mutiplicity of references. Realism's *making* of private meanings is subordinated to its *matching* of meanings against available common norms of usage. ... Symbolical fictions [on the other hand] grow 'beyond the world of common indication'. This is why they occasionally contain prophetic insights which are denied to realism. ... Just so their language displays an originality and a creativeness that leaves the common usage of a given age behind, though it may provide a later age and *its* realism with new linguistic forms.
>
> (1973, 84)

This rationale, advanced by a 'pro-Realist' in support of an explicitly anti-Realist mode of narrative and unmistakably an argument for a kind of fiction that would be *radical* in its function, is one that neither *nouveau roman* nor *Tel Quel* radical theories could conceivably openly adopt, since it rests on the assertion of fiction's ability to 'intimate' transcendental meanings. It's couched in the very idiom that neocosmic reasoning, as we've seen in Chapter 2, might appropriate in its defence. Neocosmic fiction, however, may be yet more 'radical' than either Realist or anticosmic theory would allow. One of its peculiarities is that, abandoning or even in revolt against the mystique of homology (where 'form' must match 'content'), it frequently tends to say anticosmic things even while it posits a cosmos. Narratatively stable texts as early as *Voyage to Arcturus*, in spite of or by means of their failure to meet customary standards of mimesis and even of 'good literature', avail themselves of 'the marvellous' to articulate schematically, with great conceptual resolving power, the incompleteness of customary conceptual models (social, religious, ethical, aesthetic) of believing and reasoning.[5] Rather than 'totally closed', by reminding the reader that they differ from given customs of modelling, they could be argued to recall persistently the plurality of possible models. In any case, a narrative of this sort may not only say it is 'about' something; it may admit as one of its features that it is about both more than it *can* say and more than it *wants* to say. That is, it is an overture – literally an opening – to those things which it cannot control (for example the undecidability of facts) *even while* it postulates an ordered universe. This, as we've seen, appears to enact a crucial contradiction which is categorically repugnant to the rigorous homological attitude intrinsic to much anticosmic theory.[6] Anti-Realism contains the curious phenomena: a deliberately disordered (anticosmic) narrative mode founded on an abhorrence of disorder, and a narrative mode founded on order (neocosmic) that is deeply tolerant of disorder.

A mordant response to neocosmic fiction launched by serious criticism – and there's no intelligence in pretending now that anticosmic theory, for all that it repels the idea, is not itself indefatigably serious if not solemn – is that the aspects of it just discussed stem from constitutional naiveté. Certainly anticosmic texts are among the most sophisticated forms in Western literature. As I've pointed out, though, the display of sophistication is itself a rhetorical mode, by which a work may choose – or *not* choose – to gain its effects. There may actually be at least two kinds of sophisticated narrative stance. One (which we might call 'naivist' or 'primitivist') that claims knowledge on the basis of experience, such as neocosmic fiction may often seem to do; and one (of a sceptical sort) that claims 'not to know', as anticosmic writing often does – on the basis of experience. Both arrogate *sagesse* to themselves, and it may not be as obvious as one would like which is ultimately the more logically convincing, though the latter is sure to be more rhetorically persuasive *to a certain audience*. What are we finally to do with a literature that claims to be most knowing, yet whose most paramount 'knowledge' is that knowing is impossible?

Setting aside this merely logical difficulty, however, the serious critic will point out that neocosmic fiction makes continual use of childish and sentimental kitsch literary formulae, borrowing (as writers as different as Calvino, Golding, Fuentes, Nabokov and Borges do) from the traditions of historical and exotic-locale romance, science-fiction, and the tales of mystery and the supernatural, for not always plainly parodic purposes. The problem of its relation to children's literature is one that must eventually be explored, and it's clear that neocosmic narratives frequently have great appeal for children. For the moment it's worth observing that, while anticosmic fiction may well be argued to be invaluable in preparing the next generation to fend off the delusions which an established culture perpetuates, of the literally thousands of anticosmic works now in circulation not one seems to have been written for children. Assuming that writers of anticosmic texts are not simply too tender-spirited to whisper despair to young minds, the rationale would be that children are not yet sophisticated enough to understand them – which sends us back to the problem: sophistication as a literary 'good' or norm necessitates a certain conventionality on the part of the literary text. Texts that can 'work' would be only those which their readers had in some sense already read, had been prepared for by other similar utterances. We don't like to think of revolutionary books as ones that can preach successfully only to the converted, but in some sense they always are. In anti-Realist texts of both kinds, then, the conventional element differs only as to kind and not in degree (as we've already observed in considering the banality of anticosmic narratives' context and pretexts).

A further, pragmatic value thus accompanies neocosmic writing to which anticosmic narrative – with its insistence on homology – has little access. The former has the potential (because it's willing to be synthetic and heterologous) to move freely between thoroughly traditional ways of addressing its reader ('naive', 'archetypal', 'sentimental', even morally prescriptive – in the manner of wholly traditional tales) and the most 'subversive' concepts ('sophisticated', 'phenomenalistic', 'morally neutral', 'anarchic', 'indeterminist'). It would modulate with candid ease and challenge readers to follow these modulations without requiring them by some inhering doctrine to resolve them.

Having in 1971 published a collection significantly called *Anti-*

Story, energetically heralding a post-war fiction that was 'Against Mimesis ... "Reality" ... Event ... Subject ... the Middle Range of Experience ... Analysis ... Meaning ... Scale' (xv–xxiii), Philip Stevick in 1981 wrote for a reappraisal of sentimentality.

> A plain equating of sentimentality and mendacity obscures more than it clarifies. It implies that truth lies only within those areas that are ironic, tough, Apollonian, guarded, understated. ... Literature that overvalues irony ... is in danger of attending too little to the richness of texture, indeed the wholeness of vision, which unabashedly sentimental works can contain.

Writers in the 1980s, he suggests, have "learned all there is to learn about hardness, dryness, and ritual despair ... about ironic poise and Olympian detachment from the classic modernists ... a way to make fiction intricately and seriously superficial". For the radical formalist this is revisionist stuff, though not for the political radical (it opens the way towards political action not possible for the committed formalist). But with it comes: "What we need to do is to accommodate ourselves to the possibility that fiction ... may move, even within the same work, between modes more conventional and less conventional and that such a rhythm does not, itself, vitiate the work" (Stevick, 1981, 70–1, 149–50, 68–9). This last observation, making less aggressive claims and without justifying naive utterances in themselves, is likely to prove in future a pervasive rationale for an anti-Realist fiction that is less nervously fretful to prove its own circumspection and (admittedly spurious) analytic purity. One that is less breathlessly zealous to exclude, as theoretically subversive, varieties of discourse (materials of experience, as Stevick might say, whether 'transcendental', 'sentimental' or other) which its theories both cannot resolve and declare it should neither exclude nor try to resolve.

But with such allusions to 'superficiality', the 'transcendental' and the 'sentimental' we stand on the brink of what's no doubt the most potent and the most common charge that anticosmic thinking in its early phase lays at the door of its partner in anti-Realism. The alternative-worlds mode, says the anticosmist, in an all-too-human yearning for closure (and finding closure inaccessible in reality), turns us to 'fantasy' for *escape*. One may indeed find some anticosmists still today ready to insist that the popularity of neocosmic fiction, whose readership remains after a third of a century many times the size of their own, could be accounted for by this factor alone.

The 'retreat into a book' has always promised one answer to those forms of discontent with the present world which both neocosmic and anticosmic theories themselves bring to the fore.[7] The difficulty is that there is obviously no hope of our finally identifying escapism exclusively with the allure of the uncustomary, which might have seemed to make neocosmic fiction especially answerable.[8] "I am in the midst of love-making", wrote Flaubert as he worked on *Madame Bovary*:

> I am sweating and my throat is tight. This has been one of the rare days of my life passed completely in illusion from beginning to end. At six o'clock this evening, as I was writing the word "hysterics," I was so swept away, was bellowing so loudly and feeling so deeply what my little Bovary was going through, that I was afraid of having hysterics myself. ... No matter; it is a delicious thing to write, whether well or badly – to be no longer yourself but to move in an entire universe of your own creating. Today, for instance ... I was also the horse, the leaves, the wind. ...[9]

This kind of experience of books doesn't end with the writer, as we well know from the centuries-long testimony of readers of *Realist* fiction. Neocosmic narrative, in this perspective, might be regarded as no more than a natural continuation of an appeal to escape 'universally present in art'.

There *is* an 'escapist' function latent specifically in the reading of the uncustomary which has made neocosmic fiction and its forerunners the butt of traditional Realist criticism for a century and a half and of which Robbe-Grillet (as a logical 'representationalist' successor to Realism) has simply reminded us. "Here was a man", Colin Wilson says of Lovecraft, "who made no attempt whatever to come to terms with life. ... Oppressed by the ordinary, Lovecraft keeps declaring passionately that the extraordinary exists. ... [He] creates 'other worlds' in a fervor of spite."[10]

By arousing that sense of doubleness (of the other, the metaphorical, the allegorical) the uncustomary seems to attract us away from the physical world into some imaginary metaphysical landscape or imagined psychological 'inscape'. Under the heading of the problem of 'the imagination' – a faculty frankly acclaimed by anti-Realists of both persuasions, as we saw at the start – opponents often level their heaviest charge against neocosmic literature. The term is used without methodical punctilio as shorthand variously for all writing of a nonsense-grounded kind, the intimation being conventionally that it has been acquired in some unitary and unambiguous way from – an already otherwise discredited – Romanticism. No argument based on the fact that we have mental experiences other than those directly generated by the senses is in any way bound intrinsically to theories of 'the imagination', and the failure to see this constitutes an important flaw in the case put by neocosmic fictions' adversaries. But the conception is so deeply entrenched a feature of western culture's outlook, wherever culture is suspicious of fictional undertakings, of the escapist menace of imaginative activity, that it merits attention.

The case, as famously put by Sartre, separates imaginative consciousness from conception and perception. In Sartre's view, as a basis for the *representation* of reality imagination "suffers from a sort of essential poverty"; the image "teaches nothing . . . never reveals any aspect of the object. . . . No risk, no anticipation: only a certainty" (1940, 8–9). This notion, which is later echoed in Barthes (and in writers on fantasy such as Jackson), fundamentally makes of products of the imagination artefacts that – however pleasurably creative – only encourage us to stray from reality into the mind's own nether reaches. (In some sense, as Sartre would say, "I have an image" = "I see nothing"; psycholinguists frequently remind us of the notion when they tell us that we cannot imagine a thing when we are in its presence.) Wallace Stevens offers a parallel in his trouble in deciding if his appeal to the imagination is "a poetics of courage and high risk, or simply a poetics of cowardice".[11] Thus any 'imaginative' fiction – how we might manage exactly to discern it from other kinds remains an enigma – puts us on the perilous track of escape insofar as we see it as something other than 'the (nonserious) *play* of imagination'. But the escapist charge runs deeper than merely the arraignment of ill-placed seriousness. Imaginative literature – as Erich Heller would put it, echoing the secret sentiment of many – *competes* with reality (Heller, 1965). The question to answer is precisely: can fictional narrative replace reality in our minds?

As it happens, the neocosmic fictionalist is far from the only one having a vested interest in the answer to this question. As soon as we begin to talk about a book's creating something that was not there before – rather than merely reiterating what was already there – we must confess that 'non-referential' texts, however much they may pretend to stand free and innocent, are equally implicated, adding as they do to the impedimenta of our experience and informing our relationship to the world of experience at large.[12] Even within the nonrepresentational, commutative view, any idea we may have formed of a horse may influence any idea we may have of a hobby horse (or of a horse in a painting or in the book we read), *and vice versa*. And to the extent that we hold an interest – find a functional value – in the created object, the force of our commitment to it may be precipitously potent. The more we pretend we don't take it referentially, then, the *more* we may avoid applying to a fiction's 'events' all the tests for truth (accuracy, compatibility and so on) that go with referential thinking. We're in the very 'serious' position now of having to consider that our picture of reality may genuinely be in jeopardy of being replaced by the work of art. The hobby horse may override the horse. We're in risk of believing what we want to believe, not only in our reading but in the life that inseparably adjoins it. The spectre of escape into fiction is now gravely with us, or so it seems.

The arguments by which fictionalists may offset this anxiety are as follows.

In the *commutational* view, fiction doesn't replace reality because what in the text appears to compete with reality (looks different from reality) may 'allure' us by virtue of its very resemblance to what is of interest in reality.[13]

A second, *political* argument (and any omen of escapism in culture is of the most intimate concern to anyone taking a political stance) would point out that, in practice, the case for utopian writing (and 'anti-escapists' are habitually inclined to object that fiction is dangerous because it ensnares us in utopian fantasies) like dystopian writing – whether it's been that of a Reformationist, an Augustan, a Marxist or a situationist – has always been not that it replaces reality with a dream but that it forcefully augments culture's awareness of the nature of its own actualities and of what kind of *polis* can 'in fact' – quite pragmatically – be made within and of them.

A third, *semiotic* argument – a 'supplementarist' one, to appropriate Derrida's term – is that, as can be seen from the deconstructionist's point of view, insofar as neocosmic fiction is likely to be implicated by its commutative function in the hazard of escapism, anticosmic fiction (as well as Realism) is perforce equally implicated for the same reason. There is no way one might distinguish how neocosmic fiction could 'add to the muck' of signs, of experience (as Barthelme would put it) without admitting that all other writing does the same.[14]

A fourth, *ontological* argument, reveals a further dimension. No alteration of *what* one reads, with or without explicit escapist implications – no discarding of a neocosmist text, for example, in favour of an anticosmic one – can dispel the escapist implications of the fact *that* one reads. The notion that while one reads one is not living in the world in the 'normal' way is not only one that its critics often charge anticosmic (conspicuously bookish) fiction with, but is something that anticosmic theory likes to repeat (reading, for example, displaces presence). To be reminded within the text that one is reading, a reminder which after all is swiftly recognized as a regularized convention of the text's own, provides no reassuring hedge against this 'escapist' effect of all reading. Once again, escape is a property of the act of reading and not of one text as against another.

A fifth, *psychological* view comes in two parts. The first of these points out that even the most hard-bitten theories of the operations of mind have never suggested that it is the appeal of the-thing-substituted-for-the-real that instigates escapism. Quite differently, no one who smokes cigarettes doesn't seek oral gratification elsewhere, no child who likes riding a hobby horse can be expected to be turned *by this experience* against real horses. In psychological hypotheses concerned with escape mechanisms, fugues are generated by other, highly specialized mechanisms – deeper-lying retardant neuroses, for example – involving unmistakable *obstructions* of desire, and not at all by the surrogate itself.[15] Any recourse to a psychological theory of flight may take escape-into-fiction as a symptom, but is obliged finally to look entirely elsewhere for a cause.

But, with respect to how the mind actually works in practice, 'normal' as well as 'abnormal' psychology has an argument to propose. The cat doesn't eat the ball that it has chased as though it were a mouse; the child seeking a pacifier as a substitute for a nipple in its comforting capacity (if, in other words, it's not hungry) does not expect it to (does not show frustration when it doesn't) provide milk. Both cat and child 'use' these fictions – if fictions they are – with realistic awareness of the constraints appropriate to them. While as examples these may seem strained, the apprehension underlying them can be vital, and the more immediate relevance of this becomes apparent when we meet its counterpart in anthropological accounts.

In western traditional thought from the time of the Stoics through Bacon and Vico to Frazer, Lévy-Bruhl and Durkheim, it was broadly (though not universally) maintained that non-scientific beliefs couched specifically in those narrative forms called myths were man's initial, 'pre-logical' attempts to explain the origins and qualities of the natural universe, and that through a process of evolution these had been replaced by the experimental and rational procedures of scientific thought itself. This has proved to be a naive historical scenario. Since the time of the work of Bronislaw Malinowski (whose terms, quoted now, are unquestionably rebarbative but do not vitiate the force of his main argument), field study has provided data to the effect that "every primitive community is in possession of a considerable store of knowledge, based on experience and fashioned by reason", and that so-called 'savage' groups make everyday use of "an attitude of mind wholly akin to that of a modern man of science".[16] "Yet", Malinowski wrote, "mixed with all their activities there is to be found magic" whose underlying convictions and practical uses are equally widespread.[17] Side by side with his magical beliefs and practice, in other words, the 'native' "knows as well as you do that there are natural conditions and causes, and by his observations he knows that he is able to control these natural forces by mental and physical effort. His knowledge ... is sound and proof against mysticism" (1925, 28). In a given culture seemingly incompatible beliefs, incorporated in diverse narratives, persist successfully alongside one another, simultaneously, and are – without replacing or endangering the respective viability of each – each ready to be adopted according to their functional utility in the face of overriding immediate needs.[18]

The sixth, *complementarist* argument – one on which the physical sciences also daily rely – is then this. Whether or not substitution takes place, the coexistence of the manifold data of experience *always* involves mutual exclusivity, in the totality of that experience. We are made 'safe' enough from escapist oblivion to entertain alternate possibilities posed in a book by the fact that mutually exclusive percepts do not actually exclude one another in the way we might think they do. First, because no percept ever 'lives alone' in our minds, proof against the tests of other percepts; and second because every percept has a chance to gain vigour in our thinking when it's needed, if we are properly prepared – largely by fiction-making itself – to let it.[19] When we read – even when we 'believe in' a fiction – our minds are not empty of other possibilities: we are aware of them, weigh them, and act at each 'moment' as if one possibility is in sum more believable than others. We might imagine that we believe only one thing at a time, and that what we do when we come to believe something else is to discover, for the first time, this second, better possibility; but there is probably rarely an occasion when this is in fact anything like the case.

One believes more wholeheartedly in one thing, at a given time, than in another. Thus when we read we are in a position to 'believe' what we read until a change of context requires us to shift our commitment to another belief.[20] A created text – like any other object – certainly risks shaping our thinking as to what to look for in reality (and it's true that we tend to find what we look for as opposed to what we aren't looking for). But it's equally plain that our beliefs are models of reality only, and when a belief-model fails to work we repair, revise, improve it. Ideas are 'made' and in this respect are different from works of fiction only in degree and not in kind. 'Making' of ideas and 'making' of texts both have viability not because we believe the thing made is perfect but because, first, it is useful when it matches with or relates intelligibly to other things and, second, because we are ready to remake it. The two activities – the being ready to believe and the being ready to disbelieve – form two mutually dependent and equally essential aspects of one indispensable activity fundamental to our way of holding ideas to be true; that is, conditional (or frame-linked) believing.

There is no dim hope of perfection, completeness, this argument says, in an either/or conception of thinking. Completeness, even as an eidolon, is intelligible only within the framework of the notion that for each apperception its alternative – its comple-ment – must be fully entertained. (Here, of course, is where on that peculiar chart of certain modes of intentionality, p. 144, the 'boxed' area at its centre suggests a fifth, 'complementary' mode, taking as its motivation the free synthetic modulation among systematic/non-systematic, referential/non-referential perspectives.)

There seems to be no example of an anti-Realist on either side who would reject (or admit to rejecting) this last angle of view. Nevertheless, wouldn't such an apparently functionalist paradigm seem to put us into the hands of artists ready to seize the opportunity to manipulate our 'desires' (our desire to believe, for example, what it's momentarily expedient for us to believe) – and hence to lead us through the back-door into something *like* escape from ultimate reality, such as that might be? Unquestionably. But, as the artist subscribing to the idea would argue, not with the effects we often (and anticosmists always) ascribe to the notion of escape: that is, seclusion, entrenchment and fixation. In anti-Realist writing each text, whether anticosmic or neocosmic, in some important sense repulses its own isolation and autonomy. *Realist* fiction, says its opponent, by assuring us that it only replicates what we already think – that is, by appearing to have switched from a substitutional to a representational mode – threatens to replace reality with 'smuggled untruths'. The *anti*-Realist text, by its heterogeneity, its strangeness, it is proposed, prompts our awareness that it is a substitute, attracts to it further substitutes (provokes us to say "but also ..."), and thereby engages us in a continuing dynamic condition of complementary thinking. It aims to let us not rest in that vacuous repose of singleminded evasion but instead, in a kind of *Aufhebung*, it instigates a dialectic between itself and its past and forthcoming alternatives. Anticosmic literature, of all literature, hopes to elude the perils of escapism on the ground that it is anti-systematic, that it refuses to support a single coherently illusionistic cosmos into which we might irretrievably escape. But this hope, it would seem now, is equally delusive. No work 'containing its own critique' does not also institute a programme of attitudes which remains unproblematized.

Having argued this, I must say that I'm not happy with it. Not because I believe that any text evades erecting a system into which the reader may escape (since no text can be absolutely complementarily 'open' and heteroglossic, can jump indefinitely out of itself, as post-graduate enthusiasts sometimes proclaim). But rather, because there is a kind of circularity about complementarist motivation that invites an attitude of quietism that is genuinely escapist. *Some work*, it expects (hopes), will safeguard us against the delusions of another, and hence *writing as a class* of activity ensures us against escapism even while no one text can do so. We are encouraged thus to rest assured, relying on a fantasy of completeness (a complete and completely read literature) to rescue us from the errors promoted by the portion of it we're looking at. This seems to me not to state all that it's necessary to say. There is an effect accompanying certain kinds of writing that this book in its panoptic mode can't substantially illustrate. No matter how it tries, even the 'most anticosmic' text finally and logically can't, because of its own inevitable specific integrity, overthrow the very thing 'systematicity' as a whole. A work can at most throw into question other specific previously compelling systems by inserting its admittedly limited processes of disruption into the particular custom of discourse which is theirs and which it inherently selects as its target-discourse. Thus it may positively 'explode' (as popular critical idiom puts it) the escape-value of a *particular* paradigm – theological, ethical, economic, political, psychological – external to it, even while it entices us into its own always questionable illusions. And some (for example anti-Realist) texts do appear ready to promote *this* prophylactic against certain forms of escapism more than other (for example most Realist) texts are inclined to do.

It seems clear that if anticosmic writing tends in ways such as this to 'err on the side of caution', neocosmic writing will err on the side of recklessness. Particularly in the light of the history of our doubts about traditional positivism, any literature that pretends even momentarily to be 'positive' – to reorientate rather than disorientate, to invite the revaluation rather than the devaluation of shapes and relations – must be suspect. One answer would be that anticosmic fiction is brilliantly proficient in – and in fact highly specialized for exactly the activity of – shattering our sluggish habits of thought, but is inclined (for motives of parsimony for which there are undoubted long-standing philosophical good reasons) to stop there. Neocosmic thinking may say: 'Down with the concern-at-all-costs with consistency – its discovery, its absence or failure – and finesse'. This sounds ominous. Fiction cannot 'substitute' for reality in the long run. Yet it *can* replace one sense we have of it with another; we can't afford to hide from the fact that it can in-form/re-form our view of things. Here's risk indeed. But it's the confusion of 'views', the failure of clear sight, that is the threat, and not the outright replacement of one view with another. And it's not self-evident that any one kind of view – for example an entirely 'self-problematizing' one, if that were truly possible, which we can now regard with scepticism – would be guaranteed to be 'the best'. We may or may not agree with Hassan, committed to the radicalization of literature, when he says (perhaps to the surprise of some) that

> we cannot expect the avant-garde . . . to obey the same logic, assume the same forms. For instance, the new avant-garde need not have a historical consciousness, express recognizable values, or endorse radical politics. It need not shock, surprise, protest. The new avant-garde may not be an 'avant-garde' at all: simply an agent of yet invisible change.
>
> (1975, 42)

But we may see the force – in his argument for literature as an agent of change – of his essential conception: "innovate or die". And for this project (as Hassan's lines hint) we may have a wider range of ways to proceed in literature than anticosmic argument may typically tell us.

What Stern says, as we recall, is that "The realistic writer has no contribution to make to any discussion about 'models of reality', for he has no doubt about the singularity of the world in which realism lives, in which we all live" (54). This is surely the place at which anti-Realism takes its leave from Realism, and the heart of matter.

Fictionalists – indeed artists over all – have, finally, never been good at constructing satisfactorily, internally cogent philosophies. What they have been good at is putting ideas to the proof, the test, of (what seems like) experience. Of what it feels like to 'be experiencing' them as they unfold in the contexts of specified actualities. We need to decide: just what risks, in truth, do they put us to in the process? If we look to thinkers – logicians, say, and scientists – vocationally dedicated to the anxiety that we make no mistakes, we find them repeatedly giving us one answer. As Quine the post-positivist sceptic puts it, speaking of that thing which every logician and scientist ultimately must acknowledge is a basis of his discourse, metaphor "flourishes in playful prose and high poetic art ... it is vital also at the growing edges of science and philosophy" (1978, 161–2). We needn't in any technical sense identify fiction strictly with metaphor. R. R. Hoffman (1980, 414) says that "to have a metaphor means to have hope". The idea of 'alternative-model-making' is what's at issue. "There is no limit to the metaphors by which we can effectively convey what we know," the philosopher A. Kaplan writes; "it would be rash indeed to attempt a priori to set limits on the fruitfulness of models" (1965, 287, 292). "The empiricist", wrote Hans Reichenbach, "is allowed to use a synthetic principle, because he does not assert that the principle is true or must lead to true conclusions or to correct probabilities or to any kind of success; all he asserts is that employing the principle is the best he can do. ... The scientist resembles a gambler more than a prophet ... his goal is staked higher – the goal of foretelling the rolling dice of the cosmos ... what he asserts is that positing the conclusion is a means to his end" (1951, 247–9).

These proposals seem to suggest that some risks are worth taking. But, standing before the precipice, maybe there's another, safer way left. We have available one ultimate prophylactic against the hazards that come of thinking and saying parlous or uncertain thoughts – one that anti-Realist, narratological conceptions of writing themselves provide *par excellence*: the notion that each idea we entertain is, after all, 'mere words'. But why do we speak/write *as though* we also experience events on planes outside language? The assertion leaves us with all the explaining yet to do. Another objection, an assurance actually, is that no text definitively closes our experience any more in fact than any text definitively opens it. They merely offer *plans*, as Lem might say, for closedness and openness which they can never wholly achieve.[21] We can read – and write – without fear. We can seek, this argument would say, not to hold signs in tremulous awe but to *capture* them *in their illusory states*, to manipulate them freely, to generate new provisional customs for the relating of ideas. We need, it might say, to dare to enter the realm – at the 'growing edges' of experience – of the hypothetical and to think (dare one say 'feel'?) it through. This is where Ronald Sukenick would say "The less we use our imagination the more somebody else is going to use it for us – by manipulating us".[22] Denying mimesis itself, in this sense, is to deny one of the principal modes of action by which we may test that very language that, we're told, demands testing. We may deplore the fact of 'absence' – the disappearance of the 'thing' behind the 'sign' – but in this respect absence is the *gift* by which language makes possible universes of growth, of revolution, relatively free of instant destruction at every turn, including such revolutions as those to which the indeterminist gives faith when he or she speaks rather than keeping silent. It provides for trial without error. Whether this were an appeal to Keats' notion of negative capability or to Wittgenstein's of perspectivist 'seeing-as', for example, the argument for fiction is in this limited way the same as those we've seen for the projects of deductive reason and inductive experience, of logic and of science. The danger, if not disaster, would lie in pre-setting prohibitions on the models we may try; not in being bold but in not being bold enough. The case would be that there's no safety for us in a literature that takes cover behind the excuse of 'pure chance', and that doesn't freely and avowedly take chances. That what's wanted is a fiction that takes risks, not to denounce or abjure its own influence but – by full-blooded modelling and ceaseless counter-modelling – to assume the positive burden of them.

Can we be accused of having appeared hard on anticosmic, and 'soft on' neocosmic writing? It may in fact be that few fictionalists acting as 'neocosmists' have so far shown the kind of rational grit we feel a need for; those premisses, irresistible particles of reasoning, that the more one chews them over the less arbitrary and more inevitable they seem: so far, that is, at least. But as to 'experiential grit', some may find less in the quotidian *histoires* and the aleatory discursive word-play most typical of anticosmic narrative than they would have desired. Certain kernels of experience are hard enough to crack the teeth of any rational theory of being-and-saying we may devise, and where fiction fails to remind us of these, to try our bite upon them, it may seem suet if not softsoap indeed. By experiential grit I refer not only (for that would mean a gross under-representation of what's involved) to the articulation of physical, but – equally – of ideational events; of that fresh, richly and finely evolved 'thickness' of cognitive conjecture of which literature alone (as an art) is capable. Whether in a spirit of passionate, ironic, or whimsical venturousness, there may appear to be few occasions in fiction outside the neocosmic where the reader can try his or her mind against such 'eventuations' as those (of Abbott) in which 'people' strive imprisoned within the lines and circles of a two-dimensional reality; or (in Lindsay) of the corpuscular torrent of Matterplay or the shock-death of music issuing from a liquid-metal lake; or (in Borges) the suffocation in the flood of phenomena, or the nonextended nonperduring coins of an ideal universe, or the transmogrifications of an unaltered story by its myriad scribes; or (in Calvino) of a human's retreat into the earth's chasms from the world of colours, a human's self-dismantlement, the congealing of forms around scratches in space, the discovery of inside and outside, the deductive and inductive search for an exit through expanding/shrinking space-time-book, or the interminable instant of a lion's leap, or the creation of a dusty road and a battle out of paper and ink; or (in White) the material slaughter of a fictive beast, or an automaton life among ants; or (in McElroy) the brain's engendering its organs of sense, knowing and self-destruction; or (in Fuentes) the black beaches and white jungles of a New World, the solid swim in a sea of pearls, the multiple of births in history yet out of time. One writes 'to the moment' and will expect writings to evince their historical moments. The intimation here would be that in recent moments the rationalist enchantment has discovered itself – and laid its spell – everywhere, and that it may be difficult to find in discourse anywhere except in fiction (and perhaps specifically in neocosmic fiction) the full 'experiential ground' from which reason(s) should spring.

An incisive feature of the anti-Realist trend in fiction has been the co-existence side by side within it of two such counterpoised modes. Instincts for equilibrium are alive and well and living – if not in all canonical literature – in the world of writing that plays around it. Since each text is in fact its own particular mélange of premisses and intentions – having thought a little about the possibilities, such as those scanned here – the reader is left to glean the actualities in each case.

But as even some of the few allusions above obviously suggest, neocosmic and anticosmic writing find it increasingly hard to stay apart. In logic alone the former has to accept that discourse is a force for information outside the 'substance' it would report, and the latter has to believe that there is a world of systematic relations (e.g. linguistic relations and those massive cultural systems that support language) outside its own discourse, before either can make sense of the idea of the writing of anything including itself. There appears a growing impulse toward the fusion of anticosmic and neocosmic 'motivations'. Isolated critics, looking close, think they see now "parallel worlds" between say Pynchon and Lovecraft (Meikle, 1981). Nabokov plays not just the Realism-busting game; he aims toward "not text, but texture. ... Not flimsy nonsense, but a web of sense. ... Some kind of correlated pattern in the game" (1962, 53). Cortázar's composition of *Rayuela* is disruptively paratactic –

but as one of his characters makes plain, he believes in the bridging of those voids:

> Giving coherence to the series of pictures ... meant filling in with literature, presumptions, hypotheses and inventions the gaps between one and another photograph. ... The bridges ... would have to be presumed or invented by the reader. ... The book would have to be something like those sketches proposed by Gestalt psychologists, and therefore certain lines would induce the observer to trace imaginatively the ones that would complete the figure. But sometimes the missing lines were the most important ones, the only ones that really counted. ...
>
> (1963, 468–9)

Vonnegut, in a characteristically American way for example in *Slaughterhouse-5* (and in a way peculiarly reminiscent of Continental Romanticism's appeal to what it once called a theory of the 'grotesque'), works with marked fluidity – and not without tactical grace – back and forth along the scale from nonfictionalistic mimesis (Dresden) to 'the marvellous' (Tralfamadore) to metaleptic passages of self-reflexive 'authorial' commentary ("there are almost no characters in this story ..."). Barth offers as background to the reading of his fiction a theory which he believes to make possible an "anti-illusionist" kind of narrative that can preserve "storytelling" – or a tension between the two – in which "the aesthetic pleasure of complexity, of complication and unravelment, suspense, and the rest" has continuing value (Bellamy, 1974, 7–10). Pinget's *Graal Flibuste* appears as what Mercier perplexedly calls one of "the rare works of fantasy written by the New Novelists ... sheer storytelling for its own sake"; "to draw parallels with the fantasy worlds of J. R. R. Tolkien or Lord Dunsany would be misleading, however: Pinget does not burden himself with a plot or consistent morality. His chief delight seems to lie in the creation of new words and images, which in turn beget new gods and a new flora and fauna" (Mercier, 1971, 16, 384–5). Mercier's difficulty underscores a fact that anti-Realism in general insists we remember: that notions of '-isms' do not define authors so much as they help us to perceive strands in (or form relations with) texts. Not only have both Pinget *and* Tolkien actually written many different kinds of texts, but so have Barth, Calvino, Nabokov, Cortázar, Borges, Robbe-Grillet, Sollers and most of the others we've examined[23] – neocosmic in vein here, anticosmic in vein there, seemingly working toward some alloy of these elsewhere.

For any who are keen to make headway as their literary biographers and for us in our present context, what's most crucial is that *as authors*, over-all, what they seem always finally to have put first in deciding what and how next to write – as the essentially anti-Realist impulse in them would have made sure – was not the conception of some 'right model' to hold to, but rather the *act of model-making*. That *Graal Flibuste*, like some of the later fiction of that other 'New Novelist' Robbe-Grillet, happens to feel more 'fantastic' is inevitable but is not the objective. In the act of creation – a massively prominent *topos* throughout the fiction we've considered – there would seem to some to lie an answer to the state of Creation. Having made the point – by way of *histoire*-troubled and/or *discours*-troubled narrative – that language is a troubled medium, the anti-Realist appears liberated to move on toward expressly 'new world-generative' writing.

Meanwhile, the strategies and themes of anti-Realism have already begun to be assimilated by fictions of more widely disseminated sorts, whose intentions are not in the same way problematic. A new popular formulaic narrative in a half-dozen languages, often vivid often banal, is already with us.[24]

As I warned, much has been simplified here, much omitted in the name of (my – problematic – idea of) clarity. Put thus simply, anti-Realism is no longer a movement. An impulse that was always there has come out of the closet, and is now an established tradition living alongside Realism. If there was ever a moment when texts subverted Realist principles in ways that were free, nonaligned, self-determining, unconventionalized and at the disposal of the unique playful spirit of each writer and reader unfettered by the constraints of any custom, that time does not now exist and is at best a chapter of bygone literary history if not of literary mythology. This may or may not be a logical conundrum. For many, in any event – whether 'neo-' or 'anti-cosmic' (whether blazoned with the motto *Vive la différence* or *Vive la différance*) – anti-Realist practice is the only way we can do what we want or need to do in narrative. Its practitioners will never, however – any more than Realists – do it without presenting not only the world but themselves with complications.

Many anti-Realists would feel it ultimately mistaken to argue at length for theirs – any more than for Realists' – as a better form of literature. The reason is that anti-Realism is just another set of forms of human discourse – of humans addressing, and on the whole seeking to influence, one another's thoughts and actions; that discourse is not some 'canon' of texts selected and to be preserved at all costs because of what they are as things; that, instead, the array of all discourse (of which any literary canon is only a small part, or indeed is only the reflection of a changing conception about discourse) should be ever stretched and kept flexible not as an object but as a human right. Like various other isolated human institutions (the family, science, marriage, career) that have in recent centuries been compulsively laden with the burden of sanctity once extended to the holy – as though it might manage to 'contain' all our spiritual and other displaced yearnings – 'Literature' too can eventually break down under the strain. This doesn't signify that certain written things cannot be especially prized. It means plainly – and anti-Realists aren't the only thinkers to have argued this by now, though they started it – that the word 'Literature' as commonly propounded in for example traditional academic settings can't suceed in embracing them all. We can name whatever measures we like by which to gauge what it is we esteem in our reading – that it 'moves' us by its 'subject matter', that it gives us new insight into matters of fact, that it gives us aesthetic pleasure by its form and texture, that it provokes us to think and/or 'imagine', to 'modulate' from frame to frame, that it gives us some magisterial model of investigation or synthetic power, for instance. Yet there is probably no one who won't then have in candour to cite among his or her own cherished exemplars, according to any criterion of force or beauty he or she chooses, some work which no conventional teaching institution would consign to Literature. (Following just those criteria I've mentioned I would personally have to name not only a particular few novels but certain pieces of writing in the fields called vernacular architecture, philosophy, mathematics, logic, genetics, pyschology, archaeology, information theory, history, geography, art theory, language study, regional sociology, regional cookery, a confessional memoir, a certain well-known bible, a collection of letters, a political tract, a travel guidebook, a dictionary, a suite of foreign correspondence press reports.) Insofar as it thinks of itself as Literature, anti-Realist writing by some of its own arguments is compelled to waive any claim to being the only best kind of writing.

Again, this is not to say that there is no differentiation to be made between say fiction and fact or between a fiction and its criticism. Where there will in the past have been rivalries in the name of Literature, and Literature will have claimed fiction and not fact as its own, it's now to say rather that there is *no contest* between them when it comes to questions of value. Not because they don't occasionally compete but because they *always* compete and neither can manage to be adjudged as having won. They are always at some level making the same appeals – that they are internally valid and can be connected in some vital ways with our actual experience, and are always only finally informing us as to how to think and feel, and are doing so by fundamentally the same means.

This book has been not about truth or value, but about usage. About one body of writing's inclination, for one thing, to replace a given set of conventions inherited from another, not with a radical dissolution of conventionality but with a new set of conventions, whose special preoccupation was with how to dissolve conventions. It's cause for very real apprehension that on one front in anti-Realism a central strategy along these lines has been to define the thinking it seeks to replace, and then to offer as its own alternative theory that *from now on* definitions were not to be accredited as meaningful. By its own rules such indeterminist theory proposes that definitions are a matter of usage, even while it is essentially a doctrine proposing the eventual indifference of usage as a ground for positive judgement. We may object that it puts theoretical speculation entirely out of touch with those very actualities that make every book 'the way society speaks to itself'. But there's yet a deeper import in the historical phenomenon which this theory is. The strategy I've mentioned is in one sense acceptable. Within a certain frame of reference it's perfectly correct to behave in a way that in another frame of reference would – as 'self-contradictory', for example – be incorrect. It is, in other words, a matter for individual 'choice of frames' whether we subscribe to it or not. What bears remembering is that the ultimate choice (the choice not to define) offered under this doctrine entails the relinquishment of decision as a basis for action, even while – so long as we live – we shall act as though we continued to believe in it.

There is something urgent to be said about recent writers' anxieties concerning such dichotomies – disparities – as those suggested by 'decision v. hesitation', 'homology v. heterology', 'analysis v. synthesis', '*histoire* v. *discours*', 'fact v. fiction'. For one pressing reason at least, they may reflect an intuition about the nature of human experience that closes upon us as it never has before. We may believe with many that writing – and reading – and thinking about how we write and read – are essentially there to lead us to fruitful discoveries about 'the functioning of our own faculties of perception'. It may be no accident that, as Iser and Culler point out, this is itself largely a twentieth-century scenario of what literature's for (Culler, 1983, 78–9). I genuinely have reservations about bringing up science in a 'serious' way in a book that is about 'art', but I'm afraid I must for the very reason that there is a deep dis-parity between these that may never be overcome and that is the exact subject of the intuition at hand.

Where, in what form, does our 'experience' actually take place? Here is a narrative: "it is raining". Here is another narrative: "neuro-terminal $A7k4^2mn_3$ releases transmitter at synapse $2111g^{14}$ activating neuro-receptor set $S3r7^9ox_6$". There is every reason to believe – and no convincing evidence to dispute – that when the mind 'perceives' an event in the first narrative's form, the event happening in the brain is very likely to have occurred in a form more precisely to be described by some narrative (though more complicated) like the second. There is no rain falling in the brain but a firing of neurons. Both narratives (rain falling, neurons discharging) are, it should be pointed out, entirely consistent with the same single system of explanation of events (involving causality, gravity, conservation of energy and so forth). There is no paradoxical, undecidable conflict of models here. Yet they are two thoroughly distinct and non-isomorphic, non-homologous modes of 'eventuation'. The first is in the mode in which we 'normally, naturally', consciously perceive events 'from the inside', subjectively, 'from within our minds'. The second, equally 'real' as a general model, is in the mode in which the constitution of the same events by the same brain at the same time would be observed by say a neurophysiologist 'objectively' from the 'outside'.

The implications are enormous. As Hassan points out (showing signs of awareness of these) by quoting an expert in the field, a scientist can already say 'We are now talking to the brain without the participation of the senses. This is pure and direct communication – I call it nonsensory communication."[25] There is no dodging the fact that by means of chemical, electronic, surgical and other intervention – both at genetic developmental stages and at stages involving the living individual subject – what we 'think from the inside' can now be manipulated by other human beings who are 'outside', without any regard for the processes of mental eventuation humans have always considered the necessary and eternal conditions of perceiving and thinking. In place of the sequence of ideas 'it is cloudy, it is growing cold, it is going to rain, it is raining', the experimenter – to put crudely what is rapidly becoming a far from crude experimental activity – can pass a current through a cranial electrode and the subject 'feels wet'. In addition to this, data once so far beyond anyone's capacity to resolve in a lifetime as to have been accepted as categorically indeterminate, as if metaphysically inscrutable to 'natural' man, can now be recuperated – decisions can be provided meeting all previously agreed standards of resolution – by computer systems within a matter of minutes or seconds. Belletrists will find comfort in insisting that 'these things take time, there are snags, it will never really happen', but this moment of solace is likely to be briefer than they imagine. There is every possibility that the closer we come to thinking accurately – in the terms of a causal system consistent with the ones we use to understand how things work in external actuality – about what makes us think 'it is raining', the further we'll be from thinking 'through the mind' – that is, in the language literature unqualifiedly presumes to be 'the language of the mind'.

'Hold on', we can say. 'Maybe the "natural" language in which the mind speaks to itself is not the "scientific" language in which we might talk about *how* it speaks to itself – but we will *always* deal with reality by *thinking things through* in the language by which it speaks to itself.' But are we sure even now that this means what it did before? To take a thoroughly commonplace example: what have we actually decided, at present, to be the exact significance for us of the multitude of cases we know of a person (not excluding perhaps ourselves and often strongly justified) who – instead of 'thinking through' his or her relations to his or her self, society, the nature of being, mother, God, the party, the president, the boss, the meaning or non-meaning of life – swallows a pill and 'feels directly better', with 'thinking' supervened?

The greatest question before us pertaining to how we're to relate to thinking in the future is: do we have an ethical or other obligation to deal with (understand, facilitate, ply) the processes of mind in a way that takes as its basis the processes of consciousness itself, in preference to any other? What happens to writing is in this context a minor matter, but one of no small interest. There are two kinds of reality operating in the mind at once, and one of these can never be approached by literature, even while the number of other institutions in society that can approach and manipulate it grows day by day. Literary dilemmas relating to homology, to unity of *histoire* and *discours* – and the anguish many seem to feel when these appear to crumble – may be more serious than we've thought. Anti-Realism's cultivation of illusionist naiveté on one hand, and on the other of a full-scale narrative technology for the problematization of the always previously assumed necessity that we cope with subjectively experienced crises by fighting things out within the frame of subjectivity – that we resolve the crises stemming from our illusions by working them out through illusion – rehearse a dumbshow on the page that is yet to be performed (or addressed) *viva voce* in life. What, for instance, is to be the place, in this double perspective, of radical action, of literary or any other sort?

The vibrant activity of indeterminist critical discourse, of which voluminous examples now fill our shelves, shows itself caught in the toils of that deepening dilemma. Not least in its persistent adoption of those naive modes of belletrist *écriture* – in volume upon volume of critical and philosophical essays – which its kindred fiction throws into doubt or disavows.[26]

Among the eminent achievements of this book is that it has consistently left out – and couldn't have included – the most important thing. In discussing anti-Realist fiction as a 'problematizing' one, it has omitted any description of the specific *struggle* (as if all its texts were fixed and comfortable from start to finish in their various activities of problematization) of which each is an enactment. That is, I've left out, essentially, the narratives. How each book comes to – how it in fact shows the eventuation of – its answers and questions is something others will need continually to uncover. *This* book's particular kind of 'eventuation' – the sort of model *it* is – is here to be seen, but is itself obviously problematical. It adopts hypersystematic differentiative strategems (juxtaposing contrasting 'premisses', 'strategies', 'modes') in the name of 'perspective'. It games with language, appropriating rhetorical tactics (the repeated use of half-quotation-marks around words, parenthetical phrases, locutions such as 'in this view' and 'this argument would say') to bring persistently to mind that there are multiple, alternative, complementary 'meanings' in and around utterances all the time, and to hint at another kind of 'transparency' than the one anti-Realism has sometimes condemned. That is, if *this* model seems (in truth must be) its own limited kind, it wants to be so in a special spirit.

In our time it's become a custom, as the easiest (and most swiftly endorsed as suitably sophisticated) way out of a bind in our reading, to treat some or all-but-one of the competing models within a text as either ironically or parodically motivated, and this is frequently far from being a sufficiently sophisticated kind of reading. What is often more likely the case is that a text – such as this one – gives models which (however 'thick' and fast they come) it sets against one another not because an ironist's or parodist's choice is intended but because it quite 'simply' desires its reader not to allow any of them to become opaque. It wishes its models to be taken neither as solid 'goods' nor as solid evils in themselves, blocking our view of the realities/possibilities which they're there to help us to see. This work's intention is thus to be transparently 'usable'. Yet *that* constitutes a (meta)model that threatens to become opaque. I have now further initiated an 'outside' commentary on *its* limitations and evident attitude and have so begun to subtilize its opacity into transparency (and could delight in doing that at length). But I couldn't keep on jootsing out of my skin in this way indefinitely if I wished. Quite apart from the fact that (as I've argued) no one could, I don't wish to. I call a conditional halt; I affirm that this set of utterances, like all utterances, is propaganda. It is hereby 'put into circulation' as a model among models, as part of my transaction with the wor(l)ds around me, and the ways in which it is itself fiction remain to be negotiated.

Much anti-Realist fiction is superb at reminding us that writing and its experience is to be endlessly renegotiated. Whether the pondersome plethora of 'traditional' criticism on 'classic' texts through the ages is not lumbering proof that we've inveterately done this anyway – or whether, as some fear, a literature that devotes itself literally *ad infinitum* to reminding us that we must do it does not inure us to its own desired effect (such that it finally only serves, ironically, to 'flatter our presuppositions', our late-twentieth-century habits of thinking in this very respect) – remains to be seen. But there are even more serious difficulties – or ones from which we may die laughing – in both supporting and attacking the foundations of anti-Realism. The grounds for decisions based on probability, for example, on which depend not only notions of usage and the recognition of contexts and frames but in fact all statements (all efforts to communicate) by both indeterminists and their opponents, are not altogether secure. Nor is there, perhaps, any particular reason why learning, growing, change – or survival itself or any artistic or other qualitative augmentation of the life of survivors – should go on.

What are they to do who're slightly less sceptical than this – those, for instance, who care about life and ask what is writing's rôle in it? Throw up their hands in bewilderment? 'Literature is not to be thought of as a tool.' We listen to this, some of us, with powerful sympathy. We even ignore that those who feel it most passionately are often those who elsewhere claim that it *is* a tool – in the hands of the opposition – and who with greatest application appropriate it as an instrument to propagate their views. What if – just suppose, imagine – what if writing is *not* without some effect beyond its manifestation of its own formliness speaking to itself? What if by some chance it might (also) serve? Acts of communication and their associated dilemmas involve all other matters, but are not superordinate to them. It could be reasoned that we are, like it or not, part of the fabric of the colossal and precipitous pyramid of our culture and its discourse, and are to be monstrously crushed by its weight only and exactly insomuch as we mystically invest it with the dumbfoundingly phantasmic gravity of some immutable edifice in the constitution of whose alien stuff we have no rôle or effect. Who is 'behind' language but ourselves?

If there's any sense in these ideas, what needs to be fought for is not the 'destruction' of language but how to make communication acts stick to the truths and possibilities our contexts spell out for us; a thing which any thoroughgoing problematization of communication itself can logically only cover over or leave untouched. A contemporary critic, talking of what he takes to be two basic conceptions of reality, "reality as hard-rock *donnée*, and reality as a projection" of the imagination of the fantasist, argues that there is an alternative to these: "the concept of reality as a communal formulation.... The cooperative processing of experience by the individual and his culture". The 'new realist' – 'resisting the domination of the present' and 'the pretensions of relevance' – can freely exploit and explore "the fractures and pliancies in his subject matter", "the slackness which betrays the spent dogma", and the "flaws induced by the heat of social change" (Goldknopf, 1972, 192–4). This notion is a challenge, and not an easy one to meet. Our situation seems to demand that we do not hold back, that we mell and grapple with our words. We may find it perplexing to the point of dismay that, as another recent author says, mind – and we can as readily say art or writing – "fits the world and shapes it as a river fits and shapes its own banks" (Dillard, 1982, 15). We can wonder and must continually ask 'Which is the "cause"?' and are obliged to confirm that, simply, we never get out of the stream, we are particles of it. But, to shift the metaphor, while we may long to make our way 'outside' to live safe in exile from our history and even our discourse and discover we never shall, we can (to paraphrase Guevara speaking as an active revolutionary) prize the luck that has us living in the heart of the beast.

But even now, it would be daft not to expect rapid further transformations in our situation and outlook bringing with them further revolts in narrative. Such as ones concertedly relinquishing the overriding thematic priority given in the recent past to the putting-into-question of language, in favour of other preoccupations. We can anticipate for example that fiction (always in certain ways slow on the uptake) may begin to reflect a consciousness of the problem – towards which thinkers in other fields have now for some time been moving – not of disorder but of why 'so much order' appears, and why theoretical and experimental observations repeatedly turn up systems of 'closure' where they were least expected.

Ready cases come to hand. In mathematics' and information theory's exploration of stochastic processes, conventional ideas of chance and of entropy – once thought to be inimical to organized systems – themselves prove to be qualified by larger systematic functions. Mathematicians and engineers play increasingly with 'tangles' (such as 'gordian knots' and 'regular polylinks') displaying theoretical and pragmatic orderliness and utility (e.g. Holden, 1983); and recent theorems concerning the ordering of sets associated with partition theory, which has had increasing impact on physics, have started to produce 'surprise' responses to common assumptions about undecidability and infinitude.[27] In physics, mechanics and information mechanics new conceptions – for example affecting 'vortex flow' and 'cellular automata' – have arisen from the observation of previously unpredicted dynamic systems beginning in random initial states and evolving highly ordered structures.[28] In the same disciplines 'chaos theory' has emerged to demonstrate the practicability – for instance in engineering – of 'compliant systems' where indeterminacy would previously have been thought to leave organized structures incapable of survival (cf. Thompson, 1983). In linguistics and logic, a growing array of parallel theories have sprung up to the effect that diversity and context-boundness may be systematically contained. Ranging in subject matter from 'creole languages' to 'vagueness', in advanced studies old notions of innate ideas are being revived in more subtle form and vagueness itself has come to be characterized as a specifiable, analysable and necessary phenomenon in discourse (cf., e.g., Ballmer, 1983; Bickerton, 1983). In psychology and ethnology, arguments recur to suggest that, beyond cultural divergences, 'mental sets' predispose the mind toward certain 'closural tendencies' visible in humans in infancy. Phenomenalist notions are increasingly challenged in favour of a new technical movement startlingly called 'psychological realism', and illusions (visual, for example) have been shown to coincide with certain 'regularities in the external world', such that our inferences may be demonstrated to bear 'nonarbitrary relations to the real world'.[29] And an entire field of thought has come to the fore, bringing together under the name of 'synergetics' specialists in disciplines including physics, chemistry, bio-chemistry, genetics, zoology, meteorology, topology, sociology, whose concern is to corroborate, analyse and explain the spontaneous formation of well-organized structures out of random or chaotic states.[30]

We shouldn't be astonished to find some new 'gaming' fiction mimicking such fresh hypotheses just as fiction has mimicked the now conventional hypotheses on undecidability and uncertainty. We may soon discover in these new '*jeux de mondes*' the diction that those more recent world-views have begun to adopt and produce – 'joint probability', 'self-organization', 'stochastic system', 'recurrence time', 'dissipative structure', 'static instability', 'chaotic dynamics' and the like – together with a distinctive matching galaxy of fresh images and *topoi*. There's no patent reason to expect that any of these ideas will prove more or less true, out of their context, than any of those we've so far observed. But who knows?

For the moment, perhaps never in history has so much been so fancifully, portentously and hypnotically staked on whether the writer ought to hope to have it inscribed on his or her tombstone or book's endleaf: '*It made a difference*.' Culture will decide, and culture's in our hands. For good and ill, we've technically both loosened up and tightened up our ways of reading and writing in readiness for what's to come. A future work of fiction may be a chart of manifold vectors, a 'loom' of many warps and wefts, sometimes a wonder book, a domesday book, a bestiary, a dictionary, a search ephemeris, a wind-rose. It may be idiosyncratic, maybe cryptic, it may be pellucid and sleek, it may be many-faceted and multi-coded, richly saturated in eloquence of incident, elasticity of action, plasticity of sign and image, a prismatic book. But this too is a fantasy. There'll never be just one utterance, but a tide of them, coming deep and swift and relentless. A *language*, that is – now of ecstatic naturalism, now cannily anti-natural but at last unleashed and luminous – for a new, as yet un-uttered world. What difference *can* it make? Time, as we give it tongue, will tell.

One might have closed on that note. In the rhapsodic language of a book modelled from beginning to end on the happy dream of 'an open mind'. Throughout, I've dwelt on a literature whose concerns are with the vast reaches of ontological thinking and the close quarters of formal play. The book has joined with anti-Realism in its overriding silence regarding the missing middle – the middle distance of history and of present acts, to which Realism had addressed itself and which anti-Realism sees as a nightmare from which we might and must all awaken. The question now to ask is whether the project of the open, indeterminate mind is all that it seems. And – coming to the brink – whether it's what the voice we hear calls for, as the future opens its mouth to speak.

NOTES

Foreword

1 Ronald Sukenick, "The new tradition in fiction", in Federman, 1981, 37. Sukenick refers to *Tristram Shandy*, as Barth does to *Don Quixote* (Barth, 1967), as evidence of the antiquity of this alternative tradition. Others will point considerably further back, as we'll see.
2 For an example of the conflation of fiction and theory and of arguments for theoretical discourse as the manifestation of creative activity comparable with that of the writing of fiction, see e.g. Bruss, 1982.

Introduction

1 My intention in this book in using the words 'movement' and 'tradition' is to take as a starting point what J. Hillis Miller has in mind when he says of "periods" that they "differ from one another because there are different forms of heterogeneity, not because each [period] held a single coherent 'view of the world'" (1975, 31). It's doubtful there are ideas of "forms of heterogeneity" that aren't models positing world-views. Miller presents a fine corrective to the anti-Realist version of Realism described here, hinting (via classic anti-Realist strategies) 'Realism' to be a straw man, i.e. containing its own negation.
2 Susan Sontag, interviewed in Bellamy, 1974, 120.
3 Not 'anti-realists' because they are not to be identified as writers against 'reality', nor 'Anti-Realists' for I'm not interested in attributing to them the

status of a single monolithic school. The term, speaking generally, is not one I've coined. It has been in use in criticism since the 1960s, and not only among its devotees (cf. Stern, 1973, e.g. 59).

4 In Britain *famous* targets have been Trollope, Bennett, Galsworthy, Maugham, and in America Dreiser, Sinclair Lewis – and the long roll of 'best-selling' fictionalists. Cf. parallel 'high' and 'low' lists of favourites advanced by Realist criticism itself, from W. Somerset Maugham's *Great Novelists and their Novels* to F. R. Leavis's *The Great Tradition*.

5 Two examples will suffice: they may ignore the rejection by certain leading 'Realists' of the epithet 'Realist' (see Flaubert), however acclaimed by most it had been; and they will attribute to various Realist works the programmatic intentions of Naturalism. *In re* the latter, for instance, the response would be that the 'Naturalist school' represents, as often happens in history, the late *rationalization* of a generic impulse, a world-view whose fundamental tenets were in virtual force for a long period in advance of its systematic articulation by writers such as Zola. That, as Damian Grant argues in his summary of the Realist movement (quoting in support writers as diverse as P. Martino, Philip Rahv, Harry Levin, J.-H. Bornecque, P. Cogny), the Naturalist formulation was in all essentials the "more positive definition" by which "the naturalist initiative" "achieved", carried "the pointers in realist theory to their logical conclusion" (Grant, 1970, 33ff.). A close study of the theoretical expressions of those commonly nominated as Realists is likely to show this to be right. Thus of Flaubert: where he speaks specifically of positivism, of materialism, and of realism (e.g. to George Sand, 10 September 1870; to Maxime du Camp, 29 September 1870, in Flaubert, 1953, 227, 230) he condemns them outright. Yet these expressions are consistently ones framed by discourse directed against not their philosophical premisses but their adoption as shibboleths for a philistine cultism. In practice – and in his correspondence otherwise – he can be cogently argued to have been a mechanist, a materialist determinist, and a genuine mimeticist in the terms set out in the following pages.

6 "The basic convention which governs the novel – and which, *a fortiori*, governs those novels which set out to violate it – is our expectation that the novel will produce a world" (Culler, 1975, 189). There's a long tradition in modern criticism to revert to this kind of pairing; typical examples appear in Josipovici's *The World and the Book* (1971) and Stevick's citing – out of his long list of popular metaphors for the thing 'novel' – "world" and "game" as his two favourites (Stevick, 1981, 11–13). He proffers contemporary writers as different as Gass and Butor, each both a fictionalist and critic, as prizing the 'world' metaphor. Barthes' assertion that "The book *is* a world" (my italics) – which he elaborates by saying "the critic experiences before the book the same linguistic conditions as does the writer before the world" – is characteristic, and something Josipovici takes him to task for (Josipovici, 1971, 271). There is an attempt to outline "a formal ontology of fictional worlds" in Martinez-Bonati, 1983.

7 The interchangeability of these pairs is only rough and ready. Apart from

technical differences commonly cited, I use the word '*histoire*' in preference to 'story' for the reason that it carries the double connotation of both 'the story told' and of the larger aggregate of all the givens of the 'world' in which the 'story takes place' which we associate with the business of 'history'. The inadequacy of the English word 'story' shows up, for example, when we smile slightly (as we're meant to) at James's phrase 'the story of the story'.

8 Since this is intended purely as an introductory outline serving as a schematic basis for later discussion, and not as a demonstrational argument, I refer to specific textual instances in this chapter only for *illustrative* purposes to avoid confusion as to my meaning. Though the accuracy/inaccuracy of the propositions put forward here can't be taken as evidence on its own that anti-Realists would/wouldn't hold to them, certainly it should affect one's decision as to whether they *ought* to, and the reader will wish to test them against his/her own reading of Realist fiction.

9 The famous opening passage of Balzac's *Le Père Goriot* has come to be a *locus classicus* for this argument. "... Yet in 1819, the time when this drama begins, an almost penniless girl was living there. ... Will it be understood outside Paris? One may doubt it. Only between the heights of Montmartre and Montrouge are there people who can appreciate how exactly, with what close observation, it is drawn from life" (Balzac, 1834, 27). The reader's 'own actual world' is given as the subject; a 'real' time ("1819") and place ("Paris, Montmartre/Montrouge") are identified as the setting; and the novel's fidelity to that world is asserted ("close observation ... drawn from life"). The subsequent long and detailed description of the rooms of the pension Vauquer, presented as empty of people, vividly betokens what recent criticism has often referred to as the attribution to the world portrayed of the quality of being 'always already there' – a solid, sharply definable, autonomous 'reality' whose existence has no need of the mind to confirm it.

10 In his interesting rationale for the realism of *The Lord of the Flies*, Stern says that "The island ... is a complete world. ... The question, 'How will these boys behave in this situation?' receives a complete answer" (21). "What Mr Golding has done is to take the boys and their situation absolutely seriously. This is what enables him 'to see the thing through, all the way to the end' (as Henry James would say), to create a world composed of nothing but the consequences of their given situation" (1973, 24). Barthes and Hamon will underscore this notion – perhaps first accentuated by Auerbach – of the "*sérieux*" as a fundamental intention in Realism. "Man's epistemological situation is firmly and unproblematically given" (Stern, 1973, 115–16). Realism in this view, then, necessitates some uniform system for the organization of what's observed. If in the 'classical' or 'medieval' era this was a theological or moral system, "must science accommodate itself to morality?" Flaubert asks. Rather, "the Absolute" is "to be measured in terms of the material "relentless evolution of things. ... It is high time for sociology to find inspiration in" Darwin. (Flaubert, 1953, 263; quotations from Flaubert cited in this chapter, unless otherwise indicated, are from the same collection of letters.)

In the following notes I cite Flaubert in particular as the writer (so often called the master Realist) most likely to present initial confusion to those seeking to reconcile anti-Realist views of Realism with the ones apparently held by those considered Realists – confusion for reasons indicated above and because of equally passionate formalist (and nihilistic?) inclinations in him which anti-Realists will adopt as signs of his avuncular if not paternal status in their own lineage. The famous 'split' within Flaubert was his own most conscious and obsessive theme, and no one would systematically argue that this second aspect of his approach to literature is typical of Realism. That was *his* point, and it's mine.

11 Cf., e.g., Brunetière's avowal that Realism was on the way to becoming in art what positivism was in philosophy (e.g. in *Le Roman Naturaliste*, 1883). Anti-Realist writers will reaffirm that it would be largely impossible to read Stendhal, Balzac, Flaubert, Eliot, as well as Tolstoy and Zola, without taking into full account the extent to which their rich historical and/or quasi-scientific contextualization of experience is offered by them as informing their work and as their century's positive gift to what Erich Heller calls "the passion for understanding, the desire for rational appropriation, the driving force toward the expropriation of mystery" (1965, 95). Cf. Flaubert: "The leading characteristic of our century is its historical sense. This is why we have to confine ourselves to relating the facts – but *all* the facts"(171). The two muses of the modern age are history and science. "The brand-new dogma of equality [like the old dogma of religion] is given the lie by experimental psychology and by history" (248). In anti-Realism's view Realism is not merely an expression of an empiricist urge to assemble data such as would spring, for example, from the spirit of scepticism of a Francis Bacon. Its impulse is to secure a sense of the data of experience as aspects of a cosmic order – what has been called the nineteenth century's "*orgeuil de tout comprendre*" (cf. Grant, 1965, 35ff. on this point). To 'totalize' – to assemble into a meaningful totality – reality.

12 Stern: "*Realism in literature* connotes a way of depicting, describing a situation in a faithful, accurate, 'life-like' manner; or richly, abundantly, colourfully, or again mechanically, photographically, imitatively" (40); "if [a writer] allows the meaning to exceed the concrete details, underscoring their intimatory functon – the making at the expense of the matching – he will be moving toward symbolism" (which Realism can intermittently accommodate but must not – to remain itself – give way to) (122); "No content or image of transcendence and no object of religious faith can be a concern of realism" (47); Realism "refus[es] all invitations to journey into the ineffable" (184).

13 "No lyricism, no comments, the author's personality absent" (Flaubert, 127).

14 "There are in me, literarily speaking, two distinct persons: one ... who would like to make you feel almost *physically* the things he reproduces" (Flaubert, 125–6).

15 "The truth is that Shakespeare's conception of Hamlet reaches into the remotest corners of the human soul"; "I have always endeavored to penetrate

into the essence of things and to emphasize the most general truths" (Flaubert, 153, 247).

16 "The more banal and generalized it is, the more typical it becomes", Zola quoted in Grant, 1970, 31. In choosing as his first major representative 'realist' text passages from *The Pickwick Papers*, Stern says he does so "because there is nothing grand or passionate about them. They are set in the modest regions of life, of social and emotional life alike" (4). We should note that Stern elsewhere (109) says that "The realist ... isn't concerned to show 'the average' or even the 'typical' ... even though a social historian may find that 'Julien Sorel is a typical product of the post-Napoleonic age'. The average is boring ... the typical is boring". This insistence (an anti-Realist might say), characteristic of Stern's apologia – that Realism isn't concerned with boring X (for which he has elsewhere commended it) because "to call a work 'realistic' is to commend it" and no commendable activity can be boring – is not helpful, but its intention is not as naive as it seems, but simply confounds two crucially different issues. Stern feels that Realism is not concerned with the average or typical because the 'unboring' Realist *particularizes*: no real individual is average or typical; Realism is interested in the tension between the particular (individual) and the general (collective). This is a common Realist view. But – as Stern is the first to argue – this tension is 'meaningful', as he would say, *because* both the individual and his circumstances *are probable* – are to be found through and through 'the everyday world'. Gawain, Una, Lucifer, Tristan are *not*. (As he'd put it, a Realistic text would 'break down' if Lucifer were to appear on the scene in all his burning glory.) And not only because they are 'improbable' in a Realist context, but also because they are *generalized* in a way that Emma, Julien, Anna Karenina are not.

Stern is fighting a Realist's battle against the generalization ('universalization') of characters and events associated with Classicism. Curiously, it's a battle which even Classicism (or neo-Classicism) would have no interest in fighting, since nothing was further from the mind of a (neo-)Classicist than the idea that by 'general, universal types' he/she meant anything like the 'average' or the 'typical'. The critic has here fallen foul of a predicament that plagues students and scholars alike when confronted with the likelihood that Realism is interested in the probable or the 'normal'. 'But the characters in *Madame Bovary* are not all alike – they're unique!' they feel like crying. It stems from a confusion – due to the ambiguity of our vocabulary – of the terms of two quite different sets of categories: (1) typical (average, probable) *versus* exceptional, eccentric, and (2) typical (generalized, universal) *versus* particularized (unique). Emma, Charles, Rodolphe, Léon, Homais and Rouault are all different, seen 'particularly', and yet none are (or are meant to be) *eccentric* in the more or less 'normal conditions' of *Madame Bovary* in ways that Milton's Lucifer would be. We may feel that the Realist/Romantic battle actually centres on the values expressed in category (1) and the Realist/Classicist battle on those in category (2). In any case, in the end, the anti-Realist says, the Realist invariably argues that his/her aim is precisely to particularize the typical and probable (cf. the terms of Flaubert's praise for Turgenev).

Cf. the work of Georg Lukács, whose powerful acclamation of Realism is inseparable from his insistence on its revelation of the typical.

17 "What informs [Dickens'] evocations is always an unabating *interest* in this world and this society as a thing real and, as to its reality, wholly unproblematical" (Stern, 1973, 5).

18 E. M. Forster's notions of character in this respect exemplify an orthodox Realist attitude.

19 A significant feature of critical arguments given *for* the flood as Eliot writes it (e.g. in Barbara Hardy, Laurence Lerner) is that it plays an integral part in the book's over-all poetic unity; that is, that on some other plane it contributes to the *cosmic* aspect of the novel.

20 "There *is* one area in which [realism] is most fully at home: it is where human relationships are formalized and protected against the caprice of solipsism, in the social institutions of a given age" (Stern, 1973, 91). Stern cites a few of those indicated below, but does not examine them systematically.

21 A term for which – unlike the preceding one, usefully used by Philippe Hamon – I must take the blame; there being a good deal against it and only a few things to be said for it on *formal* grounds (beyond the motive of word-gaming that lies behind all the neologisms in this book). One of the best being perhaps that once we've uttered the notion of 'megastory' the worst damage has been done, i.e. in our raising external verifiability/non-verifiability as a criterion of classification (as Hamon himself does), as we see in great detail later.

22 In the respect *referred to here*, the *nouveau roman* can be considered a logical historical extension of Realism, and as such is often properly spoken of as *chosisme*.

23 Grant, 1970, 25. For Flaubert, "poetry is only a way of perceiving external objects, a special sense through which matter is strained and transfigured without being changed" (147).

24 Each unit within the segment – beginning with the first phrase "Obliged to" – expresses the limits of that 'mind', or of some function of it, in the context of some other function that threatens to 'absorb' it. 'Julien' is composed of a multiplicity of mental–sentimental functions operating simultaneously. The mind struggles to 'contain' itself, but must fail. His 'feeling' (for Mathilde) makes it impossible to think; his thinking makes it impossible to feel – or affirm his feeling; his fantasies alternately (in the past/in the present) distract him from thinking or feeling/are driven to distraction by thinking or feeling. But – we say, as the chapter's epigraph suggests – this then is 'a portrait of infatuation'; somewhere, at some (further?) level he perceives this; hence his "absurd extreme of self-depreciation" ("*excès de modestie ridicule*"). Here, we may think, is even another Julien, one who might well have reason to 'depreciate' himself: the one whose mind has in the past been "taken off those feelings" by "ambition, and the minor triumphs of vanity",

by "pride" and "presumption". But does the character Julien depreciate himself for this? *Who is it* that sees Julien in this way? Have we ever been '*in Julien's mind*', as the saying goes, at all? With a chilling turn of phrase the narrator makes it plain: "This individual whom we have seen. . . . " Finally we stand with the narrator, fully outside the 'person' Julien is. It is the objectivist narrative, alone, that finally contains him.

25 The manuscript, deed, contract, bond, warrant, licence, formula, blueprint, plan, map, portrait, photograph, relic or souvenir, signature or seal, ring, fingerprint, footprint, birthmark, bloodstain, certificate of birth, marriage, death, of kinship, membership, affiliation. . . .

26 Barthes has been particularly influential on this point. He cites examples from *Madame Bovary* in which (he feels) "the signified is expelled from the sign". 'Concrete details' here "finally say nothing but this: *we are the real*". ". . . The 'real' is supposed to be self-sufficient . . . strong enough to belie [*démentir*] any notion of 'function'. . . . the *having-been-there* of things is a sufficient principle of speech [*un principe suffisant de la parole*]" (Barthes, 1968, 147–8).

"If you knew me better you would know that I abhor ordinary existence" writes Flaubert concerning *Madame Bovary*. "But aesthetically, I desired this once – and only this once – to plumb its very depths. Therefore I plunged into it heroically, into the midst of all its minutiae, accepting everything, telling everything, depicting everything" (Flaubert, 176).

27 77. Positive redundancy combats the inevitable 'noise' that surrounds all reading and thinking, its repetition in different forms of like classes of data establishing a sense of pattern and coherence. Hamon – with less obvious recourse to the notion of what is after all in Stern's view at least partly a thematizing process (intimation) – puts it this way: "the text then presents itself as surcoded (a trait of mass-communication: the receiver having no access to code A will have access to code B . . .)" (Hamon, 1973, 427; "le texte se présente alors comme surcodé (trait de la communication de masse: le recepteur qui n'aura pas accès au code (a) aura accès au code (b) . . .)").

28 This tenet is implicit in philosophical endeavour throughout the eighteenth and nineteenth centuries down to and including Hegel, and lies behind the major Realist tradition of 'chronicle-novels', from Balzac's conception of the *Comédie humaine* through Zola's Rougon–Macquart series and Trollope's Barsetshire chronicles, to the flood of European and American *romans-fleuves* of our own century.

Recent criticism has often proposed that at the heart of Realism there lies a fundamental antithesis between the impulse to 'describe', to impart information, and the impulse to satisfy the requirements of narrative readerliness. (E.g. in Hamon, 1973, which is interestingly – and often imaginatively – modified by Brooke-Rose, 1981. Hamon is a proponent – in a self-confessedly 'helter-skelter' way – of the analytic notions of defocalization, demodalization and disambiguation to which I refer later with fewer reservations than I hold with respect to his more generalized conception discussed here.) I believe this reflects a crude misunderstanding. The theory is fundamentally a permutation of the basic idea that art is a continual manifestation of the tension between order and disorder, which must certainly be true in a broad and profound sense. But it fails to explain what characterizes Realistic literature in particular and, I feel, actually misrepresents it. The information motive is – with the 'probabilistic' and 'totalistic' – only one intention within the aim to appear rationally comprehensive. A contribution distinguishing Realism is its special appearance of presenting the infinity and complexity of ordinary human life and of still managing to find a way (a cosmic view) to resolve it all into order. It claims to make intelligible (readerly simplicity of narration) what the reader agrees to be probable (*readerly* richness of description). Order – in formal beauty and referential 'truth' – is the ultimate pursuit, and the *semblance* of plurality and exhaustiveness acts in its service. For the Realist the real difficulty lies in having an orderly preconception of an already-there cosmos to 'declare'' and that for an 'objective' writer in an era especially ready to demand objectivity of him, not disorder but the risk of *hyper-order* (heavy thematic structure, schematic symmetry of the sort attributable for example to traditional Christian narrative or to a neoclassicist – that 'overburdening of intimation' Stern describes as anti-realistic), is his/her genuine problem: one which the simulacrum of uncontrolled infinite diversity will be there to mask.

In this sense, the descriptive function is an aspect of readerliness and not its arch-antagonist. If the emphasis in nineteenth-century Realism were on the newness of its information, it would reach towards what the theorists I've mentioned agree that it shuns: the exotic. *René* and *Atala* and *Paul et Virginie* richly provided that. (While a Realist text so often gives detailed data on, for instance, how a local doctor, craftsman, farmer performs his job – as Hamon and others point out – this is not to teach its reader something unsettlingly new. To the contrary, it is the elaboration of what the nineteenth-century reader commonly recognizes; it is a dilation and consolidation of the reader's own experience. A Realist world is one in which essentially subtle mutations take place within a narrowly confined armature of routine – of people working, playing, conversing, eating, sleeping. Few characters in nineteenth-century fiction are explorers or – for all that – 'Red Indians', unless the text is frankly not Realist but, in opposition, frankly Romantic.) Rather, more often it offers *description* as a wonder *in itself*; the sustained reassertion of its descriptive powers, however wonted their subject. It aims to restore and affirm its reader's sense – and sense of the importance – of the known, and its 'knowability'. Hence Stern's – and many others', as we'll find – anxiety about Realism's potential for banality.

29 Thematic "intimations and distant echoes of infinity that stir behind, beyond". "What realism cannot do is to allow these glimpses and intimations to dominate a fictional structure ... until they and not 'the reach of common indication' become the true theme of the fiction" (Stern, 152–3)

30 Classic studies piloting criticism's exploration of this area were, of course, those of Booth and Genette.

31 Here Genette would *not* use "voice" but "mood".

32 As if, first of all, by the grace of this doubleness of voice or vision, where two possibly even mutually exclusive propositions are offered side by side, the immediate illusion (Julien's feelings) and the circumambient illusion (the narrator's view of Julien's vanity and pride) are allowed to coexist without harm or prejudice to one another. And as if, secondly, the pretence of *self-effacement* – which is always a condition of irony, in contrast to the assertion of personality that appears to accompany the assertion of an exclusive opinion, even when it's satirically expressed – carries with it the warranty, the imprimatur and seal of objectivity which the over-all Realist context has promised.

33 They do not appear in my list of typical thematic *topoi*, and that's my point. This distinction between theme and proposition is a central subject of Chapters 2 and 4.

Culler cites in Stephen Crane's "The open boat" what he considers an example of an irony of "uncertainty": "'These waves were most wrongfully and barbarously abrupt and tall, and each froth-top was a problem in small-boat navigation'." Here, Culler suggests, "unable to arrest the play of meaning and compose the text ... as spoken from an identifiable position by someone with identifiable attitudes", the reader finds language putting "everything to the test with a distance and detachment that is unjustifiably cruel"; he finds "the action of irony itself ... a means of hesitation" (Culler, 1975, 158–9). In my view this is an insightful reading that falls just short of the point. In the true spirit of Realism, the passage reveals a narrative voice that – through the medium of an admittedly rather coarsely Dickensian irony – declares itself free of the sway of the potentially emotionally affective qualities of the event described, and sets out not to evoke uncertainty but finely to assure us as to the *certainty* of its own detachment. As we must have already glimpsed, Realism's 'objective voice' has little to do with 'factuality' and a great deal to do with a *rhetoric* of imperturbable neutrality. There may well be "unjustifiable cruelty" here, entirely analogous to that which we recognize when, at the point of her gruesome death, Flaubert's narrator says of Emma "Doubtless she was finding again ... the lost ecstasy of her first flights of mysticism and beginning to see visions of eternal blessedness" (Flaubert, 1857, 335). (The reader may wish to review Culler's *Flaubert: The Uses of Uncertainty* in this light.) The point about the Crane (and the Flaubert) is that, far from producing no "positive precipitate", as Culler says, the irony of both texts disengages quite specific – and similar – propositions concerning the relations between the posture of detachment and the sources of cruelty. Our knowledge (were we allowed it) of both Flaubert's and Crane's other work and external statements would positively reinforce this view. The matter confirms (against Culler's opinion) Barthes' idea that even in its *irony* Realism is far from resisting 'premature closure' and *is* inclined to posit the existence of a 'superior truth' within the ken of the narrator. That there is no perception of irony until there is the apprehension of an overarching 'better (more accurate and complete) knowledge'.

34 A few of these and subsequent examples set within a specifically semi-

ological context (if, as he says, fairly haphazardly) appear in Hamon, 1973.

35 Free indirect discourse is not merely an idiosyncrasy of Realism; it's the seal of its whole narrative procedure and outlook. An irony of this melding of disparate 'knowings' in one apparent intelligence is that the narrator's sense of gravity of the character's insentience is often thus the basis of *our* first mistaken sense of the character's perspicuity. By the sheer linguistically-contrived contiguity of Julien Sorel's and his narrator's 'minds' Julien is lent a semblance of wit or wisdom that's not his, or is his only only on narrative sufferance. It's a price the narrator pays – to the inattentive reader – for his/her own concealment. Thus one literary biographer actually writes that Stendhal's "novels, like his letters and his journals, are largely records of psychological experiments. . . . Julien Sorel is an embodiment of . . . his clear, cold mind, incisive and dangerous"(!) (Richardson, 1971, 301).

36 Loaded modifiers such as wonderful, terrible, huge, tiny, beautiful, heartless, delicious, poor, clever, luxurious, great, tragic, grotesque, comic, good, bad; nouns like saint, coward, beauty, hag, horror, miracle, fate, blessing, ordeal; verbs like torment, triumph, ruin, adorn, blunder, lavish, waste, bewitch, corrupt, ennoble, pry, mortify, violate, sneak, surrender, usurp. A hint of the genuine pervasiveness of free indirect discourse is disclosed in how often we do find just such terms in Realist fiction – that they have come under its precious shelter. Their appearance is one of the first and most incisive clues, in fact, that free indirect smuggling is afoot.

37 Thus Auerbach is enthusiastically ready to include Woolf – and Stern to include Golding – among Realists. In spite of Gerald Graff's presumptively reasonable argument that we should seek continuity between Modernism and post-war anti-Realist thinking, in the context of western literature as a whole it's symptomatic of the tangentiality, at best, of the rôle of Modernism in any revolt against Realism that among the majority of contemporary writers we're to discuss – certainly among west-Europeans and Latin-Americans – the very term or concept 'Modernism' in the sense used in English-speaking countries has scarcely any signification at all.

38 Cf. Edmund Wilson's famous book of that title, or Virginia Woolf's standard discussion of Modernism as a process for the imitation of the mind's direct experience, "On modern fiction".

39 It's no accident, though it may seem eccentric, that one recent summary of Tolkien's position in fiction's history says that "another literary movement: realism" held sway in his time, preoccupied with "everyday" ugliness, hopelessness, waste, misery – "the frank, rounded portrayal of life . . . wallowed down in the ironic mode" – and declares that the prime exemplar of this 'realist' spirit is the Modernist novelists' poetic counterpart, T. S. Eliot (Rogers, 1980, 37–40).

40 G.-Albert Aurier, from "Les peintres symbolistes", *Revue Encyclopédique* (Paris, April 1892), trans. H. R. Rookmaaker, *Symbolist Art Theories*, 1; in Chipp 1968, 93–4.

41 *Die Gegendstandslose Welt*, Bauhausbuch 11 (Munich, 1927, trans. from

the Russian), trans. H. Dearstyne, *The Non-Objective World*, Chicago, 1959; in Chipp, 1968, 341–3.

42 Picasso to Marius de Zayas, published in trans. in *The Arts*, New York, May 1923 ("Picasso speaks"), in Goldwater and Treves, 1945, 416.

43 From J. L. Martin, Ben Nicholson and Naum Gabo (eds), *Circle: International Survey of Constructive Art*, London, 1937; in Chipp, 1968, 336.

44 Published in J. L. Martin, Ben Nicholson and Naum Gabo (eds), op. cit., reprinted in Piet Mondrian, *Plastic Art and Pure Plastic Art*, New York, 1945; in Chipp, 1968, 355, 359.

45 Mondrian, quoted in Goldwater and Treves, 1945, 428 (Goldwater and Treves give no further source data).

46 Mondrian, *Plastic Art and Pure Plastic Art*; in Chipp, 1968, 352.

47 Naum Gabo, "The Realistic Manifesto" (1920), trans. in Sir Herbert Read and Leslie Martin, *Gabo*, 1957; in Chipp, 1968, 328.

48 Mondrian, *Plastic Art and Pure Plastic Art*; in Chipp, 1968, 353.

49 Catalogue of the Forum Exhibition of Modern American Painters, New York (Anderson Galleries, 13–15 March) 1916; in Chipp 1968, 320–1.

50 Wassily Kandinsky, "Über die Formfrage", *Der Blaue Reiter*, Munich 1912, trans. K. Lindsay, "On the problem of form"; in Chipp, 1968, 170.

51 Mondrian, from "de nieuwe beelding in de schilderkunst", *De Stijl* 1, Amsterdam, 1919, trans. M. Seuphor, "Natural beauty and abstract reality", *Piet Mondrian, Life and Works,* n.d.; in Chipp, 1968, 321–3.

52 That is, through the fusion of subjective intuition with that objectivity with which Naturalism has sought to replace it.

53 Zavarzadeh, 1976, 19; Z's quotation is from J. Ellul, *The Technological Society*, New York, 1964, 79.

54 It's difficult to see how the "self" can (without a theory more complex than Stern is willing to give) be fragmented into "episodes" – and impossible to imagine it fragmented into "linguistic ploys".

Chapter 1

1 This paraphrase is given by Borges (in English) in "An autobiographical essay", Borges, 1970, 171.

2 "Event": from here on I frequently use this word in a way different from that intended for it in paragraphs above. I don't now invariably mean it to refer to an 'event in the story' – as an event happening, for example, to some continuous character – any more than a modern physicist speaks of 'an event in the continuing life of a uniquely identifiable particle' (which would at best be a fiction in much the way that a novel's character is), but rather very approximately in the way that a physicist might use it to denote a datum *occurring to the observer (to the reader) at a given point in his/her observation (reading).* Thus we stand free to ask whether 'a thing that happens' in a text happens at, for example, the level of the story or at the level of the telling of the story: whether the minimal segment by which it's constituted is (in old-

fashioned terminology) a complex narrative 'scene', an expository passage of description or argument, a lexeme, a punctuation point, an orthographic device, a typographical space. It's in this non-prejudgemental – or at least perhaps less prejudiced – sense that I use the word 'event' (or 'datum'); not to forestall but to open the way toward more precise descriptions as the need arises.

3 Interviewed in Bellamy, 1974, 56. Cf. his similar statement of 1973 quoted in Klinkowitz, 1975, 3.

4 "El milagro secreto" ["The secret miracle"], Borges, 1964, 91; cf. *Obras completas* (Borges, 1974), 510.

5 Note 2, above.

6 Cf., e.g., not only James Gunn's history of science fiction, *Alternate Worlds*, but (already referred to) Hooper's posthumous edition of C. S. Lewis's essays and stories, *Of Other Worlds* (title taken from *The Faerie Queene*); W. H. Auden's *Secondary Worlds* (a term Auden takes from Tolkien); and David Ketterer's *New Worlds for Old*.

7 As Vivian Mercier says of the linguistically, narrationally most 'radical' among those discussed in this section, Pinget's *Graal Flibuste*, it is "a fantasy, but the freedom granted to [its] matter is counterbalanced by the secret classicism of [its] manner" (Mercier, 1971, 383).

8 When, e.g., either for comic or serious or even arrogant or cynical reasons, we imitate an actor playing a rôle, a comedian telling a joke, a scientist describing an experiment, a professor expounding a theory, a mechanic explaining how a thing works, a lawyer pleading a case, a judge rendering a judgement, a father laying down the law.

9 My dramatization of a 'shift in Flaubert's procedure' was of course only a fiction – but we've a famous mass of biographical evidence that his daily effort was endlessly and agonizingly directed along just such lines.

10 Calvino, 1960 (p. 8 – "Be', per uno che non esiste, siete in gamba!"; Weaver's translation "You seem in fine form" has its own advantages, obviously, p. 289).

11 We may feel that 'form and content' can't be separated. But in a text that says 'a suit of armour moves but no human being is there', no rule of how customarily-reliable descriptive language works is violated, but only a rule of how life works as represented in Realist discourse. If writers persist in doing this, we may cease to attribute the property of mimesis to language of this sort; and much anti-Realist fiction will aim precisely toward that end. Yet the effort to do so reflects an anxiety not to show that form and content are the same but, to the contrary, to save the notion of mimetic discourse's formal independence of content, e.g. of referents other than itself.

12 E.g. the first lines of "Tutto in un punto" ["All at one point", 1965]: "Through the calculations begun by Edwin P. Hubble on the galaxies' velocity of recession, we can establish the moment when all the universe's matter was concentrated in a single point, before it began to expand in space." Without further allusion to this pre-text, the story begins: "Naturally, we

were all there – *Old Qfwfq said* – where else could we have been? Nobody knew then that there could be space."

13 Cf., e.g., the difference of views represented by T. Todorov and Darko Suvin, especially as Brooke-Rose tangles with it (1981).

14 Cf. C. S. Lewis in conversations recorded in Lewis, 1966.

15 "I conceived of the eye-encephalon link as a kind of tunnel dug from the outside by the force of what was ready to become an image, rather than from within by the intention of picking up any old image" (Calvino, 1965, 182).

16 Pinget will indeed not have missed the etymology/analogy in the surname Astaire. Whether he knew, in addition, that Adele had another name, Ann, and that Fred's only daughter was called Ava, is something for film-lit. buffs to play with.

17 The Müller connection is explicit. A Monsieur Muller, the narrator tells us, who "distinguished himself by linguistic works at the University of Agapa, affirms that the roots *pil* and *piv* are identical, both derived from the indogomorrhean *pis* (wet); thus Pivons-Trassoulle and Pilon would be one and the same god" ["s'est distingué par des travaux linguistiques à l'université d'Agapa, affirme que les racines *pil* et *piv* sont identiques, toutes deux dérivées de l'indogomorrhéen *pis* (mouillé); ainsi Pivons-Trassoulle et Pilon seraient un seul et même dieu" (56)]. Pinget's title, *Graal Flibuste*, obviously enriches the 'pleasure of the text': as we've seen, the novel wants us to work backward to the creative sources of the word as well as forward through its proliferative permutations. The Dutch sense of the term producing our 'freebooter' is in fact (*vrijbuit*) *booty*: the grail, dare we say, of the pirate roaming free, raiding the shores of language's bounteous potential. But more, it has come, in some languages, to refer us quite specifically to the act of *filibustering*: the delaying ('deferring') action of endless utterance, the deliberate obstruction of legislation, of rule-making, the forestalling of decision (of 'closure', as anti-Realists will come to say); the consuming, gaining, 'killing' of time precisely by the generation of words and more words.

18 Calvino, 1967 (163; Weaver's translation, 158, of "*iper-romanzo*" as "super-novel" I think misses Calvino's point).

19 "Non avevo pensato neanche per un minuto al bene e al male. . . . Avevo usato un ben noto contrasto narrativo per dare evidenza a quel che mi interessava, cioè il dimidiamento / Dimidiato, mutilato, incompleto, nemico a se stesso è l'uomo contemporaneo" (Calvino, 1960, xi–xii). Perhaps significantly, this passage does not appear in current English-language editions.

20 Sontag, 1969, 14. Sontag's statement is presented in the context of her argument against interpretation. If we accept (as she clearly does) the line of thought from Bacon and Vico to German Romantic theory and its heirs in Lévy-Bruhl *et al.* on the nature of primitive mentality, analytical interpretation as the supportive activity underlying mimesis may well not always have been an essential function associated with the production of what we call art. But it's most likely that *the notion 'art'* itself *comes with* the interpretative way of regarding artefacts and would probably be a conception altogether foreign to just that kind of mentality Sontag has in mind. Yet more than this:

inasmuch as such a distinct mode of thinking has ever operated (where interpreting artefacts is not or was not the rule), the idea that mimesis (or a cosmic motive generally) is not an urgent motive among those thinking in that way runs counter to all the evidence we have – particularly if we include the "expressionist" urge among mimetic intentions as Sontag does. What's more, as it happens, observations in the field among modern tribal groups tend to suggest that the activity of interpretation – the attribution of natural, metaphysical and communal meaning – may recurrently have been a vital part of those rituals associated with the manufacture and celebration of artefacts. I mention this not as a 'defence' of mimesis, but to put Sontag's view fully into the kind of perspective which the foundations of her own argument logically entail. Unfortunately for anti-mimeticists or 'anticosmists' inclined to appeal to her rationale for support, it cannot wholeheartedly provide it.

21 Brooke-Rose, 1981, 362. She is paraphrasing Yuri Lotman.

22 Cf. Barthes: "the text needs its shadow" – "some ideology, some mimesis, some subject" (1973, 53). Culler: "For all its opposition to models of intelligibility and coherence, the radical novel relies on the link between the text and ordinary experience just as traditional novels did" (Culler, 1975, 191). Butor: the "system of significations within the book will be an image of the system of signification within which the reader is caught in his daily life", quoted by Heath, 1972, 39, in setting out "the area of the work of the nouveau roman", where such "projections" remain "ceaselessly to be remade". Sollers, perhaps ostensibly the least referentialist of our writers, will say repeatedly that the text cannot escape that 'quotidian reality'; cf. Sollers, 1981b.

23 There is a latent, crucial suggestion here of a necessary relationship of a unified kind between what we say and how we say it, between 'form' and 'content' – but more of that later.

24 For all their non-Realist qualities, the following complete narratives by Enrique Anderson Imbert (1961) and Gerhard Rühm (1970) are of this kind.

"Taboo"

His guardian angel whispered to Fabián, behind his shoulder:

"Careful, Fabián! It is decreed that you will die the minute you pronounce the word *doyen*."

"Doyen?" asks Fabián, intrigued.

And he dies.

"The lion"

The lion began to suck his wife. This made him so wild that he entered her with his whole head and lacerated her with his teeth until he was carrying only her mane around his neck.

25 Bory, 1973, 38–41, 45. Kostelanetz indicates (xxi) that this text, copyrighted by Bory in 1971, had not been published in French. NB "proposition", line 6, should no doubt read "preposition", just as in subsequent lines not

reproduced here "and adjective" and "aordinal number" should read "an adjective" and "ordinal number". I.e. where custom is not there to help recuperation, even the accurate registration of the text by a second 'scribe' becomes problematical.

26 A situation fiercely defied by anti-Realists with thunderous mechanical manoeuvres but one ultimately accepted; cf. Barth in Bellamy, 1974, 4. Authors of shuffle novels universally attest that while *they* do not order their passages linearly, the work is not read until someone (e.g. the reader) has done so.

27 Fourteen pages into the novel the narrator says "something happened". The death which we learn on the last page had been the 'happening' 'explains' the novel's intervening bizarre events, but only insofar as 'death' means 'change' – a conception which the last page itself in thematic terms explicitly repudiates. Cf. the epigraph (prefiguring Sollers' Day/Night nexus): "Human existence being an hallucination containing in itself the secondary hallucinations of day and night . . . it ill becomes any man of sense to be concerned at the illusory approach of the supreme hallucination known as death." (Readers conscious of the boom in O'Brien editions in the 1970s and struck with the similarity between motifs of his and of Beckett and post-war anti-Realists should be aware that he was writing *The Third Policeman* in the late 1930s.)

28 These examples – or versions of them (I've meddled with a few) – appear in Hofstadter, 1981, 1982; the second is an oft-quoted one by W. Van Orman Quine. Hofstadter, January 1982, contains a 1800-word 'story' in a self-referential mode by David Moser. For further samples, and for detailed background discussion of the whole problem of recursive processes in language, one can scarcely find more inventive argument than that in these and other essays by Hofstadter (e.g. those particularly associated with the matter of computer languages, September 1982, January, February and March 1983, in the same journal), as well as, of course, his provocative volume of 1979. For an exploration of Hofstadter's notion of 'tangled hierarchies' as background to a literary text, Sorrentino's *Mulligan Stew*, Brown, 1982, offers an interesting example. See also Hofstadter, 1985.

29 Mauriac, 1963, 197; trans. Mercier, 1971, 346.

30 Cortázar, 1956; brought forward by Genette in *Figures* (III, 1972). The device itself was of course fundamental to the strategy of, for example, Pirandello long before in e.g. "La tragedia d'un personaggio" ["The tragedy of a character", 1911, first published in book form in *La Trappola*, Milan, 1915].

31 The Roussel example appears in his *Impressions d'Afrique* [*Impressions of Africa*] a text – along with *Locus Solus* – much in the minds of Continental anti-Realists. Culler's appears in Culler 1975, 107.

32 From *Rayuela* (Cortázar, 1963, 237). That this is a translation (G. Rabassa) is of course crucial.

33 Mercier's paraphrase of an interview between Butor and F. C. St Aubyn (29).

34	I	She	He	I	He	She	She	I	He
She	1	5	13	21	29	27	19	11	3
He	9	33	37	45	56	51	43	35	7
I	17	41	57	61	69	67	59	39	16
He	25	49	65	73	77	75	63	47	23
I	32	53	72	80	81	79	71	55	31
She	24	48	64	76	78	74	66	50	26
He	16	40	60	68	70	62	58	42	18
She	8	36	44	52	54	46	38	34	10
I	4	12	20	28	30	22	14	6	2

Baudry, 1967; reproduced by Ricardou in Federman, 1981, 126; typography in the French original is slightly different, the format the same.

35 The phrase is Sollers' as translated by E. Freiburg from Ricardou, 1971 – a brief but, as always with Ricardou, thoughtful introduction easily available to readers in English in Federman, 1981, 127.

36 Cortázar, 1963, 191; chapter 34 continues in this way for six-odd pages. Note that narrator's intention is explicitly mimetic, however: he and the character Maga "form a pattern" in their relationship, a "Brownian motion", travelling on parallel tracks in opposite directions.

37 It goes without saying that, should I for sheer syntactic ease speak of 'neocosmists' and 'anticosmists' (or 'indeterminists', for example) this is not because I think for a minute any human is ever one of these, except in the loose and no doubt vacuous sense that we call a performer in a play of Shakespeare's a Shakespearean. I refer only to the narrator of a given text momentarily characterized as engaged in a neocosmic or anticosmic (or indeterminist) writing model.

38 Elsewhere an intuition has been proposed that recent fiction may be inclined to 'fork' as I'm suggesting. Cf. Kennard (1975) who extends an idea borrowed from Elizabeth Sewell and taken up by Ihab Hassan. Hassan writes "The novel may be a form undergoing deep mutations. I hope that the result will be something rich and strange. / Here is my Map of Vanishing Fiction. / Imagine two lines meeting at some point in the future. Call the left line the Novel of Silence, or as Barth would say, the Literature of Exhaustion. Call the right line the Fantastic Novel" (1975, 104–5). Their 'cases', lines of thought, and conclusions, however, are – insofar as they're not rather more diffuse, as this quotation indicates – quite their own. As will already be seen from the foregoing pages, their objectives are different, and I'm not sure that Kennard's discussion (of Heller, Purdy, Burgess, Barth, Murdoch, Golding and Vonnegut) or Hassan's (of e.g. Joyce, Beckett, and Vonnegut as 'science fictionist') are likely to integrate with the present one into a single picture of anti-Realism, which is all to the good. I'm in general sympathy with Kennard's view, but her argument presents serious problems (cf. reviews of Kennard, 1975, and of the related work, Stark, 1974, in Nash, 1977a, 1977b). They should be read for their respective merits in their own right. I'm forever indebted to students and teachers (including Judy Rawson, Jennifer Lorch,

Donald Ranvaud and Sergio Sokota) whose lively discussion with me in seminars on the subject of anti-Realism since 1970 has provided a stimulating – not to mention eternally forbearing and good-humoured – setting for the development of the thinking set forth here, though I must take full blame (they'll be relieved to hear me say) for all its defects.

39 Nor is there any room for escape, here, by means of some redefinition of our terms. It would be impossible for me to suggest (looking at things from the other angle, as it might be tempting to do in the hope of saving ourselves infinite trouble) that perhaps, then, 'neocosmic' and 'anticosmic' are false distinctions. However passionately those who acclaim an anticosmic mode, under whatever heading, there is scarcely any way we could ascribe the overriding attributes of anticosmic fiction to Borges's many "straightforward stories" or to Calvino's *Il barone rampante, Il visconte dimezzato*, or to the bulk of his short fiction (cf. his fifty-odd stories in *I racconti*, Turin, 1958). The term "straightforward stories" is Borges' own, applied by him to "The intruder" ("La intrusa") – "perhaps the best I have ever written" (Borges, 1970a, 203) – and to the entire collection of stories appearing in *El informe de Brodie*; cf. his preface to the English edition, *Doctor Brodie's Report*, 1970.

Chapter 2

1 This case highlights the problem of authorial intention, since Sollers 'speaking as himself' (if that is possible) has since its first publication changed his position on just such subjects. Far from dissolving authorial intentionality, the issue merely makes it clearer that – as Sollers' texts (in *all* his phases) assert – historical/biographical context is inscribed in what is said.

2 While I propose that, as to writers' motives, we 'have their word for it' and cannot properly choose to 'hear' some words and not others, we nevertheless retain the right not to '*take* their word for it' unproblematically. This is another question.

3 For guidelines, in other words, as to how to find flaws in this book's eventual conclusions, the secret would lie in this: look for oversimplification. I mean more than the bare fact that no one novel is an 'archtext' containing all and nothing but neocosmic or anticosmic features; that goes without saying. Rather: while I adopt concrete evidence from specific cases, I lean with predeliberation towards those cases that look to express not average but ultimate attitudes; statements and procedures seeming to me to embody what's quintessentially implicit, logically immanent, in each anti-Realist gesture considered. Merely test cases, these, and hostages to time.

4 "The subject", Lewis himself announces, "still awaits its Aristotle" (Lewis, 1966, 17).

5 15. This motive echoes T. H. White's, who in speaking of his own *England Have My Bones* says it is "a book about things, for people who have lost them", "an empirical book, an attempt to return to the various world" (quoted in Manlove, 1976–7, 68; "*The Book of Beasts* ... White's translation

of a medieval bestiary, was done out of what White shared with his source – 'a reverence for the wonders of life' ... "; 71).

6 Cf. Robbe-Grillet's early arguments for a new novel: "To be able to look at things is, after all, our best weapon." "What must be saved is ... 'the earth, the stone, the ash. *It is your duty to bring about the salvation of space and time*' "; "every man in his turn has to reinvent the things around him"; "there is no doubt that we need to return to the real" (1962, 94, 114, 118, 154).

7 Lewis, 1966, 30. "The real victim of wishful reverie does not batten on *The Odyssey*, *The Tempest*, or *The Worm Ouroboros*: he (or she) prefers stories about millionaires, irresistible beauties, posh hotels, palm beaches and bedroom scenes – things that really might happen, that ought to happen, that would have happened if the reader had had a fair chance."

8 Lewis, *An Experiment in Criticism*, 1961, cited in White, 1969, 57.

9 From a letter, quoted in White, 1969, 67.

10 As a character, Weston, says in Lewis's *Perelandra*, quoted in White, 1969, 58.

11 White, 1969, 66, describing the subject-matter that concerns Edmund Fuller and Lewis.

12 Fiction adopts "the fabulous", as Robert Coover says, "to probe beyond the phenomenological, beyond appearances, beyond randomly perceived events, beyond mere history" (Coover, 1969, 78).

13 Calvino 1967–8, 99. Calvino cites as vital Gombrich's *Freud and the Psychology of Art*.

14 "If you have a religion it must be cosmic" (Lewis, 1969, 16).

15 Cf. Abrams, 1953. It's no surprise that for a movement concerned to find a way out of Realism there should be great allure in such a conception when "the most significant element in the fabric of realist theory", as Damian Grant says, "and that which contains the most serious implications, is its habitual suspicion of the imagination" (Grant, 1970, 29; he is speaking specifically of mid/late-nineteenth-century Realism).

16 The dynamics of this – under the designation of "active imagination" – as a functional procedure fundamental not only to art but to the psychological processes of transformation is argued throughout the works of Jung, the foundations of whose theories in German Romantic theory support English thought under the same influence, e.g. via Coleridge.

Mervyn Peake writes in enumerating the stages of evolution of the Gormenghast trilogy: "1) No initial conception of plot. 2) The characters 'took their way'. 3) on the *qui-vive* while waiting for opportunities for the imagination to take its course" (Watney, 1976, 128). "Somehow the image", Borges says of his writing of "El hombre en el umbral" ["The man on the threshold", 1970a], "of an apparently helpless old man holding a secret power impressed itself on my imagination. I wove this image into the present story" (Borges, 1970a, 199). "What the three stories have in common", says Calvino of the short novels of which *I nostri antenati* [*Our Ancestors*] is composed, "is the fact that they had a very simple, very obvious image or situation as their point of departure. ... The tale is born from the image, not from any thesis which I want to demonstrate, and the image extends a network of meanings" (Calvino, 1960, ix).

17 "If pressed, scientists generally admit ... that theories are not THE TRUTH, that theories are functional or 'instrumentalist' fictions. It's not that the theory is WRONG. ... It's that theories are not entirely true. ... It is debatable on logical and philosophical grounds whether any theory can be true. ... The best we might say ... is that any theory (verbal, mathematical, metaphysical) is to some degree 'truthlike' or has some verisimilitude", Hoffman (whose references in this passage are to Carnap, Nagel and Popper), 1980, 401.

18 For examples of contemporary theoretical objections to deviationism – which certainly has appeal to some neocosmists – see Iser, 1976, Fish, 1970. Readers interested in recent deviationist argument itself – addressed specifically to 'postmodernist' issues and neatly skirting if not resolving certain problems for which Iser takes Lotman to task – should see Lyotard, 1979, to which Carol Watts (whose current study of deviationist thought in the eighteenth and twentieth centuries promises to break new ground) has generously alerted me.

19 In spite of what I've said of the three 'green objects', no event can be taken solely on its own as customary. There is nothing uncustomary about 'green sun' in a Realist text if it's the product of some character's mind, as we've noted – if in other words it is psychologically naturalized. Lines about Freud and psychoanalysis (in a Realist novel) or lines about Merlyn and King Arthur's knights (in a 'romance') may both seem to be guaranteeably customary in their respective traditions. But when lines on Freud and psychoanalysis appear in a text making appeal to the 'romance' tradition they become uncustomary – yet this happens 'seriously', and with touching coherence, in *The Once and Future King* (White, 1962, 302). The relation between givens within a text defines the degree to which they are customary/uncustomary in the context of other texts. 'Custom' is not here a matter simply of 'what is customary in a given period'. Chaucer's Prologue and his Knight's Tale refer their reader to two quite different customs. While it is sometimes useful to identify the cultural moment with which a particular repertoire may be especially associated, it is our recognition of the repertoire itself that most informs us of what we may be asked to regard as 'acceptable/unacceptable'. A feature of anti-Realism is that it may indeed lay before us a 'tangled hierarchy' of repertoires within one text. But it reminds us with clarity that we have conventionally regarded these repertoires as distinct customary sets. A problem for anti-Realism will eventually be that the procedure itself constitutes a distinct custom.

20 Quoted from a letter (1972) in Federman, 1981, 5.

21 Again, here as elsewhere, any 'experience' for the reader that may be suggested to underlie the uncustomary must be taken figuratively. Not that we take fictional events only *as if* they are actually occurring, which is a different matter to be discussed in its own right later. Rather, I mean that whatever 'happens' in the story is not a first-order sensation but may only

constitute a linguistic formula for a way of thinking about, of perceiving, experiences. In concert with this: in such contexts as the present one, where I say we take the text 'seriously' I mean it in the sense used in recent pages (cf. pp. 116–17), and not 'explained away' as metaphor, hallucination, arbitrary gibberish, etc. (This is deliberately a different application of the word 'serious' from that used by, for example, certain speech-act theorists – cf. Searle, 1979, 60.) Thus where I've said we can't take the text 'pragmatically', one *may* (as Searle would) take empirical tests of it to refer to actuality, but we *are not required* to and I do not mean them to. The test-ground intended is that in which we assess the relationships between *words* according to their degree of customary/uncustomary usage – here specifically against the background of Realist convention. This is in no fashion meant to recommend some impossible artificial divorce between fiction and actuality but solely for immediate purposes to provide an economically workable basis for comparison within the range of written narratives.

22 Abrams, 1953, 27, 327. Abrams's extensive account of this anti-mimetic 'heterocosmic' impulse and the permutations of its intimate relation to notions of the text as non-teleological and autonomous is of course a classic among straighforward *précis* of complex philosophical issues in the history of pre-Modern literature, and is not offered here as definitive.

23 The phrase is a frankly Kantian one, coined by Eliseo Vivas, *The Artistic Transaction and Essays on Theory of Literature*, Columbus, Ohio, 1963, quoted in Lentricchia, 1980, 19.

24 A statement of Krieger's subsequent disappointment with Gombrich for having in his view abandoned the anti-representationalist position appears in Krieger, 1984.

25 Eco is persuasive in explicitly supporting Gombrich in detail on this functionalist point. See e.g. Eco, 1976, 209–17.

26 In the matter of low versus high literature, for example – including such otherwise seemingly shallow or empty literary phenomena as the appeals to 'horror', 'mystery', 'the supernatural' – it would help to explain how both pulp and much of Shakespeare are founded on the same fundamental patterns (as to story, for example, and character types) and get away with it. In the matter of this perspective's clarifying the action texts actually initiate in our minds (whatever their claims): it might hope to have effect in cases where, in the past (from Marlowe's *Dr Faustus* and Goethe's *Werther* to Brecht's *Mutter Courage* and, say, Robbe-Grillet's *Le Voyeur* or *L'Année dernière à Marienbad*) the history of the work's reception tells us of audiences having been 'moved' in directions which the (con)texts have quite explicitly stated were not intended. On the matter of indeterminacy, as Gombrich says, "in the sphere of art it has been shown that the same triangular shape which is the favourite pattern of many adjoining American Indian tribes is given different meanings reflecting the main pre-occupations of the people concerned" (218). When the same stick may in different contexts serve as a horse, a sword, a sceptre, "seen from the point of view of 'abstraction' . . . such a convergence of meanings onto one shape offers considerable difficulties, but from that of

psychological 'projection' of meanings it becomes more easily intelligible" (217). The extent of the appeal (across a population) of a work of art about which uniformly approving spectators *disagree* as to what if anything it might 'represent' indicates that the foundation of the appeal cannot be any standard mimetic one. To find out where the appeal lies one must begin to enquire not what range of outward forms the pattern may resemble but what range of functions it might serve. To do this, the argument might say, would require sophistication – in a new area, that is – which we at present have scarcely thought to develop, but no more than that of another kind, the referential kind, which a long and almost monolithically mimesis-orientated culture has intricately evolved by which to discover – or to think it discovers – the representation of springtime or grief in certain colours in an 'abstract' painting or in certain tonal effects in a symphony.

There is nothing *prima facie* indeterminately circular about this attention to the specific 'desires' of writer/reader, according to the argument. I do not have to share the desires of a devotee of crime novels in order to form a hypothesis as to what functions they may serve for a devotee to which he/she could agree, any more than I need ever have enjoyed a hobby horse or a stick-sword or a pacifier (significantly called a dummy in Britain) to estimate usefully what a child derives from one of these. I have only to observe how he/she 'uses' it. And it would be callow to pretend that most of our descriptions of literature have not been in large part – more than we commonly admit – primitive descriptions of our uses of it. These suggestions would seem to place the quality of what gets written into the hands of readers: what readers want is all they should have. But in fact the way it works is that the writer sets out to give the reader what will answer to that desire he/she wishes to induce in him or her. One of the principal functions of mimesis – which is only a rhetorical strategy, we recall, and not an act of transcribing – is to persuade the reader of the compelling nature of a fictional world in which the fictional desiderata are indeed desirable – and the fact that readers accept Realist texts as realistic attests to the effectiveness of this strategy.

This is not, then, a theory of archetypes, whose entire operation, from Bastian onward, has been to argue for fixed 'formal pre-dispositions' universally to be found throughout the population. To the contrary, it is 'conditionally indeterminist', an odd conception we'll come back to.

27 Stern, 1973, 156. Stern speaks here of the 'polemics' of Robbe-Grillet, Sarraute and Barthes.

28 Collingwood, 1938, 43. Contemporary literary history likes to suggest that recent theory has invented outright the idea that "no discourse refers unproblematically to a nondiscursive object that is the ground of the discourse", as Lentricchia puts it (1980, 189). The naive referentiality of fiction was already in jeopardy as an assumption not only when Sterne and Diderot spoofed it but when Rabelais did; Thomas Nashe knew perfectly well what he was doing – with poetic and comic force – in his "Hero and Leander" and "The Pope and the herring".

29 Such a scheme does not address itself to the question of whether the test

is mimetic. As indicated in the Introduction, in principle all sorts of texts may be mimetic/non-mimetic, in varying degrees.

30 "Whence the inanity of the question, 'What does the Iliad signify?'" Moritz requires, as Todorov points out, "a new class of signs, characterized by their intransitivity"; "the presence of the morpheme *allos* [in the word allegory] may suffice to account for the animosity that Moritz bears toward it: allegory requires something beyond itself"; for Schelling, too, whom Todorov quotes, "mythology is not *allegorical*; it is tautegorical. ... the gods ... signify only what they are" (Todorov, 1977, 159–64).

31 A great deal of energy has recently been put into arguments on 'the mimetic fallacy', to the effect that (as Thomas Twining had already noted in the eighteenth century) all texts are really 'diegetic' (and consequently subject to the liabilities of propositional paraphrase) except those that register direct speech, and exercises such as those of Henry James, Joyce, Woolf, and Compton-Burnett directed toward the elimination from fiction of all but direct speech are in part founded, at deep levels, on a search for a workable tautologic autonomy of composition. There is, however, at least one major difference. The programmes of James *et al.* rest on *systems of characterization*, and on the discrete and orderly separation of 'speaker' from 'speaker', each having a fixed identity fictionally 'drawn' by someone, namely the author, from whom each is in turn by that very act subsequently distinguished. The 'abolition of character' (of which more later) in anticosmic fiction will be set in train specifically to shift the accent further onto (tautologic) narration itself.

32 102. Of the work of Raymond Roussel (whose play with "Napoléon premier" we've noted, and whose writing Foucault has called "a language which says only itself") he says that "all that is left is things themselves, objects, actions". Cf. p. 95. The Foucault translation appears in Culler, 1981, 261; the Robbe-Grillet in 1962, 97.

33 This extends to the extinction of the notion of the *author* as producer of the text – a notion only contributing, the argument says, to the process by which our expectations are illusorily organized around referential ideas of fixed historical and biographical identity and motivations. 'An author", says Sollers, "is not really the cause of what he writes but its product; thus, he is incessantly potential and plural in relation to his writing" (Sollers, 1969c, 66).

34 Cf. German version in *Gesammelte Gedichte und Visuelle Texte*, Reinbek, 1970, 30; trans. R. Waldrop, in Russell, 147. For a common experience of the thetic quality of an artefact at work, consider the case of playing cards. In any of the many variations of solitaire (or, significantly, 'patience'), a sense of gratification arises *in time*, chronologically, as it may in reading a Realist novel. But now one is moving not toward a *completeness of 'meaning'* but toward the maximization, the optimization of one's 'hand', of the sequence of cards as they 'turn up'. Whereas both kinds of activities 'turn' on the relationship between the items within the collection of givens, by contrast with the claims of the Realist novel, one would never imagine the cards – either separately or in sum – to depend on any significant reference to

the outside world. There *are* potential analogies of a referential sort in the cards – for example ones having to do with social/sexual hierarchies (jack or knave, queen, king) – but these do not appear to have substantial effect *as points of external reference* in determining how the game is to be played or what the player's optimal achievement might be. In *spite* of this – and here is what makes the game's operation thetic rather than propositional – the further along one plays (as the cards turn up and one finds fitting places for them), the more rewardingly systematic and orderly one feels it to be. One's activity in playing seems in a limited way, thus, to be 'meaningful'. The process is one in which the 'text' (the total card-pack) and the 'reader' (reading his/her hand) collaborate. There are several ways of 'winning', along several 'tracks' – in terms, for instance, of straights, suits, colours, numbers of a kind, faces of a kind – yet these do not depend solely on 'how the player sees it' but are determined by constraints imposed by the nature of the deck of cards, the set of rules of the particular version of the game one has preselected from among those to which the deck lends itself, and the chance sequence in which the cards appear. In standard fiction, the writer (as Fielding might have said) acts as Fortune, stacking the deck. But *however* the cards appear, because of the *nature of the cards and the sets of rules attaching to them*, there appears to be no chance that some pattern and consequent reward will not reveal itself. One takes 'pleasure' (one feels it's worth doing this thing) from the fact that one can expect neither to be able to create out of the air a second queen of spades, on one hand, nor, on the other, to be unreasonably confronted with an unlimited number of such things as aces of rabbits – that, in other words, there *is pattern, within a variety of possibilities*.

35 A common mistake is to confuse overdetermination with redundancy. Redundancy involves the reiteration of a sign (signifier and signified having similar relations each time); overdetermination is a product of the mutiplicity of possible signifieds for a signifier. For the indeterminist, redundancy of meaning must be impossible, since every signifier-utterance appears in a new context and can in no way be a simple 'repetition'.

36 "Le concept d'*inter-textualité* (Kristeva) est ici essentiel: tout texte se situe à la jonction de plusieurs textes dont il est à la fois la relecture, l'accentuation, la condensation, le déplacement et la profondeur. D'une certaine manière, un texte vaut ce que vaut son action intégratrice et destructrice d'autres textes" (*Théorie d'ensemble*, 1968, 75).

37 Derrida, 1967c. NB this translation, which is Culler's (1975, 247), is more liberal than literal. "L'absence de signifié transcendental étend à l'infini le champ et le jeu de la signification" (original, 411). Cf. Bass translation (280).

38 'Outside' does not here concern only the case of referential texts. If I write "xeylint" and you do not accept it tautologically but ascribe *any* meaning to it, referentially significant or otherwise, that meaning is external to the word.

39 Since by its own reasoning utterances – including those of an extra-textualist as he/she argues – cannot *present* us with the gap between themselves and

what is 'extra' to them, extratextualist indeterminist writing will continually borrow the strategies of intertextualist-orientated texts to *represent*, to evoke the impression, of it. Indeed, the intentions of the former 'disappear into' the latter, only to appear repeatedly in statements *about* what concerns it – largely in the form of critical (for example, post-structuralist) theory.

40 Ehrmann, 1971, 251. As Hassan says in his project for an "anti-art", "Art cancels itself. The Tinguely machine works to destroy itself. ... The last sentence of Beckett's *How It Is* tells us that the book is about 'how it wasn't'" (1967, 21).

41 Federman, 1981, 309. As the speaker in a Barthelme 'story' reports, "Each angel, Lyon says, knows all there is to know about himself and every other angel. 'The world of possible knowledge must appear to him as an ordered set of facts which is completely behind him, completely fixed and certain and within his grasp. ...' / But this, too, no longer obtains" (Barthelme, 1970, 131).

There are other such systems. Historical thinking may be taken as merely another customary way of determining what interpretation – meaning – of a text is the appropriate one. Balzac's and Tolstoy's historicist fictional visions of the organization of human experience and action are in this view merely underwritings of that other institution, (pseudo-)non-fictional history, by which a culture lays down its particular authorized mythos and ethos. So writers such as Ehrmann, Sollers and Federman will say that a task of literature is to free itself from history. Like those of psychology, arguments from history may now equally be used as evidence that any text's 'meaning' is *in*determinate: inasmuch as we acknowledge that an utterance exists in history and is subject to the fluctuations of interpretation history entails, we acknowledge that the utterance does not have a fixed meaning. I concentrate on the issue of psychology here only because assaults directed against it (as the 'field' of scrutiny taking mind itself as its object) provide the most penetrating and all-embracing – and perhaps logically superordinate – model for attacks on other systems traditionally ordering our perceptions. This book has itself an historicist (diachronic) cast to its argument as well as a synchronic (taxonomic) one, and is subject to debate for that among many reasons.

42 This is all the more the case where – for example in Vonnegut, Barthelme – it relinquishes the claim to be anti-expressionist.

43 Quoted by C. J. Rawson in his review of Iain McGilchrist's *Against Criticism*, *Times Literary Supplement*, 11 June 1982, 627.

44 Sarraute 1956, 88. Cf. Claude Mauriac's *L'Agrandissement*: 'When we walk in the street, we know nothing of the passersby. ... We know nothing of their identity. ... No one is still present to himself, lost as each one is in his 'thoughts', obscure mental and bodily stirrings that are mingled indissolubly", trans. Mercier in Mercier, 1971, 331, from which the subsequent phrase about Sarraute is taken, 128. It's indeed possible to argue that what ultimately distinguishes the *nouveau roman* from Ricardou is in this sense only the dissolution of *story*, inasmuch as this was traditionally linked to a dramatic concept of conflict and accommodation between distinct beings. Psycholog-

ism, at a generic level, remains essential. Robbe-Grillet further shows the transitional nature of the *nouveau roman* between Modernism and extreme anticosmism when he stresses – though for altogether simple motives (he's *defending* his work against the charge that it's anti-human, a defence that *Tel Quel* will reject) – that his subject *is* subjectivity (cf. 1962, 138–9).

45 Dillard, 1982, 55. It has recently become common for scientists to speak of deliberately 'blinkering' themselves in this way; but it has long been normal for them to speak freely of, for example, being able to 'do chemistry' (at molecular levels) without concerning themselves with quantum (i.e. subatomic) physics.

46 Anticosmically-inclined stories by Barth, Calvino or Borges may seek to communicate the same thing, using different models. A neocosmic story by Williams, Lewis or Lindsay may adopt the same model as one of the others' or of Dante's or Bunyan's to say a competing thing, yet 'knows' that it cannot make sense unless the other's is taken seriously. The relationship is not one of thesis and antithesis but of complementarity.

47 I speak here of Calvino as neocosmist when he writes, for instance, *Il cavaliere inesistente*, and it's what we've seen him say about his treatment of good and evil figures in that book that I have in mind. Cf. Lewis: "It is absurd to condemn [forms of fiction such as Lewis's] because they do not often display any deep or sensitive characterization. They oughtn't to. It is a fault if they do. ... To tell how odd things struck odd people is to have an oddity too much. ... He ought to be as nearly as possible Everyman or Anyman. ... Character can apparently be reduced, simplified, to almost any extent with wholly satisfactory results. The greater ballads are an instance" (Lewis, 1966, 64–5).

48 The thrust of an anticosmic text's intention can be illustrated by contrast with an example from cinematic practice. Laurence Olivier was by his own account keenly aware of the 'artificiality' which his intended popular mass audience would assign to the language of *Henry V* at the start. While he planned his closing battle sequences to take place in the most naturalistic setting possible – in a landscape meticulously chosen (in Ireland) to resemble a 'typical medieval' English one – he deliberately opened with sequences set against a patently 'false' painted theatrical backdrop. Gradually the stage setting is traded for a progressively more 'realistic' scene. By degrees, the audience is persuaded that for all its artificial-seeming conventions the Shakespearean text – enacted by 'real flesh-and-blood people' – is more 'natural' than its theatrical context. An anticosmic text seeking to *de*-naturalize 'nature' sets its foundation sequences in a 'natural-seeming' setting and moves gradually toward the increasingly 'artificial' re-presentation of it – that is, toward alerting the reader to the artificial (culturally determined) nature of what he/she assumes to be 'natural'.

49 Echoing Lewis (one of his avowed influences), Borges – noted for 'yarns' as (neo)cosmic as any we might imagine – confidently declared "I haven't created a single character, as far as I am aware" (interview, *Arena*, BBC television, 26 October 1983).

50 Part of the 'wonder', 'play', 'dislocation' or 'hesitation' the text solicits stems from our persisting awareness not merely that what is extraordinary here is logically consistent within the text but that it is out of the ordinary with reference to what we 'normally read'.

Chapter 3

1 At this point the notion of 'thematic *topos*' comes to the proof. A reader reared solely on traditional Realist principles of textual interpretation will find it deeply perplexing to discover Calvino in his (English) preface to *I nostri antenati* [*Our Ancestors*] saying that one of its novels (*Viscount*) revolves around "themes of incompleteness, bias, the lack of human fullness", another (*Baron*) around "themes of isolation, distance, difficulties in relationships", the third (*Knight*) around "themes of empty forms and the concrete nature of living, awareness of being in the world and building one's own destiny" – only then to say that "the reader must interpret the stories as he will", for example "as existential or as structural works, as Marxist or neo-Kantian, Freudianly or Jungianly" (ix–x). Anti-Realist literature abounds with such occurrences (see as further examples Borges' 'analyses' of his stories offered as an appendix to the American edition of *El aleph* [*The Aleph*], Nabokov's 'explications' of his fiction, etc.). What is to be made of authorial statements in which the writer tells what his 'themes' are, and then says that these do not tell us what we are to understand his works to 'mean'? Clearly we need to think about 'themes' in a different way.

We've long been encouraged to treat textual 'images' and 'motifs' as somehow 'neutral' entities capable someway of objective description prior to any interpretation we may put upon them, and to treat 'themes' differently as ideational data inextricable from meaning and interpretation. (Emma Bovary – I oversimplify drastically the common view for the sake of a clearer outline – cannot sort out what is 'real' and what is 'illusion'; therefore, since she's the central character, the book *Madame Bovary* is 'about' the tension between reality and illusion. The thematic *topos* 'reveals' unmistakably the over-all 'theme'.)

Calvino's point is precisely that this is naive if not unintelligible. In many anti-Realist contexts we are invited to consider the possibility that it may be open to the text itself finally to imply (e.g. of such constellations as 'reality versus illusion'): 'Ah, but those are *only* themes', in the way that 'themes' (*or* motifs) in a musical composition are only aural patterns, definitely recognizable as organized and even orderly, but not necessarily ideologically controlling the other aural data which the piece, taken linearly for example, contains as a whole. (Some music theorists interested in the more 'programmatic works' might argue that this is not the true picture of how we hear music, but the notion is, I think, essentially appropriate.) In such a perspective in particular, one is free to regard *topoi* as they are, *in situ*, without prematurely begging questions as to whether they have propositional or even thetic intention. The decision as to what is the *topos*'s 'true' function in the text as a totality is something for the reader to make out in his/her detailed and finally synthetic thinking about the specific text. This operation does not give us a way of deciding at what point a thesis or a proposition (an ideational system) found broad enough ultimately to encompass all a text's *topoi* may or may not become so broadly encompassing as to be empty. (We can by now easily conceive of a text whose broad – 'governing' – thesis might be: 'This is a text' or 'This writing is writing.' What is the exact status of thematic *topoi* in such a text?) Nor does it yet answer – though without bringing it to bear we have always actually been in no real position to *ask* – whether fictional wholes themselves do indeed ever 'control' their parts in the way that has been traditionally believed.

An important part of the intention of *this note* is to indicate that the chapter we're now entering is meant not to organize the reader's final conceptions as to what the texts in hand are 'about' – how they operate to govern or not govern their *topoi* – but, expressly, to discover what the latter may on their own *be*, as they 'come along'. This procedure itself rests on decisions of my own, regarding certain anti-Realist theories, which will later become apparent. It's worth mentioning, meantime, that no reading of any text, however indeterminist, has ever dispensed with accounts of thematic *topoi*.

2 E.g. "The story of a panic"; *Gone to Earth; St Mawr* and *The Fox*; "Spotted horses" and "The bear".

3 Mark Rose, *Science Fiction: A Collection of Critical Essays*, Englewood Cliffs, NJ, 1976, 4, cited in Brooke-Rose, 1981, 80.

4 The worlds, divided in space, of earth and Tormance, the twin suns of Arcturus, the two realities of the palpable world and of invisible truth (*Arcturus*); the two worlds of the planet Winter (*Left Hand of Darkness*); the 'home' and 'wilderness' worlds of Middle Earth (*Lord of the Rings*); the mountain and the plain of Buzzati's *Il deserto dei Tartari* [*The Tartar Steppe*] (with its desert frontier) and *Bàrnabo delle montagne*, the house and forest of his *Il segreto del Bosco Vecchio*; the farmland and the wild mountain of Bosco's *Le Sanglier* and his 'Hyacinthe' series; the domesticated land and the 'wilderness' through which Molloy and Moran, respectively, travel (*Molloy*); the hall of Hrothgar and the wild lair of Grendel (*Grendel*); the world of earthly society and that of the baron in the trees (*Barone rampante*).

5 In *Lord of the Rings*, Tom will not cross his own frontiers; in the 'Hyacinthe' series the children are forbidden to cross the stream of la Gayolle. Cf. the perpetual hostility between the people of Karhide and Orgoreyn (*Left Hand*), the elves and dwarves (*Lord*), "the immortal feud of Gael and Gall" (*The Once and Future King*).

6 The hidden doors in *Lord* (as well as in *Pale Fire*); the river between the Old and the New People in *Inheritors*; the desert between the army of 'the civilized world' and that of the Tartars in *Deserto* which it's the role of the protagonist to guard; the great sea between the Old and the New Worlds in *Terra nostra*; the vast ice sheet between nations which the protagonist must finally cross in *Left Hand*.

7 *Tunnels* in *Pale Fire, Lord of the Rings*, "Il conte di Monte Cristo" (Calvino) whose imprisoned characters seeking an escape tunnel test the modes of knowing evoked, in turn, by conceptions of empirical and inductive thinking, of space, time, history, and fiction, and Cortázar's *Rayuela*, where humans are likened to 'sandhogs', each under the mountain of reality digging a private tunnel in the dream of meeting some other tunnel leading to some final truth (378–9). *Bridges* and forking paths in previously mentioned texts by Bosco, Buzzati, Borges, Tolkien, Le Guin.

8 Butor's *L'Emploi du temps*, Sollers' *Le Parc*, "Il conte di Monte Cristo", *Pale Fire, The Third Policeman, Terra nostra*. In *Pale Fire* see e.g. 129–30.

9 In the long catalogues of furniture in *L'Inquisitoire*, of the people observed by the narrator ("I saw ... I saw ... I saw ... ") from his window in *Pale Fire*, of beasts in *Graal Flibuste* and of architecture and décor in Robbe-Grillet's fiction. The strength of commitment to both the last-mentioned intentions is accentuated in the film of *L'Année dernière à Marienbad*, where we perfectly well *see* the details of the scene, yet are extraordinarily obliged to hear them inventoried in a parallel 'narrative' voice-over; the *film* script's special force derives from its manner of presenting us with two progressively divergent 'texts', aural and visual.

10 Forces associated with specific beasts ranging from, *for example*, those of pure destruction; the raw *vis vitae* of nature in its brute creative forms; the assertion of individual ego; the transcendence of ego in an intermediate realm of cultural action; the activation of energies on an undifferentiated (and morally in-different) plane of universal and timeless being. (This hierarchical disposition of symbolic forms is treated at length in Cristopher Nash, "A modern bestiary: the encounter between nature and culture in the English, American, French and Italian novel, 1900–1950", PhD dissertation, New York University, 1970.)

11 Jackson, 1981, illustrates the importance of vision in 'fantasy' e.g. in Hoffmann, MacDonald, H. G. Wells, Valery Brussof, Stevenson: cf. 43–5.

12 Cf. e.g. Woolf, *To the Lighthouse, Mrs Dalloway*. The Hamon phrase appears in Hamon, 1973, 430; he recites numerous studies on the Realist preoccupation with windows.

13 For extensive use of windows and optical instruments see e.g. the latter text for binoculars and kaleidoscopes, Calvino's "Gli anni-luce" ["The light-years", 1965] for the telescope and "I cristalli" ["Crystals", 1967], for crystals and numerous texts by Robbe-Grillet (e.g. especially the window in *La Jalousie*) and Nabokov (e.g. "Perfection" for spectacles), the lens in *Arcturus*, etc.

14 Cf. cases at these extremes: Sollers' *Le Parc* "constructed", as Ricardou reminds us, "according to the two sides of Day and Night"; "We are nothing other", as Sollers himself says, "than this nocturnal and diurnal movement of the *lisible* and the *illisible* in us, outside of us" (Ricardou, 1967, 275; Sollers, 1968b (*Logiques* 240, trans. mine)); Le Guin's *The Left Hand of Darkness*, whose title points the way to its fundamental theme: "*Light is the left hand of darkness / and darkness the right hand of light. / Two are one, life and death.* ... It is yin and yang. ... Both and one. A shadow on snow'" (199, 225). The

background 'myth' on which the story of Gardner's *Grendel* is founded is of "an ancient feud between two brothers which split all the world between darkness and light"(34). The dynamic play of forces in the 'New World' of *Terra nostra* is characterized in terms of reversals of the customary rôles of black and white in nature: cf. especially 428, 453, 459, 502, 508. NB *Third Policeman*, whose light/dark figuration, deepening as the book progresses – "'Do not worry if you think it is dark . . . because I am going to light the light and then mangle it for diversion" – is prefigured by its epigraph: "Human existence [is] an hallucination containing in itself the secondary hallucinations of day and night (the latter an insanitary condition of the atmosphere due to accretions of black air . . .)", 92, iii. Other examples – not to mention the most obvious set 'foreshadowed' in *Pale Fire*'s central figures 'Shade' and 'Gradus' – will appear as we go along.

15 Cf. e.g. Baudelaire and subsequent *symbolistes*' beliefs concerning the operation of synesthesia.

16 See e.g. Ricardou on *Le Parc* (1981), Derrida on the "tache rouge" in *Nombres* (1969).

17 See e.g. Attebery, 1980, Rogers, 1980.

18 See Brooke-Rose, 1981, 273–88. The word "green" itself, she points out, occurs 127 times. Cf. the work of William H. Gass, a professional philosopher and fictionalist influential among American anti-Realists who has written extensively on the metaphorical functions of colour; see e.g. his *On Being Blue* ("blue is the color of the mind in borrow of the body; it is the color consciousness becomes when caressed; it is the dark inside of sentences", 58).

19 Robbe-Grillet 1962, 87–8. "We can be more definite about a form, for instance, than a colour, which changes with the lighting, the background, and the person looking at it" (87). Hence his preoccupation with the geometrics, as opposed to the chromatics, of visual experience.

20 Note Alan Garner's oft-praised (potentially neocosmic) novel *Red Shift*, appropriating the astro-physicist's term.

21 As has been observed for some years, for example, by Todorov and others.

22 E.g. the forest or desert or sea or waste of *Lord of the Rings, The Once and Future King, Left Hand of Darkness, Voyage to Arcturus, Segreto del Bosco Vecchio, Last Unicorn, Sanglier, Inheritors, Barone rampante, Mare verticale, Mar delle Blatte*, Borges's "Inmortal", *Graal Flibuste*, Barth's "Night-Sea Journey", or *Terra nostra*. It's a commonplace that – in anti-cosmic as much as in Modernist fiction – the 'civilized' world its very self may now be offered as a 'jungle' in which the protagonist is regarded as estranged. There is scarcely any way in which neocosmic 'worlds', any more than anticosmic worlds, might be accurately described as 'safely stable'. At their most 'positive', what they propose and what anticosmic models eschew is the *possibility of equilibrium* (homeostasis) and the feasibility that by a continuing and concentrated act of imagination and will this equilibrium may be recovered. More often than not, incidentally, their narrative conclusions additionally suggest the likelihood of further future repetitions of the disrup-

tion of that equilibrium. This is evident throughout the most optimistic work of writers from Lewis and Tolkien to Bosco, Buzzati, Calvino and Fuentes.

23 Pynchon's *V*, *Pale Fire*, *Se una notte d'inverno*.

24 *Se una notte d'inverno*, Borges' "La muerte y la brújala" ["Death and the compass", 1964], numerous works by Robbe-Grillet, for whom the detective story 'takes over the place formerly held in fiction by the love story' (cf. his essay in *Critique*, Nov. 1951, 1002, paraphrased here by Mercier, 1971, 185).

25 Not only in those characters whose whole function is to 'watch' – e.g. in *Le Sanglier*, *Deserto dei Tartari* – but in the 'window people' of Sollers, Mauriac, Robbe-Grillet's image of the *Voyeur*, the many prying folk motivating Pinget's narratives, Nabokov's Kinbote, the 'old people' of *The Inheritors* whose closing life is given to gazing from the trees into the world of the 'new ones', Molloy in long passages of his observation of 'A and C', and the nameless observer in space who torments the narrator of "Gli anni-luce".

26 E.g. texts by say Barth, Cortázar, Nabokov, Vonnegut, Gardner, O'Brien and Beckett in which the plot itself is woven about the pronouncements of some oracular character (e.g. Tiresias in Barth's "Echo" and his Polyeidus in "Bellerophoniad", *Rayuela*'s Morelli, the dragon in *Grendel*, *Pale Fire*'s Shade, Bokonon in Vonnegut's *Cat's Cradle* and his Tralfamadorians. NB the "voice" that pursues the protagonist – an extremely popular parallel 'figure' in anti-Realist fiction acting as alter ego or psychopomp – in *The Third Policeman* and *Molloy*, 'a character' that is in the ultimate logic of the latter novel superordinate to both Moran and Molloy themselves. NB the frequency of appeal among anti-Realists – on both sides – of the textual formats and vocabularies associated with prophecy in the literature not only of scientific futurology but of such occultist modes of prediction as those offered by the tarot and *I Ching*.

27 E.g. 264ff. Cf. Nabokov's uses of "the magic key" in *Pale Fire*, e.g. 100–3, 111; in *Rayuela* Horacio "guesses that in some part of Paris, some day or some death or some meeting will show him a key; he's searching for it like a madman. . . . He is looking for the black light, for the key" (133).

28 Borges, 1970a, 13, 10. Awkward in English, this translation is nevertheless (importantly) correct (*contiene*; i.e. the crucial antecedent is not "points" but "one"): cf. *Obras completas*, 1974, 623.

29 Calvino, 1965, 52, 51. Guglielmo Biraghi elaborates exactly this motif in his story "Decantazione" (1972).

30 Vonnegut, 1969, 3, 62–3. Cf. *Terra nostra*, where the magus "aspir[es] from the beginning and to the end of time the impossible: a perfectly simultaneous narration" (636).

31 E.g. '*anachronistically*': Sir Walter Raleigh has an accordion (*Cien años de soledad*); a magician defends a unicorn with "secret judo holds" (*The Last Unicorn*); King Arthur lives in the fifteenth century, and Freud is adduced in his support (*The Once and Future King)*. E.g. '*anatopistically*': characters climb a ladder onto the moon (*Cosmicomiche*); a man's blood flows through a village to his mother's house (*Cien años de soledad*); a two-dimensional

house has people living within it (*The Third Policeman*). These departures from the 'acceptable' are not the same as those we find, for example, in fictional 'alternative histories' such as Lem's *The Star Diaries*, Olaf Stapledon's *Last and First Man*, or Philip K. Dick's *The Man in the High Castle*. While a cosmic systematicity may operate in both to normalize much that is uncustomary, events such as the ones given here retain an essential trace of the anomalous which is vital to anti-Realism and which the alternative history makes every effort to exclude.

32 E.g. Merlyn is born in the future and moves backward through time (*Once and Future King*), De Selby would see into the past progressively via a series of mirrors and move forward sideways in time in his sausage-shaped universe (*Third Policeman*), characters or events become 'unstuck' or stopped in time (*Last Unicorn, Slaughterhouse–5, Third Policeman, Cosmicomiche, Ti con zero, Ficciones*).

33 Wart lives among ants (*Once and Future King*), a protagonist travels in a country where no animal is bigger than a man's thumb (*Third Policeman*), where a house – or a universe – has no depth (*Flatland*) and no breadth (*Cosmicomiche, Third Policeman*) or no matter (*Ti con zero, Cosmicomiche, Ficciones*).

34 The type is most simply articulated in *Last Unicorn*, ostensibly the tale of the wanderer's quest for 'a place in the modern world' for the unicorn, a creature essentially described as one "racing to catch up with the time when she had known nothing at all but the sweetness of being herself" (68–9).

35 "Axolotl" (1951), Cortázar, 1956; "Cockroaches", *The Street of Crocodiles* (1934, 1963) trans. C. Wieniewska in Rabkin, 1979.

36 Cagnon and Smith (1981) are effective on this "central theme of arbitrarily exchanged identities" in Le Clézio (225). Their straightforward translations are used here (220, 224).

37 "That idea of otherness which is what we are always trying to grasp": cf. p. 104.

38 Ludovico's desire for "a place of common encounters" in *Terra nostra* is a response to the *angst* started up by the conviction that "One day we were one. Today we are other" (Fuentes, 1975, 683).

39 Nabokov, 1975, 113–14, 118, 121. Nabokov is quick to point out that the story was written in 1926 (published first in Paris 1927) "at least a dozen years" before Sartre's *La Nausée* [*Nausea*].

40 Calvino, 1979, 39. For further decisive examples of the 'other' or 'double' *topos* see e.g. Borges' "El otro" ["The other", 1975], "Borges y yo" ["Borges and I", 1964] and Nabokov's "Conversation piece" (1959) and *Ada*.

41 "To erase this distinction itself, to resist separation and difference, to rediscover a unity of self and other", as it's put by Jackson (52), for whom the notion of otherness is essential to her argument on the special merits of the 'new', 'real' fantasy of modern times with its contrary emphasis on estrangement. No need to argue that – as Jackson sees and as Robert Rogers emphasizes in *The Double in Literature* (1970) – the figure of the double

persists throughout fiction. Narratives turning on the *topos* of the yearning-for-the-Other are not – as Jackson frequently seeks to make out – *prima facie* demonstrations of faith in the *attainability* of transcendent unity, with all the philosophical 'wetness' she associates with that idea.

42 Doubleness of identity is obviously not the only but merely the most dominant form of the split-identity *topos*. *Pale Fire*'s Shade 'resembles at least four people' (209); Odon in the same book is "mosaic-faced" (209) – cf. the same motif in Biraghi's *Lo sguardo nel buio*. For Borges' writer addressing Shakespeare in "Everything and nothing" (the title is thus in English in the original, *El Hacedor*, 1960; *Obras completas*, 803–4): "among the forms of my dream are you, who like myself are many and one" (Borges, 1964, 249). In Robbe-Grillet's *La Maison de Rendez-vous* and Baudry's *Personnes* 'persons' are ceaselessly becoming other 'persons'. And, above all, *Terra nostra*'s entire narrative fabric is built upon the predication of the simultaneous coexistence – and the perdurance through time – of the multiple identities of the same 'person'. The fact that anti-Realist fiction persists in selecting the 'binary' mode as its favoured means of promulgating the apprehension of uncertainty (and its accompanying moral and psychological aporia) – as indeed *Terra Nostra* itself does in its long and controlling passages on the figures of "Smoking Mirror" and his double – bears watching for philosophical reasons, as we'll see.

43 "For mimesis inevitably produces a double of the thing, the double being nothing a non-being which nevertheless is added to the thing", *Thru*, 106. Among anti-Realists the *nouveaux romanciers* will often retain for the mirror its Realist signification. E.g. Mauriac in *La Marquise sortit à cinq heures*: the narrator-as-Mauriac calls his "a novel in which, however, nothing has been invented, a labyrinth of mirrors capturing some of life's sensations, feelings and thoughts" (310; in Mercier's translation, 342). This serves as further evidence of the transitional or intermediate status of the *nouveau roman*. Observe Fuentes' ironic line in *Terra nostra*, "he gazed with fascinated pride into a mirror that *an inattentive visitor might mistake* for a book" (388; italics mine).

44 Thus Sukenick: "Rather than serving as a mirror ... fiction adds itself to the world, creating a meaningful 'reality' that did not previously exist" (in Federman, 1981, 5). Cf. Nabokov's manifold allusions to mirrors and "mirror-play", e.g. in *Pale Fire* and the early short fiction, as a game of illusions.

45 So, examining his own eyes minutely in a mirror, the narrator of *Le Parc* observes that it is "impossible to see the eyes themselves without the eyes remaining open and commenting, attempting to formulate almost hypnotically the following thought: "I now see what makes me see' ..." (34). So for Ricardou "the novel is thus no longer [Stendhal's] mirror taken out for a walk; it is the result of internal mirrors ubiquitously at work within the fiction itself. It is no longer representation, but self-representation" (1971, 130).

46 Thus Borges' St Paul in "El espejo de los enigmas" ["The mirror of

enigmas"]: "We see everything backwards" (1964, 211). And in *Pale Fire*, "'Kinbote means regicide ...'. 'Yes, a king's destroyer'" says Kinbote, the supposed exiled king. "A king who sinks his identity in the mirror of exile is in a sense just that" (210).

47 Cf. Barth: in "the mirror-maze he saw once again more clearly than ever, how readily he deceived himself with supposing he was a person" (1968, 90). Fuentes: "They permitted me to look at myself in the mirror; I did not recognize myself, nevertheless I have no other proof of my existence"; "the youths held the mirror before my face; I screamed, horrified to see that face I could not recognize as mine" (1975, 270, 196). Federman: "he saw himself in the mirror, and that's when the shock came, the shock of not recognizing himself" (1971, 136). In Biraghi the crisis initiating the writing of the stories in *Lo sguardo nel buio* is that the writer–protagonist (finding it impossible to compose a 'unitary cosmos'), looking in a mirror, finds his face strangely deformed; "a mosaic, athwart which so many different faces sought simultaneously to efface themselves" (7; trans. mine). In Saviane's *Il mare verticale* the protagonist, returned from his journey through the eras of human evolution, in the last pages sees his face in a mirror, a "human face but not his, a visage of wax" (197–8; by a pun in the word "*cera*" which my translation cannot capture, "look" or "appearance" and "wax" are significantly interchangeable). The contemporary parallel in psychological theory is Lacan's view that the individual human mind at a formative stage passes universally through a tripartite "mirror phase" [*stade du miroir*] involving recognition of the other as self but as other (cf, Lacan, 1949). Compare Brooke-Rose's novel *Thru* which, commencing with a section organized around perceptions and verbal play associated with an automobile's rearview mirror and evoking specifically the *topoi* of mirror-multiples and mirror-reversals, recurs insistently to the mirror as organizing/disorganizing image.

48 Calvino, 1979, 166. Manlove, 1983, has useful things to say about the rôle of the mirror in this respect in earlier fantasy fiction.

49 In *The Third Policeman* De Selby's most "notable investigation" is "of the nature of time and eternity by a system of mirrors", the upshot of which is that what one "sees is not a true reproduction of himself but a picture of himself when he was a younger man" (56). In *Rayuela*, "the King puts a mirror to his face, but this face is Karma. ... The King of the Dead looks into the mirror, but he is really looking into your memory" (157). In *Terra nostra* the most insistently recurrent narrative image is probably the mirror through which the king is "resolved" and, in horrific sequences, is progressively in "the dyssymbolic light of refractory years ... pursued by the past of his future" (181–2).

50 Cf. Borges' *El libro de los seres imaginarios*, a modern teratology.

51 Sources of the first four examples are self-evident; the remaining eight clusters (along with many other examples) appear in *Left Hand, Graal Flibuste, Arcturus, Terra nostra, Mar delle Blatte, Giles Goat-Boy, V, Segreto del Bosco Vecchio* (and *Once and Future King*).

52 Cf. *Lord of the Rings, Once and Future King, Place of the Lion,*

"Axolotl", "Cockroaches", *Cosmicomiche, I nostri antenati* ("I dinosauri" ["The dinosaurs", 1965], *Visconte dimezzato*, "La spirale", "Giochi senza fine" ["Games without end", 1965]) and *Plus*.

53 Note e.g. the extraordinary uses put to the *topos* of political revolution in *Pale Fire, Giles Goat-Boy, Se una notte d'inverno, Thru, Barone rampante, Terra nostra, Catch-22, Left Hand, Chimera, Mare verticale* and many stories by Borges.

54 When Robbe-Grillet – notorious for sustained experimentation with these features in his fiction – so early (1951) declared that the detective story was replacing the love story he made clear that lover and mistress were to find as their substitutes murderer and victim, and that (as Mercier translates it) "the 'act' *par excellence* is no longer the possession of a body but its destruction" (see 233n).

55 E.g. there's the obvious attack on those institutions that taught us that the world would be pleasant if only its covenants were kept. At another level there's the ultimate revulsion against the spirit of Realistic determinism itself, against any sign of resignation to mechanistic nature's own 'lack of taste', its arbitrary and indiscriminate indifference.

56 *Arcturus*, 286. Cf. the 'bone-masks' the 'new people' appear to wear in *Inheritors* and the succession of masks throughout *Terra nostra*.

57 23, 236. Cf. James Brackman, *The Put-On: Modern Fooling and Modern Mistrust* (New York, 1972)

58 Resembling laughing mechanical Fat May in *Lost in the Funhouse*, a tour-de-force in the surcharging of a brief text with an encyclopaedic display of broad and concealed allusions to forms of pretence. As *Pale Fire*'s Kinbote says of Gradus, the man who hunts the king whom Kinbote himself would be, he "spiritually did not exist. Morally he was a dummy pursuing a dummy" (218).

59 NB Robbe-Grillet's enthusiasm (1954) for this aspect of *Mahu* – see his essay "A novel that invents itself" (1962), now a theme that has been the basis of more than one work of critical theory.

60 Cf. Lovecraft's Necronomicon, and further examples in *Se una notte d'inverno*, Borges' "Tlön", "El acercamiento a Almotásim" (1970a), "Examen de la obra de Herbert Quain" ["An examination of the work of Herbert Quain", 1962], Lem's "Gruppenführer Louis XVI" (1971), O'Brien's *The Third Policeman* (De Selby's writings) and, of special interest in his *At Swim-Two-Birds*, "Characters should be interchangeable as between one book and another. . . . The modern novel should be largely a work of reference" (1939, 25).

61 Mauriac 1963, 309–10; trans. Mercier, 1971, 342.

62 *Necronomicon* 1978 (including essays by Colin Wilson, L. Sprague de Camp, Christopher Frayling, Angela Carter).

63 Vonnegut 1969, 70; it establishes, if nothing else in the text had, the questionable status of Billy's Tralfamadorian vision.

64 As described in *The Sirens of Titan* (1959). Farmer/Trout's *Venus on the Half-Shell* appears in 1975.

65 "Total freedom is total paralysis in literature" (Lem, 1971, 409).
66 Where the Thesean allusion is made explicit in Robbe-Grillet's preface, in which he makes specific reference (in the French original) to a "*dédale*".
67 In which 'maze' the writer decides finally to remain, as an artist, to "construct funhouses for others and be their secret operator" (1969, 94).
68 "Tlön is surely a labyrinth, but it is a labyrinth devised by men, a labyrinth destined to be deciphered by men" (1964, 17).
69 Cf. the close of Borges' "La muerte y la brújala": "'the next time I kill you . . . I promise you that labryinth, consisting of a single line which is invisible and unceasing" (1964, 87).
70 "A labyrinth, after all, a place in which, ideally, all the possibilities of choice (of direction, in this case) are embodied" (Barth, 1967, 34).
71 For Robbe-Grillet, "the whole film" of *Marienbad* "deals with a reality which the hero creates out of his own vision, out of his own words. . . . A perfect labyrinth [*dédale*] of false trails, variants, failures and repetitions!" (1962, 10). Saviane's 'king' at the close of *Il mare verticale* sees that at each ambush, each resolution concerning what he has seen and been, there surge forth only "labirinti di pensiero" (177).
72 The protagonist of "Abenjacán" ["Ibn Hakkan"] dies ensnared in the bolt-hole he has constructed of the labyrinth designed for his escape from his assassin.
73 Examples of both strategies are described in Chapter 1. Cf. Hofstadter's discussions of 'jootsing', jumping out of conceptual systems into 'ever wider worlds' (1982). While the heraldic formula '*mise-en-abîme*' is a favourite emblem in current French literary theory, there are good examples of its use not only among more recent American writers but with even more technical/etymological precision in Spanish – e.g. *Terra nostra*, "This is where we live, in an abyss which is the very center, the blind spot, the motionless heart of the heraldic field" (325).
74 "Not one Thalia joined to another – but a Thalia *within* a Thalia, like the dolls-within-dolls" ("Petition", Barth, 1968, 66). "A body with another body inside it in turn, thousands of such bodies within each other like the skins of an onion, receding to some unimaginable ultimum? Was I in turn merely a link in a vast sequence of imponderable beings, the world I knew merely the interior of the being whose inner voice I myself was?" (*Third Policeman*, 102–3).
75 Cf. Peake's plan for an autobiography/novel to be called *Chinese Puzzle*, meant to start "Box within box like a Chinese puzzle – so it seems to me, was my childhood" (quoted in Watney, 1976, 31, 167). Cf. the shoebox parcel of letters – as well as the living scenes within paintings, photos – in *Dans le labyrinthe*. In *Pale Fire*: the Prince's toy-circus-in-a-box (101) and the painting in the palace showing a bronze box, the visible side of which turns out to be 'real metal', yet behind which there is (as the fact of its being in a painting should have warned us) "nothing . . . except the broken bits of a nutshell", still another emblem of the empty container (106). In *Third Policeman*: not only (obviously) the box – money/omnium – that's the object of the

protagonist's search, but the several-page sequence on MacCruiskeen's chest, from which he 'progressively' extracts thirty-two identical but smaller chests, the last of which are seen only through a magnifying glass, to which are added five more that no glass can reveal, another "nearly as small as nothing" still in the process of manufacture, "the dear knows where it will stop and terminate" (61–5).

76 The latter appears (1967) under the fictitious 'authorship' of "Honorio Bustos Domecq" – names appropriately taken from two of the 'real' authors' grandfathers. Cf. Márquez's "story about the capon, which was an endless game in which the narrator asked if they wanted him to tell them the story about the capon, and when they answered yes, the narrator would say that he had not asked them to say yes, but whether they wanted him to tell him the story of the capon, and when they answered no ... and when they remained silent ... and no one would leave because the narrator would say that he had not asked them to leave ... and so on and on in a vicious circle that lasted entire nights" (1967, 44–5). Here, as in the prefigurative Silone's "Polikusc'ka", containing a retelling of Tolstoy's "Polikushka" – and *not* as in the standard tradition of the story within a story (e.g. Fielding) – infinite regress is importantly concerned with the (re)making of the *listener*'s reality. A close parallel is to be found in Fuentes' passage in *Terra nostra* following the line "And it is the narration, not the dream, that is infinite" (653–4).

77 *Thru*, 66–7; "Life-Story" (1968), 125; *Se una notte d'inverno*, 260. One of the most aggressive exercises in polemically explicit metalepsis appears in *Lost in the Funhouse* itself, from the fifth sentence onward. *Cavaliere inesistente* is full of examples, as is indeed its less theoretically self-conscious counterpart, *The Once and Future King*. Note *Thru*'s parody of the *regressus* itself, e.g. "shared pursuit of the same insistently mise-en-abysmal dialogue with recursivity to right or left that is almost preventing the idyll from developing its fixed motifs" (124).

78 Quoted in McGilchrist, 1982, 193. See Chap. 2, Note 43.

79 Manlove, 1983, in his chapter "Circularity in fantasy: George MacDonald", 70. An earlier discussion appears in Manlove, 1976–7.

80 At the close of Borges' "*Deutsches Requiem*": "I rejoice in the fact that our destiny completes its circle and is perfect" (1964, 147). In *Terra nostra*: "only what is circular is eternal and only the eternal is circular" (392).

81 "The drama has never taken place; it is the circular delirium that Kubin lives and relives endlessly", Borges, "El milagro secreto" (1964, 91).

82 *Terra nostra*; "'I am convinced'", as Toribio says, "'that everything is spherical and that everything spins in circles; everything is movement, incessant, circular ...'", 349.

83 Borges' "La esfera de Pascal" ["The fearful sphere of Pascal", 1964, 192].

84 Nabokov in his introductory note to "The Circle", 1973, 254.

85 Part of a quotation from O'Brien appended as a "Publisher's Note" to the novel, 173. Barth and Borges give us versions of *The Thousand and One Nights* in which "the queen may persist and the motionless king hear forever the truncated story ... now infinite and circular" (Borges, 1964, 25; cf. Barth,

1967, 33–4); the mystics in Borges' "La biblioteca de Babel" claim the centre of their circular chamber to be a circular book that "is God" (Borges, 1964, 52) and the speaker in his "El jardín de senderos que se bifurcan" can think of nothing in the way of an infinite book but "a cyclic volume, a circular one" (1964, 25).

86 I.e. the "serpent biting its tail type" by which Nabokov classifies his "The circle" and *The Gift* (1973, 254). Cf. E. R. R. Eddison's novel *The Worm Ouroboros*, New York, 1926, 1962, and Borges's essay on the uroborus in *El libro de los seres imaginarios*. It's to this figure, of course, that Coleridge refers in the passage cited on p. 196.

87 E.g. coins in Borges' "El Zahir" ["The Zahir", 1964], "Tlön". Spheres: "El Aleph", "Los teólogos"; Biraghi's "Ruggine" in *Lo sguardo nel buio*.

88 E.g. in *Voyeur* the protagonist's journey is to sell watches; in *Third Policeman* (which ends, after all, with the question "Is it about a bicycle?") his journey is *first* to recover his watch; note again the double-circle motif (bicycle, watch/band) which becomes eminently clear (if deliberately still a puzzle) in O'Brien's: "'Why should anyone steal a watch when they can steal a bicycle?' ... 'Who ever heard of a man riding a watch down the road or bringing a sack of turf up to his house on the crossbar of a watch?'"(53). In *The Last Unicorn* we read "'The way is through the clock. ... You simply walk through the clock and there you are'" (136). In Pinget's *Passacaille* the clock may in fact be the dominant image – culminating at one stage with the tearing off of its hands.

89 Manlove notes in his authors "not only a circular mode of 'There and Back Again', but a spiral one, whereby the return is at a higher level of insight" (1983, 71). While for Cortázar (quoting Anaïs Nin) "the spiral was a labyrinth" (1963, 470), such variations on the circle motif often raise provocative questions as to the possibility of there being (enigmatically) progress still – via a kind of 'open-ended' (upward/outward, downward/inward) circularity. Permutations of this possibility appear, for example, in De Selby's notion that in a sausage-shaped universe one may have the impression of moving on a sphere but may turn in a 'second direction', into an effectively different-seeming world, however circular; and in Sollers' (important?) 'admission that "by making a circular trip in the universe ... you would return to your point of departure, not identical to yourself, but *symmetrical* to what you were at the start": quoted by Ricardou from *L'Intermédiaire* (1967, 275); and, of course, in Calvino's vision in "La spirale" (1965) of the making of the spiral as an emblem of self-expressive growth.

90 Cf. also (K)yK and Xlthlx (not only "w" but "y" and the thorn "th" being equally 'absent' from Italian). Large-scale circles and solar patterns formed of words appear on the pages of *Thru*. "Look shall we buy that one which is not your discourse but a disc-organized trompe l'oeil" (124).

91 E.g. the item "*Male*" in *Pale Fire*'s 'glossary' (244). The latter two texts are classics in their provision not only of data whose utility is subsequently denied (e.g. the close of the commentary on line 231 in *Pale Fire*) but in their 'denying' the utility of data whose relevance is subsequently clear (e.g.

Kinbote's failure to 'see' what "the Toothwart White" 'means' – 147 – when it's 'no doubt meant', I'd say (playing Nabokov's game), to refer to "the White twins" – 150 – etc.).

92 E.g. *Molloy, The Third Policeman, Slaughterhouse–5, Catch–22, Thru*, "Il sangue, il mare" ["Blood, sea", Calvino, 1967]. D. Rogers (who has given a paper on "Vehicles of transportation in the fiction of Lewis and Tolkien", 1970) argues for this feature in Tolkien (1980, 137).

93 With *Plus*, of course, as the ultimate case, in which the body is 'amputated' to leave only the protagonist's 'immobilized' brain.

94 Cf. Calvino's essay on "The narrative form as a combinative process" (1967–8).

95 As it indeed is in its own way in traditional Surrealism, whose express influence on Sollers is considerable.

96 "I see I see myself as a halt narrative" (Barth, 1968, 32–3).

97 Pynchon, 1963, 53. Cf. the closing line of Beckett's trilogy: "I can't go on, I'll go on" (1953a, 579).

98 Compare the enormous narrative burden they carry in Realism from Flaubert to Dostoevsky. In both the fiction of 'the marvellous' and the fiction of 'hesitation', should we care to use these distinctions, they serve only as prolegomena to 'serious action' in a 'real' (within the text) world whose deranged or oneiric qualities themselves – manifestations of the uncustomary 'taken seriously' – are what matters.

99 *Grendel*, 99; *Pale Fire* (with less force but equivalent connotation), 187. Cf. the incessant appearance in Beckett of cognates, e.g. taken at random, "Here then were two incompatible bodily needs, at loggerheads. Such things happen" (1951, 97).

100 Sollers, 46. Lem: "What then remained? For a sound mind, nothing but to keep silent" (1971, 354).

101 The passage in fact appears also in *The Book of Merlyn* as now (posthumously) published, with little alteration to the portions quoted (115). The interpretive lines cited are from Manlove, 1983, 113. He here points out that in other notes White had written "The wind in this place had no human characteristics. ... It was mindless, in a country without mind." Cf. his similar statements recorded in Manlove, 1976–7, 81–3, where the background to the "mad black wind" phrase, plainly deeply imbedded in the White hagiography, is somewhat different from that described in Manlove, 1983. The reader coming new to the silence motif will find a great deal of literary-critical material devoted to it, beginning at least with the vital work of Maurice Blanchot (e.g. *Le Livre à venir* and *l'Espace littéraire* [*The Space of Literature*]) and flourishing in poststructuralist discourse on the topic in the recent past. Among early American texts Sontag's "The aesthetics of silence" (1967) and Hassan's *The Literature of Silence* (1967) are celebrated.

102 Molloy, who certainly considers killing himself, thinks "But I must first wait. To be sure there is nothing more I can acquire, or lose, or throw away, or give way" (108). *Murphy*, the Beckett protagonist coming closest to

suicide, does so in the book in which Beckett's fiction is closest to nineteenth-century Realism in both chronology and mode.

103 E.g., as we've noted, the mirror, the window. We must accept that it is not possible to so 'cook the books' as to make these differences dissolve. The issue is one of narratively functional patterns and how they differ. We cannot make anti-Realist and Realist texts the same by saying that the former are 'actually Realistic (or trying to be realistic) but only happen to be using metaphors in a more intensive way' or that there may be frequent references ('metaphorical, of course') to circles or labyrinths in Realist fiction too. Any fictional fixture may be (also) regarded metaphorically. But the fact is that there is no 'circular labyrinth', whose circularity is irreducibly indispensable to the narrative, in Realist fiction, nor is there nor can there in its very logic be a narratively functional anachronism or anatopism or *lieu théatral*.

104 See the first footnote to this chapter.

105 Problems ensuing from this are central to discussion in the coming chapters.

Chapter 4

1 Any lapse of perspective referred to here is one of few in a book remarkable for its clarity and frequent brilliance, and stems from the nature of the book itself: it is a collection of diverse essays and itself no attempt at a 'systematic' study of anti-Realism as such – something Brooke-Rose may well be inclined to reject.

2 "Everything is full, existence everywhere, dense and heavy and sweet" (149); "I am in the midst of Things"; "'What filth! What filth!' . . . tons and tons of existence, indefinitely: I was suffocating" (Sartre, 1938, 180, 193).

3 My translation; consider the ambiguity of "facts"/"events", where the original reads "questo gorgo dei fatti" (198).

4 *Castello*, 1976, 126. Hugh Kenner, among many, speaks of such narrative efforts to exhaust the permutational possibilities within a predetermined set (in Scholes, 1964).

5 Leonard B. Meyer, 1967, 292–3. Meyer quotes from T. W. Adorno.

6 Often of particular attraction to anti-Realists in the notion of entropy as expressed in Pynchon's story "Entropy" is the way that it turns Realist aspiration on its head. As the 'narrative' of nature's progression unfolds, "galaxy, engine, human being, culture, whatever" degrade to "the condition of the More Probable", to – as Rosemary Jackson paraphrases it – "a zero point of non-difference" (167). Realism's principles of probabilism and exhaustiveness here nullify its declarative and objectivist (i.e. differentiational) principles.

7 From *L'Avenir de la science*; written 1848–9 at the height of Positivism (*Kapital* published this year), it was first printed in 1890, at which time Renan declared that he had changed his mind on the grounds, among other things, that his statements had shown "an exaggerated optimism". Trans. in Grant, 1970, 34.

8 Numerous critical works – of which Rose, 1979, is but one example – make much of the connections between referential anti-Realism and the literature of parody.

9 The notion of post-war American narrative as a struggle to insert a fiction between us and reality is taken up in Pütz, 1979. In line with my suggestion of the possibility of American representational fiction's offering a 'counter-description' in response to actuality, an extension of the idea may lead to what we might call a recurrent 'rhetoric of retaliation'. At its most pessimistic the fiction of Barthelme or a Pynchon – not to mention Burroughs – may acclaim its own utility under some satisfyingly ambiguous motto such as: It 'serves' us right.

10 This latitude of sources of 'information' acceptable in the synthetic view may seem surprising or abhorrent to contemporary minds, but it is philosophically correct. While analytic/synthetic debates come down to arguments over the relative validity of 'deductive' versus 'inductive' evidence, nothing in the logic of the question requires that the provenance of 'induced' data be based in empirical observation of the sort that conventional science, for example, seeks. The latter presumption is, of course, typical of contemporary and not all pro-synthetic thinking.

11 Peirce, 1878, 297. NB Kant's terms, usually translated as "explicative" and "ampliative", and Popper's regular use of "ampliative" as a synonym for "synthetic" in e.g. Popper, 1972.

12 See e.g. his use of this distinction in *Expositions*, as quoted by Mitchell (1966, 103–4) where he speaks further of "Schoenberg, who is both".

13 The reader familiar with the debate between speech-act and deconstruction theory will recognize the importance of this position. In contemporary literary-philosophical discussion the word 'seriousness' is chronically used in two different and conflicting ways. As we've seen (Chapter 2), to take a text seriously may mean to decline to take it literally but to paraphrase it; with semantic gravity (attributing a burden of meaning) to reinterpret it. By contrast, in the present pages 'serious' implies 'to be taken as fact' as opposed to 'as whimsical' – or as 'primary' as opposed to 'secondary' or 'merely tropistic' – for the duration of the reading. The point being that *no* distinction is intended in narrations with synthetic intentions between *degrees of truthfulness*. (The synthetic attitude, for example, is ready to acknowledge the force of *aprioristic* analytic-bases for assessing the truth of statements. It may argue these to be incomplete; so may it argue *a posteriori* ones to be in some way incomplete; the synthetic rationale seeks the accommodation of apperceptions divergent as to source but – in its view – equally necessary. This 'taking the uncustomary seriously' that neocosmic fiction requires in the first instance places the latter in a particular position in the history of twentieth-century literary exploitations of 'non-standard' juxtapositions of material. I've said that the uncustomary in neocosmic narrative is not merely uncustomary but is a coherently integrated articulation of the uncustomary (another way of saying 'serious'). This sets it apart from uses of the unfamiliar in say Dada and much Surrealistic literature.

14 The idea of 'posture' is crucial. Orientations discussed here must not be confused with what philosophers often but not universally believe is an *authentic* distinction – where analytic knowing is drawn from the internal workings of a linguistic system and synthetic knowing derives from this plus genuine data from our experience of 'reality' outside that system. The 'new' data introduced in "La distanza della Luna" is still entirely contained within a language-system, Calvino's text – as indeed, many will argue, are all data once they appear in an utterance. Any distinction between texts having purely analytic and purely synthetic effect is itself largely metaphorical. In any case it is far from clear that in *any* discourse, fictional or otherwise, authentic analytic relationships are nearly as ready to hand as is commonly thought. There are persuasive arguments to the effect that no utterance can be purely analytic except a tautology (see e.g. Eco on 'iconic signs', 1976, and Rosen, 1980). Disputes in recent decades, for example, between analytic and phenomenological schools of thought make evident this uncertainty. Considerations of the rôle of the uncustomary in discourse are vital here. What is analytically true in the language of one culture may not be so in another. 'God' may be 'the creator' in one culture but in another there may be many 'gods' who are not; 'flight' may be a property of birds and not of humans in one culture and not in another. This will of course be one of the principal 'truths' explored by a language-conscious fiction. For historical, ideological reasons a contemporary narrative that is 'analytically orientated' will take data as customarily related in Realist texts as though they were unproblematically in keeping with 'the natural language' – and should thus be analytically consistent – and interrogates their relations, showing them to be unstable. But this procedure – while it is 'analytical' in the sense that it's critically dissective – is of course then historicist and hence synthetic in its essential function.

15 I choose this particular quotation – from the close of Romanos' *Quine and Analytic Philosophy* (1983, 194) – for the express purpose of signalling the persistence in recent times of the attitude among philosophers. NB it comes in a text whose aim is "to reveal clearly the implausibility and meaninglessness of the analytic conception of language" (xvi).

16 *Paracriticisms*, 67. Kennard subsequently adopts this notion (1975).

17 Henri Poincaré, "Mathematical creation", an essay delivered early in this century as a lecture before the Psychological Society of Paris, reprinted in unattributed translation in Newman, 1956, 2041.

18 Christ himself cannot resist the gift; viz. his use of curses in his childhood to wither, blind and strike dead those who unwittingly bump into him, etc., in the Gospel of Thomas. Happily, within these same apocryphal tales he eventually restores his victims to themselves – by the same procedure.

19 Williams, 1965, 202–4. In *Secondary Worlds*, W. H. Auden, much aware of Williams, at length expresses faith in the power of names not only to evoke but to create the individual's private – as opposed to social – identity.

20 "To change this rock into a jewel, you must change its true name", says

his master. "And to do that ... is to change the world", Chapter 3; quoted in Shippey, 1977, 151.
21 Kellman, 1980, gives much attention to "the act of naming".
22 Quoted in Carpenter, 1977, 172. Tolkien's fascination with names and his use of them is a continual topic of popular critical investigation.
23 Thus Borges' many stories of worlds contained within libraries, within books, within single words in themselves. The opening premiss of Calvino's essay on "narrative as a combinative process" is a classic statement: "1. Once upon a time a member of the tribe began to declaim a sequence of words.... The real purpose was to see how far words could be linked up; to test their reciprocal fertility. And to arrive at a rational account of [tribal man's] cosmos.... Each animal, object and relationship would acquire beneficent and maleficent powers, which came to be called magic ones but could really be described as narrative powers, because they constituted the inner potentiality of a word set in narrative, the faculty of linking with other words at the level of continuous discourse" (94–5). Lem, in his story "Gigamesh", plays with the idea of a book that is "the largest logogriph in literature, a semantic monster rebus" that unites "in one novel the entire world of man"; "the letter (L) is to the name (Gigamesh) as Lucifer is to the events of the novel.... Through 'Logos' L indicates the Beginning (the Causative Word of Genesis)", etc. (Lem, 1971, 381, 379, 374). Thus in Nabokov, not only does a word in Shade's poem ("lemniscate") have "no real meaning" for its 'editor' and has instead arisen from the poet's having "fallen under the spell of misleading euphony"; more, "the force propelling" one of the characters (Gradus) described in the 'commentary' "is the magic action of Shade's poem itself". I.e. (as adjoining notes neatly reveal) the language of the poem appears by its very nature to 'create' words for the sake of their own effect, and in fact 'creates' events in the world outside it (110).
24 Pinget, 1952; cf. Chapter 31, "The name".
25 Jackson discusses these nineteenth-century forerunners briefly, along with the notion of literary 'thingless names", 38–40. Anticosmic fiction's persistent exploration of the possibility of breaking our habitual reliance on names as a basis of knowing (of fixing identities, truths) – nicely explored by Ricardou (e.g. 1971) – is an expressive demonstration, by inversion, of the writer's obsession with the power of names.
26 Calvino, 1965, 146, 148. Ricardou, for example, rather inaccurately speaks of such efforts in *Tel Quel* literature – of which this is in a sense a figurative 'representation' – as the narrative's travelling "back and forth, from fiction to narration" (1971, 131). Barth, apart from his practical experiments with this process, allegorizes it in his story "Water-message" (1968).
27 Federman, 1981, 303; the punctuational oddities are in Federman's text.
28 *Nicocles*, reproduced in *Antidosis*, quoted in Kennedy, 1963, 8.
29 It is characteristic of both 'literary' and 'philosophical' discourse, in other words, that they base the idea of the centrality to thought of language on the conviction that thinking itself is to be regarded as the *mind addressing itself*, *form*ulating its experiences.

30 60–1. "This all-powerful, anonymous language and thought ... reign inside and outside, from public information to the mutest intimacy, with an exaggerated visibility which renders them invisible. Our identity depends on it.'

31 In the way Ehrmann feels writing should in future be read, the text would lose "the sacred character which in our culture we have been pleased to confer upon it. Sacred (public) language and ordinary language cease to oppose one another like an aristocrat and a plebian" (1971, 241). Read William Burroughs: "Word authority more habit forming than heroin no this is not the old power addicts talk I am talking about certain exercise of authority through the use of words authority words habit more forming than heroin" (1973, 198).

32 In Sollers' view of the conventional habit of seeing the literary work as a 'product', "a sort of fetishism of the work, as dogma and as absolute, is constituted"; "increasingly sure of themselves, bourgeois journalists judge from above and decide with enviable impunity"; the reader is left the slave of the authorized interpretation of the text. "We must pose the problem from within language. ... To the extent that we value the product, we suppose the existence of the academy; we favor the collection of fixed, rigidified things in the pseudo-eternity of value, whereas what we seek should carry us beyond all value" (1968b, 63, 66, 68).

33 "Our shit is our history", says Ehrmann; "our history is our undoing" – since it acts as the group's narrative formulation of experience (as Tolstoy, Joyce, Sartre and others have in fact long declared) (1971, 251).

34 In "western thought", says Jochen Gerz, "the external world is such as it is 'said' to be. In replacing it with its own interpretation ... our language mechanically assures the domination of representation over life." "Our language assumes this domination by division. It divides life into 'reality' and 'idea'. ... The individual becomes dependent on it and is forced to abandon his rights in the world" (Gerz, 1981, 279). "Signs are a mass of all of history's messages" says Ehrmann. Meaning "cuts, disposes, executes, meaning is never legitimate. That is why it is advisable to denounce it rather than submit to it. ... Let that tyranny be a terror" (1971, 249).

35 Hassan, 1967, 82. Cf. Ehrmann, " 'the author' is no longer to be found at the origin of the 'text' " (1971, 237).

36 *Lois*, trans. W. H. Matheson, E. Kafalenos in Russell, 1981, 119. Motives for the onslaught on the psychological recuperation of narratives can be seen more fully in the present context. To 'analyse' narrative as the product of a unified psychological entity would amount to reductive declarative paraphrase according to some fixed limited system of assessment; to attribute rondeur or depth of an external referential sort; to take insufficient account of supra- or extra-personal processes operating through the text (ontologically linguistic, formal, social, metaphysical). It should be said that Beckett's trilogy is clearly an 'intermediate' work; but we can now perceive in it the thrust of its adoption of 'free direct discourse', its movement toward a 'post-Modern disembodied voice'. Sollers' persistent appeal to Mallarmé

(undoubtedly reflecting the influence in this sense, however indirect, of Blanchot) constitutes only one of many traces in anticosmic narrative of the earlier *symboliste* effort in poetry to rid writing of the '*je*'. The fact that current criticism so regularly takes the presence of some 'disembodied' voice as proof of the eviction of 'character' (cf. Brooke-Rose's discussions on the subject, 1981, 322ff.) discloses how difficult it is to throw off *Realism*'s dicta as to what actually constitutes character in the first place. (Who says that material being – i.e. location in time and place – is an indispensable feature of 'characterizable' discourse?)

37 "C'est la Narration qui parle ... la voix n'est pas ici l'instrument, même dépersonalisé, d'un *secret*: la *ça* qui est atteint n'est pas celui de la personne, c'est celui de la littérature ..." (Barthes, 1979, 21).

38 1962, 146. The historical place of Robbe-Grillet's statements on the subject is important. As the publication in 1968 of *Théorie d'ensemble* (with essays by Sollers, Derrida, Kristeva, Ricardou as well as Barthes, Foucault and others) manifestly articulated, the *Tel Quel* movement was in large part founded to express the conviction that he, Sarraute *et al.* hadn't gone far enough. As Heath recounted it (1972), the *nouveau roman* still clung to a "positivist ideology", hovering "between a survival from psychologism, the stress of mental life, and a decoratively structural 'descriptivism'" (222) of which the lines just quoted do indeed show traces. As Ricardou phrased the difference between *nouveau roman* and *Tel Quel*, "the former subverts the category of character, the latter abolishes it. The former tends to formalize its fiction, the latter, with more violence, its narration. The former turns the process of representation against itself, the latter nullifies it. ... For anti-representation, self-representation is still too representative" (1971, 133).

The 'Sollers' of whom I speak in the immediately following pages is Sollers as described by himself down to the moment of personal and intellectual crisis *c.* 1970 and as acclaimed and rationalized by his colleagues Derrida, Kristeva, and late Barthes (whose appraisals of his work Sollers has vigorously applauded). He has also appeared in a series of different and profoundly propositional, politically referential 'states'. Further discussion of the complex implications of his work appears in a sequel to this volume, alluded to elsewhere.

39 *Drame* (1965), 157–8. "Il se réveille un matin dans ce qu'il a écrit. A la lettre: sans transition en ouvrant les yeux, le récit continue, se répète. ... Il sort an effet du texte, naturellement, il vient d'en toucher l'existence autonome, directe." Cf. *Terra nostra*: "aspiring from the beginning and to the end of time the impossible: a perfectly simultaneous narration. He was paper. ... When they killed him and threw him into the sea, he was again paper" (636).

40 *Thru*, 32. The following two selections appear on 84 and 106.

41 In Russell, 1981, 92, 93. Analogous short selections from additional writers appear in Russell and in Kostelanetz, 1983.

42 Cf. Ehrmann, "The 'writer' is therefore neither *inside* nor *outside* his language. ... Far from appropriating language in order to immobilize it, the

'writer' suspends language in order to transmit it. By putting it back into circulation" (1971, 243).
43 *City Life*, 117, 109, 112–13. NB in this story's perhaps characteristically American closing view, language is (a) a matter of pragmatic rhetoric, more or less *effective*, to be contrasted, set over against, (b) a pre-existent, 'rock-solid' reality (118).
44 Foreshadowings of this have long been with us in fiction (e.g. in Kafka) even before 'who is doing what where and when' was so clearly in doubt, and are characteristic of even the most straightforward narratives of Robbe-Grillet:

> The blue sedan is going to crash into a roadside tree whose rigid foliage scarcely shivers under the impact, despite its violence.
>
> The car immediately bursts into flames. The whole brush is illuminated by the crackling, spreading fire.
>
> (1957, 113–14)

What criticism unflaggingly likes to call a 'Kafkaesque' oneiric quality in art stems in fact more often than not from some abandonment of the representation of resistance, tension or stress that we customarily associate with 'natural' processes. It is not in *change*, merely, that causality manifests itself but in processes associated with some exercise of *force* – tensions we experience in contemplating forces for change in their competition with forces (e.g. gravity) resisting change. What happens often in linguistically transformational narrative (and its forerunners) is that 'natural' forces for change appear to operate 'weightlessly', without resistance, as if – quite literally – by fiat. Contemporaneous cinematic techniques echoed this – in e.g. the slow-motion sequences of violent destruction seeming to happen effortlessly, peacefully even, at the close of *Easy Rider* and *Zabriskie Point*.
45 This recurrent anecdote has been recorded (by D. A. Pennebaker) on film in at least one case as told by Billy Whitelaw in conversation with Alan Schneider – Beckett's principal English-language actress and director – during a production of *Rockaby*.
46 Consider the narrative (of which there are different and longer versions) persistent among children in anglophone countries:

> 'Twas early in the morning in the middle of the night
> And two dead boys got up to fight.
> Back to back they faced each other,
> Drew their swords and shot each other.
> A deaf policeman heard the noise
> And came and killed the two dead boys.

Part of the satisfaction – relevant to the present issue – for young tellers and listeners is that there is not merely nonsense here but a play between that and elements of 'heightened verisimilitude' which the 'nonsensical' arrangement itself 'produces'. E.g. lines 3–4: pre-war boys had often enough performed mock sword and pistol 'duels', the latter starting back to back, in a manner of which this could easily be taken as a condensed – and hence 'extra-sharp, extra-real' – reproduction.

47 Cf. the work of Federman, Roche, Brooke-Rose, Sollers. Barthes is explicit, if not persuasive, in his praise of this aspect of Sollers' writing, e.g. 1979, 66–7. Calvino's *Se una notte d'inverno* and Brooke-Rose's *Thru* make an express thematic *topos* of the matter.

48 This helpful pairing of terms Lavers uses in 1982, 66.

49 "'Literature' has no rightful existence of its own. ... Critical reading is but an invention and an inventory of literature. ... 'Literature' then does not distinguish itself from other systems of signs as a privileged mode of discourse, but *is a particular manner of reading and deciphering signs*. ... Now, signs, *all signs*, are open to a new reading" (Ehrmann, 1971, 248).

50 "Il y a donc un changement constant, un chaos, à la limite. Mais visant une sorte de lieu absolu, homogène?" "Une homogénéité indescriptible!" (Sollers, 1981b, 179). I have not seen the transcription of the English-language interviews of which Sollers'/Hayman's published book is a translation, and am consequently particularly uncomfortable with the translations I offer in the present text. What, for example, was the original English for "à la limite"?

51 There exists a way of describing a large number of such 'a-nonymous' procedures: nouns/pronouns are used as 'technonyms' (names relating their subjects to their contexts – e.g. 'father', 'king') rather than conventionally as 'autonyms' (names 'belonging' in stable ways to fixed subjects – e.g. 'John', 'King John'). But this should be watched: it is a *rationale* that the discourse-centred text may resist as such.

52 Ricardou, 1971, 133.

53 "On assiste à un combat fou entre l'«inconclusion» des attitudes ... dont la succession est toujours ouverte ... et le poids de l'Image, qui tend invinciblement à se solidifier; car le destin de l'Image, c'est l'immobilité"."Le scandale sollersien vient de ce que Sollers s'attaque à l'Image, semble vouloir empêcher à l'avance la formation et la stabilisation de toute Image" (1979, 88–9). I say that he 'partially' perceives the issue only because, while I feel that the intention is clearly there and is reinforced by his statements elsewhere, his immediate aim is a defence of narration (as '*écriture*') against the image as a societal product, rather than of narrative as something that may be ontologically inimical to the image. This is a crucial and complex subject, and my aim here is merely to broach it.

54 In the conventional rhetoric of narrative copia, e.g. in Rabelais and Boccaccio, there are always formulae for halting the inventory without rescinding the implication that its subject is infinite; that is, without admitting closure. "But why do I expand in so many words?" says the narrator terminating the famous catalogue of Ceperello's vices in the *Decameron*'s first tale. "I could cite you a thousand other examples and references, but here is not the place", says *Gargantua*'s narrator. The verbal inventory itself, we see,

is (arbitrarily) ended, while the *point* – the infinity of its object – has been made. The intention in the mind of the personified narrator takes precedence over the actual subject itself, whose relevant properties his/her abbreviated inventory has satisfactorily exhausted. Now, in the case of a language-orientated fiction, since the subject is language itself, such an act is philosophically impossible. ("Perchè mi distendo io in tante parole?", Boccaccio, 1349–51, 48. I deliberately translate the perfectly idiomatic "distendo" with the rather woodenly literal "expand" – expatiate – to invite the pro-narratological reader to explore the interestingly pleonastic self-referential aspect of the original; is the text speaking to, extending, itself? "Mille aultres exemples et lieux à ce propos vous pourrois-je exposer, mais ce n'est ici le lieu", Rabelais, 1539–64, 35. Would the same reader like to play with Rabelais's recursive 'other places/this place'?)

55 *Paracriticisms*, 13; see also his *The Literature of Silence*.

56 Beckett, 1951, 164. On 'filibustering' cf. Chapter 1, n.17.

57 Cf. the artist's problem in *City Life*'s closing story: "The empty canvas remains. So (usually) he makes a mark on it. ... Then he is profoundly depressed because what is there is not what he meant"; he will eventually "wrest something from nothing" with his "marks", but never the thing intended (170–3).

58 410, 414, 353–4. We must regard with caution any idea of Lem's "play" as having intentions identical to those of other mentioned texts evoking the same theme. His attitude toward narratology in the present sense is ironic. This tricky aspect of such works is in fact part of the hollow interplay of texts – of which Lem himself is fully aware.

59 Repeated in Federman's essay, "Fiction today ...", 1981, 301.

60 On the depotentiation of language by language's recursive internal circulation: in *Thru*, a 'character' says "Literature is the servant of the bourgeoisie", another answers, "Well maybe we are too literary to swallow your cliché" (92). Here one 'literary' – but also culturally received – verbal convention is 'attacked' by another. Both 'happen' to be '*about*' literature – and what's more, both are contained within a literary work. Which diction is 'right'? Conditions are such that there appears to be no way to decide. The text would oblige us to suspend commitment to terms either of which we may have felt acceptable before.

61 For seminal critical expositions along parallel lines see, e.g., the later work of Barthes and Derrida, 1967a and 1967c.

62 References here to an 'expected' class of readers of course raises crucial questions – as indeed does the whole matter of the unnaturalizability of signs generally (just how indeterminate *are* 'incomprehensible signs' – e.g. nonsense words – really?). For the moment it suffices to say that it would be nonsense to pretend that Sollers did not have a specific class of readers in mind when he introduced his ideogrammes. This *might include* readers whom he might expect to understand Chinese, but even if this were the case it is hard to stretch our conception of the text's intention to the point where we imagine it to be *equally* addressed to readers who understand *only* Chinese,

let alone those who read neither Chinese nor French. The element of indeterminacy he has in mind could of course best be confirmed in cases where no one could understand *any* word of his text, but we have no evidence of his taking an interest in such an enterprise. He wants a substantial modicum of determinacy.

63 Quoted in Hassan, 1975, 82.

64 Since, for example, the first impact of the seminal views of such as Booth and Barthes.

65 Who in fact gave many years' energy to the exploration, in his anagrams, of the fictionally creative effect of lexical permutations.

66 Obvious illustrations of the affiliation in this regard of two such otherwise deeply opposed outlooks appear in Gerald Prince's *A Grammar of Stories* (cf. review in Nash, 1976) and Derrida's *De la grammatologie* [*Of Grammatology*].

67 Nabokov, 1962, 151. "I abhor such games", adds Kinbote; but his incessant observations on the figural quality of his story betrays him.

68 I use the term 'aesthetic' now in a deliberately more conventional sense than that called upon by Iser, for whom it means "the realization accomplished by the reader" (1976, 21). It is, as is seen below, the applicability/inapplicability of conventional aesthetic notions of form to anti-Realist fiction that needs in the first instance to be tested.

69 As my treatment of the Elba palindrome shows, this is not to say that such formal traits may not be inextricably connected with the text's communicational effect. It's also far from saying that for a formal intention to seem *present* the artefact must display some 'universally agreed and unchanging' relational traits such as symmetry, etc. It is offered only as one rough and ready, provisional *test* of intention. That is, on the assumption that each new artefact seeks to 'communicate' or evoke in the perceiver some 'new datum' of experience, where such predictive, independently specifiable patterning appears and especially where the artefact can be conceived in any way as capable of communicating its semantic properties without it, one test of its having formal intent is tentatively satisfied. If there seems to be question-begging here, it throws into doubt only the precise nature of the relation between 'form and content' and does not itself pre-empt the logic of our enquiring into the formal properties of texts. If we find semantic implications thrust upon us, we shall have to find a way, eventually, of living with them.

70 Without this new dimension, "increasingly, men will ask machines to make them forget machines. . . . We should not be surprised if the accent is henceforth placed increasingly with perfunctory, confused haste on Epinal's surrealism, the fantastic, the neobaroque, cheap sexuality" (Sollers, 1968b, 62).

71 Cf. e.g. Sontag's essay called (NB) "On style" (1969) and "The aesthetics of silence" (1967), and Barthes's *Le Plaisir du texte* [*The Pleasure of the Text*, 1973].

72 Anti-Realist reticence on the subject of aesthetics is well-illustrated in the case of the work of Kostelanetz, a professional critic, fictionalist and

anthologist devoted particularly to avant-garde literary theory and practice. When he comes to edit a collection of no fewer than forty-five essays dedicated specifically to "*Esthetics Contemporary*" (1978), while among the authors he includes – and among the artists referred to by them – there are a number of writers *mentioned*, there is no essay by or in any significant way about any contemporary writer. This does not mean that he or other writers have nothing to say on the subject of aesthetics in literature (he refers the reader at the start to Sontag's "The aesthetics of silence" which he omits because it is "available elsewhere"), but it does acknowledge the scarcity of statements within the realm of avant-garde literature having the status (the 'reproduction-worthiness', if nothing else, in the economy of his book) of those made in the fields of music, the 'visual arts', and the cinema.

73 Lest this last pair seem less familiar than those preceding, cf. Breton's "beauty will be convulsive or will not be at all", last line of *Nadja*, 1928.

74 This pretence of realistic 'objectivity' is of course no proof of neutrality but is only a by-now familiar habit of the book and merely another way of stacking the cards. It takes no special objectivity or insight or subjective paranoia on my part to be persuaded that others will be ready with alternative stacks.

75 For detailed analyses of Sollers' texts, for example, as explorations of the notion of "*la surface*" ("*la nappe sollersienne*") cf. Derrida, 1969, and Barthes, 1979.

76 "In a sense they are all ready-made caricatures here, nothing to invent", says *Thru*'s narrator, telling of "the short plump demagogue and his lanky henchman" and of "the tense young man" and "the middle-aged chairman", 24. The line is reminiscent, again, of Calvino's explication of his appropriation and exploitation of 'flat' conventional personifications (the villain, the hero) for the purpose of exploring not ethical but formal relations.

77 Brooke-Rose, 1975, 56, 100, 36. Cf. these typical examples from Sollers (for which no translation is needed) "les poissons putréfiés les nations poudrées pakhad pakkah pakh effroi fosse filet qui fuit devant l'effroi tombera dans la fosse et en remontant de la fosse il sera pris dans le filet seul pourra s'en tirer l'incestant l'athlettre"; "je m'incarne tu t'incarnas il se réincarne nous carnavalons ils s'encarnent nous montons la garde aux lucarnes chacun à son créneau de chrono chacune à son chromo pro domo et le temps s'en va par rafales chacun chacunant chacune en chacun chacune menant chacun en cabal", *Paradis*, 56, 122.

78 "Ma matière est forme en soi" (*Lois*, 121). The line is immediately followed with: "There's nothing formal in all this. Even less anything formalist. It's an instantaneous association. . . . The thing conditions itself and brings itself to its conditions. . . . I have as a base only my own nullity." ("Tout cela n'a rien de formel. De formaliste, encore moins. C'est une association instantanée. . . . La chose se conditionne et s'oppose à ses conditions . . . je n'ai pour base que ma propre nullité") (121). Here the reciprocal formal patterns (inversion, evocation/revocation, etc.), typical in this literature, give the lie to any propositional repudiation of form itself.

79 For a classic example, note the use of the ellipsis (. . .) in *Le Parc*.
80 I mean 'stability' here in every sense. The reader early comes to recognize that 'someone' – some reliable enunciator – is there (posing questions and/or indicating that something is expressly missing) and that this someone so-characterized will never let him/her down.
81 In Sollers "et" is on occasion supplemented by the iteration of "cependant" and "car", "puisque" and "mais". In Pinget, "ou", "ou que", "ou alors", "mais que", "pour ce qui est", and "et" amass to the point of tirelessly rhythmical redundancy.
82 Derrida, 1969, 315. "Not a single atom of *Numbers* escapes this play of recurrences."
83 Binary systems may appear privileged insofar as they may be used to evoke the perception of difference/*différance*, of identity/otherness, violations of the rule of non-contradiction, and the problem of presence/absence; and nothing is 'complete' until it is seen as containing what is other than itself, in a way that 'merely' stochastic systems may not. This in no way annuls, however, the special consciousness such discourse imposes on us of a systematically symmetrical structuration of experience.
84 I owe this phrase to a draft of P. S. O'Rourke, "The construction of self-identity as a narrative pre-condition in Proust's 'A la recherche du temps perdu' and Beckett's 'Trilogy'", thesis (MA), University of Warwick, 1986.
85 The *topos*, not discussed in detail here, is common; the convergence of narrative 'lines' on Malta in *V* and on Shade's death in *Pale Fire* are only two obvious examples ("Thus, some time in the morning of July 21, the last day of his life", Kinbote says as *Pale Fire* draws to its close, ". . . two silent time zones had now merged to form the standard time of one man's fate" (214). Cf. related palindromic procedures in, e.g., Butor's *L'Emploi du temps* and Pinget's *Quelqu'un*. A Dickens may certainly seem to be drawn toward similar patterns, but never with the insinuation, persistent here, that the space between the 'making forces' of fatality and those of narration itself is bridged by a somehow identical perfection or causal filiation.
86 Derrida, 1969, 307. The analysis is not exactly correct: it is true of every sequence of which the heading leads with a 'whole' number 4 (e.g. "4.64" but not "1.49"); the exactitude of the text's regime is greater than Derrida registers.
87 Derrida, 1969, 350–1, 348; "*quadrature*" appears in the original, 231.
88 See *Thru*, 90. Thus, as Derrida says of *Nombres*, the text is "a machinated structure", the "product of an arithmetic operation" (308).
89 "A mathematical demonstration", as Poincaré wrote, "is not a simple juxtaposition of syllogisms, it is syllogisms *placed in a certain order*, and the order in which these elements are placed is much more important than the elements themselves" (trans. G. B. Halsted, "Mathematical creation", in Newman, 1956, 2042–3).

That Sollers' intention is 'straightforward' and not ironic is beyond dispute. As Derrida sees in elaborate detail, in one way the *linguistic* text of *Nombres* is devoted to the discursive unfolding of the transformational potential of 'numbers' ("nombre", "nom", "ombre", etc.); the number 4, for example, is not 'just' a figure that must appear in the 'natural order' of any 'normal' series of numbered *headings* but is an incessant thematic *topos* within the narrative, which – while famously 'without identifiable story or characters' – is itself repeatedly described as an articulation of 4-ness (the 4 angles of the square – the "*cadre*" – of the page, of the die, and so forth). Sollers' fascination with non-determinate processes, exemplified by his recurrence to the motif of dice, is clear. But the non-stochastic *regularity of that recurrence* to this and other specific motifs seen in sum is overwhelming. (Cf. Brooke-Rose's 'dice-like' use of the *pun* to ironize the stability of utterances – showing by the pun the potential for multiplicity in utterances. The periodicity of her reversion to puns – departing distinctly from the usage of 'classic' fiction where the occurrence of puns is variously proportioned and timed to the fluctuation of 'moods' in which at the level of *histoire* the pun would/would not be 'fitting' – makes of the device a formal *constant*, not to say a stable thematic *topos*.) When a Sollers text speaks of its numeration as 'arbitrary' it does so not in the sense of 'capricious' or 'inconsequential' but of 'pure' and 'transportable', such that Sollers uses the same system concertedly, with analogous significations, in several texts. Once again, there is the 'motivation' of an *analytic* relation between all the parts of the total text.

90 "Je voulais qu'il y ait la certitude géometrique la plus poussée"; "j'ai pensé des journées, des mois, à imaginer que j'étais en train d'écrire réellement un cube"; "j'ai l'impression de toucher, en traçant les mots, un fond géometrique, algébrique" (1981b, 107, 105, 100–1).

91 "La musique est ici plus près de moi que vous ne le serez peut-être jamais" (1972, 118); "Oh! Tout est musique. . . . Je prends la musique comme logique" (1981b, 181).

92 1973, 114 (first printed in *Incontri musicali*, August 1959). So he constructs his lecture along the following lines: "There are four measures in each line and twelve lines in each unit of the rhythmic structure. There are forty-eight such units, each having forty-eight measures. The whole is divided into five large parts, in the proportion 7, 6, 14, 14, 7. The forty-eight measures of each unit are likewise so divided. The text is printed in four columns to facilitate a rhythmic reading" (109). "Subdivision involving a square root is the only possible subdivision which permits this micro–macrocosmic rhythmic structure. . . . It makes very little difference what I say or even how I say it. At this par-ticular moment, we are passing through the fourth part of a unit which is the second unit in the second large part of this talk" (112). It should be mentioned that, not shown here, in the text phrases are spaced rhythmically on the page.

93 It would be faint- if not false-hearted of the present text not to be the first to point out its own gestures in the direction of ordinal formliness, and should be subjected to the same scrutiny.

94 Cf., e.g., *Nombres*. They are occasionally drawn at some 'point' as open-ended; but in such cases the lines drawn to these points are, again and for no

logical but only conceivably some aesthetic reason, equivalent in length and parallel or balanced in orientation.

95 Many further examples appear in Kostelanetz's anthology 1973, in his *Future's Fictions*, New York, 1970, and in Russell, 1981.

96 Sollers, 1960, 49; this passage trans. in Heath, 1972, 134.

97 *Le Parc*, 72–3. Italicizations of English words here and in adjoining quotations mine.

98 "Il faudrait refoudre complètement la rythmique" (1981b, 106).

99 "Comme une expérience mystique" (1981b, 116).

100 "Vous avez remarqué l'emploi très déliberé du rythme. Je tente d'intégrer différentes traditions métriques. ... C'est la métrique et la rythmique" (1981b, 217).

101 "Ecoutez, l'essential est la perception que l'écrivain a de la répétition. Que pense-t-il de la répétition; comment l'utilise-t-il; et comment se situe-t-il par rapport à ses propres répétitions?" (1981b, 238).

102 "Il y a à la fois le rythme, la danse, le roulement des syllabes et l'interprétation des évènements. Le roulement continu des mots correspond à une sorte d'immobilité maximale. ... L'idée, c'est de faire sentir le sujet comme ayant sa circonférence partout et son centre nulle part" (1981b, 126–7).

103 "Est-ce le «vrai» que vous cherchez?" ... "Oui, la beauté et la splendeur de la vérité, certainement. ... La «beauté», la «splendeur» ne sont plus des valeurs mais un rayonnement, une force abstraite" (1981b, 233–4).

104 Cf., e.g., those many others bearing on textual efforts toward *semiotic* – bearing on consonance of imagery, etc. – 'harmony' (a word prized by Sollers, for one), another favourite topic of aestheticians which, involving as it does the *compatibility* of elements in a work, could be adequately treated only if we were to regard (as criticism elsewhere no doubt must) the entire idiom of each individual text in great detail.

105 Ricardou, 1971, 123. There is nothing that says that mimetic – e.g. representational – fiction must be formally orderly. The fictionalist or theorist claiming that there is only displays a special predisposition toward a concern for formal order.

106 Sollers likes to point out that rules are made to be broken and that we cannot experience play until we are made aware of the rules we are breaking: e.g. 1981b, 98–9.

107 There are reasons in fact to speak of narration-centred fiction as a 'steady-state' mode – as we'd expect of an analytic modality, one not subject to referential (synthetic) contingency – for all that at another level it wants to be transformationally dynamic. In "La Dissémination" [*Dissemination*, 1969] – so massively detailed an analysis of *Nombres* as to be longer than the novel itself, and endorsed as nothing less than "*grand*" by Sollers – Derrida never discusses any developmental feature in the book, even while he speaks at every turn of an active interplay between its marks. This befits Derrida's own idea of the impossibility of any 'originary' event, no priority/posteriority, even though it may sit awkwardly with our own knowledge that at the end of

any reading of a text our state is unquestionably altered from the one that obtained prior to the reading. A feature of anti-Realist fiction *is* that a text's semantics often change but that at the level of discourse it is progressively *consolidated*. Not only in its extra-linguistic (e.g. arithmetic) but in its linguistic notation (e.g. labyrinth, mirror, square, etc.) it often becomes deeply redundant. We don't find as frequently as we might expect, and as we *do* find widely in Modernism, the shifting of central motifs that made William York Tindall so unhappy with Lawrence's *St Mawr* (Tindall, 1954, vi). The relations between many of the narration's sequential 'points' (as e.g. in all squares, whatever their size) remains remarkably stable.

108 "Je dis du livre de Sollers qu'il est beau. ... Je désigne par là ... une plénitude matérielle de plaisirs" (Barthes, 1979, 55ff.). It is Barthes' essay on *Drame* in that volume that Sollers calls "un grand article" (1981b, 82). Barthes' theoretical expressions, as well as the totality of his criticism, are of course surcharged on every page with the narrative vocabulary of aesthetic evaluation – viz. "the physics of bliss", and so forth.

In this paragraph the spectre of 'mechanical' perfection as 'beauty' rears its head once again – as does the ghost of the narrator-as-living-being which the narratologist had thought he/she had in theory laid to rest.

109 Klinkowitz on Federman: "literature fails when it claims to represent the other, so in his own novel he simply lets it represent itself. As such it is a system, an esthetic one" (1981, 178).

110 Lentricchia, 1980, 169. Lentricchia calls American post-structuralists "the new aesthetes" (186).

111 In the case of Sontag's open 'defence' of the 'aesthetic' aspect of literature in recent times, a logical weakness is that it quickly turns 'seriously' to propound the *utility* of literature's stimulating greater responsiveness to the world of sensuous experience. A *strength* in this defiant act of defence becomes clear at the very moment we realize that it is the latter she's arguing for, in fact, and not actually 'pure aesthetic' experience. While she obviously recognizes the contradiction (aesthetics not to be defended as useful) – "we are stuck with the task of defending art" (1969, 14) – it's not clear that she's aware she has left the real problems of aesthetics largely untouched.

112 *Thru*, 100; by contrast, the narrator argues, it must be "the text that generates the passion acceptable in the text".

113 From a different angle Lyotard (1979) touches on the problem raised in these pages, in his discussion of 'the postmodern condition'. "I see a much earlier modulation of Nietzschean perspectivism in the Kantian theme of the sublime. I think in particular that it is in the aesthetic of the sublime that modern art (including literature) finds its impetus and the logic of avant-gardes finds its axiom" (77).

114 That is (to put the strongest case possible): formal *symmetry* is in fact an inevitable outcome of narrativity, since – whether for 'natural biological' (Lévi-Strauss) or cultural (Derrida) reasons, by the rule of *difference* if no other – the trace of every assertion's opposite is present within it.

115 For reasons previously described and because – in answer to the

'strongest case' put in the previous note – while the *trace* of an assertion's antithesis may be implicit, quite simply nothing says that the text must enunciate it. (Moran does not have to say 'it was raining/it was not raining'.) That will always be a matter of choice for the enunciator, and specifies his/her interest.

116 Cf. Cristopher Nash, forthcoming volume assessing 'the limits of anti-Realist revolt'.

Conclusion

1 1981b, 100; Hayman's and Philip Barnard's translation, from their (1983) edition of 1968c, xviii.

2 See Chapter 4, n. 116.

3 Ambiguous narrative has always had the capacity for simplicity of form, as Dante, Spenser, Milton and indeed most pre-nineteenth-century realist literature shows. In the case of neocosmic fiction, its uncustomary signs necessitate complex procedures for their naturalization, while its form remains quite stable. The theses imbedded in an equivocal discourse, by contrast, may be 'deeply simple" and we should not feel we are missing something when we feel unable to find there a 'message' as complex as the 'form'.

4 By no means all 'radical' programmes have rejected simplicity. Sontag, for example, has insisted that "it is possible to elude the interpreters" who endanger our sense of the "being itself" of things "in another way, by making works of art whose surface is so unified and clean, whose momentum is so rapid, whose address is so direct that the work can be ... just what it is". "Certain kinds of overviews, for example – which scant the minutiae of feeling altogether – are, I am sure, at least as valid"; "I do not share [Sarraute's] contempt for the novelist's effort to transmute the watery shapeless depths of experience into solid stuff, to impose outlines, to give fixed shape and sensuous body to the world" (1969, 21, 115–16).

5 A large part of the work of Calvino, Borges, Nabokov, associated in all central ways with the neocosmic modality, is commonly and intelligently argued by its analysts to fit this description.

6 I.e., that a text should not work according to different sets of principles simultaneously, and specifically that a work's form must match – and indeed recapitulates – its sense. Utterances must enact what they appear to purport, must perform what they mean. Thus a text that is orderly in its form 'smuggles' to us a faith in a transcendent order, whatever may be 'said' locally within it. The problem of homology/heterology in recent narrative theory is a principal subject of the work referred to in Chapter 4, n. 116.

7 "The aesthetic creative impulse is building unawares a third joyous realm of play and of appearance", as Schiller put it, "in which it releases mankind from all the shackles of circumstance and frees him from everything that may be called constraint, whether physical or moral"; art enables "indifference

towards reality" (1794–5, 125, 128). For Schopenhauer the function of art was conceived as "the deliverance of man from the chain of vulgar realities which binds us to this phenomenal world" (W. S. Lilly, quoted in Grant, 1970, 48). "The liberating function of art", Borges says somewhere, "lies in its singular capacity to 'dream against the world', to structure worlds that are otherwise."

8 The most vehement spokesman in fiction's history for escape from reality may of course be Flaubert, whose correspondence (from his "*tour d'ivoire*") is rent at every turn with its mordant cry. "If you knew me better you would know that I abhor ordinary existence" (1953, 176); "I have a hatred of life. There: I have said it; I will not take it back" (123); "What is natural for me is unnatural for others – I am at home in the realm of the extraordinary and the fantastic, in flights of metaphysics and mythology. *Saint Antoine* ... was an outlet for my feelings; I had only pleasure in writing it, and the eighteen months spent writing its five hundred pages were the most deeply voluptuous of my entire life" (148). The 'uncustomary' aspect of *La Tentation de Saint Antoine* [*The Temptation of Saint Anthony*] does not set it categorically apart from Flaubert's other writings and motives. There is every evidence – as the main-text quotation below shows – that, in his revulsion from 'ordinary existence', he could not have found the passion to have "plunged into it heroically, into the midst of all its minutiae, accepting everything, depicting everything" (176) in *Madame Bovary* had he not converted it from 'reality' into his own private illusion.

9 Flaubert 1953, 162–3. While we recall that Flaubert himself opens the way toward anticosmic thought: most revealing about his famous "what I should like to write, is a book about nothing" (126) is that it comes in the personal setting of the equally famous "agonies of Art" (*les affres de l'Art*) cry, written either four or two days before (12 or 14 January 1852, 16 January 1852, both to Louise Colet), in which he had described his "mortal depression" following Bouilhet's criticism of one of his characters, and the struggle with "my accursed Bovary". It falls in the context of an expression of his utter exhaustion with the ordeal of mimesis. The "*livre sur rien*" passage obviously provides *aperture a sinistra* and *a destra* both – towards anticosmic literature (which he did *not* ever write, though *symbolistes* were soon to try something like it) and toward neocosmic fiction which in the form perhaps of *Salammbô* and certainly of *Saint Antoine* he did approach. The explanation of the choice lies certainly in this matter of the context from which his protest against Realism springs: *not* from any suspicion of the reality of actuality *or* of art's capacity to represent it, but in his revulsion against the demand that the art do only or even largely the representational (referential) things. For him the anguish lay not in the impossibility of mimesis but in the insufficiency of it. Flaubert's was the 'Bletchley-station' crisis neatly – if naively – expressed by Tolkien. (*Pace* Jonathan Culler, to whose book *Flaubert: The Uses of Uncertainty* the reader should be referred.)

10 Wilson, 1962, 27–9; the Lovecraft quotation is given, 23, without source.

11 The phrase is Lentricchia's (1980, 33).

12 For Derrida, giving general support to anticosmic theory, the act of

'saying something more', whether we pretend or not to be saying it about the world, is an act of saying something about the world: that the world prior to that text was *incomplete* in exactly those respects in which the text would appear to wish to complete it.

All texts are parts of a chain of "supplements and substitutional significations" (Derrida, 1967a, 158–9). NB the link with commutative theory. Following Borges, even 'identical' utterances are such substitutions – as e.g. in the case of his Pierre Menard's twentieth-century verbatim 'writing-out' of *Don Quixote*, since its writing context is a new one.

13 This seems to me the weakest argument because it still hinges on the work's subordination of certain 'truths' in reality to others. But it is stronger than any speculation of the popular sort to the effect that 'abstract' art or 'fantasy' *dismisses* the truths of reality by drawing us into some totally non-contingent vacuum of 'pure illusion'; to the contrary, the text depends, in this view, on crucial aspects of the spectator's volitional engagement with reality.

14 The appeal of the autonomy of a book's 'world', for instance, is not something the anticosmist might accuse the neocosmic text of without, as we know, being tarred by the same brush. "When we write, we do merely that" says Todorov " – the importance of the gesture is such that it leaves room for no other experience. . . . For writing to be possible, it must be born out of the death of that which it speaks about" (Todorov, 1970, 175).

15 When the surrogate may seem to come in time to displace the desire for other objects or activities, psychological theories tend to agree, this is 'because' not of a greater value intrinisic in the former but of complications (e.g. inhibitions) residing in the attitude of the individual regarding the latter.

16 Malinowski, 1925, 26. While as a mode of demonstration of the universal nature of thought his procedures of extrapolation present other problems as do certain aspects of his own special conclusions, contemporary anthropological views have not abondoned his general observations as to material evidence.

17 Thus "a superficial observer might be led to assume that the mystic and the rational behavior are mixed up, that their effects are not distinguished by the natives and not distinguishable in scientific analysis. Is this really so?" Malinowski, among many, proceeds to demonstrate that his subject groups are, e.g., "expert fishermen, industrious manufacturers and traders" with "extensive knowledge of the classes of the soil, of the various cultivated plants, of the mutual adaptation of these two factors", of "a clear knowledge of weather and seasons" and, in the design and construction of goods and implements, such as the canoe, of "empirical knowledge of material, of technology, and of certain principles of stability and hydrodynamics", of "buoyancy, leverage, equilibrium" together with "a whole system of principles of sailing, embodied in a complex and rich terminology", which "they can also explain . . . in clearly mechanical terms" (Malinowski, 1925, 30, 34).

18 Thus put in simplistic terms, when within the confines of our own 'civilized' culture we say 'love makes the world go round', 'economics rules our lives', 'all thinking is governed by language', and 'physical laws determine

psychic behaviour' we are entertaining narratives between which there is unquestionable tension, yet we move freely among them in our actions without being 'untrue to ourselves'. The crucial problem with this perception is of course that some 'meta-narrative' seems required to provide 'information' as to which 'need' necessitates the application of which code. But the point at this stage is clear: when Sidney declared that "the Poet ... doth grow in effect into another nature: in making things either better than nature bringeth foorth or, quite a new, formes such as never were in nature ... so as he goeth hand in hand with nature ... freely raunging only within the Zodiac of his owne wit", he set forth much of the spirit that was to infuse the neocosmic mode. When Erich Heller, having in his essay on 'the Realistic Fallacy' espoused exactly that 'inwardness' which the fictionalist might offer as an alternative to 'outward' representationality – precisely the inwardness to which Sidney undoubtedly refers when he speaks of the zodiac of the poet's own wit – he nevertheless concludes with colourful intensity that "the economy of the world cannot support forever the expensive households of so many creators competing with Creation itself" (Heller, 1965, 98). Outward truth (reality) and inward fiction (and potential escape) stand opposed. A critic of Heller's is accurate in saying that this is "as if the two must be thought of as alternatives, straining against each other in some kind of ontological tug-of-war" (Grant, 1970, 67). The special insight (or intention) in Sidney's lines lies in that other phrase: the poet "goeth hand in hand with Nature". Which side is Sidney on? is the question that's plagued analysts of Sidney's *Defence* for centuries; that of 'real' nature (and of mimesis), or that of 'wit' (of 'invention')? But Sidney's answer must be clear. He says 'hand in hand', and that's what he means.

19 As we read, we do so 'as if' what we read has some reality, even though in some sense we think that it does not. "Although ... we may say that we believe in something 'as if' it were true," Michael Beldoch has written, "these are in fact mutually contradictory states of mind. At the moment that we *believe* in something it *is* true; the moment that we add *as if*, we cease to believe" (Beldoch, 1975, 117). But this, however commonsensical it may superficially seem, is a coarse misrepresentation of the texture of our thinking. I don't believe that the route I walk along is a safe one because another possibility simply never enters my head, but because alternative beliefs suit the context of my immediate experience less well though equally believable, and I may not be surprised to find that the path presents me with dangers I had decided it was less worthwhile to concern myself with. Our decisions are based not on clear mutually exclusive beliefs but on beliefs that are 'believable enough' to permit statistical risks.

20 We do not 'merely make sense' of the words without believing; this would probably be impossible, in fact; we inevitably believe all kinds of things in the act of reading: at the very least that the words have a characterizable relationship to one another, that they are 'meant' in ways comparable with the ways the same words are meant when we use or hear them used elsewhere – and no doubt much more, but these are enough to establish the

rule. To distinguish as antithetical the kinds of 'believing' I've cited – i.e. believing in the functionality of the *discours* – from 'believing at the level of the *histoire*' is likely to turn out to be specious.
21 Cf. Lem's narrator's passage on consciousness cited p. 194.
22 Quoted in Pütz, 1979, 18; source not given.
23 Cf. the latter's recent novels *Femmes* and *Portrait du Jouer* in confessedly Realist format.
24 Perhaps the best-known writer in English at whose absence here some readers may wince, John Fowles, is an example of these. (The Fowles case is argued in Brooke-Rose, 1981.) Readers will recall in any event that, since this is not meant to be a study of all anti-Realists but of kinds of anti-Realists, I've selected as samples those texts that seemed to present the most usefully incisive illustrations.
25 Dr José Delgado, Yale Medical School, quoted in Hassan, 1975, 92.
26 Christopher Norris's apparent hope of defending deconstructionism from a question similar to this last one (as raised in a slightly different way by Habermas under the heading of the 'transcendental *tu quoque*' – the suggestion that certain sceptics "demand that their texts be properly understood – or at least intelligently read – while ostensibly denying the power of language to encompass any such end") – on the grounds that the deconstructionist position (a) is "hard-won by arguments" and that it (b) only *suspends* but doesn't deny "the commonsense view that language exists to communicate meaning" (Norris, 127–8) – is likely to disappoint indeterminists as half-hearted (though it may well be the best case to be made), even were it to be treated with the seriousness its largely sentimental basis may barely merit. Seeming "quaintly moralistic" as Norris confesses, (a) makes appeal to a notion of (con)sequentiality of assertions and a conception of priority – of the *origination* of determinate conclusion in determinate assertions – incompatible with the specifically Derridan logic Norris thinks to defend. And (b) attributes to Derrida a view ("commonsense") which, if he were to acknowledge it, would leave the entire matter a non-issue, and any mere 'suspension' of it implies the postulation of simply two determinate attitudes (holding/not holding with common sense) subtended by a third (holding contradictory attitudes is an interesting thing to do, for determinate reasons if 'interesting' is to be a comprehensible term) which would be intractable to deconstruction.
27 E.g. in the work of G. Cantor, J. B. Kruskal, N. Dershowitz and Z. Manna, R. M. Smullyan, R. L. Goodstein, H. Steinhaus, F. R. Berlekamp, R. L. Graham, M. Warmus, H. A. Rademacher. A brief survey appears in Gardner, 1983.
28 E.g. the work of E. Fredkin, N. Margolus, T. Toffoli, G. V. Vichniac. A brief survey appears in Hayes 1984.
29 On 'closural tendencies', cf. Michael, 1953, Bruner and Minturn, 1955, Fautz, 1958. On 'psychological realism', cf. Verbrugge, 1980. On illusions, cf. Hoffman, 1983.

30 The seminal figure in this area has been Ilya Prigogine, whose works the interested reader should consult. 'Synergetics' was coined by Herman Haken, who has since edited a number of collected essays on the subject (e.g. Haken, 1978). See also the work of E. Jantsch (e.g. 1980).

BIBLIOGRAPHY

The purpose of the following is not to give an exhaustive survey but solely to provide details of texts specifically cited in the main body of this book. In those instances where further works have been referred to (for example in the notes) but have not been treated as essential to my central argument, bibliographical data are given not here but at the point of reference (except where – for instance in the citation of the King James version of the Bible – they are so familiar as to need no further documentation). Every effort has been made to use those editions most readily accessible at the time of writing, both in terms of language (where translations exist) and physical availability, to contemporary English-speaking readers.

Unless otherwise indicated, works are ordered here under their authors – and identified in the text – by the dates of their original appearance in book form. (Thus, in the main text, the book in which a short work – whether fiction or essay – is to be found is signalled by the date in parentheses immediately following the short work's first mention.) Full details of anthologized texts (noted as available in collections such as Federman 1981, Russell 1973) are given under their authors' names. Where separate short works by one author have come commonly to be known as parts of a single, widely circulated volume (for instance essays by Robbe-Grillet in *Pour un nouveau roman*), I give here details simply of the volume. Where published translations have been located and quoted, page references are to these, while the dates indicate the original sources; where in a few cases editions – and, more frequently, printings – other than the earliest have proved more suitable, dates of those actually used are given and are signalled in square brackets when this would not otherwise be clear. The scholar will wish assiduously to check these against other versions. In the main text I have at the point of first allusion included the translator's English title (in square brackets) for each work for which I've found record of a published translation, but since it's not my purpose here to endorse translations at all costs, I provide full bibliographical data only for those versions I have myself examined. Exceptionally, texts originally published in other than Western European languages are referred to by their translators' English titles – for example stories by Stanislaw Lem discussed in this volume, all of which may be found in Lem 1971.

In certain cases recourse has been had to passages by authors not normally expected to be part of every reader's strictly 'literary' repertoire (for example from art theory, mathematics, information theory, physical sciences); selections in these instances have been taken wherever possible from easily obtained standard collections (such as Chipp 1968, Newman 1956) or journals (such as *Scientific American*), indicated below. Since the quality of translations in such cases is extremely variable, the reader is encouraged to compare these with other versions published within the relevant fields. This applies as well to quoted correspondence, for instance that of Flaubert (where, for example, the widespread Pléiade French edition should be consulted in any event). The layperson (like myself) will count on the specialist scholar to point out my errors, and the latter should be reminded that our gratitude is as deep as it often seems slow in coming.

Abbott, Edwin A. (1884) *Flatland: A Romance of Many Dimensions* (no place given); repr. Oxford, 1962.

Abrams, Meyer Howard (1953) *The Mirror and the Lamp: Romantic Theory and the Critical Tradition*, Oxford and New York.

Addison, Joseph (1712) *Spectator*, 419; repr. in Donald F. Bond (ed.) *The Spectator*, Oxford, 1965, 570–3.

Althusser, Louis (1969) *Lénine et la philosophie*, Paris; trans. B. Brewster, *Lenin and Philosophy and Other Essays*, New York, 1971.

Attebery, Brian (1980) *The Fantastic Tradition in American Literature: From Irving to Le Guin*, Bloomington, Ind.

Auerbach, Erich (1946) *Mimesis; darstellte Wirklichkeit in der abendländischen Literatur*, Bern; trans. W. R. Trask, *Mimesis: The Representation of Reality in Western Literature*, Princeton, 1953.

Bakhtin, Mikhail Mikhaĭlovich (published as by V. N. Vološinov) (1929/30) *Marksizm i filosofija jazyka*, Leningrad; trans. L. Matejka and I. R. Titunik, *Marxism and the Philosophy of Language*, New York, 1973. Authorship not proven.

Ballmer, Thomas T., and Pinkal, Manfred (1983) *Approaching Vagueness*, New York, Amsterdam and Oxford.

Balzac, Honoré de (1834) *Le Père Goriot*, Paris; trans. M. A. Crawford, *Old Goriot*, Harmondsworth, 1951.

Barth, John (1967) "The literature of exhaustion", *Atlantic Monthly*, 220 (August), 29–34; appears in Raymond Federman, *Surfiction: Fiction Now . . . and Tomorrow*, Chicago, 1981, 19–33.

Barth, John (1968 [1969]) *Lost in the Funhouse*, New York.
Barth, John (1972 [1973]) *Chimera*, Greenwich, Conn.
Barth, John (1977) "The literature of replenishment; postmodernist fiction", *Atlantic Monthly*, 245 (January), 65–71.
Barthelme, Donald (1970 [1976]) *City Life*, New York.
Barthes, Roland (1964a) "Eléments de sémiologie", *Communications*, 4, 91–135; trans. A. Lavers and C. Smith, *Elements of Semiology*, London, 1967.
Barthes, Roland (1964b) *Essais critiques*, Paris; trans. R. Howard, *Critical Essays*, Evanston, Ill., 1972.
Barthes, Roland (1968) "L'effet de réel", *Communications*, 11, 84–9; trans. R. Howard as "The Reality Effect" (in Howard's translation of Barthes' *Le bruissement de la langue* [Paris 1984]), *The Rustle of Language*, Oxford, 1986, 141–8.
Barthes, Roland (1970) *S/Z*, Paris; trans. R. Howard, *S/Z*, London, 1974.
Barthes, Roland (1973) *Le plaisir du texte*, Paris; trans. R. Miller, *The Pleasures of the Text*, London 1976.
Barthes, Roland (1975a) "Introduction à l'analyse structurale des récits", *Communications*, 8; trans. S. Heath, "Introduction to the structural analysis of narratives", *Image, Music, Text*, Glasgow, 1977.
Barthes, Roland (1975b) *Roland Barthes par Roland Barthes*, Paris; trans. R. Howard, London 1977.
Barthes, Roland (1979) *Sollers écrivain*, Paris.
Bate, W. J. (1963) "Keats's 'Negative Capability' and the Imagination"; repr. in John S. Hill (ed.), *The Romantic Imagination: A Casebook*, London, 1977.
Baudry, Jean-Louis (1967) *Personnes*, Paris.
Beagle, Peter S. (1978 [1982]) *The Last Unicorn*, London; repr. 1982.
Becker, George J. (1963) *Documents of Modern Literary Realism*, Princeton.
Beckett, Samuel (1931 [1957]) *Proust*, New York and London.
Beckett, Samuel (1938 [1963]) *Murphy*, London.
Beckett, Samuel (1949) "Three dialogues with Georges Duthuit", *Transition 49*, 5 (December), 97–103; repr. in Martin Esslin (ed.), *Samuel Beckett: A Collection of Critical Essays*, Englewood Cliffs, NJ, 1965.
Beckett, Samuel (1951) *Molloy*, Paris; trans. P. Bowles with S.B., New York, 1955. English citations in this book affecting *Molloy* and the next two texts are from *Molloy, Malone Dies, The Unnamable: A Trilogy*, Paris, 1959.
Beckett, Samuel (1952) *Malone meurt*, Paris; trans. S.B., *Malone Dies*, London, 1958.
Beckett, Samuel (1953a) *L'innommable*, Paris; trans. S.B. *The Unnamable*, London, 1958.
Beckett, Samuel (1953b [1963]) *Watt*, Paris; repr. London, 1963.
Beldoch, Michael (1975) "The therapeutic as narcissistic", in R. Boyers and R. Orrill (eds), *Psychological Man*, New York, 1975.
Bellamy, Joe David (1974) *The New Fiction: Interviews with Innovative American Writers*, Urbana, Ill.
Bettelheim, Bruno (1976) *The Uses of Enchantment: The Meaning and Importance of Fairy Tales*, New York.

Bickerton, Derek (1983) "Creole languages", *Scientific American*, 249, 1 (July), 108–15.

Bigelow, Charles, and Day, Donald (1983) "Digital typography", *Scientific American*, 249, 2 (August), 94–105.

Biraghi, Guglielmo (1972) *Lo sguardo nel buio*, Milan.

Bloom, Harold (1975) *A Map of Misreading*, New York.

Boccaccio, Giovanni (1349–51) *Decameron*; C. Segre (ed.), Milan, 1972.

Borges, Jorge Luis (1974) *Obras completas 1923–72*, Buenos Aires. Many essays and stories referred to have long Spanish-language publishing histories – some first appearing in book form not later than 1936 – too complex to record individually here. Those in the first four volumes below are in *Obras completas*. In the main text, to facilitate general-reader reference,dates supplied are those of publication in the following more readily accessible collections rather than those of first printing. The 1964 and 1970a English-language collections represent special selections authorized by J.L.B. and do not precisely correspond with any published originally in Spanish.

Borges, Jorge Luis (1962) *Ficciones*, ed. A. Kerrigan and trans. A. Kerrigan, A. Reid, A. Bonner, H. Temple and R. Todd, New York.

Borges, Jorge Luis (1964) *Labyrinths: Selected Stories and Other Writings*, ed. and trans. D. A. Yates and J. E. Irby, New York.

Borges, Jorge Luis (1970a) *The Aleph and Other Stories 1933–69*, ed. and trans. N. Thomas di Giovanni with J.L.B., New York.

Borges, Jorge Luis (1970b) *El informe de Brodie*, Buenos Aires; trans. N. Thomas di Giovanni with J.L.B., *Doctor Brodie's Report*, New York, 1972.

Borges, Jorge Luis (1975) *El libro de arena*, Buenos Aires; trans. N. Thomas di Giovanni, *The Book of Sand*, London, 1979.

Borges, Jorge Luis, with Guerrero, Margarita (1967) *El libro de los seres imaginarios*, Buenos Aires; trans. N. Thomas di Giovanni with J.L.B., *The Book of Imaginary Beings*, London, 1970.

Bory, Jean-François (1973) "Post-Scriptum", trans. D. Higgins, in Richard Kostelanetz (ed.), *Breakthrough Fictioneers: An Anthology*, West Glover, Vt, 1973, 38–45.

Bosco, Henri (1932) *Le Sanglier*, Paris.

Bosco, Henri (1937) *L'Ane Culotte*, Paris.

Brooke-Rose, Christine (1975) *Thru*, London.

Brooke-Rose, Christine (1981) *A Rhetoric of the Unreal: Studies in Narrative and Structure, especially of the Fantastic*, Cambridge.

Brown, Harold I. (1982) "Self-reference in logic and Mulligan Stew", *Diogenes*, 118 (Summer), 121–42.

Bruner, J. S., and Minturn, A. L. (1955) "Perceptual identification and perceptual organization", *Journal of General Psychology*, 53, 21–8.

Bruss, Elizabeth A. (1982) *Beautiful Theories: The Spectacle of Discourse in Contemporary Criticism*, Baltimore and London.

Burroughs, William S. (1967) "Word authority more habit forming than heroin", from *San Francisco Earthquake #1*, in Richard Kostelanetz (ed.),

Breakthrough Fictioneers: An Anthology, West Glover, Vt, 1973, 198–202.
Butor, Michel (1954) *Passage de Milan*, Paris.
Butor, Michel (1957a) *L'Emploi du temps*, Paris; trans. J. Stewart, *Passing Time*, New York, 1960.
Butor, Michel (1957b) *La Modification*, Paris; trans. J. Stewart, *Second Thoughts*, London, 1959, and *A Change of Heart*, New York, 1959.
Butor, Michael (1960) *Degrés*, Paris; trans. R. Howard, *Degrees*, New York, 1961.
Buzzati, Dino (1933) *Bàrnabo delle montagne*, Milan.
Buzzati, Dino (1935) *Il segreto del Bosco Vecchio*, Milan; repr. with *Bàrnabo delle montagne*, Milan, 1957, the edition cited in this text.
Buzzati, Dino (1941) *Il deserto dei Tartari*, Milan; repr. in *Il deserto dei Tartari e dodici racconti*, Rome, 1966.
Cage, John (1961 [1973]) *Silence: Lectures and Writings by John Cage*, London.
Cagnon, Maurice, and Smith, Stephen (1981) "J. M. G. Le Clézio: fiction's double bind", in Raymond Federman (ed.), *Surfiction, Fiction Now . . . and Tomorrow*, Chicago, 215–26.
Calvino, Italo (1960) *I nostri antenati*, Turin; trans. W. Weaver, *Our Ancestors*, London, 1962 [1980]; orig. pub. separately as *Il visconte dimezzato, Il barone rampante, Il cavaliere inesistente*, Turin, 1951, 1957, 1959, and trans. W. Weaver, *The Cloven Viscount, Baron in the Trees, The Non-Existent Knight*, London, 1962, 1959, 1962.
Calvino, Italo (1965) *Le cosmicomiche*, Turin; trans. W. Weaver, *Cosmicomics*, New York, 1968 [1970].
Calvino, Italo (1967) *Ti con zero*, Turin; trans. W. Weaver, *t zero*, New York, 1969 [1970].
Calvino, Italo (1967–8) "Cibernetica e fantasmi", *Le conferenze dell'Associazione Culturale Italiana*, 21, 9–23, and in I.C., *Una pietra sopra*, Turin, 1980; trans. B. Merry, "Notes towards a definition of the narrative form as a combinative process", *Twentieth-Century Studies*, May 1970; an abbreviated version (based on "Appunti sulla narrativa come processo combinatorio", *Nuova Corrente*, nos 46–7, 1968) appears in Raymond Federman (ed.), *Surfiction: Fiction Now . . . and Tomorrow*, Chicago, 1981, 75–81.
Calvino, Italo (1973) *Il castello dei destini incrociati*, Turin; trans. W. Weaver, *The Castle of Crossed Destinies*, New York and London, 1976.
Calvino, Italo (1979) *Se una notte d'inverno un viaggiatore*, Turin; trans. W. Weaver, *If on a Winter's Night a Traveler*, New York and London, 1981.
Campbell, N. R. (1970) "What is a theory?", in Baruch A. Brody (ed.), *Readings in the Philosophy of Science*, Englewood Cliffs, NJ.
Carpenter, Humphrey (1977) *Tolkien*, Boston.
Chipp, Herschel B. (1968) *Theories of Modern Art: A Source Book by Artists and Critics*, Berkeley, Los Angeles and London.
Collingwood, Robin George (1938) *The Principles of Art*, Oxford.
Coover, Robert (1969) *Pricksongs and Descants: Fictions*, New York.

Cortázar, Julio (1956) *Final de Juego*, Mexico (City); trans. P. Blackburn, *End of the Game, and Other Stories*, New York, 1967.
Cortázar, Julio (1963) *Rayuela*, Buenos Aires; trans. Gregory Rabassa, *Hopscotch*, London, 1966 [1967].
Culler, Jonathan (1975) *Structuralist Poetics: Structuralism, Linguistics and the Study of Literature*, London.
Culler, Jonathan (1981) "Towards a theory of non-genre literature", in Raymond Federman (ed.), *Surfiction: Fiction Now ... and Tomorrow*, Chicago, 255–62.
Culler, Jonathan (1983) *On Deconstruction: Theory and Criticism after Structuralism*, London.
Dallmayr, Fred R. (1981) *The Twilight of Subjectivity: Contributions to a Post-Individualist Theory of Politics*, Amherst.
Derrida, Jacques (1967a) *De la grammatologie*, Paris; trans. G. C. Spivak, *Of Grammatology*, Baltimore, 1976.
Derrida, Jacques (1967b) 'Différance", *La Voix et la phénomène: Introduction au problème du signe dans la phénomenologie de Husserl*, Paris; trans. D. B. Allison, "Differance", *Speech and Phenomena and Other Essays on Husserl's Theory of Signs*, Evanston, Ill., 1973.
Derrida, Jacques (1967c) *L'Ecriture et la différence*, Paris; trans. A. Bass, *Writing and Difference*, London, 1978.
Derrida, Jacques (1969) "La dissémination", *Critique*, 260–1 (February–March), 98–139, 215–49; trans. (based on *La Dissémination*, Paris, 1972) B. Johnson, *Dissemination*, London, 1981.
Derrida, Jacques (1977) "Signéponge", *Francis Ponge: Colloque de Cérisy*, 1, Paris; trans. R. Rand, *Signéponge/Signsponge*, New York, 1984.
Dillard, Annie (1982) *Living by Fiction*, New York.
Eco, Umberto (1976 [1977]) *A Theory of Semiotics*, London.
Ehrmann, Jacques (1971) "La mort de la littérature", *"Textes" suivi de la Mort de la littérature*; trans. A. J. Arnold, "The death of literature", in Raymond Federman (ed.), *Surfiction: Fiction Now ... and Tomorrow*, Chicago, 1981, 229–53, and (in a different version) in *New Literary History*, 1971, 3 (Autumn), 31–48.
Eliot, T. S. (1960) "Shakespeare and the Stoicism of Seneca", *Selected Essays*, New York.
Eliot, George (1871–2 [1965, Harmondsworth]) *Middlemarch*, London.
Emerson, Caryl (1983) "Outer and inner speech", *Critical Inquiry*, 10, 2 (December), 245–64.
Emrich, Wilhelm (1958) *Franz Kafka*, Bonn; trans. S. Z. Buehne, *Franz Kafka: A Critical Study of His Writings*, New York, 1968.
Farmer, Philip José (1975) *Venus on the Half-Shell*, New York.
Fautz, R. L. (1958) "Pattern vision in young infants", *Psychological Record*, 8, 43–7.
Federman, Raymond (1971) *Double or Nothing*, Chicago.
Federman, Raymond (1973) "Dashing from Don to Tioli", in Richard Kos-

telanetz (ed.), *Breakthrough Fictioneers: An Anthology*, West Glover, Vt, 1973, 260–3.

Federman, Raymond (1976) *Take It or Leave It*, New York.

Federman, Raymond (ed.) (1981) *Surfiction: Fiction Now . . . and Tomorrow*, Chicago; includes his two essays "Surfiction – four propositions in form of an introduction", 5–15, and "Fiction today or the pursuit of non-knowledge", 291–311.

Feyerabend, Paul K. (1981) *Realism, Rationalism and Scientific Method*, Cambridge.

Fish, Stanley (1970) "Literature in the reader: affective stylistics", *New Literary History*, 2 (1970–1), 123–62.

Flaubert, Gustave (1857) *Madame Bovary*, Paris; trans. A. Russell, Harmondsworth, 1950.

Flaubert, Gustave (1953) *The Selected Letters of Gustave Flaubert*, trans. and ed. F. Steegmuller, New York.

Foucault, Michel (1969) *L'Archéologie du savoir*, Paris; trans. A. M. Sheridan-Smith, *The Archeology of Knowledge*, New York, 1972.

Fuentes, Carlos (1975) *Terra nostra*, Mexico (City); trans. M. S. Peden, Harmondsworth, 1976 [1978].

Gale, George (1981) "The anthropic principle", *Scientific American*, 245, 6 (December), 114–22.

Gardner, John (1972 [1973]) *Grendel*, London.

Gardner, Martin (1983) "Mathematical games", *Scientific American*, 249, 2 (August), 8–13.

Gass, William H. (1976) *On Being Blue*, Boston, Mass.

Genette, Gérard (1968, 1969, 1972) *Figures I, II, III*, Paris; partially trans. in J. Lewin, *Narrative Discourse*, London, 1980, and A. Sheridan, *Figures of Literary Discourse*, New York, 1982.

Gerz, Jochen (1981) "Towards a language of doing", in Raymond Federman (ed.), *Surfiction: Fiction Now . . . and Tomorrow*, Chicago, 1981, 279–81.

Golding, William (1962 [1963]) *The Inheritors*, New York.

Goldknopf, David (1972) *Life of the Novel*, Chicago.

Goldwater, Robert, and Treves, Marco (eds) (1945 [1976]) *Artists on Art*, London.

Gombrich, E. H. (1951) "Meditations on a hobby horse or the roots of artistic form", in L. L. Whyte (ed.), *Aspects of Form, A Symposium on Form in Nature and Art*, London; repr. in *Meditations on a Hobby Horse and Other Essays on the Theory of Art*, London, 1963.

Goodman, Nelson (1955) *Fact, Fiction, and Forecast*, Cambridge, Mass.

Gordon, Giles (1973) "Genealogy", in Richard Kostelanetz (ed.), *Breakthrough Fictioneers: An Anthology*, West Glover, Vt, 15.

Graff, Gerald (1979) *Literature Against Itself: Literary Ideas in Modern Society*, Chicago.

Grant, Damian (1970) *Realism*, London.

Guyotat, Pierre (1970) *Éden, Éden, Éden*, prefaces by Michel Leiris, Roland Barthes, Philippe Sollers, Paris.

Haken, Hermann (1978) *Synergetics: An Introduction: Nonequilibrium Phase Transitions and Self-Organisation in Physics, Chemistry and Biology*, 2nd edn, Berlin, Heidelberg and New York.

Haken, Hermann, and Wagner, M. (eds.) (1973) *Cooperative Phenomena*, Berlin, Heidelberg and New York.

Hamon, Philippe (1973) "Un discours contraint", *Poétique*, 16, 411–45.

Hassan, Ihab (1967) *The Literature of Silence: Henry Miller and Samuel Beckett*, New York.

Hassan, Ihab (1975) *Paracriticisms: Seven Speculations of the Times*, Urbana, Ill., Chicago and London.

Hawkes, Terence (1977) *Structuralism and Semiotics*, London.

Hawthorne, Nathaniel (1850) Preface to *The Scarlet Letter*, London; repr. Harmondsworth, 1970.

Hayes, Brian (1983, 1984) "Computer recreations", *Scientific American*, 249, 5, 16–24, and 250, 3, 10–16.

Heath, Stephen (1972) *The Nouveau Roman: A Study in the Practice of Writing*, London.

Hector, L. C. (1966) *The Handwriting of English Documents*, London.

Heisenberg, Werner (1930 [1956]) "The uncertainty principle", trans. C. Eckart and F. C. Hoyt in *The Physical Principles of Quantum Theory*, Chicago; repr. in James R. Newman (ed.), *The World of Mathematics*, 4 vols, New York, 1956, 1051–5.

Heisenberg, Werner (1958a [1963]) *Physics and Philosophy – The Revolution in Modern Science*, London; 2nd edn, London, 1963.

Heisenberg, Werner (1958b) "The representation of nature in contemporary physics", *Daedalus*, 87, 3 (Summer), 95ff.

Heissenbuttel, Helmut (1981) "Mainclausestation", trans. R. Waldrop in Charles Russell, *The Avant Garde Today*, Urbana, Ill., 1981, 109.

Heller, Erich (1963 [1965]) "The fallacy of Realism", in George J. Becker (ed.), *Documents of Modern Literary Realism*, Princeton, NJ; repr. in *The Artist's Journey into the Interior*, New York, 1965.

Heller, Joseph (1961 [1964]) *Catch-22*, London.

Hemingway, Ernest (1944 [1962]) *The First Forty-Nine Stories*, London.

Hemmings, F. W. J. (ed.) (1974) *The Age of Realism*, Harmondsworth.

Hoffman, D. D. (1983) "The interpretation of visual illusions", *Scientific American*, 249, 6 (December), 137–44.

Hoffman, Robert R. (1980) "Metaphor in Science", in R. P. Honeck and R. R. Hoffman, *Cognition and Figurative Language*, Hillsdale, NJ, 393–423.

Hofstadter, Douglas R. (1979) *Gödel, Escher, Bach: An Eternal Golden Braid*, Harmondsworth.

Hofstadter, Douglas R. (1981, 1982) "Metamagical themas", *Scientific American*, 244, 1 (January), 34–41; 246, 1 (January), 12–17; 247, 3 (September), 18–31.

Hofstadter, Douglas R. (1985) *Metamagical Themas*, New York.

Holden, Alan (1983) *Orderly Tangles: Cloverleafs, Gordian Knots, and Regular Polylinks*, New York.

Honeck, R. P., and Hoffman, R. R. (eds) (1980) *Cognition and Figurative Language*, Hillsdale, NJ.

Imbert, Enrique Anderson (1961) "Taboo", in *El Grimorio*, Buenos Aires; trans. I. Reade, in *The Other Side of the Mirror*, Carbondale, Ill., 1966.

Iser, Wolfgang (1976) *Der Akt des Lesens: Theorie aesthetischer Wirking*; trans. W. Fink, *The Act of Reading: A Theory of Aesthetic Response*, London, 1978

Ivanov, V. V. (1976) "The significance of M. M. Bakhtin's ideas on sign, utterance, and dialogue for modern semiotics (1)", in Henryk Baran (ed.), *Semiotics and Structuralism: Readings from the Soviet Union*, White Plains, NY, 310–67.

Jackson, Rosemary (1981) *Fantasy: The Literature of Subversion*, London.

Jameson, Fredric (1982) "Toward a new awareness of genre", *Science Fiction Studies*, 9 (November), 322–4.

Jantsch, Erich (1980) *The Self-Organizing Universe: Scientific and Human Implications of the Emerging Paradigm of Evolution*, Oxford.

Johnson, Mark (1980) "A philosophical perspective on the problems of metaphor", in R. P. Honeck and R. R. Hoffman (eds.), *Cognition and Figurative Language*, Hillsdale, NJ, 47–67.

Johnson, Samuel (1750) *Rambler* 4; in A. Chalmers (ed.),*The British Essayists: with Prefaces, Historical and Biographical*, vol. 19, London, 1817, 20.

Josipovici, Gabriel (1971) *The World and the Book: A Study of Modern Fiction*, London.

Kagle, Steven (1977) "Science fiction as a simulation game", in Thomas D. Clareson (ed.), *Many Futures, Many Worlds: Theme and Form in Science Fiction*, Kent, Ohio.

Kaplan, A. (1965) *The Conduct of Inquiry*, San Francisco.

Kellman, Stephen G. (1980) *The Self-Begetting Novel*, New York.

Kennard, Jean E. (1975) *Number and Nightmare: Forms of Fantasy in Contemporary Fiction*, Hamden, Conn.

Kennedy, George (1963) *The Art of Persuasion in Ancient Greece*, Princeton, NJ.

Klinkowitz, Jerome (1975) *Literary Disruptions: The Making of a Post-Contemporary American Fiction*, Urbana, Ill.

Klinkowitz, Jerome (1981) "Literary disruptions: or, what's become of American fiction?", in Raymond Federman (ed.), *Surfiction: Fiction Now ... and Tomorrow*, Chicago, 165–79.

Kostelanetz, Richard (1971) "Twenty-five fictional hypotheses", from *Panache*; appears in Raymond Federman (ed.), *Surfiction: Fiction Now ... and Tomorrow*, Chicago, 283–6.

Kostelanetz, Richard (ed.) (1973) *Breakthrough Fictioneers: An Anthology*, West Glover, Vt.

Kostelanetz, Richard (1981) "New fiction in America", in Raymond Federman (ed.), *Surfiction: Fiction Now ... and Tomorrow*, Chicago, 85–100.

Krieger, Murray (1983) "Thematic underside of recent theory", *New Literary History*, 15, 1 (Autumn), 119–36.

Krieger, Murray (1984) "The ambiguities of representation and illusion: an E. H. Gombrich retrospective", *Critical Inquiry*, 2, 2 (December), 181–201.

Kristeva, Julia (1969) *Semiotikē: Recherches pour une sémanalyse*, Paris.

Lacan, Jacques (1949) "Le Stade du miroir comme formateur de la fonction du Je, telle qu'elle nous est révélée dans l'expérience psychanalytique", *Revue Française de Psychanalyse*, 13, 449–55; also in *Ecrits*, Paris, 1966; trans. J. Roussel, "The mirror-phase", *New Left Review*, 1968, 51, 71–7.

Landolfi, Tommaso (1975) *Il Mar delle Blatte, e altre storie*, Milan.

Lavers, Annette (1982) *Roland Barthes: Structuralism and After*, London.

Le Clézio, J. M. G. (1963) *Le Procès-verbal*, Paris.

Le Clézio, J. M. G. (1970) *La Guerre*, Paris; trans. S. W. Taylor, *War*, London, 1973.

Le Guin, Ursula (1969 [1971]) *The Left Hand of Darkness*, London.

Lem, Stanislaw (1971) *Doskonała próznia*, Warsaw; trans. M. Kandel, *A Perfect Vacuum*, in *Solaris: The Chain of Chance; A Perfect Vacuum*, London, 1979 [1981].

Lentricchia, Frank (1980) *After the New Criticism*, London.

Lesser, Simon O. (1962) *Fiction and the Unconscious*, New York.

Lessing, Doris (1973) *Briefing for a Descent into Hell*, London.

Lewis, C. S. (1966) *Of Other Worlds: Essays and Stories*, ed. W. Hooper, London.

Lindsay, David (1920 [1972]) *A Voyage to Arcturus*, London.

Lyotard, Jean-François (1979) *La Condition postmoderne: Rapport sur le savoir*, Paris; trans. G. Bennington and B. Massumi, *The Postmodern Condition: A Report on Knowledge*, Manchester, 1984.

Macpherson, James (1760–3 [1926]) "The songs of Selma", *The Poems of Ossian*, Edinburgh.

McElroy, Joseph (1977) *Plus*, New York.

McGilchrist, Iain (1982) *Against Criticism*, London.

Malinowski, Bronislaw (1925, 1926) "Magic, science and religion", "Myth in primitive psychology", in *Magic, Science and Religion*, New York, 1954.

de Man, Paul (1971) *Blindness and Insight: Essays on the Rhetoric of Contemporary Criticism*, New York.

Manlove, Colin Nichols (1976–7) "Flight to Aleppo: T. H. White's *The Once and Future King*", *Mosaic*, 10, 2 (Winter), 65–83.

Manlove, Colin Nichols (1983) *The Impulse of Fantasy Literature*, London.

Marinetti, Filippo Tommaso (1912) *Zang Tumb Tumb*, Adrianople.

Márquez, Gabriel García (1967) *Cien años de Soledad*, Buenos Aires; trans. Gregory Rabassa, *One Hundred Years of Solitude*, London, 1970 [1978].

Martinez-Bonati, Felix (1983) "Towards a formal ontology of fictional worlds", *Philosophy and Literature*, 7, 2 (October), 182–95.

Mauriac, Claude (1959) *Le Dîner en ville*, Paris; trans. M. Lawrence, *The Dinner Party*, New York, 1960.

Mauriac, Claude (1961) *La Marquise sortit à cinq heures*, Paris; trans. R. Howard, *The Marquise Went Out at Five*, New York, 1962.
Mauriac, Claude (1963) *L'Agrandissement*, Paris.
Meikle, Jeffrey L. (1981) "'Other frequencies': the parallel worlds of Thomas Pynchon and H. P. Lovecraft", *Modern Fiction Studies*, 27, 2 (Summer), 287–94.
Mellard, James M. (1980) *The Exploded Form*, Urbana, Ill.
Mercier, Vivian (1971) *The New Novel from Queneau to Pinget*, New York.
Meyer, Leonard B. (1967) *Music Arts and Ideas*, Chicago.
Michael, D. N. (1953) "A cross-cultural investigation of closure", *Journal of Abnormal Psychology*, 48, 225–30.
Miller, J. Hillis (1975) "Deconstructing the deconstructors", *Diacritics*, 5 (Summer), 24–31.
Miller, J. Hillis (1982) *Fiction and Repetition: Seven English Novels*, Oxford.
Mitchell, Donald (1966) *The Language of Music*, London.
Nabokov, Vladimir (1955) "On a book entitled *Lolita*", *Lolita*, New York.
Nabokov, Vladimir (1959) *Nabokov's Dozen: Thirteen Stories*, London.
Nabokov, Vladimir (1962 [1973]) *Pale Fire*, London.
Nabokov, Vladimir (1969 [1970]) *Ada*, Greenwich, Conn.
Nabokov, Vladimir (1973) *A Russian Beauty and Other Stories*, London.
Nabokov, Vladimir (1975) *Tyrants Destroyed and Other Stories*, London.
Nagel, Ernest, and Newman, James R. (1956) "Goedel's proof", in Newman (ed.) *The World of Mathematics*, 4 vols, New York, 1956, 1668–95.
Nash, Cristopher (1976) review of Gerald Prince, *A Grammar of Stories: An Introduction, Yearbook of English Studies*, 204–6.
Nash, Cristopher (1977a) review of Jean E. Kennard *Number and Nightmare, Forms of Fantasy in Contemporary Fiction, Yearbook of English Studies* 1975, 331–2.
Nash, Cristopher (1977b) review of John Stark, *The Literature of Exhaustion: Borges, Nabokov and Barth, Yearbook of English Studies*, 1974, 331–2.
Nash, Cristopher (1980) "Myth and modern literature", *The Context of English Literature: 1900–1930*, London, 160–85.
Necronomicon, The (1978 [1980]) ed. George Hay, London.
Newman, James R. (ed.) (1956) *The World of Mathematics*, 4 vols, New York.
O'Brien, Flann (1939 [1967]) *At Swim-Two-Birds*, Harmondsworth.
O'Brien, Flann (1967 [1974]) *The Third Policeman*, London.
Oxenhandler, Neal (1981) "Listening to Burrough's voice", in Raymond Federman (ed.), *Surfiction: Fiction Now . . . and Tomorrow*, Chicago, 1981, 181–201.
Norris, Christopher (1982) *Deconstruction: Theory and Practice*, London.
Peirce, Charles Santiago Sanders (1878) "The probability of induction", *Popular Science Monthly*, 12 (April 1878), 705–18, repr. in Max H. Fisch (ed.), *Writings of Charles S. Peirce: A Chronological Edition*, vol. 3, Bloomington, 1986, 290–305.

Penn, Julia M. (1972) *Linguistic relativity versus Innate Ideas: The Origins of the Sapir-Whorf Hypothesis in German Thought*, The Hague and Paris.

Pick, J. B., Wilson, Colin, and Visiak, E. H. (1970) *The Strange Case of David Lindsay*, London.

Pinget, Robert (1952) *Mahu ou le Matériau*, Paris; trans. A. Sheridan-Smith, *Mahu or The Material*, London, 1966.

Pinget, Robert (1956) *Graal Flibuste*, Paris.

Pinget, Robert (1958) *Baga*, Paris; trans. J. Stevenson, London, 1967.

Pinget, Robert (1959) *Le Fiston*, Paris; trans. R. Howard, *Monsieur Levert*, New York, 1961, and R. N. Coe, *No Answer*, London, 1961.

Pinget, Robert (1962) *L'Inquisitoire*, Paris; trans. D. Watson, *The Inquisitory*, London, 1966.

Pinget, Robert (1965) *Passacaille*, Paris; trans. B. Wright, *Recurrent Melody*, London, 1975.

Pinget, Robert (1968) *Le Libera*, Paris.

Popper, Karl (1972 [1973]) *Objective Knowledge: An Evolutionary Approach*, Oxford.

Prince, Gerald (1973) *A Grammar of Stories: An Introduction*, The Hague.

Prince, Gerald (1980) review of Gérard Genette, *Narrative Discourse*, *Comparative Literature*, 32 (Fall), 413–17.

Pütz, Manfred (1979) *The Story of Identity: American Fiction of the '60s*, Stuttgart.

Pynchon, Thomas (1963 [1966]) *V*, Harmondsworth.

Quine, W. V. (1978) "A postscript on metaphor", *Critical Inquiry*, 5, 1978, 161–2.

Rabkin, Eric S. (ed.) (1979) *Fantastic Worlds: Myths, Tales, and Stories*, Oxford and New York.

Rabelais, François (1539–64) *Gargantua et Pantagruel* in *Oeuvres complètes*, ed. Jacques Boulenger and Lucien Scheler, Paris, 1955.

Raval, Suresh (1981) *Metacriticism*, Athens, Ga.

Reichenbach, Hans (1951 [1963]) *The Rise of Scientific Philosophy*, Berkeley, Los Angeles and London.

Restle, F., and Brown, E. (1970) "Organization of serial pattern learning", in G. H. Bower (ed.), *The Psychology of Learning and Motivation: Advances in Research and Theory*, vol. 4, New York.

Ricardou, Jean (1967) "Les allées de l'écriture", *Problèmes du nouveau roman*, Paris, 56–68 (and not, as suggested in Federman 1981, in *Pour une théorie du nouveau roman*); trans. E. Freiberg, "Writing between the lines", in Federman 1981, 263–77.

Ricardou, Jean (1971) "Nouveau roman, Tel Quel", *Pour une théorie du nouveau roman*, Paris, 234–65; trans. E. Freiberg in Federman 1981, 101–33.

Richardson, Joanna (1974) *Stendhal: A Biography*, London.

Robbe-Grillet, Alain (1953) *Les Gommes*, Paris; trans R. Howard, *The Erasers*, New York, 1964.

Robbe-Grillet, Alain (1955) *Le Voyeur*, Paris; trans. R. Howard, *The Voyeur*, London, 1958 [1959].

Robbe-Grillet, Alain (1957) *La Jalousie*, Paris; trans. R. Howard, *Jealousy*, New York, 1959.
Robbe-Grillet, Alain (1959) *Dans le labyrinthe*, Paris; trans. C. Brooke-Rose, *In the Labyrinth*, London, 1967.
Robbe-Grillet, Alain (1961) *L'Année dernière à Marienbad*, Paris; trans. R. Howard, *Last Year at Marienbad*, New York, 1962.
Robbe-Grillet, Alain (1962) *Pour un nouveau roman*, Paris; trans. B. Wright, *Snapshots and Towards a New Novel*, London, 1965.
Robbe-Grillet, Alain (1965) *La Maison de Rendez-vous*, Paris; trans. R. Howard, New York, 1966 and, London, 1970, as *The House of Assignation*.
Rogers, D. W. and I. A. (1980) *J. R. R. Tolkien*, Boston, Mass.
Romanos, George D. (1983) *Quine and Analytic Philosophy*, Cambridge, Mass.
Rose, Margaret (1979) *Parody/Meta-Fiction*, London.
Rosen, Stanley (1980) *The Limits of Analysis*, New York.
Rühm, Gerhard (1970) "Der Löwe", *Knochenspielzeug*, Düsseldorf 1970; trans. E. Williams, "The Lion", in Kostelanetz 1973, 5.
Russell, Charles (1981) *The Avant-Garde Today*, Urbana, Ill.
Said, Edward (1975) *Beginnings; Intention and Method*, New York.
Sanguineti, Edoardo (1967) *Il giuoco dell'Oca*, Milan.
Sanguineti, Edoardo (1970) *Il giuoco del Satyricon*, Turin.
Sarraute, Nathalie (1956) *L'Ere du soupçon*, Paris; trans. M. Jolas, in *Tropisms and the Age of Suspicion*, London, 1963.
Sartre, Jean-Paul (1938) *La Nausée*, Paris; trans. R. Baldick, *Nausea*, Harmondsworth, 1965.
Sartre, Jean-Paul (1940) *L'Imaginaire*, Paris; English edn. intro. Mary Warnock (no trans. given), *The Psychology of Imagination*, London, 1972.
Saviane, Giorgio (1979) *Il mare verticale*, Milan.
Schiller, Friedrich (1794–5) *Über die aesthetische Erziehung des Menschen*; trans. R. Small, *On the Aesthetic Education of Man*, New York, 1965.
Scholes, Robert (ed.) (1964) *Learners and Discerners: A Newer Criticism*, Charlottesville, Va.
Scholes, Robert (1977) "Toward a semiotics of literature", *Critical Inquiry*, 4 (Autumn), 105–20.
Scholes, Robert (1979) *Fabulation and Metafiction*, Urbana, Ill.
Scholes, Robert, and Kellogg, Robert (1966) *The Nature of Narrative*, New York.
Searle, John R. (1979) *Expression and Meaning*, Cambridge.
Sellin, Bernard (1981) *The Life and Works of David Lindsay* (trans. from the French by K. Gunnell), Cambridge.
Shelley, Mary (1818 [1969]) *Frankenstein or the Modern Prometheus*, London.
Shippey, T. A. (1976–7) "The magic art and the evolution of words: Ursula Le Guin's Earthsea Trilogy", *Mosaic*, 10, 2 (Winter), 147–63.
Sidney, Sir Philip (1595) *The Defence of Poesie*, London; repr. in Albert Feuillerat (ed.), *The Prose Works*, vol. 3, Cambridge, 1963.

Simon, Claude (1960) *La Route des Flandres*, Paris; trans. R. Howard, *The Flanders Road*, New York, 1961.
Simon, Claude (1969) *La Bataille de Pharsale*, Paris.
Sollers, Philippe (1960) "Sept propositions sur Alain Robbe-Grillet", *Tel Quel*, 2 (Summer), 49–53.
Sollers, Philippe (1961) *Le Parc*, Paris; trans. A. M. Sheridan-Smith, *The Park*, London, 1968.
Sollers, Philippe (1965) *Drame*, Paris.
Sollers, Philippe (1968a) *Nombres*, Paris.
Sollers, Philippe (1968b) *Logiques*, Paris; the essay "Le roman et l'expérience des limites", trans. C. Grahl, "The novel and the experience of limits", in Raymond Federman (ed.) *Surfiction: Fiction Now ... and Tomorrow*, Chicago, 1981, 59–74; also trans. P. Barnard with D. Hayman, in Sollers, 1968c; except where otherwise noted, page references are to Grahl's trans.
Sollers, Philippe (1968c) *L'Ecriture et l'expérience des limites*, Paris; trans. P. Barnard, in D. Hayman (ed.), *Writing and the Experience of Limits*, New York, 1983.
Sollers, Philippe (1972) *Lois*, Paris.
Sollers, Philippe (1981a) *Paradis*, Paris.
Sollers, Philippe (1981b) *Vision à New York: entretiens avec David Hayman*, trans. from English by P. Mikriammos, Paris.
Sollers, Philippe, with de Haes, Frans (1983) "Femmes et paradis", *L'Infini*, 2 (Spring), 32–43.
Sontag, Susan (1967) "The aesthetics of silence", *Aspen*, 5–6; repr. in *Styles of Radical Will*, New York, 1969.
Sontag, Susan (1969) *Against Interpretation and Other Essays*, New York.
Stark, John (1974) *The Literature of Exhaustion: Borges, Nabokov and Barth*, Durham, NC.
Stendhal (Henri Marie Beyle) (1830) *Le Rouge et le Noir*, Paris; trans. M. R. B. Shaw, *Scarlet and Black*, Harmondsworth, 1963.
Stern, J. P. (1973) *On Realism*, London.
Sterne, Laurence (1759–67) *The Life and Opinions of Tristram Shandy*, London; repr. Harmondsworth, 1967.
Stevick, Philip (ed.) (1971) *Anti-Story: An Anthology of Experimental Fiction*, New York and London.
Stevick, Philip (1981) *Alternative Pleasures: Post-Realist fiction and the Tradition*, Urbana, Ill.
Sukenick, Ronald (1976) "Thirteen digressions", *Partisan Review*, 43, 1, 90–101.
Sukenick, Ronald (1981) "The new tradition in fiction", in Raymond Federman (ed.), *Surfiction: Fiction Now ... and Tomorrow*, Chicago, 35–45.
Tanner, Tony (1982) *Thomas Pynchon*, London.
Théorie d'ensemble (1968) Collection "Tel Quel" (a collective project, essays by Michel Foucault, Roland Barthes, Jacques Derrida, Jean-Louis Baudry, Jean-Joseph Goux, Jean-Louis Houdebine, Julia Kristeva, Marcelin Pleynet,

Jean Ricardou, Jacqueline Risset, Denis Roche, Pierre Rottenberg, Philippe Sollers, Jean Thibaudeau), Paris.

Thom, René (1983) "Stop chance! Silence noise!", trans. R. E. Chumbley, *SubStance*, 40, 12, 3.

Thompson, J. M. T. (1983) "Complex dynamics of compliant off-shore structures", *Proceedings*, Royal Society of London, A387, 407–27.

Thurley, Geoffrey (1983) *Counter-Modernism in Current Critical Theory*, London.

Tindall, William York (1954) preface to D. H. Lawrence, *The Plumed Serpent*, New York.

Todorov, Tzvetan (1970) *Introduction à la littérature fantastique*, Paris; trans. R. Howard, *The Fantastic – A Structural Approach to a Literary Genre*, Ithaca, NY, 1973.

Todorov, Tzvetan (1971) *Poétique de la prose*, Paris; trans. R. Howard, *The Poetics of Prose*, Ithaca, NY, 1977.

Todorov, Tzvetan (1977) *Théories du symbole*, Paris; trans. C. Porter, *Theories of the Symbol*, Oxford, 1982.

Tolkien, J. R. R. (1937 [1975]) *The Hobbit*, London.

Tolkien, J. R. R. (1964) *Tree and Leaf*, London.

Tolkein, J. R. R. (1965) *The Lord of the Rings*, New York. (Published as first authorized edition.)

Verbrugge, R. R. (1980) "Transformations in knowing: a realist view of metaphor", in R. P. Honeck and R. R. Hoffman, *Cognition and Figurative Language*, Hillsdale, NJ, 87–125.

Vološinov, V. N. *see* Bakhtin, 1929–30.

Vonnegut, Kurt, Jr (1959 [1967]) *The Sirens of Titan*, London.

Vonnegut, Kurt, Jr (1969 [1970]) *Slaughterhouse–5*, London.

Vonnegut, Kurt, Jr (1971) *Happy Birthday, Wanda June*, New York.

von Neumann, John (1947 [1961]) "The mathematician", in *Works of the Mind*, R. B. Heywood (ed.), Chicago; repr. in *Collected Works*, A. H. Taub (ed.), vol. 1, Oxford, 1961, 1–9.

Walsh, Chad (1979) "C. S. Lewis: the man and the mystery", in Mark R. Hillegas (ed.) *Shadows of Imagination: The Fantasies of C. S. Lewis, J. R. R. Tolkien and Charles Williams*, Carbondale, Pa.

Watney, John (1976) *Mervyn Peake*, London.

Watt, Ian (1957) *The Rise of the Novel: Studies in Defoe, Richardson and Fielding*, London.

White, T. H. (1958 [1962]) *The Once and Future King*, London and Glasgow.

White, William Luther (1969) *The Image of Man in C. S. Lewis*, Nashville and New York.

Wilde, Alan (1981) *Horizons of Assent: Modernism, Post-Modernism and the Ironic Imagination*, Baltimore.

Williams, Charles (1931 [1965]) *The Place of the Lion*, London.

Wilson, Colin (1962) *The Strength to Dream: Literature and the Imagination*, London.

Zavarzadeh, Mas'ud (1976) *The Mythopoeic Reality*, Urbana, Ill.

Ziolkowski, Theodor (1982) introduction to Hermann Hesse, *Pictor's Metamorphoses and Other Fantasies*, trans. R. Lesser, London.

INDEX

In the interests of economy, below are indicated the locations of *primary* discussions only. Where for example references to the Notes (307ff.) are concerned, these are largely confined to those *leading* topics and authors there to which the reader might not have been led naturally by main-text entries. Thus C.S. Lewis's narrative theories are considered in the main text and no reference is given here to Notes where remarks – *or specialist sources, or alternative theories* – simply amplify that discussion, since these can be found via the main text on Lewis; on the other hand, 'oneiric' effects of Kafka's and Robbe-Grillet's work – or, say, Laurence Olivier's 'naturalization' of *Henry V* – are considered solely in Notes, which are therefore signalled here.

Author index

Subject index